T0155949

Lecture Notes in Computer Science

Lecture Notes in Artificial Intelligence   14695

Founding Editor

Jörg Siekmann

Series Editors

Randy Goebel, *University of Alberta, Edmonton, Canada*
Wolfgang Wahlster, *DFKI, Berlin, Germany*
Zhi-Hua Zhou, *Nanjing University, Nanjing, China*

The series Lecture Notes in Artificial Intelligence (LNAI) was established in 1988 as a topical subseries of LNCS devoted to artificial intelligence.

The series publishes state-of-the-art research results at a high level. As with the LNCS mother series, the mission of the series is to serve the international R & D community by providing an invaluable service, mainly focused on the publication of conference and workshop proceedings and postproceedings.

Dylan D. Schmorrow · Cali M. Fidopiastis
Editors

Augmented Cognition

18th International Conference, AC 2024
Held as Part of the 26th HCI International Conference, HCII 2024
Washington, DC, USA, June 29 – July 4, 2024
Proceedings, Part II

 Springer

Editors
Dylan D. Schmorrow
Soar Technology Inc.
Orlando, FL, USA

Cali M. Fidopiastis
Katmai Government Services
Orlando, FL, USA

ISSN 0302-9743   ISSN 1611-3349 (electronic)
Lecture Notes in Artificial Intelligence
ISBN 978-3-031-61571-9   ISBN 978-3-031-61572-6 (eBook)
https://doi.org/10.1007/978-3-031-61572-6

LNCS Sublibrary: SL7 – Artificial Intelligence

This Springer imprint is published by the registered company Springer Nature Switzerland AG
The registered company address is: Gewerbestrasse 11, 6330 Cham, Switzerland

If disposing of this product, please recycle the paper.

Foreword

This year we celebrate 40 years since the establishment of the HCI International (HCII) Conference, which has been a hub for presenting groundbreaking research and novel ideas and collaboration for people from all over the world.

The HCII conference was founded in 1984 by Prof. Gavriel Salvendy (Purdue University, USA, Tsinghua University, P.R. China, and University of Central Florida, USA) and the first event of the series, "1st USA-Japan Conference on Human-Computer Interaction", was held in Honolulu, Hawaii, USA, 18–20 August. Since then, HCI International is held jointly with several Thematic Areas and Affiliated Conferences, with each one under the auspices of a distinguished international Program Board and under one management and one registration. Twenty-six HCI International Conferences have been organized so far (every two years until 2013, and annually thereafter).

Over the years, this conference has served as a platform for scholars, researchers, industry experts and students to exchange ideas, connect, and address challenges in the ever-evolving HCI field. Throughout these 40 years, the conference has evolved itself, adapting to new technologies and emerging trends, while staying committed to its core mission of advancing knowledge and driving change.

As we celebrate this milestone anniversary, we reflect on the contributions of its founding members and appreciate the commitment of its current and past Affiliated Conference Program Board Chairs and members. We are also thankful to all past conference attendees who have shaped this community into what it is today.

The 26th International Conference on Human-Computer Interaction, HCI International 2024 (HCII 2024), was held as a 'hybrid' event at the Washington Hilton Hotel, Washington, DC, USA, during 29 June – 4 July 2024. It incorporated the 21 thematic areas and affiliated conferences listed below.

A total of 5108 individuals from academia, research institutes, industry, and government agencies from 85 countries submitted contributions, and 1271 papers and 309 posters were included in the volumes of the proceedings that were published just before the start of the conference, these are listed below. The contributions thoroughly cover the entire field of human-computer interaction, addressing major advances in knowledge and effective use of computers in a variety of application areas. These papers provide academics, researchers, engineers, scientists, practitioners and students with state-of-the-art information on the most recent advances in HCI.

The HCI International (HCII) conference also offers the option of presenting 'Late Breaking Work', and this applies both for papers and posters, with corresponding volumes of proceedings that will be published after the conference. Full papers will be included in the 'HCII 2024 - Late Breaking Papers' volumes of the proceedings to be published in the Springer LNCS series, while 'Poster Extended Abstracts' will be included as short research papers in the 'HCII 2024 - Late Breaking Posters' volumes to be published in the Springer CCIS series.

I would like to thank the Program Board Chairs and the members of the Program Boards of all thematic areas and affiliated conferences for their contribution towards the high scientific quality and overall success of the HCI International 2024 conference. Their manifold support in terms of paper reviewing (single-blind review process, with a minimum of two reviews per submission), session organization and their willingness to act as goodwill ambassadors for the conference is most highly appreciated.

This conference would not have been possible without the continuous and unwavering support and advice of Gavriel Salvendy, founder, General Chair Emeritus, and Scientific Advisor. For his outstanding efforts, I would like to express my sincere appreciation to Abbas Moallem, Communications Chair and Editor of HCI International News.

July 2024   Constantine Stephanidis

HCI International 2024 Thematic Areas and Affiliated Conferences

- HCI: Human-Computer Interaction Thematic Area
- HIMI: Human Interface and the Management of Information Thematic Area
- EPCE: 21st International Conference on Engineering Psychology and Cognitive Ergonomics
- AC: 18th International Conference on Augmented Cognition
- UAHCI: 18th International Conference on Universal Access in Human-Computer Interaction
- CCD: 16th International Conference on Cross-Cultural Design
- SCSM: 16th International Conference on Social Computing and Social Media
- VAMR: 16th International Conference on Virtual, Augmented and Mixed Reality
- DHM: 15th International Conference on Digital Human Modeling & Applications in Health, Safety, Ergonomics & Risk Management
- DUXU: 13th International Conference on Design, User Experience and Usability
- C&C: 12th International Conference on Culture and Computing
- DAPI: 12th International Conference on Distributed, Ambient and Pervasive Interactions
- HCIBGO: 11th International Conference on HCI in Business, Government and Organizations
- LCT: 11th International Conference on Learning and Collaboration Technologies
- ITAP: 10th International Conference on Human Aspects of IT for the Aged Population
- AIS: 6th International Conference on Adaptive Instructional Systems
- HCI-CPT: 6th International Conference on HCI for Cybersecurity, Privacy and Trust
- HCI-Games: 6th International Conference on HCI in Games
- MobiTAS: 6th International Conference on HCI in Mobility, Transport and Automotive Systems
- AI-HCI: 5th International Conference on Artificial Intelligence in HCI
- MOBILE: 5th International Conference on Human-Centered Design, Operation and Evaluation of Mobile Communications

List of Conference Proceedings Volumes Appearing Before the Conference

1. LNCS 14684, Human-Computer Interaction: Part I, edited by Masaaki Kurosu and Ayako Hashizume
2. LNCS 14685, Human-Computer Interaction: Part II, edited by Masaaki Kurosu and Ayako Hashizume
3. LNCS 14686, Human-Computer Interaction: Part III, edited by Masaaki Kurosu and Ayako Hashizume
4. LNCS 14687, Human-Computer Interaction: Part IV, edited by Masaaki Kurosu and Ayako Hashizume
5. LNCS 14688, Human-Computer Interaction: Part V, edited by Masaaki Kurosu and Ayako Hashizume
6. LNCS 14689, Human Interface and the Management of Information: Part I, edited by Hirohiko Mori and Yumi Asahi
7. LNCS 14690, Human Interface and the Management of Information: Part II, edited by Hirohiko Mori and Yumi Asahi
8. LNCS 14691, Human Interface and the Management of Information: Part III, edited by Hirohiko Mori and Yumi Asahi
9. LNAI 14692, Engineering Psychology and Cognitive Ergonomics: Part I, edited by Don Harris and Wen-Chin Li
10. LNAI 14693, Engineering Psychology and Cognitive Ergonomics: Part II, edited by Don Harris and Wen-Chin Li
11. LNAI 14694, Augmented Cognition, Part I, edited by Dylan D. Schmorrow and Cali M. Fidopiastis
12. LNAI 14695, Augmented Cognition, Part II, edited by Dylan D. Schmorrow and Cali M. Fidopiastis
13. LNCS 14696, Universal Access in Human-Computer Interaction: Part I, edited by Margherita Antona and Constantine Stephanidis
14. LNCS 14697, Universal Access in Human-Computer Interaction: Part II, edited by Margherita Antona and Constantine Stephanidis
15. LNCS 14698, Universal Access in Human-Computer Interaction: Part III, edited by Margherita Antona and Constantine Stephanidis
16. LNCS 14699, Cross-Cultural Design: Part I, edited by Pei-Luen Patrick Rau
17. LNCS 14700, Cross-Cultural Design: Part II, edited by Pei-Luen Patrick Rau
18. LNCS 14701, Cross-Cultural Design: Part III, edited by Pei-Luen Patrick Rau
19. LNCS 14702, Cross-Cultural Design: Part IV, edited by Pei-Luen Patrick Rau
20. LNCS 14703, Social Computing and Social Media: Part I, edited by Adela Coman and Simona Vasilache
21. LNCS 14704, Social Computing and Social Media: Part II, edited by Adela Coman and Simona Vasilache
22. LNCS 14705, Social Computing and Social Media: Part III, edited by Adela Coman and Simona Vasilache

47. LNCS 14730, HCI in Games: Part I, edited by Xiaowen Fang
48. LNCS 14731, HCI in Games: Part II, edited by Xiaowen Fang
49. LNCS 14732, HCI in Mobility, Transport and Automotive Systems: Part I, edited by Heidi Krömker
50. LNCS 14733, HCI in Mobility, Transport and Automotive Systems: Part II, edited by Heidi Krömker
51. LNAI 14734, Artificial Intelligence in HCI: Part I, edited by Helmut Degen and Stavroula Ntoa
52. LNAI 14735, Artificial Intelligence in HCI: Part II, edited by Helmut Degen and Stavroula Ntoa
53. LNAI 14736, Artificial Intelligence in HCI: Part III, edited by Helmut Degen and Stavroula Ntoa
54. LNCS 14737, Design, Operation and Evaluation of Mobile Communications: Part I, edited by June Wei and George Margetis
55. LNCS 14738, Design, Operation and Evaluation of Mobile Communications: Part II, edited by June Wei and George Margetis
56. CCIS 2114, HCI International 2024 Posters - Part I, edited by Constantine Stephanidis, Margherita Antona, Stavroula Ntoa and Gavriel Salvendy
57. CCIS 2115, HCI International 2024 Posters - Part II, edited by Constantine Stephanidis, Margherita Antona, Stavroula Ntoa and Gavriel Salvendy
58. CCIS 2116, HCI International 2024 Posters - Part III, edited by Constantine Stephanidis, Margherita Antona, Stavroula Ntoa and Gavriel Salvendy
59. CCIS 2117, HCI International 2024 Posters - Part IV, edited by Constantine Stephanidis, Margherita Antona, Stavroula Ntoa and Gavriel Salvendy
60. CCIS 2118, HCI International 2024 Posters - Part V, edited by Constantine Stephanidis, Margherita Antona, Stavroula Ntoa and Gavriel Salvendy
61. CCIS 2119, HCI International 2024 Posters - Part VI, edited by Constantine Stephanidis, Margherita Antona, Stavroula Ntoa and Gavriel Salvendy
62. CCIS 2120, HCI International 2024 Posters - Part VII, edited by Constantine Stephanidis, Margherita Antona, Stavroula Ntoa and Gavriel Salvendy

https://2024.hci.international/proceedings

Preface

Augmented Cognition research innovates human-system interactions for next-generation adaptive systems in diverse fields such as biometrics, cybersecurity, adaptive learning system design, and health informatics. Advancements in psychophysiological sensing and data analyses have led to major breakthroughs in the real-time assessment of a user's psychophysical signatures as input to human-systems leading the way for better human-system collaboration. More importantly, the use of Augmented Cognition methods and tools for studying elusive brain constructs such as cognitive bottlenecks (e.g., limitations in attention, memory, learning, comprehension, visualization abilities, and decision making) significantly contributes to a better understanding of the human brain and behavior, optimized reaction time, and improved learning, memory retention, and decision-making in real-world contexts. Each contribution paves the way for practical innovation in many fields dependent on the symbiotic relationships of human system integration.

The International Conference on Augmented Cognition (AC), an affiliated conference of the HCI International (HCII) conference, arrived at its 18th edition and encouraged papers from academics, researchers, industry, and professionals, on a broad range of theoretical and applied issues related to augmented cognition and its applications.

The papers accepted for publication this year reflect emerging trends across various thematic areas of the field. Our understanding of cognitive processes and human performance is furthered by submissions exploring topics such as impostor syndrome, academic performance, cognitive bias, cognitive-motor processes, emotional responses to music, phishing susceptibility, and the influence of educational and entertainment videos in frontal EEG activity. In addition, technological approaches for advancing cognitive abilities and performance were addressed in several articles across various contexts including cybersecurity training, situational awareness enhancement, cooperative learning, vehicle recognition, human-robot teaming, and human cognitive augmentation. A considerable number of papers discussed recent technological advancements in the AC field, exploring the impact of Artificial Intelligence and Machine Learning technologies, such as Convolutional Neural Networks and Large Language Models. Finally, applications of AC in various contexts were presented, providing insights into the challenges and opportunities in the field.

Two volumes of the HCII 2024 proceedings are dedicated to this year's edition of the AC conference. The first focuses on topics related to Understanding Cognitive Processes and Human Performance, and Advancing Cognitive Abilities and Performance with Augmented Tools. The second focuses on topics related to Advances in Augmented Cognition Technologies, and Applications of Augmented Cognition in Various Contexts.

The papers accepted for publication in these volumes received a minimum of two single-blind reviews from the members of the AC Program Board or, in some cases, from members of the Program Boards of other affiliated conferences. We would like to extend a heartfelt thank you to all the members of the AC Program Board and other affiliated conference program boards for their invaluable contributions and support. The groundbreaking work presented in this volume would not have been possible without their tireless efforts.

July 2024

Dylan D. Schmorrow
Cali M. Fidopiastis

18th International Conference on Augmented Cognition (AC 2024)

The full list with the Program Board Chairs and the members of the Program Boards of all thematic areas and affiliated conferences of HCII 2024 is available online at:

http://www.hci.international/board-members-2024.php

HCI International 2025 Conference

The 27th International Conference on Human-Computer Interaction, HCI International 2025, will be held jointly with the affiliated conferences at the Swedish Exhibition & Congress Centre and Gothia Towers Hotel, Gothenburg, Sweden, June 22–27, 2025. It will cover a broad spectrum of themes related to Human-Computer Interaction, including theoretical issues, methods, tools, processes, and case studies in HCI design, as well as novel interaction techniques, interfaces, and applications. The proceedings will be published by Springer. More information will become available on the conference website: https://2025.hci.international/.

General Chair
Prof. Constantine Stephanidis
University of Crete and ICS-FORTH
Heraklion, Crete, Greece
Email: general_chair@2025.hci.international

https://2025.hci.international/

Contents – Part II

Contents – Part I

Advancing Cognitive Abilities and Performance with Augmented Tools

Advances in Augmented Cognition Technologies

Advancing EEG-Based Gaze Prediction Using Depthwise Separable Convolution and Enhanced Pre-processing

Matthew L. Key[✉], Tural Mehtiyev, and Xiaodong Qu

Department of Computer Science, The George Washington University, Washington DC, USA
matthewlkey@gwu.edu

Abstract. In the field of EEG-based gaze prediction, the application of deep learning to interpret complex neural data poses significant challenges. This study evaluates the effectiveness of pre-processing techniques and the effect of additional depthwise separable convolution on EEG vision transformers (ViTs) in a pretrained model architecture. We introduce a novel method, the EEG Deeper Clustered Vision Transformer (EEG-DCViT), which combines depthwise separable convolutional neural networks (CNNs) with vision transformers, enriched by a pre-processing strategy involving data clustering. The new approach demonstrates superior performance, establishing a new benchmark with a Root Mean Square Error (RMSE) of 51.6 mm. This achievement underscores the impact of pre-processing and model refinement in enhancing EEG-based applications.

Keywords: EEG · Gaze Prediction · Machine Learning · Vision Transformer · EEGEyeNet · Depthwise Separable Convolution

1 Introduction

Electroencephalogram (EEG) data, with its multidimensional architecture, captures an abundance of details regarding brain functions, providing various perspectives on numerous neurological events [18,22,24]. Despite the widespread use of machine learning regression models for EEG data, their complexity and expensive data collection process often hinder these models from effectively understanding the data's complex structures [6,21]. The EEGEyeNet dataset, with its extensive collection of EEG and eye tracking (ET) data, emerges as a significant asset in this field, enabling in-depth gaze behavior study and laying the groundwork for benchmarking gaze prediction approaches [11]. Leveraging the EEGEyeNet dataset, the hybrid vision transformer (ViT) has showcased its potential in gaze prediction, challenging conventional convolution-based approaches [27]. As a contribution to the field, our study delves into how alterations in EEGViT design with additional depthwise separable convolution, combined with pre-processing techniques, can amplify the accuracy in predicting absolute eye position. Following our findings, we propose a new model which obtains better than state of the art performance on EEGEyeNet absolute eye position.

M. L. Key and T. Mehtiyev—The first authors contributed equally to this work.
Full source code is available at https://github.com/GWU-CS/EEG-DCViT.

D. D. Schmorrow and C. M. Fidopiastis (Eds.): HCII 2024, LNAI 14695, pp. 3–17, 2024.
https://doi.org/10.1007/978-3-031-61572-6_1

1.1   Research Questions

To further elucidate our direction within this evolving landscape, we formulate two
pivotal research questions (RQs):

RQ 1: In what ways does incorporating depthwise separable convolution into EEG-
based gaze prediction models influence their predictive accuracy?

RQ 2: What impact do advancements in pre-processing techniques have on the accuracy of EEG-based gaze prediction models?

2   Related Work

Gaze prediction, with its extensive applications in human behavior analysis, advertising,
and human-computer interactions, has garnered significant attention. The traditional
reliance on Convolutional Neural Networks (CNNs) for this task has been reconsidered
due to their limitations in capturing complex EEG patterns [3,17,19,28]. The introduction of the EEGViT model, incorporating Transformer blocks, represents a significant
shift, offering a promising alternative to conventional convolutional approaches [27].

The integration of ViTs with EEG-based gaze prediction marks a notable advancement, utilizing deep learning to navigate the intricacies of brain data interpretation. The
effectiveness of both pure and hybrid transformer models in gaze estimation has been
showcased, illustrating their capability in extracting detailed spatial features [5]. Such
models demonstrate the versatility of transformers, adapting well across different data
modalities and enhancing the accuracy of human gaze prediction.

Transformers have also been applied beyond gaze prediction, notably in EEG signal
analysis for tasks like epileptic seizure prediction. This broadens the scope of transformer applications from their origins in NLP to encompass the analysis of temporal
and spatial EEG signal features, highlighting their adaptability and potential in handling complex EEG data [8].

Furthermore, exploring the synergy between CNNs and transformers has opened
new avenues for EEG data processing. This combined approach leverages CNNs for
local feature extraction and transformers for global dependency modeling, as demonstrated in Transformer-guided CNNs for seizure prediction. Such innovations underline
the potential of integrating CNN and transformer architectures to achieve higher accuracy and better generalization in EEG-based applications, including gaze prediction
[5,8].

This evolving landscape underscores the promise of combining CNNs and transformers in EEG data analysis, guiding our research towards optimizing such integra-
tions. By harnessing the strengths of both architectures, we aim to set new standards
in EEG-based gaze prediction and neural data interpretation, contributing to the field's
advancement.

LARGE GRID PARADIGM

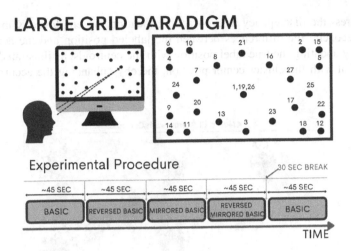

Fig. 1. Large Grid Experimental Setup: This image illustrates the schematic view of the experimental setup and the stimuli placement on the screen. It gives a visual representation of how participants interacted with the stimuli during the eye-tracking events [11].

3 Methods

Our research extends the work presented in [27], focusing on the utilization of pre-processing and depthwise-separable convolution techniques in EEG-based gaze prediction methodologies.

Data Pre-processing: Pre-processing techniques have become crucial in enhancing the performance of pre-trained vision transformer models, as noted in studies by Chen et al. [4] and Li et al. [14]. In our analysis of the EEGEyeNet dataset, we noted the presence of significant noise. During the original data collection, the EEGEyeNet procedures required participants to focus on specific target positions. Kastrati et al. [11] reported that, with the computer monitor used in the experiment, 1 pixel equates to 0.5 mm. However, we identified x and y label positions in the dataset that are as much as 100 pixels (or 50 mm) away from any known target position (Fig. 2). This significant discrepancy led us to hypothesize that participants were indeed looking at the target positions, suggesting a potential issue with the eye-tracking system. This inaccuracy leads to inherent biases in the label positions which cannot be learned during model training. These errors could be the result of the system's malfunction or improper calibration.

Another potential source of error might stem from the disparity in the granularity of the data collected. The EEG data were captured at a frequency of 500 Hz, equivalent to 500 times per second. In contrast, the eye-tracking data were recorded at a much lower frequency, once per second [11]. Therefore, if a participant's gaze was in transit towards a target point when captured, the recorded eye position might not accurately represent the entire second during which the brainwave data were collected. Unfortunately, with the available data, it is impossible to determine the exact position of the participant's eyes throughout each sample.

To address the discrepancy in eye-tracking location, we employed K-means clustering to reconcile the differences between the labeled position and the actual target position. By updating the true label position with the centroids, as illustrated in Fig. 3, we aligned it with the cluster center position, thereby enhancing the accuracy of our dataset.

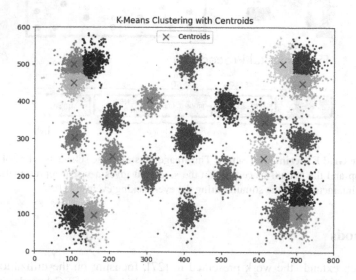

Fig. 2. Clustering illustrates the discrepancy between labeled positions and actual target positions.

Depthwise-Separable Convolutional Neural Networks (DS-CNNs): Early studies [12] highlighted that initial layers of CNNs are adept at detecting edges or specific colors in natural images. In recent years, research aiming to gain a deeper understanding of how Convolutional Neural Networks (CNNs) operate has largely shifted towards analyzing the features learned by convolutional layers rather than the weights themselves [29,30]. While examining the learned features of convolutional layers is a logical approach, the interpretation of the filter weights in the deeper layers of CNNs remains a challenge. Meanwhile, Depthwise-Separable Convolutional Neural Networks (DS-CNNs) have been rising in prominence within the field of computer vision and demonstrated state-of-the-art accuracy while requiring significantly fewer parameters and computational operations than traditional CNNs, owing to the reduced computational demands of DS-CNNs [9].

The application of depthwise separable convolution in EEG data analysis shows its potential in enhancing model performance through efficient feature extraction from multichannel EEG signals. The high accuracy rates achieved in emotion recognition tasks using publicly available EEG datasets, as cited in the works by Li et al. [13] and further supported by studies [10,25], underscore its effectiveness in reducing computational load while maintaining or improving performance score.

Building on these findings, we extend the application of depthwise separable convolution to the EEGEyeNet dataset. EEGEyeNet, being a comprehensive dataset for gaze estimation and other EEG-based analyses, could benefit significantly from the effective feature extraction capabilities of depthwise separable convolution. This approach may enhance the accuracy, especially in tasks requiring the analysis of spatial EEG signal characteristics. The potential for improved performance in EEG-based predictive modeling with reduced computational demands makes depthwise separable convolution a promising technique for exploration in this dataset.

We apply depthwise separable convolution by expanding the previous work [27] where the authors developed a hybrid vision transformer architecture named EEGViT, specifically tailored for EEG analysis. This model integrates a traditional two-step convolution operation during the patch embedding process. The first step involves a convolutional layer employing a $1 \times T$ kernel to capture temporal events across channels, acting as band-pass filters for EEG signals. Following this, the second step involves a depthwise convolutional layer with a $C \times 1$ kernel, designed to filter inputs across multiple channels at the same point in time. The model segments input images into $C \times T$ patches, which undergo a row-by-row linear projection, transforming each column vector into a scalar feature.

Building on previous study, we introduce an additional depthwise separable convolution layer in our approach. This layer incorporates both depthwise and pointwise convolutions. Following this enhancement, as shown in Fig. 4, our systematic approach for EEG data classification begins with a 2D convolution layer employing 256 filters of size (1, 36), featuring a stride of (1, 36) and padding of (0, 2). This layer is tasked with extracting temporal features from EEG signals. Subsequently, the depthwise separable convolution layer, comprising 256 filters for the depthwise part and 512 filters for the pointwise part, processes spatial information across channels. The architecture further integrates a ViT, modified with a custom depthwise convolution layer using 512 filters of size (8, 1). The process concludes with a classifier that includes a linear layer, a dropout layer, and a final linear layer, responsible for outputting logits that indicate class probabilities in a binary classification task. The incremental addition of the depthwise separable convolution layers in on the previous approach has proven to be effective in generating enhanced spatial features. These improved features effectively contribute to the model's ability to refine its performance and improve its accuracy.

Evaluation Metrics: To maintain consistency and ensure comparability with prior work, all methods, whether applied individually or in combination, will be gauged using the root mean squared error (RMSE).

Early Stopping: We employ a type of early-stopping during training to improve model performance. The SOTA EEG-ViT model was trained on a static number of 15 epochs [27]. However, the authors did not take advantage of the validation set to detect when the model was overfitting to the training data. During training, our algorithm run for 15 epochs and then output the trained model based on the epoch that has the best validation score. This will protect against overfitting and encourage higher overall accuracy.

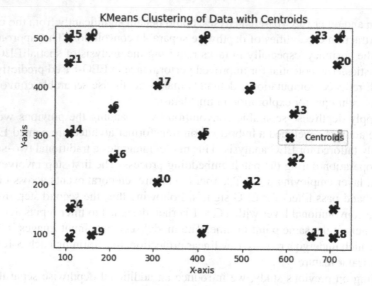

Fig. 3. The centroids used to correct training data labels.

Table 1. Descriptions of the methods used in the study.

Method	Description
Method 1	EEGViT Trained with DS-CNNs
Method 2	EEGViT Trained with Clustered Data
Method 3 (EEG-DCViT)	EEGViT Trained with Clustered and DS-CNNs

As outlined in Table 1, our study employs several methods to address the problem at hand. Each method has been tailored to optimize performance based on the specific characteristics of the dataset and the goals of the analysis.

Method 1: EEGViT Trained with DS-CNNs: This approach leverages a pre-trained EEGViT model, further refined using depthwise-separable convolutional neural networks as an additional layer. Known for their superior spatial feature extraction capabilities, DS-CNNs enable the model to effectively identify and process complex patterns in EEG channels. This method addresses Research Question 1 by demonstrating the impact of depthwise separable convolutions techniques on the accuracy score in EEG data.

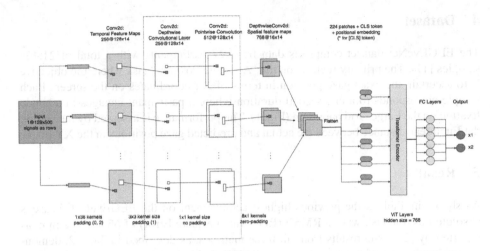

Fig. 4. EEG Vision Transformer with Depthwise Separable Convolution A specialized ViT structure tailored for raw EEG signal input. This architecture utilizes a quad-step convolution process to produce patch embeddings. The dotted outline highlights the depthwise separable convolution. After this initial step, positional embeddings are integrated and the combined sequence is subsequently passed through the ViT layers [27]. The design of the positional embedding and ViT layer is adapted from [7].

Method 2: EEGViT Trained with Clustered Data: By clustering the data prior to training, we can ensure that the model is exposed to the most representative and diverse examples. This pre-processing step helps in improving the generalization capability of the EEGViT model by focusing on the underlying distribution of the dataset. This method addresses Research Question 2 by exploring the impact of data processing step on the model performance in EEG data.

Method 3 (EEG-DCViT): EEGViT Trained with Clustered and DS-CNNs: This method, EEG Deeper Clustered Vision Transformer (EEG-DCViT), integrates the techniques of data clustering with depthwise separable convolutional neural networks (DS-CNNs) to harness the advantages of both approaches. By clustering the EEG data, the model can focus on learning from more homogeneous subsets, which improves its efficiency in recognizing underlying patterns. When combined with the DS-CNNs, known for their enhanced feature extraction with fewer parameters and computational efficiency, this strategy significantly boosts the model's capacity to identify intricate and subtle patterns within the EEG channels. This dual approach integrates the findings from both research questions to enhance the training phase, laying a robust foundation for the model. This integration aims to boost the accuracy and improve the generalization capabilities of EEG data analysis.

4   Dataset

The EEGEyeNet dataset comprises data from 27 participants with a total of 21,464 samples [11]. The primary focus is on the "Absolute Position" task where the objective is to ascertain the exact gaze position in terms of XY-coordinates on the screen. Each sample corresponds to a one-second duration where a participant engages in a single fixation on the Large Grid paradigm (Fig. 1). The performance is assessed by measuring the Euclidean distance between the actual and predicted gaze positions in the XY-plane.

5   Results

As shown in Table 2, the previous highest achievement on the EEGEyeNet dataset's absolute position task was an RMSE (Root Mean Square Error) of 55.4 ± 0.2 mm, as reported by [27]. The results from all three methods, as described in Table 2, demonstrated improved performance in terms of RMSE. In Method 1, where we implemented depthwise separable convolution, we achieved 53.5 mm. In Method 2, which applied 'EEGViT Trained with Clustered Data,' we achieved an RMSE of 53.4 mm. This result indicates the positive impact of data clustering on model accuracy. Finally, in Method 3, where we combined both methods by training the model with depthwise separable convolution on the clustered data, we achieved an even better RMSE of 51.6 ± 0.2 mm, reinforcing the effectiveness of these combined strategies.

Table 2. RMSE Comparisons for Absolute Position Task: Root Mean Squared Error (RMSE) was converted to millimeters at a ratio of 2 pixels/mm. Lower RMSE values signify better accuracy, aligning closer to true values. Displayed values represent the average and standard deviation from 5 trials. [27].

Model	Absolute Position RMSE (mm)
Naive Guessing	123.3 ± 0.0
CNN	70.4 ± 1.1
PyramidalCNN	73.9 ± 1.9
EEGNet	81.3 ± 1.0
InceptionTime	70.7 ± 0.8
Xception	78.7 ± 1.6
ViT - Base	61.5 ± 0.6
ViT - Base Pre-trained	58.1 ± 0.6
EEGViT	61.7 ± 0.6
EEGViT Pre - trained	55.4 ± 0.2
Method 1	53.6 ± 0.6
Method 2	53.4 ± 0.8
Method 3 (EEG-DCViT)	**51.6 ± 0.2**

	precision	recall	f1-score	support
0	0.64	0.67	0.66	127
1	0.67	0.76	0.71	126
2	0.66	0.84	0.74	89
3	0.59	0.51	0.55	120
4	0.92	0.64	0.75	152
5	0.50	0.45	0.47	328
6	0.48	0.55	0.51	125
7	0.88	0.85	0.87	124
8	0.58	0.38	0.46	112
9	0.80	0.83	0.81	124
10	0.49	0.56	0.52	118
11	0.64	0.71	0.67	121
12	0.57	0.59	0.58	119
13	0.38	0.35	0.36	120
14	0.45	0.50	0.47	121
15	0.57	0.41	0.48	111
16	0.43	0.53	0.48	117
17	0.49	0.51	0.50	120
18	0.40	0.55	0.46	109
19	0.75	0.58	0.66	142
20	0.61	0.50	0.55	114
21	0.62	0.83	0.71	122
22	0.46	0.51	0.49	121
23	0.54	0.68	0.60	100
24	0.56	0.39	0.46	137
accuracy			0.58	3219
macro avg	0.59	0.59	0.58	3219
weighted avg	0.59	0.58	0.58	3219

Fig. 5. Classification Performance Metrics by Cluster: This figure presents a detailed breakdown of classification metrics including precision, recall, F1-score, and support for 25 clusters, highlighting the performance of each cluster in the model evaluation.

6 Discussion

These results collectively suggest that specialized training involving data clustering and DS-CNNs can significantly improve the accuracy of deep learning models in estimating absolute positions from EEG data.

Computational Complexity: Traditionally, adding depth to vision transformers by increasing the number of convolutional layers adds computational complexity. Although our work does not include a comprehensive analysis, EEGViT has 86.0M trainable parameters, while EEG-DCViT has 86.2M trainable parameters. This results in insignificant differences in training time and memory usage.

The clustering technique runs in $\mathcal{O}(ndki)$ where n is the number of points, k is the number of clusters, d is the dimensionality of x, and i is the number of iterations that the algorithm takes to converge. In this case, the number of clusters is 25 and the number of dimensions is 2. Since these are constant, our algorithm runs in $\mathcal{O}(ni)$. Given only 21,000 data points and the hardware requirements to train EEG-DCViT, the algorithm converges within seconds.

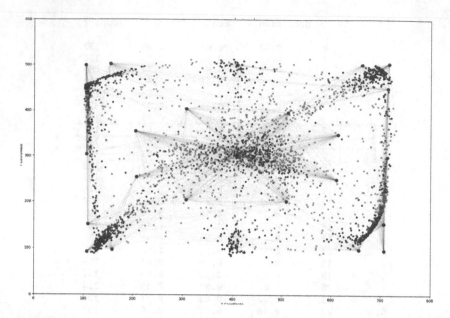

Fig. 6. Visual of Test Error for Absolute Eye Position Showing Positions within 55.4 mm RMSE (Blue) and Positions Above 55.4 mm RMSE (Red). (Color figure online)

Understanding Test Error: One of the pivotal aspects of our study was the introduction of new visualization techniques that will help both computer scientists and neuroscientists understand the test error. During our training, we discovered a way to better understand the test error. Where is the test error coming from? Which eye positions have more error? We created a new visual in order to help us answer these questions (See Fig. 6). For example, in Fig. 6, we see that the eye positions on the top left and bottom right are more difficult for the model to perform well on compared to the bottom left and upper right-hand corners. Insights from neuroscientists and other subject matter experts will be critical in order to improve performance in these positions. In this same figure, faint lines between test locations and true labels show the distance between the target and predicted values. Notably, there are fewer red lines between the "inner" positions and the "outer" positions. This could mean that the model is good at determining the difference between someone looking at the center of the screen as opposed to the outside of the screen, though we did not quantify these results.

Understanding EEG-ViT Performance: In order to understand the original EEG-ViT model, our team expanded the use of clustered eye positions shown in Fig. 3 by converting the model into a classifier. So, instead of predicting a location on a screen, the adjusted classification model would predict one of the 25 centroids shown in Fig. 3.

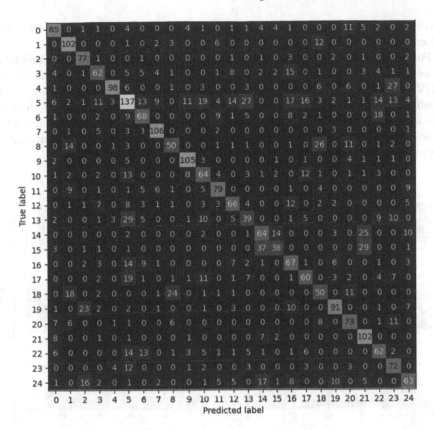

Fig. 7. Confusion matrix across 25 clusters: On the x-axis, we have the predicted values, which represent the outcomes as forecasted by our model. The y-axis, on the other hand, displays the true labels for each data point.

In the given classification report in Fig. 5, the original EEGViT model's discriminative ability is quantified across multiple classes, with individual performance metrics presented for each class. Precision, recall, and F1-scores are provided, alongside the 'support' column, which denotes the actual number of samples for each respective class. Classes 7 (participant looking straight down) and 9 (participant looking straight up) are noteworthy, with F1-scores of 0.87 and 0.81 respectively, indicating a robust predictive performance for these categories. However, there are classes with notably lower F1-scores, such as class 13, indicating potential areas for model improvement. Similarly, the confusion matrix in Fig. 7 reveals that categories 7 and 9 closely match their predictions with the true labels, while class 13 has the least number of matched predictions. The high number of matched predictions in category 5 is attributed to its larger sample size in the dataset. Notably, the central category, represented three times more frequently than others, may skew the model's predictive distribution. Future iterations of the model could benefit from a more targeted approach in feature engineering and class-specific parameter tuning to uplift the predictive accuracy for underperforming classes.

Furthermore, our team evaluated samples that were predicted with high confidence scores by EEGViT. We hypothesized that this would uncover patterns detected by the EEGViT model that are also interpretable to the human eye. We discovered similarities in samples classified with high confidence using EEG-ViT. As shown in Fig. 8, there are clear similarities in the EEG samples. The cause of these similarities is undetermined; it could be due to leakage from ocular artifacts or valuable data that requires further insight from neuroscientists.

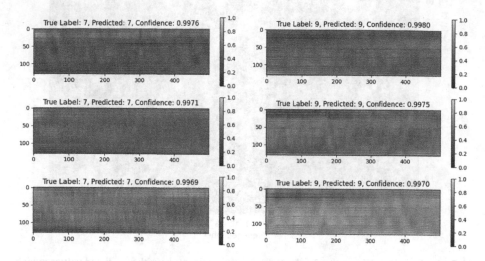

Fig. 8. Heat Map of EEG Data Samples Predicted with High Confidence by EEG-ViT Model: This figure shows samples with high confidence from class 7 (left) and class 9 (right). Class 7 displays similar bright spot in the upper left corner. Class 9 displays a similar, larger, dark spot in the upper left.

These visual tools not only facilitated a deeper understanding of the model's performance but also provided insights into the complex interplay of data features and model predictions. Visuals like this could be useful also as a communication tool between computer and neuroscientists. However, there is still a vast scope for innovation in this domain. Future research can focus on developing more advanced visualization techniques and tools that can provide even deeper insights into the workings of EEG data analysis models. This direction holds the promise of not only enhancing the interpretability of complex models but also fostering a more collaborative and intuitive approach to understanding neuroscience data.

Other deep learning approaches, [1,2,15,16,20], particularly those applied in clinical image recognition [23,26,31] could also be explored to enhance the predictive accuracy in this experiment.

Our investigation applied enhanced pre-processing strategies and architectural improvements to a pre-trained EEG-ViT model, resulting in notable performance enhancements. The integration of vision transformers with EEG data analysis in our EEG-ViT model has demonstrated a powerful synergy. Importantly, the potential of these pre-processing techniques, when applied to Convolutional Neural Networks (CNNs), should not be overlooked. Future studies could explore how these strategies might elevate the performance of CNNs in EEG data analysis without the addition of a vision transformer model. This approach could offer valuable comparative insights between Transformer-based and convolutional architectures. Another promising avenue for research involves the use of Generative Adversarial Networks (GANs) in generating synthetic EEG datasets. This could potentially address the challenges of data scarcity and diversity in EEG analysis.

7   Conclusion

In conclusion, the deployment of pre-processing and using DS-CNNs has improved the performance of EEG-based predictive models. Our proposed model, in particular, has established new state-of-the-art results, achieving a benchmark RMSE of 51.6 mm. We are optimistic that the significant performance leap made by our model will serve as a cornerstone for future developments in EEG-based brain-computer interfaces and machine learning, inspiring continued innovation and research in the field.

Disclosure of Interests. The authors declare no competing interests.

References

1. An, S., Bhat, G., Gumussoy, S., Ogras, U.: Transfer learning for human activity recognition using representational analysis of neural networks. ACM Trans. Comput. Healthc. **4**(1), 1–21 (2023)
2. An, S., Tuncel, Y., Basaklar, T., Ogras, U.Y.: A survey of embedded machine learning for smart and sustainable healthcare applications. In: Pasricha, S., Shafique, M. (eds.) Embedded Machine Learning for Cyber-Physical, IoT, and Edge Computing: Use Cases and Emerging Challenges, pp. 127–150. Springer, Cham (2023). https://doi.org/10.1007/978-3-031-40677-5_6
3. Chaaraoui, A.A., Climent-Pérez, P., Flórez-Revuelta, F.: A review on vision techniques applied to human behaviour analysis for ambient-assisted living. Expert Syst. Appl. **39**(12), 10873–10888 (2012). https://doi.org/10.1016/j.eswa.2012.03.005
4. Chen, H., et al.: Pre-trained image processing transformer. arXiv preprint arXiv:2012.00364 (2021). https://doi.org/10.48550/arXiv.2012.00364
5. Cheng, Y., Lu, F.: Gaze estimation using transformer. arXiv preprint arXiv:2105.14424 (2021). https://ar5iv.labs.arxiv.org/html/2105.14424
6. Craik, A., He, Y., Contreras-Vidal, J.L.: Deep learning for electroencephalogram (EEG) classification tasks: a review. J. Neural Eng. **16**(3) (2019). https://doi.org/10.1088/1741-2552/aba0b5
7. Dosovitskiy, A., et al.: An image is worth 16x16 words: transformers for image recognition at scale. ICLR, January 2021
8. Godoy, R.V., et al.: EEG-based epileptic seizure prediction using temporal multi-channel transformers. arXiv preprint arXiv:2209.11172 (2022). https://ar5iv.labs.arxiv.org/html/2209.11172

9. Howard, A.G., et al.: MobileNets: efficient convolutional neural networks for mobile vision applications. arXiv preprint arXiv:1704.04861 (2017). https://arxiv.org/pdf/1704.04861.pdf

10. Huang, Z., et al.: CDBA: a novel multi-branch feature fusion model for EEG-based emotion recognition. Front. Physiol. **14** (2023). https://doi.org/10.3389/fphys.2023.1200656. https://www.frontiersin.org/articles/10.3389/fphys.2023.1200656/full

11. Kastrati, A., et al.: EEGEyeNet: a simultaneous electroencephalography and eye-tracking dataset and benchmark for eye movement prediction. ETH Zurich, November 2021

12. Krizhevsky, A., Sutskever, I., Hinton, G.E.: ImageNet classification with deep convolutional neural networks. In: Proceedings of the 25th International Conference on Neural Information Processing Systems - Volume 1. NeurIPS (2012). https://proceedings.neurips.cc/paper_files/paper/2012/file/c399862d3b9d6b76c8436e924a68c45b-Paper.pdf

13. Li, Q., et al.: Multidimensional feature in emotion recognition based on multi-channel EEG signals. Entropy **24**(12), 1830 (2022). https://doi.org/10.3390/e24121830. https://www.mdpi.com/1099-4300/24/12/1830

14. Li, W., Lu, X., Qian, S., Lu, J., Zhang, X., Jia, J.: On efficient transformer-based image pre-training for low-level vision. arXiv: Computer Vision and Pattern Recognition, December 2021. https://doi.org/10.48550/arXiv.2112.10175

15. Lu, Y., Shen, M., Wang, H., Wang, X., van Rechem, C., Wei, W.: Machine learning for synthetic data generation: a review. arXiv preprint arXiv:2302.04062 (2023)

16. Lu, Y., et al.: COT: an efficient and accurate method for detecting marker genes among many subtypes. Bioinform. Adv. **2**(1), vbac037 (2022)

17. Majaranta, P., Bulling, A.: Eye tracking eye-based human-computer interaction, March 2014. https://doi.org/10.1007/978-1-4471-6392-3_3

18. Murungi, N.K., Pham, M.V., Dai, X., Qu, X.: Trends in machine learning and electroencephalogram (EEG): a review for undergraduate researchers. arXiv preprint arXiv:2307.02819 (2023)

19. Okada, G., Masui, K., Tsumura, N.: Advertisement effectiveness estimation based on crowd-sourced multimodal affective responses. In: CVPR Workshop (2023)

20. Qiu, Y., Zhao, Z., Yao, H., Chen, D., Wang, Z.: Modal-aware visual prompting for incomplete multi-modal brain tumor segmentation. In: Proceedings of the 31st ACM International Conference on Multimedia, pp. 3228–3239 (2023)

21. Qu, X., Liu, P., Li, Z., Hickey, T.: Multi-class time continuity voting for EEG classification. In: Frasson, C., Bamidis, P., Vlamos, P. (eds.) BFAL 2020. LNCS (LNAI), vol. 12462, pp. 24–33. Springer, Cham (2020). https://doi.org/10.1007/978-3-030-60735-7_3

22. Qu, X., Mei, Q., Liu, P., Hickey, T.: Using EEG to distinguish between writing and typing for the same cognitive task. In: Frasson, C., Bamidis, P., Vlamos, P. (eds.) BFAL 2020. LNCS (LNAI), vol. 12462, pp. 66–74. Springer, Cham (2020). https://doi.org/10.1007/978-3-030-60735-7_7

23. Tang, Y., Song, S., Gui, S., Chao, W., Cheng, C., Qin, R.: Active and low-cost hyperspectral imaging for the spectral analysis of a low-light environment. Sensors **23**(3), 1437 (2023)

24. Teplan, M.: Fundamentals of EEG measurement. Meas. Sci. Rev. **2**(2), 1–11 (2002)

25. Wang, X., Shi, R., Wu, X., Zhang, J.: Decoding human interaction type from inter-brain synchronization by using EEG brain network. IEEE J. Biomed. Health Inform. (2023). https://doi.org/10.1109/JBHI.2023.3239742. https://pubmed.ncbi.nlm.nih.gov/37917521/. epub ahead of print

26. Xu, K., Lee, A.H.X., Zhao, Z., Wang, Z., Wu, M., Lin, W.: Metagrad: adaptive gradient quantization with hypernetworks. arXiv preprint arXiv:2303.02347 (2023)

27. Yang, R., Modesitt, E.: ViT2EEG: leveraging hybrid pretrained vision transformers for EEG data (2023)

28. Yi, L., Qu, X.: Attention-based CNN capturing EEG recording's average voltage and local change. In: Degen, H., Ntoa, S. (eds.) HCII 2022. LNCS, vol. 13336, pp. 448–459. Springer, Cham (2022). https://doi.org/10.1007/978-3-031-05643-7_29
29. Yosinski, J., Clune, J., Nguyen, A., Fuchs, T., Lipson, H.: Understanding neural networks through deep visualization. arXiv preprint arXiv:1506.06579 (2015). https://arxiv.org/pdf/1506.06579.pdf
30. Zeiler, M.D., Fergus, R.: Visualizing and understanding convolutional networks. arXiv preprint arXiv:1311.2901 (2013). https://arxiv.org/pdf/1311.2901.pdf
31. Zhao, S., et al.: Deep learning based CETSA feature prediction cross multiple cell lines with latent space representation. Sci. Rep. **14**(1), 1878 (2024)

A Novel Loss Function Utilizing Wasserstein Distance to Reduce Subject-Dependent Noise for Generalizable Models in Affective Computing

Nibraas Khan[✉][iD], Mahrukh Tauseef[iD], Ritam Ghosh[iD],
and Nilanjan Sarkar[iD]

Vanderbilt University, Nashville, TN 37235, USA
nibraas.a.khan@vanderbilt.edu

Abstract. Emotions are an essential part of human behavior that can impact thinking, decision-making, and communication skills. Thus, the ability to accurately monitor and identify emotions can be useful in many human-centered applications such as behavioral training, tracking emotional well-being, and the development of human-computer interfaces. The correlation between patterns in physiological data and affective states has allowed for the utilization of deep learning techniques that can accurately detect the affective states of a person. However, the generalisability of existing models is often limited by the subject-dependent noise in physiological data due to variations in a subject's reactions to stimuli. Hence, we propose a novel cost function that employs Optimal Transport Theory, specifically Wasserstein Distance, to scale the importance of subject-dependent data such that higher importance is assigned to patterns in data that are common across all participants while decreasing the importance of patterns that result from subject-dependent noise. The performance of the proposed cost function is demonstrated through an autoencoder with a multi-class classifier attached to the latent space and trained simultaneously to detect affective states. An autoencoder with a state-of-the-art loss function i.e., Mean Squared Error, is used as a baseline for comparison with our model across four different commonly used datasets. Centroid and minimum distance between different classes are used as metrics to indicate the separation between different classes in the latent space. An average increase of 14.75% and 17.75% (from benchmark to proposed loss function) was found for minimum and centroid Euclidean distance respectively over all datasets.

Keywords: Machine Learning · Affective Computing · Optimal Transport Theory · Human-Computer Interaction · Wasserstein Distance

1 Introduction

Affective state can be measured and monitored in two ways: intrusively and non-intrusively. Intrusive methods measure the concentration of various hormones in

D. D. Schmorrow and C. M. Fidopiastis (Eds.): HCII 2024, LNAI 14695, pp. 18–30, 2024.
https://doi.org/10.1007/978-3-031-61572-6_2

the bloodstream that can be used to detect an affective state. For instance, cortisol levels produced by the hypothalamic-pituitary-adrenocortical (HPA) axis can be collected through samples of blood, urine, hair, or saliva and used to detect stress [5]. One of the challenges with intrusive measurement is that it is invasive and cannot be used to monitor the affective state in real time.

Non-intrusive methods, on the other hand, include the analysis of behavioral or physiological data that can lead to non-invasive real-time detection of affective states. Behavioral actions such as blink rate, facial expression, gesture, speech, and body pose have been commonly used for affective state detection [20]. However, all these actions can be masked and voluntarily controlled by a subject which reduces its reliability [7,20]. Alternatively, strong evidence suggests physiological signals to be more reliable for affective state detection due to their involuntary nature and a strong correlation of patterns in the data with different affective states [5].

Physiological signals are a response to the Autonomic Nervous System (ANS) utilizing both motor and sensory neurons to communicate and operate between the Central Nervous System (CNS) and the various organs or muscles. The ANS is composed of the Sympathetic (SNS) and Parasympathetic (PNS) nervous systems. The sympathetic nervous system prepares the body for emergency action, which results in the "fight or flight" response [18]. The response leads to an increase in measurable physiological signals, such as heart rate, blood flow, and increased muscle activation which can be mapped to different affective states. Whereas, the parasympathetic nervous system helps sustain homeostasis during rest by decreasing physiological signals and maintaining them in moderate ranges [4]. Since ANS is involuntarily stimulated, the response cannot be manipulated or masked by an individual. This has led to the popular field of affecting computing to focus on dynamically identifying different affective states using non-invasive wearable sensors that can monitor changes in physiological signals in response to a stimulus.

The ability to map patterns in physiological data with affective states has allowed for the utilization of machine learning techniques for the detection of affective states. Research in psychophysiology has led to the compilation of a comprehensive list of physiological data that can be used to monitor affective states. This list includes heart activity (ECG), brain activity (EEG), skin response (EDA), blood pressure variation (PPG), respiratory response, and muscle activity (EMG) [5]. Several datasets have been compiled by collecting physiological data while inducing an affective state. For instance, one of the state-of-the-art datasets, Wearable Stress and Affect Detection (WESAD) [19], induced amusement by making the subjects watch funny video clips and they induced stress through public speaking and mental arithmetic tasks. Meanwhile, their physiological data i.e., blood volume pulse, ECG, EDA, EMG, respiration, body temperature, and three-axis acceleration was collected and classified simultaneously. Other common datasets like Database for Emotional Analysis using Physiological Signals (DEAP) [8], Affect, Personality and Mood Research on Individuals and Groups (AMIGOS) [15], and Cognitive Load, Affect, and Stress

Recognition (CLAS) [14] follow suit by using video clips or stress-inducing tasks to collect and classify physiological data for the induced affective states.

Numerous machine learning techniques have been utilized to detect affective states from physiological data. These approaches include support vector machines (SVM), random forest (RF), k-nearest neighbors (KNN), and Linear Discriminant Analysis (LDA) that need handcrafted features from the pre-processed signal in order to remove noisy data [20]. However, there is no consensus on the list of features extracted from physiological data that can be accurately mapped to affective states which results in reduced performance [12]. Alternatively, with the advancement of deep learning, there has been an increasing interest in using deep learning techniques like long short-term memory (LSTM), autoencoders, and convolutional neural networks (CNN) [1,17]. These models allow for automatic feature extraction based on the model's ability to automatically comprehend patterns in data with respect to the labels.

Even though deep learning techniques show promise, the lack of generalisability still exists and contributes to poor performance. This is because the subjects might not exhibit the same physiological response to stimuli [12]. Thus, subject-dependent noise can lead to poor generalisability of the model. This issue can be resolved by using a loss function that filters out the features of data that are person-specific and do not contribute much to affective state detection. In other words, if each subject's data is treated as a distribution, the loss function assigns higher importance to features that are closer in distance to the group distribution (distributions of all subjects) while assigning lower importance to features that are much further apart across from the group distribution. The distance between distributions can be calculated by using the Wasserstein distance [16].

In this paper, we introduce a novel loss function that accounts for subject-dependent noise in the data to develop more generalizable models. This is accomplished by training an autoencoder model with a loss function that utilizes Wasserstein Distance to scale the importance of subject-dependent patterns to obtain a latent space with reduced dimensions and less noisy subject-independent features. The performance of the model is tested on four different datasets (WESAD, AMIGOS, CLAS, and DEAP) using the centroid and minimum distances between classes as metrics.

This paper is structured as follows. Section 2 presents an overview of existing literature that informed the development of the proposed model. This is followed by the 3 section that discusses the mathematical and algorithmic details of the model. The results are shown and discussed in Sect. 4 followed by concluding remarks in Sect. 5.

2   Background

As mentioned before, machine learning techniques for affective state detection using physiological data have been a topic of immense interest in the past few years. Kolodyazhniy et al. [9] conducted a notable study in 2011 on the topic by compiling a dataset and training several machine learning models like LDA,

Quadratic Discriminant Analysis (QDA), Multilayer Perceptron (MLP), Radial Basis Function (RBF), and KNN. They used a variety of features extracted from the physiological data to discover the features that are strongly correlated to affective state. They reported a maximum accuracy of 81.9% using KNN with 7 features on subject-dependent classification, but they reported the accuracy to go down to 78.9% for subject-independent classification.

Ever since several novel techniques have been implemented to improve the performance of subject-independent classification. Bota et al. [2] conducted a review of existing machine learning and deep learning techniques for affective state detection from 2001 to 2019. They reported lower performance for subject-independent classification as compared to subject-dependent classification for most of the models.

Li et al. [11] proposed a technique that assigned variable learnable weights to different physiological signals fed to an attention-based bidirectional LSTM model. They reported an accuracy of 81.1% for subject-independent classification using the AMIGOS dataset. However, the model's accuracy across other datasets is not known.

Reviews conducted by both Bota et al. [2] and Xin et al. [6] highlighted the lack of generalization to be a consistent issue with the existing techniques for affective state detection. This has led to several works proposing novel techniques to increase the generalization of affective state detection models.

Li et al. [13] used different automatic feature selection techniques such as Chi-Squared-Based Feature Selection, Mutual Information-Based Feature Selection, ANOVA F-Value-Based Feature Selection, Recursive Feature Elimination (RFE), and L1-Norm Penalty-Based Feature Selection. These techniques were used such that the most important features needed for affective state detection can be extracted and used to train an SVM. They reported an accuracy of 83.3% for subject-independent classification using the SEED dataset and 59.06% using the DEAP dataset.

In addition, several domain adaptation techniques are being used to select features such that the difference between the distributions of each subject's physiological data is minimized. Chai et al. [3] proposed a *Subspace Alignment Autoencoder* to minimize the distribution mismatch of the physiological data of each subject by minimizing the maximum mean discrepancy of reproduced kernel Hilbert space (RKHS). This allowed the alignment of different distributions by mitigating the subject-specific noise from the data. They reported an accuracy 77.8% using the SEED dataset.

Based on the literature survey, we identified the potential of decreasing the distance between each subject's distribution of physiological data and using the extracted features to train a more generalized model. However, this entails that a robust method needs to be chosen to calculate the distance between distributions. One such method, Wasserstein Distance, can be retrieved from Optimal Transport Theory (OTT) [16]. Wasserstein Distance allows for the calculation of the distance between distributions while also considering the geometry of the distribution (symmetrical and triangular) [10]. Kolouri et al. [10] demonstrated the potential of Wasserstein Distance to minimize the distance between an input and target distribution for generative modeling using autoencoders.

Hence, in this paper, we propose a novel loss function using Wasserstein Distance for automatic feature extraction by assigning more weight to features that are closer in distance to each other across all subjects. An autoencoder model is used to generate a latent space that excludes all the features that are influenced by subject-dependent nuances. The goal is to increase the separation between different affective states in the latent space such that a more generalized classification model can be trained.

3   Methods

3.1   Optimal Transport Theory

Optimal Transport Theory was first formalized by the French mathematician, Gaspard Monge, in 1781, right before the French Revolution [16]. The motivation to study this was to come up with a transport plan to move a mass from one point to another with minimum cost. The outcome of this study formulated a method for measuring the distance between two probability distributions. In the formulation, consider two probability measures μ and v defined on spaces X and Y respectively. μ and v have density functions f and g where $d\mu = f(x)dx$ and $dv = g(y)dy$, where $(x, y) \in X \text{x} Y$. A cost function is defined, $c(x, y)$ which finds the *distance* between a point x and y. The initial choice by Monge was Euclidean distance. A transport plan $T : X \longrightarrow Y$ allows for moving a mass, M, from X to Y such that the measure μ of the mass in space X is the same as the measure v of the mass in space Y after the mass is transported from X to Y:

$$\mu[M] = v[T(M)] \tag{1}$$

Once a plan T has been found, the cost associated with it is (The equation is adapted from [21]):

$$I(T, f, g, c) = \int_X c(x, T(x))f(x)dx^1 \tag{2}$$

While there can be many solutions to T, the aim is to minimize the overall cost (The equation is adapted from [21])

$$I(f, g, c) = \inf_{T \in M} \int_X c(x, T(x))f(x)dx,^2 \tag{3}$$

where M is the set of all transport plans T that transfers f to g. In the formulation, the optimal cost of transporting x to y is also known as the Wasserstein Distance. (The equation is adapted from [21])

$$W_p(\mu, v) = (\inf_{T \in M} \int_{\mathbb{R}^n} |x - T(x)|^p d\mu(x))^{\frac{1}{p}}, \mu, v \in \mathcal{P}_p(X),^3 \tag{4}$$

where $\mathcal{P}_p(X)$ is the set of probability measures with finite moments of order p [21]. In this paper, we will focus on using the Wasserstein Distance to measure the distance between a subject's distribution and the group's distribution.

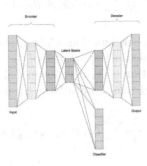

Fig. 1. Architecture of the Autoencoder model with a classifier attached to the latent space.

3.2 Models

In this work, we focus on using an autoencoder architecture to reduce noise along with our novel cost function through dimensionality reduction. In addition to a reconstruction loss, a classifier is attached to the latent space to ensure it is discriminant. Figure 1 shows the architecture of our model, and both components (encoder and classifier) are trained simultaneously. The proposed cost function is not restricted to the autoencoder model and can be used with any suitable machine learning algorithm. The following section will address how the loss function can be integrated into the autoencoder architecture. We use a standard autoencoder model with Mean Squared Error (MSE) for a baseline to compare it with our novel cost function.

3.3 Autoencoder Error Decomposition

The group reconstruction error, r_g, of the autoencoder for the subject-independent model is given as

$$r_g = \frac{1}{N} \sum_{n=1}^{N} \mathcal{L}_a(a; g_{n,x}, g'_{n,x}) \qquad (5)$$

where N is the total number of samples across all subjects, $\mathcal{L}_a$ is any loss function for reconstruction (Mean-Squared Error), and a is the encoder and decoder architecture of the network. The reconstruction error will be used in conjunction with the classifier loss. The classifier head, attached to the latent space, is used to calculate the group classifier error and subject-specific classifier error. The group classifier uses all labeled samples available across all subjects.

$$c_g = \frac{1}{N} \sum_{n=1}^{N} \mathcal{L}_c(c; g_{n,x}, g_{n,y}) * \lambda_g \tag{6}$$

where $\mathcal{L}_c$ is any classification loss function (Categorical Cross-Entropy) and λ_g is a regularizer term used to scale the importance of the group classifier error during backpropagation. The definition of λ_g is given in Eq. 11. Subject i's specific loss is computed using all labeled samples available S_i and any loss function $\mathcal{L}_c$.

$$c_{s,i} = \frac{1}{N_i} \sum_{n=1}^{N_i} \mathcal{L}_c(f; s_{n,x}, s_{n,y}) * \lambda_{s,i} \tag{7}$$

$\lambda_{s,i}$ is used to scale the importance of a specific subject in the calculation of the overall loss for backpropagation. The overall classification loss is given as:

$$c_s = \sum_{i=i}^{S} c_{s,i} \tag{8}$$

where S is the number of subjects. Optimal Transport Theory, specifically, Wasserstein Distance, is used to calculate $\lambda_{s,i}$ by measuring the distance between the group distribution and subject distribution. Equations 9 and 10 denote the formulation for $\lambda_{s,i}$.

$$\alpha_{s,i} = EMD(G, S_i) = \inf_{\gamma \in \phi(G, S_i)} \mathbb{E}_{(G,S_i) \sim \gamma}[||x - y||] \tag{9}$$

$\alpha_{s,i}$ is normalized and subtracted from 1 to ensure that the further away a subject i is from the group, the smaller the scaling factor, $\lambda_{s,i}$, is.

$$\lambda_{s,i} = 1 - \frac{\alpha_{s,i}}{|\sum_{i=1}^{S} \alpha_{s,i}|} \tag{10}$$

Finally, λ_g is determined by ensuring that the regularizer terms sum to 1.

$$\lambda_g + \sum_{i=1}^{S} \lambda_{s,i} = 1 \tag{11}$$

3.4   Datasets

Experiments in this work were conducted on popular, public physiological datasets: WESAD, AMIGOS, CLAS, and DEAP.

WESAD is a multimodal dataset for wearable stress and affect detection with data recorded using a wrist-worn device (sensors: PPG, accelerometer, electrodermal activity, and body temperature) and a chest-worn device (sensors: ECG, accelerometer, EMG, respiration, and body temperature). The dataset consists of 15 subjects (aged 24–35 years) with 100 min of data each. The dataset was recorded to detect and distinguish between three affective states: neutral, stress, and amusement which were denoted using self-reports for subjective experience during the emotional stimulus along with the study protocol of inducing emotion [19].

The AMIGOS dataset consists of data from sensors (EEG, ECG, and GSR), full-body videos, and depth videos from 40 volunteers. Data was collected while watching 16 short videos and 37 of the 40 volunteers watched 4 long videos. Both self-assessment (valence-arousal, control, familiarity, like-dislike, and selection of basic emotions) and external assessment of participants' levels of valence were used to annotate the dataset. The participants were also asked to fill forms with Personality Traits and Positive and Negative Affect Schedule (PANAS) questionnaires [15].

DEAP contains EEG, GSR, RESP, SKT, EMG, EOG, and BVP data from 32 volunteers while they were watching 40 one-minute-long music videos. Additionally, a frontal face video was recorded for 22 of the participants. The dataset was self-annotated after each video with the following labels: arousal, valence, like-dislike, familiarity, and dominance by the volunteers [8].

PPG, EEG, and GSR data from 60 patients engaged in cognitively difficult tasks was collected in the CLAS dataset. The cognitively difficult tasks used in this dataset are: Stroop test, math test, logic problem test, and emotionally evoking stimuli [14]. The dataset was labeled based on the study protocol (i.e., high cognitive load during logic and math problems and low cognitive load during neutral stimuli).

4   Results

The results presented in this work use a standard 10-fold Leave-One-Subject-Out (LOSO) where the models were trained on all subjects excluding one and tested on the excluded subject.

The dimensionality of the latent space is too high to be visualized, so Principal Component Analysis (PCA) is used to condense the space into three components. Figure 2 compares the latent space using MSE with our cost function. Figure 2(a)–2(d) shows a large overlap of classes which would lead to imprecise decision boundaries. Specifically consider Fig. 2(b) where all classes are highly interrelated. In contrast, the latent space in Fig. 2(f) shows a clear separation of classes by utilizing Wasserstein Distance. While the advantages of the novel cost function are distinct in three dimensions, the latent space has higher dimensionality, and the improvements are expressed using the Euclidean distance between centroids of classes and the Euclidean distance between closest points between different classes.

Figure 3 highlights the percent increase between the centroids of classes in all datasets with the novel cost function for training and testing data. For all datasets, there is a significant increase in the distance over MSE. Additionally, Fig. 4 shows the increase in the minimum distance between samples of classes.

The accuracy of our models is presented in Table 1 through a comparison of MSE with our novel cost function using LOSO. The table shows that the proposed cost function can achieve better performance on most datasets and performs the same as the MSE in the worst-case scenario. The experiments presented in this work were conducted on a computer with an AMD Ryzen 9 5900HX, NVIDIA GeForce RTX 3070, and 32 GB of RAM with an approximate run time of 45 min per dataset.

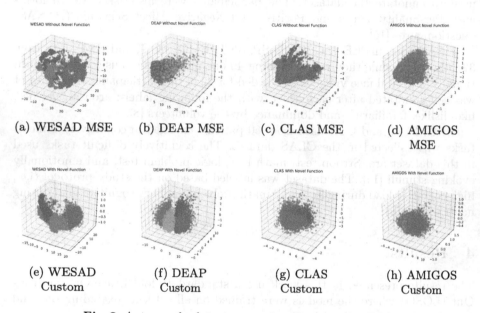

(a) WESAD MSE   (b) DEAP MSE   (c) CLAS MSE   (d) AMIGOS MSE

(e) WESAD Custom   (f) DEAP Custom   (g) CLAS Custom   (h) AMIGOS Custom

Fig. 2. Autoencoder latent space visualization using PCA

Table 1. A comparison of the accuracy between using the standard MSE for reconstruction loss and the novel cost function.

	MSE Accuracy	Novel Cost Accuracy
WESAD	80.31% ± 1.13%	84.11% ± 1.05%
CLAS	77.23% ± 0.76%	79.63% ± 0.86%
AMIGOS	79.56% ± 1.44%	79.97% ± 1.75%
DEAP	66.22% ± 1.87%	71.64% ± 1.81%

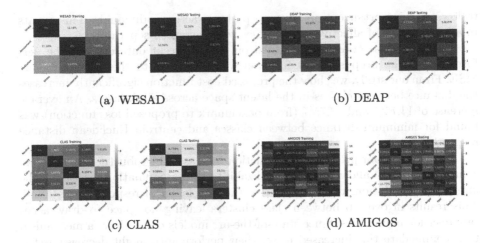

(a) WESAD   (b) DEAP

(c) CLAS   (d) AMIGOS

Fig. 3. Distance increase when using the novel cost function over MSE expressed as a percentage for training and testing data (LOSO) for class centroids.

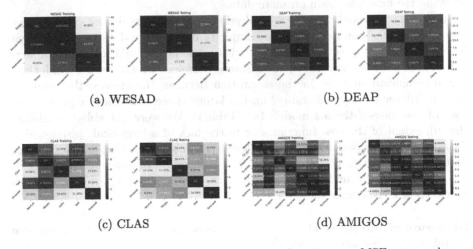

(a) WESAD   (b) DEAP

(c) CLAS   (d) AMIGOS

Fig. 4. Distance increase when using the novel cost function over MSE expressed as a percentage for training and testing data (LOSO) for the minimum distance between classes.

5 Conclusion and Future Works

The lack of generalizability of affective state detection models has been a consistent issue. It is often due to a large variation in the distribution of physiological data for a set of individuals in reaction to the same stimuli. This leads to subject-dependent noise that affects the performance of a model. Our approach employs autoencoders that can inherently reduce noise and extract relevant features through dimensionality reduction. To further reduce the subject-dependent noise, we introduce a novel cost function that uses Optimal Transport Theory to lower the importance of uncommon patterns across individuals. This results in a latent space of affective state classes with increased separability.

The model was trained and tested on four different datasets and the performance of the proposed cost function was compared to the state-of-the-art MSE. From our study, we show the proposed cost function significantly increases the distance between classes in the latent space across all datasets. An average increase of 14.75% and 17.75% (from benchmark to proposed loss function) was found for minimum distance between classes and centroid Euclidean distance respectively.

Additionally, our proposed cost function increases the robustness of affective computing models allowing for generalizability as the population increases. The larger the population, the more diverse the physiological responses to stimuli. This results in overlap between class clusters leaving no space to draw accurate decision boundaries. Since state-of-the-art models do not have a mechanism to accommodate this increased noise, their performance might decrease as the population size increases. Alternatively, our proposed loss function mitigates the effect of increased subject-dependent noise while increasing the performance by allowing the model to train on more data.

However, commonly used public physiological datasets do not contain samples from a large population as the compilation of a large dataset is expensive. In our experiments, we used datasets with a smaller population size and were still able to show an increase in the distance between classes. Even though there was a significant increase in the separation between the classes, the accuracy of a multilayer perceptron trained on the latent space was nearly equivalent to that of the state-of-the-art models (see Table 1). We were not able to highlight the full extent of the cost function due to the lack of a large-scale physiological dataset. Future works include the implementation of more complex encoder and decoder models (e.g., LSTMs and CNNs), exploration of different classifiers on the latent space to further increase the accuracy, and investigation of the cost function on a large-scale dataset.

Disclosure of Interests. The authors have no competing interests to declare that are relevant to the content of this article.

References

1. Arya, R., Singh, J., Kumar, A.: A survey of multidisciplinary domains contributing to affective computing. Comput. Sci. Rev. **40**, 100399 (2021). https://doi.org/10.1016/j.cosrev.2021.100399. https://www.sciencedirect.com/science/article/pii/S1574013721000393
2. Bota, P.J., Wang, C., Fred, A.L., Silva, H.P.D.: A review, current challenges, and future possibilities on emotion recognition using machine learning and physiological signals. IEEE Access **7**, 140990–141020 (2019). https://doi.org/10.1109/ACCESS.2019.2944001

3. Chai, X., Wang, Q., Zhao, Y., Liu, X., Bai, O., Li, Y.: Unsupervised domain adaptation techniques based on auto-encoder for non-stationary EEG-based emotion recognition. Comput. Biol. Med. **79**, 205–214 (2016)
4. Glick, G., Braunwald, E., Lewis, R.M.: Relative roles of the sympathetic and parasympathetic nervous systems in the reflex control of heart rate. Circ. Res. **16**, 363–375 (1965)
5. Greene, S., Thapliyal, H., Caban-Holt, A.: A survey of affective computing for stress detection: evaluating technologies in stress detection for better health. IEEE Consum. Electron. Mag. **5**, 44–56 (2016)
6. Hu, X., Chen, J., Wang, F., Zhang, D.: Ten challenges for EEG-based affective computing. Brain Sci. Adv. **5**(1), 1–20 (2019). https://doi.org/10.1177/2096595819896200
7. Khateeb, M., Anwar, S.M., Alnowami, M.: Multi-domain feature fusion for emotion classification using deap dataset. IEEE Access **9**, 12134–12142 (2021). https://doi.org/10.1109/ACCESS.2021.3051281
8. Koelstra, S., et al.: DEAP: a database for emotion analysis; using physiological signals. IEEE Trans. Affect. Comput. **3**(1), 18–31 (2011)
9. Kolodyazhniy, V., Kreibig, S.D., Gross, J.J., Roth, W.T., Wilhelm, F.H.: An affective computing approach to physiological emotion specificity: toward subject-independent and stimulus-independent classification of film-induced emotions. Psychophysiology **48**(7), 908–922 (2011)
10. Kolouri, S., Pope, P.E., Martin, C.E., Rohde, G.K.: Sliced Wasserstein auto-encoders. In: International Conference on Learning Representations (2018)
11. Li, C., Bao, Z., Li, L., Zhao, Z.: Exploring temporal representations by leveraging attention-based bidirectional LSTM-RNNs for multi-modal emotion recognition. Inf. Process. Manag. **57**(3), 102185 (2020)
12. Li, R., Liu, Z.: Stress detection using deep neural networks. BMC Med. Inform. Decis. Mak. **20**(11), 1–10 (2020)
13. Li, X., Song, D., Zhang, P., Zhang, Y., Hou, Y., Hu, B.: Exploring EEG features in cross-subject emotion recognition. Front. Neurosci. **12**, 162 (2018)
14. Markova, V., Ganchev, T., Kalinkov, K.: CLAS: a database for cognitive load, affect and stress recognition. In: 2019 International Conference on Biomedical Innovations and Applications (BIA), pp. 1–4. IEEE (2019). https://doi.org/10.1109/BIA48344.2019.8967457
15. Miranda-Correa, J.A., Abadi, M.K., Sebe, N., Patras, I.: AMIGOS: a dataset for affect, personality and mood research on individuals and groups. IEEE Trans. Affect. Comput. **12**(2), 479–493 (2018)
16. Monge, G.: Memory on the theory of cuttings and embankments. History of the Royal Academy of Sciences of Paris (1781)
17. Oskooei, A., Chau, S.M., Weiss, J., Sridhar, A., Martínez, M.R., Michel, B.: DeStress: deep learning for unsupervised identification of mental stress in firefighters from heart-rate variability (HRV) data. In: Shaban-Nejad, A., Michalowski, M., Buckeridge, D.L. (eds.) Explainable AI in Healthcare and Medicine. SCI, vol. 914, pp. 93–105. Springer, Cham (2021). https://doi.org/10.1007/978-3-030-53352-6_9
18. Richter, M., Wright, R.A.: Sympathetic nervous system (SNS). In: Gellman, M.D., Turner, J.R. (eds.) Encyclopedia of Behavioral Medicine, pp. 1943–1944. Springer, New York (2013). https://doi.org/10.1007/978-1-4419-1005-9_853
19. Schmidt, P., Reiss, A., Duerichen, R., Marberger, C., Van Laerhoven, K.: Introducing WESAD, a multimodal dataset for wearable stress and affect detection. In: Proceedings of the 20th ACM International Conference on Multimodal Interaction, pp. 400–408 (2018)

20. Shu, L., et al.: A review of emotion recognition using physiological signals. Sensors **18**(7), 2074 (2018)
21. Yang, Y., Engquist, B., Sun, J., Hamfeldt, B.F.: Application of optimal transport and the quadratic Wasserstein metric to full-waveform inversion. Geophysics **83**(1), R43–R62 (2018)

Enhancing Eye-Tracking Performance Through Multi-task Learning Transformer

Weigeng Li$^{(\boxtimes)}$, Neng Zhou, and Xiaodong Qu

The George Washington University, Washington, DC 20052, USA
{weigengli,nengzhou,x.qu}@gwu.edu

Abstract. In this study, we introduce an innovative EEG signal reconstruction sub-module designed to enhance the performance of deep learning models on EEG eye-tracking tasks. This sub-module can integrate with all Encoder-Classifier-based deep learning models and achieve end-to-end training within a multi-task learning framework. Additionally, as the module operates under unsupervised learning, it is versatile and applicable to various tasks. We demonstrate its effectiveness by incorporating it into advanced deep-learning models, including Transformers and pre-trained Transformers. Our results indicate a significant enhancement in feature representation capabilities, evidenced by a Root Mean Squared Error (RMSE) of 54.1 mm. This represents a notable improvement over existing methods, showcasing the sub-module's potential in refining EEG-based model performance.

The success of this approach suggests that this reconstruction sub-module is capable of enhancing the feature extraction ability of the encoder. Due to the sub-module being mounted as a sub-task under the main task and maintained through a multi-task learning framework, our model preserves the end-to-end training process of the original model. In contrast to pre-training methods like autoencoder, our model saves computational costs associated with pre-training and exhibits greater flexibility in adapting to various model structures. Benefiting from the unsupervised nature of the sub-module, it can be applied across diverse tasks. We believe it represents a novel paradigm for improving the performance of deep learning models in EEG-related challenges.

Keywords: EEG Eye-Tracking · Hybrid Vision Transformers · Multi-Task Learning · Signal Reconstruction · Unsupervised Learning · Spatio-Temporal Data Processing · Feature Extraction · Neuroscience

1 Introduction

Electroencephalography (EEG) is a powerful neuroimaging technique that plays a vital role in deciphering the complex working mechanisms of the human brain [25]. By recording the electrical activity generated by neurons, EEG provides a window into the dynamics of the brain with high temporal resolution.

D. D. Schmorrow and C. M. Fidopiastis (Eds.): HCII 2024, LNAI 14695, pp. 31–46, 2024.
https://doi.org/10.1007/978-3-031-61572-6_3

EEG has been employed in various tasks, reflecting its versatility. Researchers have harnessed EEG data for purposes such as brain-computer interfaces (BCIs) [1], sleep analysis [21], and more recently, eye movement prediction [15]. These tasks have revealed different aspects of brain function and have contributed to our understanding of the neural mechanisms underlying cognition, behavior, and sensory processing.

The challenges of EEG-based tasks are multiple, including issues related to data quality, computational complexity, and model generalization [22]. EEG signals are vulnerable to noise and artifacts, which can affect the reliability of results. In addition, the high dimension of EEG data poses computational challenges, requiring sophisticated preprocessing and feature extraction techniques.

In recent years, convolutional neural networks (CNNs) have become a powerful tool in the field of EEG research [10]. Originally developed for image analysis, convolutional neural networks have now been applied to process and interpret EEG data. These neural networks can automatically learn complex spatial and temporal patterns in EEG signals, providing a new dimension in the analysis of brain activity.

Multi-task Learning (MTL) [5], in contrast to single-task learning (STL), involves simultaneous consideration of multiple related tasks, leveraging shared information to address complex challenges. This approach capitalizes on task connections to extract complementary information, enhancing decoding model accuracy and reliability. Previous research has highlighted the advantages of multi-task EEG analysis, revealing its applications in emotion recognition [9,17], classification [3,23], and disease prediction [19].

1.1 Research Questions

Decoding EEG signals typically involves a series of steps, including preprocessing, feature extraction, and classification. Achieving successful EEG decoding in open-world scenarios necessitates careful consideration at each stage. Even when recorded under the most stringent conditions [6], EEG signals are susceptible to various artifacts such as eye blinks, muscle interference, cardiac disturbances, and electromagnetic interference.

In this context, MTL emerges as a valuable strategy for improving the feature-extracting ability of EEG decoding. By harnessing the power of multiple related tasks, MTL enhances the generalization capabilities of EEG models and mitigates the risk of overfitting, thereby contributing to more effective EEG signal analysis in open-world environments. This approach leverages the inherent connections between tasks and allows for the extraction of complementary information, ultimately enhancing the accuracy and reliability of EEG decoding models.

Our research aims to address the following questions at the intersection of Machine Learning and EEG eye-tracking:

1. Can we use EEG Signal Reconstruction as a sub-task to enhance the Transformer encoder's feature-extracting ability?

2. Which aspects of the prediction results, like specific regional accuracy or the overall prediction pattern, improved after integrating our framework?

2   Related Work

2.1   Deep Learning for EEG Tasks

Early studies highlighted the potential of Convolutional Neural Networks (CNNs) in EEG analysis. For instance, a CNN-based approach [20] is introduced for epileptic seizure classification on EEG data, utilizing the continuous wavelet transform (CWT) to convert EEG data into time-frequency domain images. Similarly, Transformer-based models [24] have shown their superiority over CNNs, RNNs, and DBNs in EEG classification, indicating the promise of the hybrid Transformer-CNN approach.

2.2   MTL for EEG Tasks

Multi-task Learning (MTL) [5] has been leveraged in various EEG signal analysis applications, including emotion recognition [9,17], classification [3,23], and disease prediction [19]. DMTL-BCI [23] employed an MTL framework to jointly optimize three modules (representation, classification, and reconstruction), outperforming state-of-the-art methods by 3.0% on BCI Competition IV dataset 2a. MIN2Net [3] utilized deep metric learning and autoencoder for subject-independent motor imagery EEG signal classification, outperforming state-of-the-art techniques by 6.72% and 2.23% on the SMR-BCI and OpenBMI datasets. Choo et al. [9] investigated the effectiveness of MTL in raw EEG-based emotion recognition, demonstrating significant classification accuracy improvements with their MTL-ShallowConvNet architecture. Furthermore, EEG-DEMTL [7] is a computation-based MTL network for assessing railway passenger comfort through EEG signals, improving the evaluation performance by 6.3% in field experiments.

2.3   Vision Transformers (ViTs)

The transformer model [26] is a deep learning model based on the self-attention mechanism, primarily used for processing sequential data. The core idea of the Transformer model is that through the attention mechanism, the model can focus on any part of the input sequence, thereby more effectively capturing long-distance dependencies within the sequence. This mechanism has led to tremendous success for the Transformer in the field of natural language processing (NLP), especially in tasks such as machine translation, text generation, and comprehension.

Building on the success of the Transformer model, Dosovitskiy and others proposed the Vision Transformer (ViT) in 2020 [12] Vision Transformer. ViT applies the concept of the Transformer to the field of computer vision, dividing

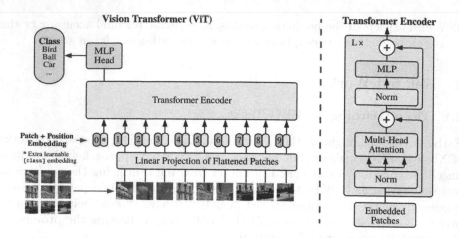

Fig. 1. Vision Transformer Encoder proposed by [12]

images into a series of small patches and feeding these patches as a sequence into a self-attention-based Transformer network. This approach allows ViT to process image data effectively, capturing complex patterns and relationships within images, thus achieving excellent performance in image classification and other visual tasks. Subsequently, ViT has also shown great potential in other areas, such as EEG data analysis, demonstrating its effectiveness in processing non-traditional visual data (Fig. 1).

Several studies have demonstrated their effectiveness regarding the application of Vision Transformers (ViT) in EEG tasks. Yang and Modesitt demonstrated the application of a hybrid ViT model, pre-trained on ImageNet, in an EEG regression task. Additionally, a bi-branch Vision Transformer-based EEG emotion recognition model, Bi-ViTNet, integrating spatial-temporal and spatial-frequency feature representations, has shown ViT's potential in handling complex EEG data [18]. EEG-ConvTransformer demonstrated improved classification accuracy over state-of-the-art techniques in five different visual stimuli classification tasks. This further proves the effectiveness of ViT models in EEG signal processing [4]. Finally, the importance of the attention mechanism in EEG signals was introduced through two ViT-based methods for the classification of EEG signals based on emotions [2].

These studies indicate that ViT models can effectively process EEG data, especially in complex tasks such as emotion recognition and visual stimuli classification. These findings support the use of ViT as a base model for multi-task learning (MTL) in EEG tasks.

3   Methods

In this paper, we plan to combine multi-task learning and Vision Transformer [11] to enhance the performance of the EEGEyeNet dataset's eye-tracking task [15].

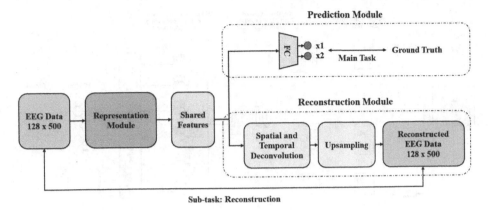

Fig. 2. Proposed MTL-Transformer Architecture: Eye Tracking and Data Reconstruction

By simultaneously addressing multiple related tasks within the dataset, we aim to improve the model's performance on the eye-tracking task. Our approach holds the potential to uncover novel connections and enhance the overall understanding of eye-tracking patterns in the context of EEG signals.

3.1   Model Architecture

Our model architecture is specifically designed to enhance performance in EEG eye-tracking tasks. The cornerstone of our approach is the introduction of a multi-task framework, which handles various sub-tasks simultaneously. This design choice is motivated by the need to capture the diverse aspects of EEG data more effectively.

Drawing inspiration from the work of Song et al. [23], our Multi-task Learning Transformer uniquely combines classification and reconstruction tasks within its architecture. By doing so, it efficiently leverages the representation module to maintain dual capabilities in feature extraction. This multi-task learning approach significantly boosts the model's ability to generalize across different EEG data scenarios.

The processing flow of our model, particularly highlighting the interaction between its different components within the multi-task framework, is depicted in Fig. 2. This illustration provides a clear visual representation of how the model integrates and processes various sub-tasks, contributing to its enhanced performance.

3.2   Representation Module

The ViT2EEG model, proposed by Yang and Modesitt [27], utilizes a hybrid Vision Transformer architecture pre-trained on ImageNet for EEG data regression tasks. It outperforms other models, including a non-trained ViT, demonstrating that models pre-trained on image data can be effectively fine-tuned

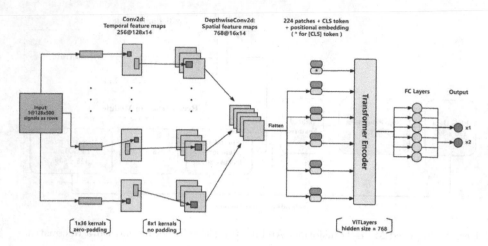

Fig. 3. Model architecture of EEG2VIT [27]. In this paper, we use the Convolution Layer and Transformer Encoder as the Representation Module

for EEG tasks. In our model architecture, we employ the Convolution Layer and pre-trained Vision Transformer (ViT) encoder, the same as the ViT2EEG model in Fig. 3. This setup has been shown to effectively capture complex patterns in data, which is essential for the reconstruction sub-module.

The input EEG data, with dimensions $1 \times 128 \times 500$, undergo a convolutional process yielding temporal feature maps of $256 \times 128 \times 14$. This is followed by depthwise convolutional layers, which further refine the spatial characteristics into feature maps sized $768 \times 16 \times 14$. The Conv2d layers utilize 1×36 kernels with zero padding, while the DepthwiseConv2d layers apply 8×1 kernels without padding, ensuring an effective spatial-temporal feature representation.

These features are then transformed into a sequence of 224 flattened patches, each integrated with a unique positional embedding. An additional [CLS] token embedding is also included, a common practice in ViT architectures to facilitate classification. The resulting embeddings are processed through a Transformer encoder, equipped with a hidden size of 768 to capture complex dependencies within the data.

The architecture concludes with fully connected layers, outputting two distinct values, which are the final inference results of the model. This innovative design leverages the strengths of both convolutional operations and transformer-based modeling to handle the intricacies of EEG signal analysis effectively.

3.3   Prediction Module

The prediction module in our architecture is designed as a sequence of interconnected layers. It comprises a fully connected layer, followed by a dropout layer for regularization, and concludes with another fully connected layer. The output of this module is articulated as follows:

$$\hat{y} = FC(dropout(FC(H^{(l)}))) \tag{1}$$

In this formulation, $H^{(l)}$ represents the output of the last layer in the encoder. The notation $H^{(l)}$ signifies the hidden representation obtained after the input data has undergone a series of transformations through the layers of the encoder neural network. Each layer in the encoder, denoted by l, contributes to shaping this representation, and $H^{(l)}$ captures the information learned up to that point. FC denotes the fully connected layers. The *dropout* function represents the dropout layer, a crucial component for preventing overfitting by randomly dropping units from the neural network during training.

For the main task of our model, the Mean Squared Error (MSE) loss is employed. This loss function is defined as:

$$Loss_{MSE}(\hat{y}, y_1) = \frac{1}{n} \sum_{i=1}^{n} (\hat{y}_i - y_{1i})^2 \tag{2}$$

Here, $\hat{y}$ is the predicted output of the network, and y_1 is the actual label for the main task. The MSE loss function computes the average of the squares of the differences between the predicted and actual values, providing a measure of the model's accuracy.

This structure ensures a streamlined flow of data through the layers, facilitating effective feature extraction and subsequent prediction.

3.4   Reconstruction Module

The reconstruction module plays a pivotal role in our system, consisting of a series of spatial and temporal deconvolution blocks designed to incrementally expand the dimensionality of shared features to reconstruct the input data effectively.

The spatial deconvolution block is crucial for spatial feature reconstruction and is defined by the following equation:

$$H_{decoder\_spatial} = Deconv\_spatial(H^{(l)}) \tag{3}$$

In this block, *Deconv_spatial* is composed of a three-layer structure: starting with a 1D Deconvolution layer with a kernel size of 1×36. This specific configuration mirrors the first convolution layer in the encoder, ensuring symmetry in feature extraction and reconstruction. It is followed by an InstanceNorm layer, enhancing the normalization of features, and a ReLU activation layer, introducing non-linearity for better feature representation.

Similarly, the temporal deconvolution block, essential for time-series data reconstruction, is formulated as:

$$H_{decoder\_temporal} = Deconv\_temporal(H_{decoder\_spatial}) \tag{4}$$

The *Deconv_temporal* block also includes three layers. It begins with a 1D Deconvolution layer, this time with a kernel size of 8×1. This dimensionality aligns with the patch size used in the Vision Transformer (ViT) encoder block, allowing for a consistent approach to handling spatial-temporal data. This layer is followed by an InstanceNorm layer and a ReLU activation layer, similar to the spatial deconvolution block.

The final step in the reconstruction process is the upsampling block, defined as:

$$\hat{x} = Upsampling(H_{decoder\_temporal}) \tag{5}$$

This block efficiently transforms the decoder output to match the original input size, ensuring the reconstructed data $\hat{x}$ is comparable to the original input x.

Lastly, we define our loss function using Mean Squared Error (MSE) to quantify the reconstruction accuracy:

$$loss\_MSE(\hat{x}, x) = \frac{1}{N} \sum_{i=1}^{N} (\hat{x}^{(i)} - x^{(i)})^2 \tag{6}$$

Where $\hat{x}$ is the reconstructed input, x is the original input, and N represents the total number of elements in x. MSE is chosen for its effectiveness in emphasizing larger errors and its suitability in scenarios where maintaining the fidelity of the reconstructed data is crucial.

3.5   Multi-task Learning Framework

In our multi-task learning framework, we aim to enhance the training of the primary eye-tracking task by integrating the losses from sub-tasks. The overall loss L of the framework is computed using the following equation:

$$L(\theta) = Loss_{MSE}(x, y_1) + \sum \alpha_i Loss(x, y_i) + \lambda ||\theta||^2 \tag{7}$$

Where x is the input EEG signal, represented as a 2D matrix. y_1 is the label of the eye-tracking task, which is also the main task. $Loss_{MSE}(x, y_1)$ denotes the MSE loss for the eye-tracking task, and $Loss(x, y_i)$ is the loss of other sub-task. Hyper-parameter α_i is utilized to balance the relative importance of the supervised and unsupervised loss. We apply l_2 regularization term with coefficient to alleviate overfitting. Our task is to minimize (θ). All trainable parameters of the network are trained in an end-to-end manner.

To evaluate different strategies within our proposed multi-task learning framework, we developed two distinct model architectures, each focusing on a separate sub-task. The first model, named MTL-Transformer, employs a reconstruction sub-task, as introduced earlier in the paper. This model aims to reconstruct the original EEG data. The second model, MTL-Transformer2, diverges by replacing the reconstruction module with a pupil size prediction module. This auxiliary subtask was introduced to explore the relevance of pupil size to the eye-tracking task. To accommodate this, we reorganized our dataset to include pupil size for each sample. Both models were measured using the Root Mean Square

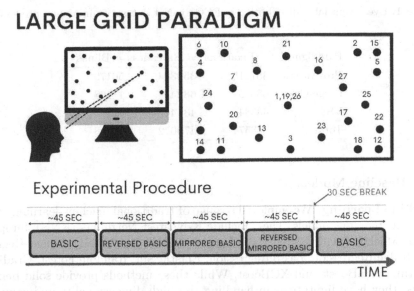

Fig. 4. EEGEyeNet Large Grid Paradigm [15]. Participants are asked to fixate on particular dots in a given period

Error (RMSE) metric to ensure a consistent and objective evaluation of their performance.

4 Experiments

4.1 Dataset

The EEGEyeNet dataset [15] offers a comprehensive resource for EEG research, featuring 47 h of high-density 128-channel EEG data, which provides detailed neural activity recordings synchronized with eye-tracking data from 356 adults. This dataset is particularly suited for our study, which aims to leverage the rich EEG data to predict behavioral responses in eye-tracking tasks. Our focus on the eye-tracking task stems from its potential to reveal how neural patterns correlate with visual attention and eye movement behaviors. Detailed information about the dataset, including the specificities of the eye-tracking tasks and participant demographics, is elaborately presented in Table 1 and Fig. 4. For our experiment, we propose a dataset split of 70% for the training set, 15% for the validation set, and 15% for the test set. This distribution is designed to maximize learning from the EEG data while ensuring robust validation and testing of our predictive models.

Table 1. Eyes event label distribution in EEGEyeNet dataset (minimal preprocessing) [15]

Paradigm	# Fixations	# Saccades	# Blinks
Pro-Antisac.	357115	358384	56179
Large Grid	68075	68245	11108
VSS	43384	43443	971
Total	468574	470072	68258

4.2 Baseline Models

Machine Learning. We employed a range of traditional machine-learning algorithms as baseline models. These include K-Nearest Neighbors (KNN), Support Vector Machines with Radial Basis Function (RBF SVC/SVR), Linear Regression, Ridge Regression, Lasso Regression, Elastic Net, Random Forest, Gradient Boosting, AdaBoost, and XGBoost. While these methods provide solid benchmarks, they have limitations in handling the high dimensionality and complex temporal dynamics inherent in EEG data.

Deep Learning Convolutional Neural Network (CNN). CNNs were effective in capturing spatial patterns in EEG data but less adept at modeling temporal dynamics.

PyramidalCNN. The PyramidalCNN, with its unique structure, offered improved performance in capturing hierarchical features, leading to better generalization [14].

EEGNet. EEGNet, designed for EEG data analysis, showed proficiency in handling both spatial and temporal features but may struggle with very large datasets [16].

InceptionTime. InceptionTime's modular architecture allowed for a robust capture of temporal dynamics, surpassing traditional CNNs [13].

Xception. Xception's depthwise separable convolutions were efficient, though they may not fully exploit the multi-channel nature of EEG data [8].

EEGViT. The EEGViT, adapting the Vision Transformer for EEG data, presented an innovative approach in modeling long-range dependencies, a common challenge in EEG analysis [27].

4.3 Implementation Details

All models in our study were trained for 15 epochs on an RTX 4090 GPU. For deep learning models, we set an initial learning rate of 10^{-4} and implemented a decay strategy, reducing the learning rate by 10% every 6 epochs. This approach is designed to balance the rate of convergence and ensure effective learning over the training period.

In our proposed model, we integrated two dropout layers with a dropout rate of 0.3, specifically in the prediction module. This rate is higher than typical settings, chosen to mitigate overfitting while dealing with the complex nature of EEG data. This dropout strategy is particularly crucial given the model's architecture and the high-dimensional feature space of the EEG signals.

5 Results

Table 2. Root Mean Squared Error (RMSE) Comparison of Baseline Models on the EEGEyeNet eye-tracking task [15]. The primary model, MTL-Transformer, demonstrates significant performance improvement, utilizing EEGViT Pre-trained as its base model. Additionally, MTL-Transformer2, which includes pupil size prediction as an auxiliary sub-task, is presented to demonstrate the scope of our experimental exploration despite its lesser impact on RMSE reduction.

Model	AbsolutePosition RMSE (mm)
Naive Baseline	123.3 ± 0
KNN	119.7 ± 0
RBF SVC/SVR	123 ± 0
Linear Regression	118.3 ± 0
Ridge Regression	118.2 ± 0
Lasso Regression	118 ± 0
Elastic Net	118.1 ± 0
Random Forest	116.7 ± 0.1
Gradient Boost	117 ± 0.1
AdaBoost	119.4 ± 0.1
XGBoost	118 ± 0
CNN	70.2 ± 1.1
PyramidalCNN	73.6 ± 1.9
EEGNet	$81.7 + 1.0$
InceptionTime	70.8 ± 0.8
Xception	78.7 ± 1.6
ViT-Base	61.5 ± 0.6
ViT-Base Pre-trained	58.1 ± 0.6
EEGViT	61.7 ± 0.6
EEGViT Pre-trained	55.4 ± 0.2
MTL-Transformer(Ours)	$\mathbf{54.1 \pm 0.2}$
MTL-Transformer2(Ours)	$\mathbf{57.4 \pm 0.3}$

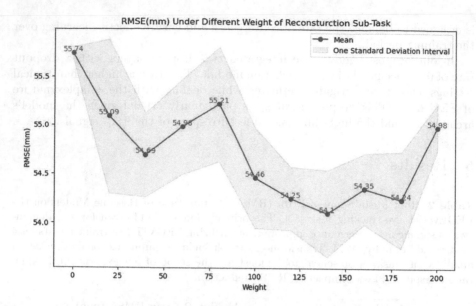

Fig. 5. RMSE(mm) Under Different Weight of Reconstruction Sub-Task

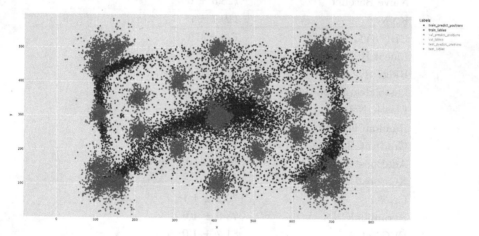

Fig. 6. Predict Gazing Position and Real Gazing Position on Training Dataset

The performance of various models on the EEG eye-tracking task is summarized in Table 2. Notably, our proposed model achieved a Root Mean Square Error (RMSE) of 54.1 mm, which slightly surpasses the current State-Of-The-Art (SOTA) model's RMSE of 55.4 mm. This improvement, although marginal, indicates the effectiveness of our model's architecture and the methodologies employed, especially in handling the complexities of EEG data in eye-tracking tasks.

Figure 5 illustrates the RMSE of our model under varying weights assigned to the reconstruction sub-task. At a weight of 0, the reconstruction sub-module does not participate in the gradient computation, and our model's results align with the EEGViT Pre-trained model, which is the base model. This parallel performance indicates that the enhancements in accuracy are not attributable to alterations in the model's structure. As the weight increases to 140, there is a discernible improvement in model accuracy, suggesting that the reconstruction sub-module contributes positively to the base model's performance. However, beyond a weight of 140, the excessive emphasis on the reconstruction sub-task seems to detract from the sub-task at hand, as evidenced by a decline in accuracy. This trend demonstrates a critical balance between the reconstruction weight and the model's focus on the primary task, underscoring the need for optimal weight tuning to harness the reconstruction sub-module's benefits without compromising the main objective.

6 Discussion

Our research presents promising implications for the field of EEG-based eye tracking. The slight yet significant improvement in accuracy provided by our model paves the way for more precise and reliable EEG eye-tracking systems. This advancement is particularly relevant in applications where minute differences in eye movement can have substantial implications, such as in neuromarketing or neurological disorder diagnosis.

Figure 6 shows the eye-tracking prediction on the training dataset. Our model demonstrates a commendable capacity to discriminate between central and peripheral points. However, it exhibits limitations in accurately distinguishing points within the intermediate regions, with a predominant aggregation of data at the center. This phenomenon may be attributed to a frequency bias towards central points, resulting in an imbalance within the dataset. To address this, future iterations of our model could incorporate weighted learning for different regions, facilitating a more balanced and nuanced understanding and thereby enhancing the model's predictive accuracy.

Looking ahead, we aim to broaden the applicability of our model by testing it on various other EEG datasets. Such an expansion will not only validate the model's effectiveness across different data types but also enhance its robustness and generalizability. This step is crucial for asserting the model's utility in diverse real-world scenarios.

Additionally, the versatility of our Multi-task Learning module is a notable aspect of our architecture. Its design allows it to be integrated as a separate module into any EEG-based task. This modular approach offers a flexible solution for improving existing EEG analysis systems, potentially transforming how EEG data is processed and interpreted in various applications.

Moreover, we attempted to leverage pre-trained language Transformer models, such as GPT and BERT, which are typically used for time-series or language tasks. However, these models generally demand substantial GPU memory capacity, which exceeds the capabilities of our personal workstations. This limitation constrained the scope of our experiments. Future work will, therefore, focus on optimizing computational efficiency, perhaps through model distillation or pruning techniques that can reduce the memory footprint of these large models.

In conclusion, while our current focus has been on EEG eye-tracking tasks, the broader impact of our work lies in its potential to revolutionize various aspects of EEG data analysis and application. Future research will delve deeper into these possibilities, continually pushing the boundaries of what is achievable in this domain.

7   Conclusion

In this study, we have demonstrated the effectiveness of integrating multi-task learning with Vision Transformers in the domain of EEG eye-tracking. Our approach has successfully employed an innovative EEG signal reconstruction sub-module, enhancing the feature extraction capabilities of deep learning models applied to this task. This sub-module, adaptable to various Encoder-Classifier-based models, facilitates end-to-end training within a multi-task learning framework and operates effectively under unsupervised learning conditions.

Our experimental results, particularly the achieved RMSE of 54.1 mm, which surpasses the previous state-of-the-art model, underscore the potential of our method in improving EEG-based eye-tracking systems. This advancement is not only significant in terms of model performance but also in its application potential across various EEG datasets and tasks.

Looking forward, the adaptability and versatility of our Multi-task Learning module open new avenues for enhancing EEG data processing and interpretation. This work lays the groundwork for future research in this area, aiming to further explore and expand the capabilities of deep learning models in the realm of neuroscience and cognitive research. We believe that our approach represents a novel paradigm in EEG data analysis, with the potential to contribute significantly to various EEG-related challenges and applications.

References

1. Ang, K.K., Guan, C.: Brain-computer interface in stroke rehabilitation. J. Comput. Sci. Eng. **7**(2), 139–146 (2013)
2. Arjun, A., Rajpoot, A.S., Raveendranatha Panicker, M.: Introducing attention mechanism for EEG signals: emotion recognition with vision transformers. In: 2021 43rd Annual International Conference of the IEEE Engineering in Medicine & Biology Society (EMBC), pp. 5723–5726 (2021). https://doi.org/10.1109/EMBC46164.2021.9629837
3. Autthasan, P., et al.: MIN2NET: end-to-end multi-task learning for subject-independent motor imagery EEG classification. IEEE Trans. Biomed. Eng. **69**(6), 2105–2118 (2021)
4. Bagchi, S., Bathula, D.R.: EEG-ConvTransformer for single-trial EEG based visual stimuli classification. Pattern Recogn. **129**, 108757 (2021)
5. Caruana, R.: Multitask learning. Mach. Learn. **28**, 41–75 (1997)

6. Chen, X., Li, C., Liu, A., McKeown, M.J., Qian, R., Wang, Z.J.: Toward open-world electroencephalogram decoding via deep learning: a comprehensive survey. IEEE Signal Process. Mag. **39**(2), 117–134 (2022)
7. Cheng, B., et al.: Evolutionary computation-based multitask learning network for railway passenger comfort evaluation from EEG signals. Appl. Soft Comput. **136**, 110079 (2023)
8. Chollet, F.: Xception: deep learning with depthwise separable convolutions. In: Proceedings of the IEEE Conference on Computer Vision and Pattern Recognition, pp. 1251–1258 (2017)
9. Choo, S., et al.: Effectiveness of multi-task deep learning framework for EEG-based emotion and context recognition. Expert Syst. Appl. **227**, 120348 (2023)
10. Craik, A., He, Y., Contreras-Vidal, J.L.: Deep learning for electroencephalogram (EEG) classification tasks: a review. J. Neural Eng. **16**(3), 031001 (2019)
11. Dosovitskiy, A., Beyer, L., Kolesnikov, A., Weissenborn, D., Zhai, X., Unterthiner, T.: Transformers for image recognition at scale. arXiv preprint arXiv:2010.11929 (2020)
12. Dosovitskiy, A., et al.: An image is worth 16x16 words: transformers for image recognition at scale. arXiv preprint arXiv:2010.11929 (2020)
13. Ismail Fawaz, H., et al.: InceptionTime: finding AlexNet for time series classification. Data Min. Knowl. Disc. **34**(6), 1936–1962 (2020)
14. Johnson, R., Zhang, T.: Deep pyramid convolutional neural networks for text categorization. In: Proceedings of the 55th Annual Meeting of the Association for Computational Linguistics (Volume 1: Long Papers), pp. 562–570 (2017)
15. Kastrati, A., et al.: EEGEyeNet: a simultaneous electroencephalography and eye-tracking dataset and benchmark for eye movement prediction. arXiv preprint arXiv:2111.05100 (2021)
16. Lawhern, V.J., Solon, A.J., Waytowich, N.R., Gordon, S.M., Hung, C.P., Lance, B.J.: EEGNet: a compact convolutional neural network for EEG-based brain-computer interfaces. J. Neural Eng. **15**(5), 056013 (2018)
17. Li, C., et al.: Emotion recognition from EEG based on multi-task learning with capsule network and attention mechanism. Comput. Biol. Med. **143**, 105303 (2022)
18. Lu, W., Tan, T.P., Ma, H.: Bi-branch vision transformer network for EEG emotion recognition. IEEE Access **11**, 36233–36243 (2023). https://doi.org/10.1109/ACCESS.2023.3266117
19. Ma, X., Qiu, S., Zhang, Y., Lian, X., He, H.: Predicting epileptic seizures from intracranial EEG using LSTM-based multi-task learning. In: Lai, J.-H., Liu, C.-L., Chen, X., Zhou, J., Tan, T., Zheng, N., Zha, H. (eds.) PRCV 2018. LNCS, vol. 11257, pp. 157–167. Springer, Cham (2018). https://doi.org/10.1007/978-3-030-03335-4_14
20. Mao, W., Fathurrahman, H., Lee, Y., Chang, T.: EEG dataset classification using CNN method. In: Journal of Physics: Conference Series, vol. 1456, p. 012017. IOP Publishing (2020)
21. Motamedi-Fakhr, S., Moshrefi-Torbati, M., Hill, M., Hill, C.M., White, P.R.: Signal processing techniques applied to human sleep EEG signals-a review. Biomed. Signal Process. Control **10**, 21–33 (2014)
22. Rashid, M., et al.: Current status, challenges, and possible solutions of EEG-based brain-computer interface: a comprehensive review. Front. Neurorobot. **14**, 25 (2020)
23. Song, Y., Wang, D., Yue, K., Zheng, N., Shen, Z.J.M.: EEG-based motor imagery classification with deep multi-task learning. In: 2019 International Joint Conference on Neural Networks (IJCNN), pp. 1–8. IEEE (2019)

24. Sun, J., Xie, J., Zhou, H.: EEG classification with transformer-based models. In: 2021 IEEE 3rd Global Conference on Life Sciences and Technologies (LifeTech), pp. 92–93. IEEE (2021)
25. Teplan, M., et al.: Fundamentals of EEG measurement. Meas. Sci. Rev. **2**(2), 1–11 (2002)
26. Vaswani, A., et al.: Attention is all you need. Adv. Neural Inf. Process. Syst. **30** (2017)
27. Yang, R., Modesitt, E.: ViT2EEG: leveraging hybrid pretrained vision transformers for EEG data. arXiv preprint arXiv:2308.00454 (2023)

Fusing Pretrained ViTs with TCNet for Enhanced EEG Regression

Eric Modesitt[1][(✉)], Haicheng Yin[2], Williams Huang Wang[3], and Brian Lu[4]

[1] University of Illinois at Urbana Champaign, Champaign, USA
ericjm4@illinois.edu
[2] University of California, Santa Cruz, USA
[3] Saint Francis Preparatory High School, New York, USA
[4] Palo Alto High School, Palo Alto, USA

Abstract. The task of Electroencephalogram (EEG) analysis is paramount to the development of Brain-Computer Interfaces (BCIs). However, to reach the goal of developing robust, useful BCIs depends heavily on the speed and the accuracy at which BCIs can understand neural dynamics. In response to that goal, this paper details the integration of pre-trained Vision Transformers (ViTs) with Temporal Convolutional Networks (TCNet) to enhance the precision of EEG regression. The core of this approach lies in harnessing the sequential data processing strengths of ViTs along with the superior feature extraction capabilities of TCNet, to significantly improve EEG analysis accuracy. In addition, we analyze the importance of how to construct optimal patches for the attention mechanism to analyze, balancing both speed and accuracy tradeoffs. Our results showcase a substantial improvement in regression accuracy, as evidenced by the reduction of Root Mean Square Error (RMSE) from 55.4 to 51.8 on EEGEyeNet's Absolute Position Task, outperforming existing state-of-the-art models. Without sacrificing performance, we increase the speed of this model by an order of magnitude (up to 4.32x faster). This breakthrough not only sets a new benchmark in EEG regression analysis but also opens new avenues for future research in the integration of transformer architectures with specialized feature extraction methods for diverse EEG datasets.

Keywords: Brain Machine Interface · EEG Regression · Vision Transformers (ViT) · Temporal Convolutional Networks (TCNet) · Feature Extraction · Neural Dynamics

1 Introduction

The analysis of Electroencephalogram (EEG) signals is a cornerstone in the advancement of Brain-Computer Interfaces (BCIs), offering profound insights into the intricate neural processes of the human brain. EEG regression, in particular, stands as a pivotal tool in both neuroscience and medical diagnostics, gaining prominence for its ability to decode complex neural dynamics. This technique plays a crucial role in a myriad of applications, ranging from pinpointing

D. D. Schmorrow and C. M. Fidopiastis (Eds.): HCII 2024, LNAI 14695, pp. 47–59, 2024.
https://doi.org/10.1007/978-3-031-61572-6_4

brain damage locations to monitoring cognitive activities and deciphering the neural basis of seizures (Subasi and Ercelebi, 2005; Sabbagh et al., 2020; Teplan, 2002). The essence of EEG regression lies in its capacity to transform raw EEG data into interpretable and meaningful information, thus providing an invaluable perspective into the brain's operations.

In the realm of machine learning, the advent of Transformer models has marked a revolutionary shift in EEG regression analysis. Initially celebrated for their breakthroughs in natural language processing, these models have been adeptly modified to cater to EEG data analysis, substantially elevating both the precision and efficiency of the analysis (Liu et al., 2022). A significant stride in this field is the adaptation of pre-trained Vision Transformers (ViTs) for EEG datasets, such as ImageNet Deng et al. (2009). The application of ViTs in EEG regression has demonstrated exceptional results, surpassing traditional methods across various benchmarks (Yang and Modesitt, 2023).

Concurrently, Temporal Convolutional Networks (TCNet) have emerged as a formidable force in the field of EEG signal processing. Exhibiting outstanding capabilities in feature extraction, TCNets excel in identifying intricate patterns and nuances in EEG data (Bai et al., 2018; Ingolfsson et al., 2020; Ingolfsson et al., 2022). Their robustness in capturing temporal dynamics and their efficacy in EEG signal handling render them an indispensable component in neural signal analysis.

This study delves into the synergistic integration of ViTs and TCNet, aiming to harness their combined strengths to substantially augment the accuracy and reliability of EEG regression. This innovative approach seeks to leverage the detailed feature extraction of TCNet and the contextual interpretation prowess of ViTs, hypothesizing a significant enhancement in EEG analysis.

Our research presents a comprehensive evaluation of this hybrid model, juxtaposing it against previous methodologies to underscore its superiority in EEG regression. We meticulously examine the performance of the ViT-TCNet combination, elucidating the contribution of each component to the overall effectiveness of the model. The implications of our findings extend beyond the confines of EEG analysis, potentially influencing a broad spectrum of data interpretation tasks in various scientific and AI-related fields.

In addition to the aforementioned aspects, a notable facet of this study is the emphasis on the processing speed of the integrated ViT-TCNet model. Speed is a critical parameter in EEG analysis, especially for real-time applications in Brain-Computer Interfaces (BCIs) where rapid response times are essential By optimizing the architecture and employing advanced techniques in model training and inference, we have successfully accelerated the processing speed of the EEG analysis. This advancement is particularly significant in scenarios where real-time data processing is crucial, such as in neurofeedback systems or in clinical settings where prompt decision-making is imperative. The increase in processing speed, achieved without compromising the model's performance, marks a substantial leap forward in making EEG-based BCIs more viable and user-friendly.

In the ensuing sections, we will outline the methodology utilized in our study, present our empirical findings, and discuss the broader implications and future research directions stemming from our work. This research not only enriches the existing literature in EEG regression but also sets the stage for future explorations into the amalgamation of advanced machine learning architectures for refined neural data analysis.

In summary, the contributions of this work can be articulated in three primary areas:

1. **Innovative Combination of ViTs and TCNet for Advanced EEG Regression**: This research marks a significant advancement in EEG regression analysis through the novel integration of pretrained Vision Transformers (ViTs) with Temporal Convolutional Networks (TCNet). This fusion harnesses ViTs' exceptional capability in processing sequential data and TCNet's robust feature extraction techniques, culminating in a notable improvement in EEG regression accuracy. In addition, we open source all of our methods and results at github.com/ModeEric/EEGViT-TCNet

2. **Enhancement of Model Processing Speed and Efficiency**: A key contribution of this study is the substantial improvement in the processing speed of the EEG analysis model. Recognizing the importance of swift data processing in real-time applications such as Brain-Computer Interfaces, the research introduces optimizations that significantly accelerate the model's performance.

3. **Ablation Studies and Future Research Directions**: The research undertakes comprehensive ablation studies to understand the individual and combined contributions of ViTs and TCNet to the model's performance. These studies offer valuable insights into the mechanics of the model, paving the way for further optimizations.

2   Related Work

2.1   Deep Learning in EEG

The evolution of EEG signal processing has been significantly influenced by the emergence of deep learning techniques. Traditional machine learning methods, while effective, often fall short in capturing the high-dimensional and complex nature of EEG data. The introduction of deep learning models, particularly convolutional neural networks (CNNs) and recurrent neural networks (RNNs), revolutionized this field. These models brought enhanced capabilities in handling large datasets, extracting relevant features, and recognizing intricate patterns in EEG signals (Subasi and Ercelebi, 2005; Sabbagh et al., 2020; Teplan, 2002). This shift not only improved the accuracy of EEG analyses but also expanded the potential applications in neurological research and clinical diagnostics.

Deep learning's impact on EEG signal processing is profound, offering new perspectives in understanding brain activity. The ability of these models to learn from data autonomously, without the need for extensive feature engineering, has opened avenues for more nuanced and detailed analyses of neural signals. This advancement is crucial in fields where EEG data plays a pivotal role, such as in the study of cognitive processes, sleep patterns, and brain-computer interfaces. The integration of advanced deep learning architectures in EEG analysis heralds a new era of innovation and discovery in neuroscience.

2.2 ViTs in Non-Image Data Analysis

Vision Transformers (ViTs), originally designed for image recognition, have demonstrated remarkable versatility by extending their application to various other domains, including EEG data analysis (Dosovitskiy et al., 2020; Wu et al., 2020; Han et al., 2022). The cornerstone of their success, the self-attention mechanism, enables ViTs to efficiently manage sequential data, a feature crucial in interpreting EEG signals Vaswani et al. (2017). This characteristic of ViTs facilitates an understanding of the complex, temporal relationships inherent in EEG data, making them an ideal choice for this type of analysis.

The adaptation of ViTs to non-image data, such as EEG signals, signifies a major shift in the approach to data analysis across disciplines. It underscores the potential of transformer models to handle diverse types of data beyond their initial scope. This cross-domain applicability of ViTs not only enriches the toolkit available for EEG analysis but also inspires innovative approaches to data interpretation. The flexibility and effectiveness of ViTs in handling sequential data pave the way for their broader adoption in various scientific and analytical fields (Fig. 1).

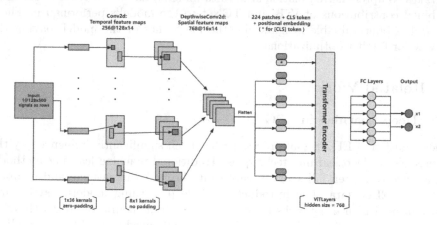

Fig. 1. EEGViT architecture, SOTA on EEGEYENET (Yang and Modesitt, 2023).

2.3 Temporal Convolutional Networks (TCNet)

Temporal Convolutional Networks (TCNet) have gained significant attention for their ability to process time-series data, particularly in EEG signal analysis.

The architecture of TCNet, with its focus on capturing temporal dependencies through convolutional layers, makes it exceptionally suited for extracting detailed features from EEG data (Farha and Gall, 2019; Hewage et al., 2020). The efficacy of TCNet in identifying subtle patterns and temporal features in complex datasets has established it as a leading tool in the field of neural signal processing.

The role of TCNet in EEG data interpretation extends beyond mere feature extraction. It involves a deeper understanding of the temporal dynamics and inherent structures within the EEG signals. This understanding is vital in applications where precise timing and sequence of neural events are critical, such as in epilepsy research or brain-computer interface development. The combination of TCNet with other advanced models like ViTs presents a promising avenue for enhancing EEG analysis, potentially leading to more accurate and insightful interpretations of neural data.

3   Methods

Our study employs an innovative approach by integrating pre-trained Vision Transformers (ViTs) with Temporal Convolutional Networks (TCNet) to enhance EEG regression analysis. This section outlines the dataset utilized, the specifics of the proposed model, and the methodology for evaluating its effectiveness.

3.1   EEGEyeNet Dataset

The data presented here is derived from the EEGEyeNet dataset Kastrati et al. (2021). The EEGEyeNet dataset encompasses recordings from 356 healthy adults, including 190 females and 166 males, aged 18 to 80 years. All individuals in this study provided written informed consent, compliant with the Declaration of Helsinki, and were compensated monetarily.

The EEG recordings in the EEGEyeNet dataset were obtained using a high-density 128-channel EEG Geodesic Hydrocel system, operating at a sampling rate of 500 Hz with a central recording reference. Eye positions were concurrently recorded using an EyeLink 1000 Plus system at the same sampling rate. This setup maintained electrode impedances below 40 kOhm and ensured accurate eye tracker calibration. Participants were positioned 68 cm from a 24-inch monitor, with their head stabilized using a chin rest.

EEG data, as recorded in the EEGEyeNet dataset, are prone to various artifacts, including environmental noise and physiological interferences such as eye movements and blinks. To address this, the dataset underwent rigorous preprocessing with two levels: minimal and maximal. The minimal preprocessing involved identifying and interpolating faulty electrodes, along with applying a high-pass filter at 40 Hz and a low-pass filter at 0.5 Hz. The maximal preprocessing, aimed at neuroscientific analyses, further incorporated Independent Component Analysis (ICA) and IClabel for artifact component removal.

The EEGEyeNet dataset also includes synchronized EEG and eye-tracking data, facilitating time-locked analyses relative to event onsets. This synchronization was stringently verified to ensure a maximum error margin of 2 ms.

The Absolute Position Task, a key component of the EEGEyeNet dataset, involved participants fixating on sequentially displayed dots at various screen positions. Each dot appeared for 1.5 to 1.8 s, located at one of 25 distinct screen positions. The central dot was presented thrice, resulting in 27 trials per block. This setup, covering the entire screen area, captured a broad range of gaze positions. Adapted from Son et al. (2020) for fMRI studies, modifications were made for EEG compatibility, including stimulus duration and repetition adjustments. The dot presentation followed a pseudo-randomized sequence across five experimental blocks, repeated six times, totaling 810 stimuli per participant.

The Absolute Position task is particularly relevant for our research as it provides a comprehensive dataset for analyzing eye movement patterns and gaze positions. The variety in dot positions and the high number of trials allow for a complete assessment of the participants' gaze behavior, which is crucial for our objective of determining the exact XY-coordinates of a participant's gaze using EEG data.

3.2   EEGViT-TCNet Model Architecture

Intending to advance EEG signal analysis, we developed the EEGViT-TCNet model, a novel architecture that combines Temporal Convolutional Networks (TCNet) with a pre-trained Vision Transformer (ViT). This model was meticulously designed to decipher the temporal dynamics and spatial characteristics embedded within EEG signals.

Temporal Convolutional Network (TCNet) Component: The EEGViT-TCNet model begins with the TCNet component, tailored to embrace the complexities of EEG data. This component is characterized by:

– **Input Layer:** Accepting EEG signals, the TCNet is prepared to handle an input dimensionality of 129, corresponding to the number of recorded EEG channels +1 for including grounding information (as done in the original EEGEyeNet paper).
– **Sequential TCNet Layers:** The architecture encompasses three layers, with the number of channel dimensions expanding progressively to 64, 128, and 256. This hierarchy is instrumental in capturing a comprehensive spectrum of temporal dependencies inherent in the EEG signals.
  - *Kernel Size:* A kernel size of 3 is uniformly applied across the TCNet layers.
  - *Dropout:* To counteract the potential for overfitting, a dropout rate of 0.75 is employed.
  - *Causality and Normalization:* The layers incorporate weight normalization alongside the ReLU activation function to enhance the model's stability and performance (Fig. 2).

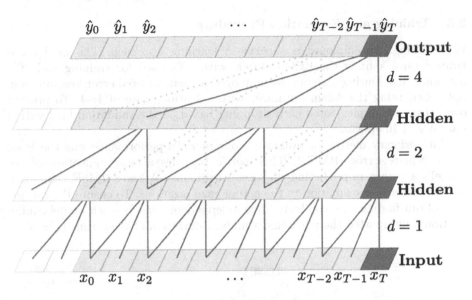

Fig. 2. An outline of the TCNet functionality (Bai et al., 2018).

Convolutional and Batch Normalization Layers: The pathway pathway we designed from the TCNet layers to the ViT involves:

- **Convolutional Layers:** Two convolutional layers connect the TCNet and ViT. The first layer, equipped with 256 filters and a kernel size of (1, 36), is succeeded by batch normalization and ReLU activation. This configuration initiates the spatial feature extraction. Subsequently, the second layer amplifies the channel dimension to 768, aligning with the ViT's input specifications. In addition, this layer employs a kernel size of (256, 1) to effectuate a spatial compression conducive to the subsequent transformer analysis.

Vision Transformer (ViT) Component: The culmination of the EEGViT-TCNet model's preprocessing lies in the ViT component:

- **EEG Data Adaptation:** Leveraging the "google/vit-base-patch16-224" model from Huggingface, the configuration is modified to fit the unique format of EEG data.
- **Patch Embeddings Projection:** This layer is reimagined as a 1D convolutional layer, directly accommodating the output from preceding stages BS ensuring the input's integration into the transformer architecture.
- **Classifier Head:** The model ends with a randomly initialized classifier layer, transitioning through a linear layer, followed by a dropout layer (p = 0.1), culminating in a linear layer that predicts the gaze XY coordinates.

3.3   Training and Evaluation Procedure

For training, we employed a supervised learning approach. The model was trained on a split of the EEG dataset, with 70% used for training and 30% for validation. During training, we employed a mean squared error loss function, optimized using the Adam optimizer with a learning rate of 1e-4. To prevent overfitting, we implemented early stopping based on the validation loss, with a patience of 10 epochs.

The primary metric for evaluating our model's performance was the Root Mean Square Error (RMSE). This metric provides a clear indication of the model's accuracy in predicting the gaze coordinates. A lower RMSE value indicates a closer approximation to the actual gaze positions. To ensure the robustness of our findings, we conducted five independent runs for each model configuration and reported the mean and standard deviation of these runs (Fig. 3).

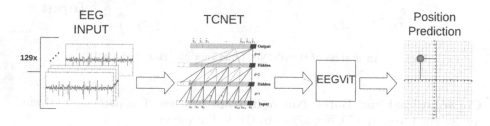

Fig. 3. An outline of our addition to EEGViT, demonstrating our distinct feature extraction methodology Yang and Modesitt (2023) Bai et al. (2018).

4   Results

Through rigorous testing and comparison, our model has demonstrated its capability to predict gaze positions with state-of-the-art precision, outperforming a spectrum of both conventional and advanced methodologies.

4.1   Performance Benchmarking

Our EEGViT-TCNet model achieved a Root Mean Square Error (RMSE) of 51.8 mm, marking a significant advancement over existing models. This performance showcases a 6.5% enhancement in precision over standalone ViT models Yang and Modesitt (2023). The stark contrast is further accentuated when juxtaposed with traditional approaches such as Linear Regression and Random Forest, where the RMSE figures exceed 115 mm.

Our model's evaluation, focusing on a single data partition divided by subject as done in Kastrati et al. (2021), demonstrates its ability to generalize effectively. This approach, where the testing data consisted of completely unseen, new groups of data, highlights the model's robustness and adaptability. Despite being tested on different subsets of subjects than what the model was trained on, it maintained consistent RMSE metrics, underscoring its sophisticated architecture's capability to handle the complexities of EEG data. This consistency in performance across various subject-based segments is crucial for real-world applications, affirming the model's potential for effective generalization (Table 1).

Table 1. Comparative analysis of Root Mean Squared Error (RMSE) across various models, highlighting the superior performance of the EEGViT-TCNet model. The values represent the mean ± standard deviation over five independent runs, illustrating the model's consistency and accuracy in the Absolute Position Task.

Model	Absolute Position RMSE (mm)
Naive Guessing	123.3 ± 0.0
KNN	119.7 ± 0
RBF SVR	123 ± 0
Linear Regression	118.3 ± 0
Random Forest	116.7 ± 0.1
CNN	70.4 ± 1.1
EEGViT (Pre-trained)	55.4 ± 0.2
EEGViT-TCNet	**51.8 ± 0.6**

4.2   Computational Efficiency and Speed Enhancement

One of the features of our EEGViT-TCNet model is its computational efficiency. In comparison to the original EEGViT architecture, our enhanced model achieves a substantial speed-up, being 4.32 times faster during inference. This improvement is not merely a testament to the model's optimized architecture but also underscores its practicality for real-time gaze position prediction applications.

The speed enhancement is achieved through key optimizations in the model's architecture, mainly through an optimization of the patch size accuracy-efficiency tradeoff. These optimizations ensure that our model not only maintains high accuracy but also operates with greater efficiency, making it well-suited for deployment in computationally expensive environments.

4.3   Ablation Studies

To assess the individual contributions of various components within our EEGViT-TCNet model, we conducted a series of ablation studies. These studies aimed to isolate the effects of specific elements of the model, such as the convolutional layers, dropout rates in the TCNet, and the use of a pretrained Vision Transformer (ViT). Each variation of the model was evaluated using the same dataset and metrics, allowing us to directly compare their performance.

Impact of Convolutional Layers. We first examined the impact of the additional convolutional layers that bridge the gap between the TCNet and the ViT on the model's performance. In particular, we analyze the results after removing all possible combinations of 1 convolutional layer (spatial, temporal, and pointwise convolution).

By removing the pointwise layer, we observed a slight increase in the Root Mean Square Error (RMSE) from 51.8 ± 0.6 mm to 52.5 ± 0.8 mm. This suggests that the pointwise convolutional layer plays a modest role in feature extraction and spatial representation, contributing to the model's overall accuracy.

For both the spatial and temporal layers we observed a significant increase in the Root Mean Square Error (RMSE) from 51.8 ± 0.6 mm to 55.1 ± 0.6 mm and 55.0 ± 0.5 mm respecitvely. This suggests that both sptial and temproal layers plays a major role in feature extraction and representation, contributing to the model's overall accuracy.

Influence of Dropout Rates in TCNet. The role of dropout rates in TCNet was another focus of our study. By varying the dropout rates, we investigated their effect on the model's capability to generalize and prevent overfitting. The original model with a 0.75 dropout rate achieved an RMSE of 51.8 ± 0.6 mm. Reducing the dropout rate to 0 increased the RMSE to 54.1 ± 0.6 mm, indicating a higher propensity for overfitting. Conversely, lower dropout rates of 0.25 and 0.5 yielded RMSEs of 52.5 ± 0.4 mm and 52.1 ± 0.4 mm, respectively. These findings illustrate a nuanced balance between dropout rate and model performance, with moderate dropout rates contributing positively to the model's accuracy and generalizability.

Contribution of Pretrained ViT. Finally, we evaluated the contribution of using a pretrained ViT in our model. By replacing the pretrained ViT with a non-pretrained counterpart, the RMSE increased to 53.2 ± 0.5 mm. This increase underscores the significance of pretraining in enhancing the model's feature recognition capabilities, particularly in the context of EEG data analysis (Table 2).

These ablation studies reveal the delicate interplay of different architectural components in optimizing the EEGViT-TCNet model for EEG regression analysis. The presence of the second convolutional layer, the calibration of dropout rates in TCNet, and the incorporation of a pretrained ViT each contribute uniquely to the model's performance. Our findings highlight the importance of these components in achieving high precision in EEG regression tasks, providing valuable insights for future enhancements and applications of the model.

Table 2. Ablation study results comparing RMSE across various EEGViT-TCNet model configurations. The values represent the mean ± standard deviation over five runs.

Model Variation	Absolute Position RMSE (mm)
EEGViT-TCNet (Ours)	**51.8 ± 0.6**
No Pointwise Conv Layer	52.5 ± 0.8
No Temporal Conv Layer	55.0 ± 0.5
No Spatial Conv Layer	55.1 ± 0.6
0% Dropout	54.1 ± 0.6
25% Dropout	52.5 ± 0.4
50% Dropout	52.1 ± 0.4
No Pretrained ViT	53.2 ± 0.5

5   Discussion

Our novel approach has not only showcased a marked improvement in regression accuracy but also set new benchmarks in processing speed and efficiency. The results obtained from this study reflect the significant potential of leveraging the strengths of both ViTs and TCNet, underscoring the profound impact that such hybrid models can have on understanding and interpreting complex neural dynamics.

The success of the EEGViT-TCNet model in reducing the Root Mean Square Error (RMSE) to its current levels emphasizes the model's capability to provide a more accurate interpretation of EEG data. This breakthrough is particularly relevant in the development of BCIs, where the precision of signal interpretation directly correlates to the effectiveness and user-friendliness of the interface. In clinical settings, the enhanced accuracy and speed of EEG analysis facilitated by the EEGViT-TCNet model could lead to more timely and accurate diagnoses of neurological conditions, potentially transforming patient care.

Throughout the research, adapting ViT to the unique nature of EEG data highlighted the complexities inherent in neural signal processing. The preprocessing of EEG signals, essential for maintaining the integrity of temporal features, posed significant challenges. This process is critical in ensuring the model's adaptability and generalizability across different subjects and experimental conditions, a vital aspect for the practical application of such technologies.

Looking forward, the field beckons for further exploration into the scalability of hybrid models like EEGViT-TCNet, particularly in handling larger datasets and assessing performance in diverse real-world scenarios. A key area of interest lies in enhancing the interpretability of these deep learning models. Improved interpretability is crucial for clinical acceptance and can lead to advancements in personalized medicine, where EEG analysis can be tailored to individual patients for monitoring or therapeutic purposes.

Moreover, the exploration of other hybrid architectures and their efficacy across various domains of neural data presents an exciting avenue for research. The integration of multimodal data sources, alongside the application of transfer learning techniques, could further refine the accuracy and applicability of EEG signal analysis methods. Such advancements could pave the way for the development of more sophisticated BCIs, offering improved interaction mechanisms between humans and machines.

6   Conclusion

This study represents a significant advancement in EEG regression analysis, underscoring the role of meticulous feature extraction in the efficacy of sophisticated computational models like Vision Transformers (ViT). The integration of Temporal Convolutional Networks (TCNet) with pretrained ViTs has unveiled the vast potential of harmonizing specialized feature extraction techniques with advanced deep learning frameworks. This synergy not only elevates the accuracy of EEG analysis but also establishes a new benchmark in the field, showcasing the profound benefits of refined feature representation.

Our findings highlight the criticality of nuanced feature extraction in interpreting complex EEG data, with the EEGViT-TCNet model demonstrating notable performance enhancements. This indicates that features, often overlooked by traditional models, can be captured and leveraged for more accurate regression analysis, suggesting a broad array of applications, from clinical diagnostics to enhanced brain-computer interfaces.

For future research, the horizon of EEG analysis and deep learning promises continued expansion and innovation. The development of increasingly sophisticated models capable of navigating the complexities inherent in EEG data is anticipated. A pivotal challenge will be enhancing the interpretability of these models, ensuring they not only perform optimally but also offer actionable insights for practitioners. For example, the performance of nearly all effective models in EEG analysis currently relies heavily on the subject-dependent nature on which they are trained, leading to the possibility of poor generalization in some instances. Moreover, integrating these advanced models into real-world applications will be crucial, extending the benefits of this research to society at large.

In sum, the fusion of TCNet and pretrained ViTs within the EEG regression domain exemplifies the transformative power of targeted feature extraction and advanced data processing. This study not only redefines the standards for EEG analysis but also lights the way for future endeavors in the realms of deep learning and neural data interpretation. As we delve deeper into the complexities of the human brain, the significance of innovative computational models grows ever more evident, harboring the potential for groundbreaking discoveries in neuroscience and artificial intelligence.

References

Altaheri, H., Muhammad, G., Alsulaiman, M.: Physics-informed attention temporal convolutional network for EEG-based motor imagery classification. IEEE Trans. Ind. Inf. **19**(2), 2249–2258 (2022)

Bai, S., Kolter, J.Z., Koltun, V.: An empirical evaluation of generic convolutional and recurrent networks for sequence modeling. arXiv preprint arXiv:1803.01271 (2018)

Deng, J., et al.: Imagenet: a large-scale hierarchical image database. In: 2009 IEEE Conference on Computer Vision and Pattern Recognition. IEEE (2009)

Dosovitskiy, A., et al.: An image is worth 16 × 16 words: transformers for image recognition at scale. arXiv preprint arXiv:2010.11929, 2020

Farha, Y.A., Gall, J.: MS-TCN: multi-stage temporal convolutional network for action segmentation. In: Proceedings of the IEEE/CVF Conference on Computer Vision and Pattern Recognition (2019)

Han, K., et al.: A survey on vision transformer. IEEE Trans. Pattern Anal. Mach. Intell. **45**(1), 87–110 (2022)

Hewage, P., et al.: Temporal convolutional neural (TCN) network for an effective weather forecasting using time-series data from the local weather station. Soft Comput. **24**, 16453–16482 (2020)

Ingolfsson, T.M., et al.: EEG-TCNET: an accurate temporal convolutional network for embedded motor-imagery brain–machine interfaces. In: 2020 IEEE International Conference on Systems, Man, and Cybernetics (SMC). IEEE (2020)

Kastrati, A., et al.: Eegeyenet: a simultaneous electroencephalography and eye-tracking dataset and benchmark for eye movement prediction. arXiv preprint arXiv:2111.05100, 2021

Liu, J., et al.: Spatial-temporal transformers for EEG emotion recognition. In: Proceedings of the 6th International Conference on Advances in Artificial Intelligence (2022)

Sabbagh, D., et al.: Predictive regression modeling with MEG/EEG: from source power to signals and cognitive states. Neuroimage **222**, 116893 (2020)

Son, J., et al.: Evaluating fMRI-based estimation of eye gaze during naturalistic viewing. Cereb. Cortex **30**(3), 1171–1184 (2020)

Subasi, A., Ercelebi, E.: Classification of EEG signals using neural network and logistic regression. Comput. Methods Programs Biomed. **78**(2), 87–99 (2005)

Teplan, M.: Fundamentals of EEG measurement. Meas. Sci. Rev. **2** (2002)

Vaswani, A., et al.: Attention is all you need. Adv. Neural Inf. Process. Syst. **30** (2017)

Wu, B., et al.: Visual transformers: token-based image representation and processing for computer vision. arXiv preprint arXiv:2006.03677, 2020

Yang, R., Modesitt, E.: ViT2EEG: leveraging hybrid pretrained vision transformers for EEG data. arXiv preprint arXiv:2308.00454, 2023

Effect of Kernel Size on CNN-Vision-Transformer-Based Gaze Prediction Using Electroencephalography Data

Chuhui Qiu$^{(\boxtimes)}$ ⓘ, Bugao Liang ⓘ, and Matthew L. Key ⓘ

The George Washington University, Washington DC 20052, USA
{chqiu,bliang271,matthewlkey}@gwmail.gwu.edu

Abstract. In this paper, we present an algorithm of gaze prediction from Electroencephalography (EEG) data. EEG-based gaze prediction is a new research topic that can serve as an alternative to traditional video-based eye-tracking. Compared to the existing state-of-the-art (SOTA) method, we improved the root mean-squared-error of EEG-based gaze prediction to 53.06 mm, while reducing the training time to less than 33% of its original duration. Our source code can be found at https://github.com/AmCh-Q/CSCI6907Project.

Keywords: Machine Learning · Deep Learning · Brain-Computer Interfaces · BCI · Electroencephalography · EEG · Gaze Prediction · Eye Tracking · Transformer

1 Introduction

Electroencephalography (EEG) is a non-invasive technique used to record the electrical activity generated by the brain. Owing to its relative accessibility, non-invasiveness, superior temporal resolution compared to other neuroimaging techniques such as positron emission tomography (PET) or functional magnetic resonance imaging (fMRI), EEG's potential extends to many different fields. One such application is the complimentary application in eye-tracking. As existing video-based eye-tracking methods rely on setting up fixed cameras and pointing them directly toward the subject's eyes, EEG-based eye-tracking may lead to a promising alternative solution that does not necessarily require fixed cameras within the subject's field-of-view.

EEGViT [16] is the current state-of-the-art (SOTA) model on EEG-based gaze prediction accuracy on the EEGEyeNet dataset [5]. It employs a hybrid transformer model fine-tuned with EEG data [7,12].

1.1 Research Question

In this paper, we propose a method that answer the following questions:

D. D. Schmorrow and C. M. Fidopiastis (Eds.): HCII 2024, LNAI 14695, pp. 60–71, 2024.
https://doi.org/10.1007/978-3-031-61572-6_5

- In CNN-transformer hybrid models, how do different convolution kernel sizes over the EEG spatial features (channels) affect the accuracy of the CNN-transformer hybrid models?
- How does this compare against a convolution over all EEG channels?

By answering this question, we investigate the effects of convolution kernels on the CNN-transformer hybrid networks.

2 Related Work

While EEG and Eye-tracking have each been studied individually for over a century, their combined use has only seen an increased interest in recent years with the aid of convolutional neural networks (CNNs) and transformers.

2.1 Dataset

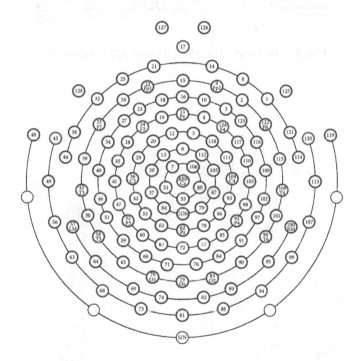

Fig. 1. Electrode Layout of the 128-channel EEG Geodesic Hydrocel system [1]

The EEGEyeNet dataset [5] offers EEG and eye tracking data that were collected simultaneously as well as benchmarks for eye movement and gaze position prediction. The EEG data of EEGEyeNet are collected from 356 participants using a 128-channel EEG Geodesic Hydrocel system, where the EEG channels are individually numbered from 1 to 128 as shown in Fig. 1. An additional reference electrode in the center make up a total of 129 EEG channels in the raw dataset.

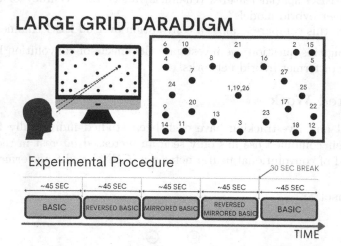

Fig. 2. The Large Grid Paradigm of EEGEyeNet [5]

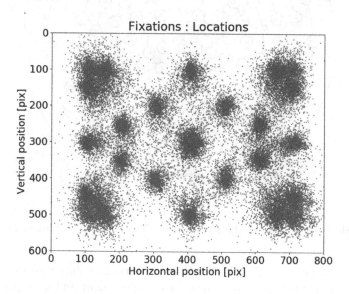

Fig. 3. Distribution of the Fixation Positions in the Large Grid Paradigm [5]

Experimental Paradigm. In one of EEGEyeNet's experimental paradigms, the participants are asked to fixate on specific dots on an "large grid" on the screen for a period as seen in Fig. 2. At the same time of recording EEG data, the participants' gaze positions are recorded. The gaze position distributions of 21464 samples can be seen in Fig. 3 [5].

2.2   State-of-the-Art

Since the publication of EEGEyeNet, several follow-up works have been made, often focusing on classification tasks (left-right or events such as blinking) [13–15]. The current state-of-the-art model in predicting gaze position is EEGViT [16], a hybrid vision transformer model fine-tuned with EEG data as shown in Fig. 4. EEGViT combines a two-level convolution feature extraction method, previously proposed in EEGNet [9] and Filter Bank Common Spatial Patterns [11] which enables efficient extraction of spatial (EEG electrodes) features for each temporal (frequency) channel, and a vision transformer using the ViT-Base model [3] pre-trained with ImageNet [2,10], to achieve a reported RMSE of 55.4 ± 0.2 mm on the EEGEyeNet dataset [16].

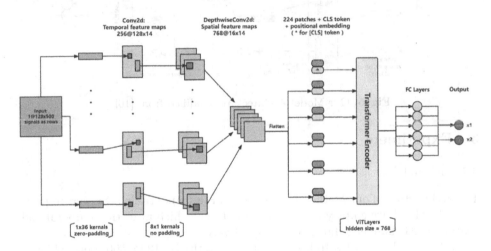

Fig. 4. EEGViT Model Architecture [16]

Table 1. Detailed Description of Our Model Architecture

Layer	Description
0	Input Size $129 \times 500 \times 1$, Zero-padded to $129 \times 512 \times 1$ on both sides
1	256 Temporal Convolution size 1×16 for Kernel and Stride, Batchnorm
2	768 Spatial Convolution size 129×1
3	ViT Model transformer, image size 129×32, patch size 129×1
4	Linear layer with 768 neurons on top of the final hidden CLS token
5	Linear layer with 1000 neurons, Dropout $p = 0.1$
6	Linear layer with 2 neurons (output)

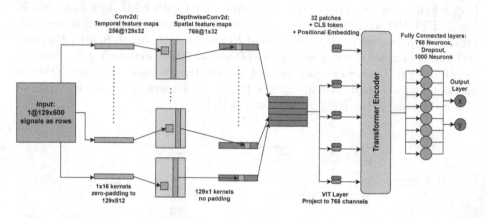

Fig. 5. Our Model Architecture, modified from [16]

3   Experiment

3.1   Model

The architecture of our Method can be seen in Fig. 5 and Table 1. Similar to prior works [9,11,16], we employ two convolution layers which filter the temporal and spatial (EEG channels) dimensions respectively.

In the first layer, a 1×16 kernel scans across the 1-s 129×500 input which is zero-padded to 129×512. The kernels effectively function as band-pass filters on the raw input signals. Our choice of 1×16 kernel is smaller than that of EEGViT at 1×36 [16] and that of EEGNet at 1×64 [9]. This provides a greater resolution of temporal features to be learned. Batch normalization is then applied on the 128×32 output [4].

In the second layer, a depth-wise 129×1 kernel scans over all EEG channels of each temporal filter. This is in contrast to EEGViT's approach, where a kernel of shape $(8, 1)$ is used [16].

Then, similar to EEGViT [16], the result is passed through a ViT transformer model, with the only difference being the shape of the input data. The base-ViT model [3] was pre-trained on ImageNet-21k and ImageNet 2012 [2,10] for image classification tasks. EEGViT [16] has previously shown that a ViT model pre-trained for image classification offers surprisingly good results when fine tuned with EEG data.

Lastly, two linear layers on top of the hidden CLS token of the ViT model output the x, y coordinates of predicted gaze position. We have additionally introduced a dropout layer to improve the robustness of the model.

3.2   Training Parameters and Software Implementation

We split the EEGEyeNet dataset into 0.7:0.15:0.15 for training, validation, and testing, and the model epoch with the lowest validation RMSE is used for testing. The split is by participant id in the original EEGEyeNet dataset to avoid leakage due to one participant's data samples appearing in more than one of training, validation, testing sets.

We included baseline ML implementations made public by the EEGEyeNet authors to be tested [5]. For EEGViT [16], we ported the authors' implementation match the setup of EEGEyeNet for training and testing in order to have the closest comparisons.

Our model and EEGViT are trained for 15 epochs in batches of 64 samples, with the Adam Optimizer [8] and an initial learning rate of 1e−4, which is dropped by a factor of 10 every 6 epochs. The model with the lowest validation error is used for testing. An example of the MSE loss during training in one of the runs can be seen in Fig. 6 and the resulting model's predictions on the testing set can be seen in Fig. 7.

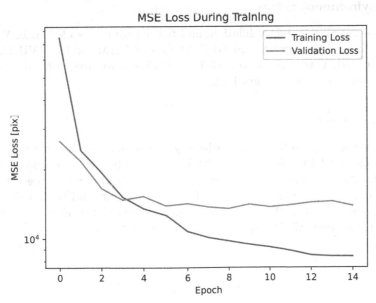

Fig. 6. Our Method's MSE Loss During Training

The full set of source code can be found at https://github.com/AmCh-Q/ CSCI6907Project.

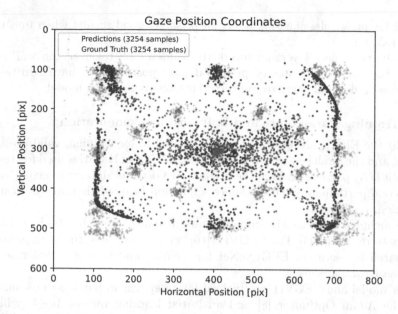

Fig. 7. Our method Gaze Position Coordinates, where predictions are colored blue, and the ground truths are colored red [6] (Color figure online).

3.3 Environment Setup

We performed all training, validation, and testing using Google Colab. We used an Intel Xeon Processor at 2.20 GHz, 51 GB of RAM, and a NVIDIA V100 GPU. For CUDA we used version 12.2, for PyTorch we used version 2.1.0, and for Scikit-learn we used version 1.2.2.

3.4 Evaluation

EEGEyeNet includes a benchmark where, given samples of shape (129, 500) collected from 129 EEG channels at 500 Hz for 1 s when the participant fixates on one location, a machine learning model is to be trained to predict the 2-dimensional gaze position (in pixels) of the participant, and the accuracy may be evaluated as either the root mean-squared error (RMSE: Eq. 1) or mean Euclidean distance (MED: Eq. 2) in pixels or millimeters.

$$\text{RMSE} = \sqrt{\frac{\sum_{i=1}^{n}((x_{i,\text{truth}} - x_{i,\text{pred}})^2 + (y_{i,\text{truth}} - y_{i,\text{pred}})^2)}{2n}} \qquad (1)$$

$$\text{MED} = \frac{\sum_{i=1}^{n} \sqrt{(x_{i,\text{truth}} - x_{i,\text{pred}})^2 + (y_{i,\text{truth}} - y_{i,\text{pred}})^2}}{n} \qquad (2)$$

Here $(x_{i,\text{truth}}, y_{i,\text{truth}}) \in \mathbb{R}^2$ is the coordinates of the gaze position collected with a video-based eye-tracker in the i-th sample, and $(x_{i,\text{pred}}, y_{i,\text{pred}}) \in \mathbb{R}^2$ is the coordinates of the gaze position predicted by machine learning models from EEG data in the i-th sample, and n is the number of 1-s data samples collected.

Five runs were run for each of the two metrics above, the mean and standard deviation of the runs were recorded, and the results can be seen in Table 2 and Table 3.

4 Discussion

In this work, we presented an algorithm for predicting gaze position from EEG signals, and Table 2 shows the comparison of accuracy against various models including the SOTA (EEGViT). As can be seen in both the root mean-squared-error (Eq. 1) and mean euclidean distance (Eq. 2) metric, our method outperforms the SOTA. This is due to the use of a spatial filtering convolution kernel of shape (129, 1), spanning all EEG channels, because the electrode layout, as seen Fig. 1, appear to be unordered and thus unlikely to be able to be learned through convolution with a smaller kernel as employed by EEGViT, and a kernel spanning all EEG channels would be able to better learn any spatial relationships between any two EEG channels at the same point in time.

We have also inspected the effect of permutation of the EEG channels and found that permuting the order of the EEG channels, either by shuffling or reordering the channels in spiral or z-order, yielded no noticeable difference in accuracy with either our method or EEGViT. We believe this means that the interactions between EEG channel signals is likely too complex and cannot be captured by convolution with a small receptive field.

Table 2. EEGEyeNet Gaze Position Scores and Standard Deviation across 5 Runs of EEGEyeNet baseline methods and EEGViT, compared against our method. Lower is better. All values are in millimeters and rounded to two decimal places. The column "Reported" contains the RMSE values that were originally reported from the respective studies.

Model	Reported RMSE	Bench RMSE	Bench MED	Study
Naive Center	–	95.85 ± 0	123.43 ± 0	[5]
Naive Mean	123.3 ± 0	95.81 ± 0	123.31 ± 0	[5]
Naive Median	–	95.79 ± 0	123.23 ± 0	[5]
KNN (K = 100)	119.7 ± 0	92.21 ± 0	119.67 ± 0	[5]
RBF SVR	123 ± 0	95.56 ± 0	123.00 ± 0	[5]
Linear Regression	118.3 ± 0	91.08 ± 0	118.37 ± 0	[5]
Ridge Regression	118.2 ± 0	90.91 ± 0	118.25 ± 0	[5]
Lasso Regression	118 ± 0	90.80 ± 0	118.04 ± 0	[5]
Elastic Net	118.1 ± 0	90.83 ± 0	118.13 ± 0	[5]
Random Forest	116.7 ± 0.1	90.09 ± 0.08	116.71 ± 0.08	[5]
Gradient Boost	117 ± 0.1	91.01 ± 0.06	117.50 ± 0.05	[5]
AdaBoost	119.4 ± 0.1	91.98 ± 0.07	119.39 ± 0.06	[5]
XGBoost	118 ± 0	91.73 ± 0	118.00 ± 0	[5]
CNN	70.2 ± 1.1	59.39 ± 0.63	70.11 ± 1.56	[5]
PyramidalCNN	73.6 ± 1.9	60.32 ± 1.67	70.86 ± 0.87	[5]
EEGNet	81.7 ± 1.0	61.92 ± 0.37	76.93 ± 0.73	[5]
InceptionTime	70.8 ± 0.8	60.32 ± 0.74	69.37 ± 0.90	[5]
Xception	78.7 ± 1.6	66.44 ± 0.80	76.77 ± 1.20	[5]
EEGViT	55.4 ± 0.2	54.41 ± 0.76	63.44 ± 0.83	[16]
Ours	–	$\mathbf{53.06} \pm 0.73$	$\mathbf{60.50} \pm 0.93$	–

In addition to measuring the accuracy of the models. We have also measured the run time of each of the models, the result of which are shown in Table 3. While slower than simpler methods such as CNN and even more considerably slower than methods such as KNN or linear regression, our method still offers an approximately 3.2 times speedup compared to the SOTA. This is due to our algorithm utilizing a much large spatial (channel) kernel, reducing the amount of trainable parameters in the model.

We were also able to confirm the findings of EEGEyeNet [5] that simple Machine learning models such as KNN, linear regression, and random forest were unable to gather meaningful information from EEG data and yielded no significant difference to naive center (where the model naively predicts the center of the screen), naive mean or naive median (where the model naively predicts the mean or median location of the training set's gaze position), while deep learning models such as CNN and EEGNet were able to yield significantly better

Table 3. EEGEyeNet Gaze Position run time (model training and validation of 21464 data samples) across 5 runs of EEGEyeNet baseline methods and EEGViT, compared against our method.

Model	Runtime [seconds]	Study
Naive Center	<0.01	[5]
Naive Mean	< 0.01	[5]
Naive Median	<0.01	[5]
KNN	0.71 ± 0.02	[5]
RBF SVR	13.23 ± 0.28	[5]
LinearReg	0.40 ± 0.07	[5]
Ridge	0.16 ± 0.01	[5]
Lasso	1.12 ± 0.02	[5]
ElasticNet	1.27 ± 0.01	[5]
RandomForest	355.90 ± 4.36	[5]
GradientBoost	816.69 ± 6.95	[5]
AdaBoost	113.31 ± 0.08	[5]
XGBoost	44.69 ± 0.43	[5]
CNN	362.71 ± 21.52	[5]
PyramidalCNN	281.84 ± 15.27	[5]
EEGNet	1696.90 ± 0.97	[5]
Xception	563.30 ± 10.59	[5]
EEGViT	2629.97 ± 5.79	[16]
Ours	812.33 ± 0.88	–

results than the naive baselines. We've also discovered that EEGEyeNet may have wrongly reported their results as "root mean-squared-error" when they may have in fact measured the mean euclidean distance error of the models, because in EEGEyeNet's source code we found that they have commented out the codes using RMSE and replaced it with MED, and that the resulting "RMSE" differs significantly with the RMSE result from our experiments, while appearing nearly identical to our "MED" measurements. Since our measured RMSE results on EEGEyeNet's models are significantly lower than reported by the authors of EEGEyeNet, the improvement made from models such as the SOTA, while still noticeable, may be smaller than what may have been believed previously.

4.1   Limitations

While the proposed method improves the accuracy and speed compared to the SOTA, the RMSE remains at approximately 5.3 cm and the mean euclidean distance remains at 6.1 cm, and training and validating the model takes an order of hundreds of seconds. This is considerable worse than commercially available video-based eye-tracking solutions in terms of both accuracy and run time. Moreover, EEGEyeNet's data was recorded in a laboratory setting and the participants were asked to stay still and have their gaze fixated on one spot on a screen, which is not reflective of most real-world application environments of eye-tracking [5]. The EEG setup is also more complex than most commercially available video-based solutions.

5   Conclusion

In this paper, we proposed an algorithm of EEG-based gaze prediction that outperforms the SOTA in both accuracy and speed. Our method improves the root mean-squared-error of the tracking to approximately 5.3 cm, and we found that having a large depth-wise convolution kernel for all EEG channels had the greatest impact. Nonetheless, EEG-based eye-tracing still has way to go and further research is needed for it to be comparable to the accuracy of traditional video-based eye tracking solutions.

Acknowledgments. This study was part of the authors' work in the course "CSCI 6907 Applied Machine Learning" in The George Washington University.

Disclosure of Interests. The authors declare no competing interests.

References

1. Bamatraf, S., et al.: A system for true and false memory prediction based on 2d and 3d educational contents and EEG brain signals. Comput. Intell. Neurosci. **2016**, 45–45 (2016)
2. Deng, J., Dong, W., Socher, R., Li, L.J., Li, K., Fei-Fei, L.: ImageNet: a large-scale hierarchical image database. In: 2009 IEEE Conference on Computer Vision and Pattern Recognition, pp. 248–255. IEEE (2009)
3. Dosovitskiy, A., et al.: An image is worth 16x16 words: transformers for image recognition at scale. arXiv preprint arXiv:2010.11929 (2020)
4. Ioffe, S., Szegedy, C.: Batch normalization: accelerating deep network training by reducing internal covariate shift. In: International Conference on Machine Learning, pp. 448–456. PMLR (2015)
5. Kastrati, A., et al.: EEGEyeNet: a simultaneous electroencephalography and eye-tracking dataset and benchmark for eye movement prediction. arXiv preprint arXiv:2111.05100 (2021)
6. Key, M.L., Mehtiyev, T., Qu, X.: Advancing EEG-based gaze prediction using depthwise separable convolution and enhanced pre-processing, preprint (2024)
7. Khan, S., Naseer, M., Hayat, M., Zamir, S.W., Khan, F.S., Shah, M.: Transformers in vision: a survey. ACM Comput. Surv. (CSUR) **54**(10s), 1–41 (2022)
8. Kingma, D.P., Ba, J.: Adam: a method for stochastic optimization. arXiv preprint arXiv:1412.6980 (2014)
9. Lawhern, V.J., Solon, A.J., Waytowich, N.R., Gordon, S.M., Hung, C.P., Lance, B.J.: EEGNet: a compact convolutional neural network for EEG-based brain-computer interfaces. J. Neural Eng. **15**(5), 056013 (2018)

10. Ridnik, T., Ben-Baruch, E., Noy, A., Zelnik-Manor, L.: ImageNet-21k pretraining for the masses. arXiv preprint arXiv:2104.10972 (2021)
11. Schirrmeister, R.T., et al.: Deep learning with convolutional neural networks for EEG decoding and visualization. Hum. Brain Mapp. **38**(11), 5391–5420 (2017)
12. Vaswani, A., et al.: Attention is all you need. Adv. Neural Inf. Process. Syst. **30** (2017)
13. Wolf, L., et al.: A deep learning approach for the segmentation of electroencephalography data in eye tracking applications. arXiv preprint arXiv:2206.08672 (2022)
14. Xiang, B., Abdelmonsef, A.: Too fine or too coarse? The goldilocks composition of data complexity for robust left-right eye-tracking classifiers. arXiv preprint arXiv:2209.03761 (2022)
15. Xiang, B., Abdelmonsef, A.: Vector-based data improves left-right eye-tracking classifier performance after a covariate distributional shift. In: Kurosu, M., et al. (eds.) HCII 2022. LNCS, vol. 13516, pp. 617–632. Springer, Cham (2022). https://doi.org/10.1007/978-3-031-17615-9_44
16. Yang, R., Modesitt, E.: ViT2EEG: leveraging hybrid pretrained vision transformers for EEG data. arXiv preprint arXiv:2308.00454 (2023)

Better Results Through Ambiguity Resolution: Large Language Models that Ask Clarifying Questions

Bernadette Tix$^{(\boxtimes)}$ (iD) and Kim Binsted (iD)

University of Hawaii at Manoa, Honolulu, HI 96822, USA
bjavery@hawaii.edu

Abstract. Here we present a pilot study on the Clarifying Questions Document Generator (CQDG), an AI document-generation application designed to ask follow-up questions to the user after receiving their initial prompt. Study participants wrote a prompt requesting the AI to generate a short document such as an email, letter, or other short document. The AI then generated follow-up questions and engaged in a short question-and-answer dialog before creating the requested document. This study examines users' willingness to engage in a question-and-answer exchange with an AI, as well as their satisfaction with the output of this exchange compared to a baseline output generated using only the users' original prompts. It was predicted that users would prefer the output that included the solicited information over the baseline result. However, the initial results suggest that there was little to no overall improvement in the final output, with about half of users preferring the baseline output to the result of the question-and-answer exchange. This paper will discuss possible reasons for this result as well as suggestions for how future systems could be improved, which will be incorporated into a larger study later this year.

Keywords: Large Language Models · Clarifying Questions · Generative AI

1 Introduction

Ambiguity has historically been a challenge in Natural Language Processing (NLP) and continues to present obstacles for modern systems. Large Language Models (LLMs) generate output by calculating a "most likely" response to any given input, with inputs usually given in the form of a prompt from a human user. However, prompts are often ambiguous, and even the best possible prediction cannot fully resolve underspecified prompts [1]. Even in a conversation between two humans, both speaking the same language and communicating clearly, misunderstandings are common. While there are many ways to resolve ambiguity in a human conversation, perhaps the most obvious way is to ask for clarification. However, commonly used LLM systems such as ChatGPT, Bard, and Bing do not ask clarifying questions in response to ambiguous prompts.

This is a problem in fields where precision is important. Detailed discussions, including follow-up questions, are a necessary part of human communication in such fields.

D. D. Schmorrow and C. M. Fidopiastis (Eds.): HCII 2024, LNAI 14695, pp. 72–87, 2024.
https://doi.org/10.1007/978-3-031-61572-6_6

Even for simple requests, a lack of follow-up questions can lead to suboptimal answers or cause the LLM to misunderstand the user's needs.

LLMs are capable of identifying ambiguity in user prompts and forming questions in response to ambiguity when prompted to do so. This has already been demonstrated with AIs answering simple ambiguous questions [2, 3], but has not yet been demonstrated with AIs intended to generate longer-form responses such as letters or documents. We propose that an LLM-based system that asks clarifying questions when needed will produce content that is more closely aligned to the desires of the human user than a comparable system which asks no clarifying questions.

2 Background

Ambiguity has historically been a challenge for NLP, including parsing [4–6], Named Entity Recognition (NER) [7–9], story understanding [10–13], and numerous other NLP tasks. In the past decade, neural models have been employed to create software that can exhibit reading comprehension-like behaviors on ambiguous, natural language text. Recurrent Neural Networks (RNN) [14, 15] and Long Short-Term Memory Networks (LSTM) [10, 16–18] demonstrated successes with specialist systems dedicated to specific NLP tasks.

Large Language Models (LLM) offer a more general solution than specialized LSTM systems. Over the past several years LLMs have improved dramatically, demonstrating state-of-the-art performance in multiple areas of NLP, matching or outperforming specialized LSTM-based systems on several NLP benchmarks [19–21] including answering questions about children's stories [22], common-sense reasoning [23], reading comprehension [24], translation, and summarization [21], among others.

Output from LLMs can be further improved by the introduction of "chain-of-thought reasoning" [25], in which the LLM is prompted to write out a full logical argument for its conclusion in small steps, rather than skipping straight ahead to the final conclusion. Chain-of-thought reasoning in LLMs leads to fewer hallucinations, more factually correct responses, more advanced reasoning, and improved ability to solve puzzles or trick questions. LLM systems operating on a chain-of-thought model also have the potential to explain the reasoning that led them to a given conclusion, which is considered to be a desirable trait in both logical and ethical reasoning, and a necessary step for humans to trust the results of an analysis [26, 27].

2.1 Context, Ambiguity, and User Needs

Understanding context is necessary for accurate reasoning and communication. When precision is needed in human communication, a wide variety of methods are used to clarify what would otherwise be inherently ambiguous language. For example, when gathering requirements for new software, a high degree of precision is needed, usually far more than is initially provided, which is the motive for the phase of 'requirements gathering' within software engineering. Requirements gathering has been researched at length, and often employs a wide variety of techniques including questionnaires, face-to-face dialogs between customer and developer, and various exercises designed to improve user engagement with the requirements gathering process [28, 29]. None of this would be necessary if software engineers could reliably get good results by simply asking users to "please state your requirements clearly!" One of the key goals of requirements gathering is to understand the context of the desired software, for example, what problem the software is needed to solve, and what specific change or improvement it is hoped the software will achieve.

Prior research in conversational interfaces has shown that better results can be achieved when the full context of a conversation is considered, not just the immediate prompt [30]. Systems such as ChatGPT are in a disadvantaged position with regards to context, as users can enter any prompt on any topic, and the LLM must provide a response with no knowledge of who the user is or why they are asking. It is unreasonable to assume that an LLM could interpret the user's intended meaning in the absence of context when this is not possible even in communication between humans, using inherently ambiguous and context-dependent language. We believe that asking clarifying questions is a skill which LLMs must master if they are to communicate clearly and precisely with humans.

2.2 Prior Work

Several recent works have addressed the concept of LLMs using clarifying questions. The CLAM architecture [2] presents a method for using an LLM to assess ambiguity, generate a clarifying question if needed, and then generate an answer based on the user's response to the question. CLARA [3] showed that a similar framework could be used to interpret user commands given to a robotic arm. ClarifyDelphi [31] uses clarifying questions to assist in context-sensitive ethical reasoning. Zhang et al. 2023 present a framework for asking clarifying questions before retrieving data from a database [32]. ClarifyGPT [33] demonstrates the benefits of asking clarifying questions for LLM code-creation tasks. Follow-up questions have been shown to be effective at steering the conversation in automated surveys conducted by LLM chatbots [34].

Our research differs from these prior works in several ways:

1. We examine the overall quality of generated text documents. The ability to create and modify original documents is a key strength of LLMs over earlier AI systems.
2. In our research, human users rate the quality of documents based on their own needs and subjective judgements. This is a realistic scenario for documents generated for human use. Prior research has relied heavily on "simulated humans" modeled by AI or automated metrics which may not reflect users' subjective experience of document quality.
3. We also examine users' willingness to engage in question-and-answer dialog with the AI. It is hoped that the AI asking follow-up questions will encourage users to engage more deeply with their own prompts and with the document creation process. However, it is also possible that users will find the process annoying or arduous.

2.3 Existing Benchmarks and Evaluation Methods

There are many benchmarks currently in use for the evaluation of LLMs. Many of the common benchmarks, such as the BLEU benchmark [35] and BERTScore [36], measure the overall quality of the generated text. However, they do not measure how well the output corresponds to the initial prompt or to a user-desired outcome. Other benchmarks test the LLM's ability to give the correct answer to questions with previously established correct answers, including numerous question-answer (QA) datasets [37]. Some QA datasets target specific types of questions, including CoQA for Conversational Question Answering [24], TruthfulQA for misleading questions [38], and the Children's Book Test for reading comprehension of short stories [22]. These styles of benchmark are poorly suited to determining whether a generated content has fulfilled a user's needs. Measuring the overall quality of the text, as BLEU and BERTScore do, does not tell us whether the high-quality text has solved the user's problem or merely provided elegant but irrelevant prose. QA datasets are only suitable for measuring the LLM's ability to produce short, accurate responses to questions with objectively right and wrong answers. This is not suitable for the evaluation of longer-form content. A letter, essay, or short story cannot be objectively classified as "correct" or "incorrect." The overall quality of such a document can only be measured subjectively, by the evaluation of the reader.[1]

Validation of generative models for visual art and music may offer some guidance here. As with long-form textual content, the quality of visual art and music cannot generally be objectively evaluated. Furthermore, such systems are most often employed in the task of generating content (art or music) from a short textual prompt, and quality of these systems must be evaluated on how closely the output matches the intent behind the prompt given to the model. Despite the challenges associated with subjective analysis by human evaluators, including higher costs and challenges with methodology and sample size, it is often the only way to gain reliable feedback on the quality of output from creative systems [39, 40]. For instance, the experiments which validated the quality of DALL-E had human evaluators rate images for both realism and accuracy relative to each image's corresponding prompt [41].

3 System Architecture

For this study we created a web-based application called the Clarifying Questions Document Generator (CQDG). The key components of CQDG are:

- A user-facing front-end.
- A back-end powered by OpenAI's GPT3.5 API.
- A database for logging results from the use of the system.

CQDG was designed as an interface between the user and the OpenAI API. CQDG applies specific prompt-engineering templates to the user's questions, prompts, and responses to induce GPT3.5 to identify ambiguity, generate follow-up questions, and ultimately produce a final output that considers both the original user prompt as well as the additional information from the ensuing conversation. In some cases, the API is prompted multiple times to produce multi-step results for ambiguity analysis before the user is shown only the final response of a small sequence of API interactions. In other

---

[1] In some cases, an objective measure may be possible for documents with a purpose, such as whether a generated resume resulted in an interview in a job application. However, in general, user assessment of document quality is subjective.

cases, the API is given a modified version of the user's original prompt decorated with specific prompt engineering to steer the response. To the user it appears as if each of their inputs is given just one output in direct response to what they wrote, just as when chatting with ChatGPT directly, although several interactions between the web page and the GPT API are actually taking place during each step of the process without being shown to the user. The process of generating follow-up questions is similar to that shown by the CLAM model (Kuhn, Gal, and Farquhar 2023) [2].

The baseline document is generated by providing the OpenAI API with an unmodified version of the user's original prompt. The experimental output, hereafter referred to as the QA Document, is generated by providing GPT3.5 with the full context of the original prompt, the follow-up questions, and all user responses. An example of a complete log of prompts and responses sent and received from GPT3.5 is provided in the appendix.

4 Methodology

4.1 Experiment Design

Since CQDG relies on user interaction in the form of question asking and answering, the use of large static databases of question-answer sets is insufficient to test this design. Direct interaction between CQDG and human users is necessary. So, participants are directed to a public website hosting CQDG, which guides them through the experiment. Participants complete the study either on a Zoom call with a researcher or in person with the researcher in the room. The participant is asked to narrate out loud their thought process and any challenges or difficulties they encounter using the system, and the researcher takes notes on any feedback given by the participants. On Zoom calls, participants are asked to share their screens so the researcher can observe their interactions with CQDG.
Step 1 Explanation and consent[2]. CQDG shows the user an explanation of the experiment, and then asks for the user's consent to participate in the study, with an explanation of what data will be collected and how it will be used.
Step 2: Demographic Questions. The user is asked a small set of demographic questions. For the small sample size of this pilot study, we were not able to draw conclusions about how different groups respond to the system. However, we hope that this data will be valuable in the full study. The demographic questions are:

• Age

  – [Numerical Input]

• Gender

  – "Female"
  – "Male"
  – "Other/Nonbinary"

---

[2] This experiment design was approved by the University of Hawaii Institutional Review Board.

- "What is your prior experience with generative AI such as ChatGPT, Bard, or similar programs?"

    - "I use generative AI regularly."
    - "I have used generative AI before, but not often."
    - "I have never used generative AI before."

- "Is English your primary spoken language?"

    - "Yes"
    - "No"

Step 3: Instructions. *The user is shown the following instructions: "Think of a writing task you would like the AI to help you produce. This can be a document you actually need (you will have the opportunity to keep the output) or something you only think up for the sake of the experiment. Either way, please think in detail about what you want the AI to write for you before proceeding to the next step. When you have a clear idea of what you want to ask the AI to write, enter a 1-sentence or 2-sentence prompt in the textbox below, asking the AI to write your document for you. The AI will ask you a series of questions, and you will then be given two versions of the document you requested, and asked for feedback on which version you prefer. "A text-entry area is provided for the user to enter their prompt.*

Step 4: Follow-up Questions. After the user enters their initial prompt, CQDG presents the user with three clarifying follow-up questions generated by GPT 3.5 based on the user's prompt, along with a text-entry field for the user to enter their response.

Step 5: Document Output. After all questions have been answered, CQDG uses GPT3.5 to generate two versions of the requested document. One version uses only the user's original prompt to generate the document (baseline). The other version additionally uses the responses to the follow-up questions (QA Document). The outputs are presented to the user in random order, one at a time. When the user is shown each document, they are asked to rate the document according to three metrics, each evaluated on a scale of 1–5:

- How close is this document to what you hoped for when you made your initial request?

    - (5) Very close to what I was hoping for.
    - (4) Somewhat close to what I was hoping for.
    - (3) A little bit like what I was hoping for.
    - (2) Not very close to what I was hoping for.
    - (1) Not at all what I wanted.

- How useful would this document be to you?

    - (5) I could use this document as-is.
    - (4) I could use this document with minimal modification.
    - (3) I could use this document with substantial modification.
    - (2) This document could be used as a general starting point but requires major revisions to be usable.

– (1) This document is not usable at all.

• How would you rate the overall quality of this document?

– (5) Excellent quality.
– (4) Above average quality.
– (3) Average quality.
– (2) Below average quality.
– (1) Poor quality.

Step 6: Optional Continuation and Exit Questionnaire. After ranking each output with the three questions listed above, the user is shown an exit questionnaire with the following questions:

• *Please rate the following statements on a scale of "Strongly Agree" to "Strongly Disagree"* (Each of the following statements is shown with 5 options and analyzed as a scale score of 1–5: 5-Strongly Agree, 4-Slightly Agree, 3-Neutral, 2-Sightly Disagree, 1-Strongly Disagree)

– It was annoying to have to answer questions even though I had already explained what I wanted the AI to do.
– I felt like the AI was more engaged with my problem because it asked follow-up questions.
– I would be willing to answer follow-up questions from an AI if answering questions led to better results.
– I liked that the AI showed me two options to pick between, instead of only picking the option it thought was best.

• Do you have any additional feedback or comments (optional)?

– A free-text entry is provided.

5 Results

A total of eight participants completed the pilot study. Although participants were not prompted to complete the study multiple times, several participants specifically requested to run the study again with different prompts immediately after completing the study for the first time. This was allowed, and the eight participants completed the study a total of fourteen times. This is not a sufficient sample size to draw statistically significant conclusions about the overall effectiveness of CQDG. However, as a pilot study, the primary goal was to inform the design of a follow-up study with a much larger sample of participants completing the study without direct supervision from the researchers.

5.1 Participant Responses

Document Ratings. As shown in Fig. 1, participant ratings for the document resulting from the question-and-answer process were similar to the ratings given for the baseline output which was generated using only the original prompts.

Exit Survey. As shown in Fig. 2, participants responded positively to the question-and-answer process overall. Participants did not express annoyance at being asked additional questions before receiving their output, and overall felt positively about the question-answering experience.

Completion Time. The average time to complete the study, measured from the acceptance of the consent to the completion of the exit survey, was 16 min 46 s. However, there was substantial variation in completion time, with the shortest time being 6 min 19 s and the longest being 41 min 35 s. This is to be expected, since participants were free to enter their own prompts and give as brief or as detailed answers as they desired for the question-answering phase. Most of the difference in completion time is explained by the difference in time spent entering answers with varying levels of detail. The longest completion time was for a user who requested a complete resume of a long musical career and gave substantial details in their prompt and answers. The shortest was for a user who requested a haiku and gave very short and general guidance in their prompt and answers.

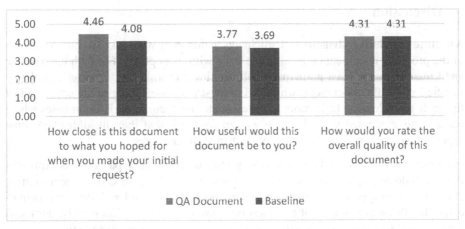

Fig. 1. Average document ratings given by participants. Note that this sample size is not large enough to be statistically significant, thus no error bars have been included.

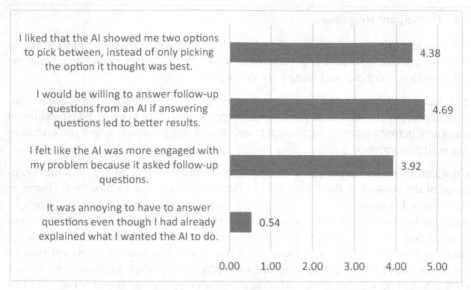

Fig. 2. Exit survey results. Overall, participants responded positively to answering questions from the AI and did not find the process annoying. Note that this sample size is not large enough to be statistically significant, thus no error bars have been included.

6   Discussion

Absolute vs Relative Measures. Participants in this study were asked to rate the quality of the produced document on an absolute scale with five options. For both the baseline and QA documents, most participants felt positively overall, but were not completely satisfied with either document, which led to most responses being in the upper half of the scale (3–5) leaving little room to differentiate the documents. Even in cases where participants expressed verbally or in written feedback that they liked/disliked some aspect of a document, this was often not reflected in the scores.

Engagement and Insight from Follow-Up Questions. Several participants expressed that the follow-up questions themselves introduced new ideas or caused them to think about aspects of their request that they had not previously considered. Participants indicated that this was a benefit of the question-answering process. Conversely, questions which asked for simple information such as the user's name or organization were not considered helpful by participants. Baseline documents often included tags such as [your name] and [name of organization] and participants did not see a benefit to giving this information in the interactive phase rather than entering the information later.

Novel Ideas in Baseline Documents. The baseline documents included a greater variety of content that did not come directly from the participants' prompts or responses. Given limited information to work with, GPT often produces plausible outputs that surprises participants or takes a direction they had not previously thought of. While this was undesired in some cases, in other cases the participants expressed finding the originality to be useful and insightful. This is in line with previous findings that LLMs often perform surprisingly well at underspecified tasks [42].

Rigid Outputs from QA Documents. Conversely, the outputs that were generated using both the original prompts as well as the questions and answers typically included far less original content and often copied pieces of the participants' answers verbatim, resulting in a document that closely adhered to the participants stated needs but offered little originality. Participants expressed valuing the insight from the questions themselves, which often contained ideas they had not thought of, but this insight and originality did not carry forward into the final output.

7 Future Work

This study was designed as a pilot for a study which will include a larger sample size and allow participants to complete the survey without the direct supervision of a researcher. Based on the results of the pilot, the larger study will:

1. Allow users to read both documents and then indicate preference for one document or the other, rather than asking users to rate the documents one at a time.
2. Use higher resolution on rating scales. The 1–5 scale proved to be insufficiently sensitive.
3. Refine the prompt engineering of the sequences input to GPT. Ideally, the final output should take participants' responses into account while retaining a degree of originality, without copying participant answers verbatim.
4. Gear questions towards encouraging users to think about their needs in ways they had not previously considered or proposing expansions or alternatives, rather than gathering information that the user could easily enter into a template form (e.g. the name of their organization).
5. Provide a way to continue refining the documents after their initial creation. Several participants, especially those with prior experience with generative AI, specifically requested the ability to continue refining the outputs they were given with new instructions.
6. Compare GPT 3.5, GPT 4, and other LLMs. GPT 3.5 was only used in this case for simplicity due to the small number of participants.
7. Conclusion

We have proposed that using LLMs to generate follow-up questions can lead to superior output for text documents generated by the LLM. However, initial results do not show an obvious advantage of the QA documents over the baseline. The primary disadvantage faced by CQDG was that the QA documents focused heavily on the users' answers and did not generate as much original content as documents generated from the prompt alone. This issue could be solved by modifying the prompt engineering in the templates that present the users' prompts and responses to the LLM. The intent behind this pilot study was to investigate users' response to CQDG and these insights will inform the design of a larger study to be conducted later this year.

Disclosure of Interests. The authors have no competing interests to declare that are relevant to the content of this article.

Appendix: Example Prompt and Response Log

An example of the QA Document generation process is shown below. This example was invented for the purposes of this paper and is not an actual entry by one of the study participants. Participants' answers are kept confidential by our privacy agreement. **Bold** text is for clarification only and is not part of the actual prompts or responses.

User Enters: Write a lesson plan on the Apollo 11 mission for a middle school science class.

Sent to GPT: You are a helpful AI assistant used to generate short documents. A user is requesting the creation of a new document. This is their request: user: "Write a lesson plan on the Apollo 11 mission for a middle school science class." Identify any areas of significant ambiguity or necessary information that has not been included, and write these out in a short list. Include exactly 3 items in the list.

GPT Response: 1. Duration and schedule: It is important to specify the duration of the lesson plan, such as whether it is designed for a single class period or a series of classes. Additionally, it would be helpful to know the desired schedule for the lesson plan, including any specific timing for different activities within the plan. 2. Required resources: Clarify whether there are any specific resources available for the lesson plan, such as textbooks, videos, or online materials. Knowing what resources are accessible will help in developing appropriate activities and assignments. 3. Prior knowledge and grade level: Identify the prior knowledge expected from the middle school students and their grade level. This will enable customizing the content and complexity of the lesson plan to suit their understanding and abilities.

Sent to GPT: Consider the following request: user: "Write a lesson plan on the Apollo 11 mission for a middle school science class." and the following identified points of ambiguity: "1. Duration and schedule: It is important to specify the duration of the lesson plan, such as whether it is designed for a single class period or a series of classes. Additionally, it would be helpful to know the desired schedule for the lesson plan, including any specific timing for different activities within the plan. 2. Required resources: Clarify whether there are any specific resources available for the lesson plan, such as textbooks, videos, or online materials. Knowing what resources are accessible will help in developing appropriate activities and assignments. 3. Prior knowledge and grade level: Identify the prior knowledge expected from the middle school students and their grade level. This will enable customizing the content and complexity of the lesson plan to suit their understanding and abilities." Respond as though this request was just made by the user. Start with a friendly greeting, then ask a respectful and concise question to clarify the user's needs, keeping in mind the ambiguity you just identified. Format your response as a numbered list of exactly 3 questions.

GPT Response: Hello! I'd be happy to help you create a lesson plan on the Apollo 11 mission for a middle school science class. To ensure I fulfill your needs, I have a few questions: 1. Duration and schedule: Could you please let me know the duration of the lesson plan? Is it designed for a single class period or a series of classes? Additionally, do you have any preferences or specific timing for different activities within the plan? 2. Required resources: Are there any specific resources available for the lesson plan, such as textbooks, videos, or online materials? Knowing what resources you have access to will allow me to develop appropriate activities and assignments. 3. Prior knowledge and grade level: Could you please clarify the prior knowledge expected from the middle school students and specify their grade level? This information will enable me to tailor the content and complexity of the lesson plan to suit their understanding and abilities. Once I have these details, I'll be able to create a comprehensive and suitable lesson plan on the Apollo 11 mission for your middle school science class.

[This response is parsed into separate questions and shown to the user]

Question 1 (Shown to User): Duration and schedule: Could you please let me know the duration of the lesson plan? Is it designed for a single class period or a series of classes? Additionally, do you have any preferences or specific timing for different activities within the plan?

User Answer: This is for a single one-hour class. Please include at least one short activity in addition to lecture and discussion.

Question 2 (Shown to User): Required resources: Are there any specific resources available for the lesson plan, such as textbooks, videos, or online materials? Knowing what resources you have access to will allow me to develop appropriate activities and assignments.

User Answer: We are going to watch a 10-min Youtube video about the Apollo program and the moon landing. Their textbook also includes a chapter on space flight.

Question 3 (Shown to User): Prior knowledge and grade level: Could you please clarify the prior knowledge expected from the middle school students and specify their grade level? This information will enable me to tailor the content and complexity of the lesson plan to suit their understanding and abilities.

User Answer: This class has students from multiple grade levels, grades 6–8. We have been covering the history of flight this quarter, and the students have made paper airplanes and launched model rockets in previous classes.

Sent to GPT: Consider the following exchange. Attempt to create the document requested by the user, considering the answers they gave when asked for details. User: "Write a lesson plan on the Apollo 11 mission for a middle school science class." assistant: "Hello! I'd be happy to help you create a lesson plan on the Apollo 11 mission for a middle school science class. To ensure I fulfill your needs, I have a few questions:

1. Duration and schedule: Could you please let me know the duration of the lesson plan? Is it designed for a single class period or a series of classes? Additionally, do you have any preferences or specific timing for different activities within the plan?"
   user: "This is for a single one-hour class. Please include at least one short activity in addition to lecture and discussion." assistant: "
2. Required resources: Are there any specific resources available for the lesson plan, such as textbooks, videos, or online materials? Knowing what resources you have access to will allow me to develop appropriate activities and assignments. "
   user: "We are going to watch a 10-min Youtube video about the Apollo program and the moon landing. Their textbook also includes a chapter on space flight." assistant: "
3. Prior knowledge and grade level: Could you please clarify the prior knowledge expected from the middle school students and specify their grade level? This information will enable me to tailor the content and complexity of the lesson plan to suit their understanding and abilities."

user: "This class has students from multiple grade levels, grades 6–8. We have been covering the history of flight this quarter, and the students have made paper airplanes and launched model rockets in previous classes."

GPT Response (Shown to User): Lesson Plan: Apollo 11 Mission
Grade Level: 6–8 Duration: 1 h (single class period) Resources:

- 10-min YouTube video on the Apollo program and the moon landing
- Textbook with a chapter on space flight

Prior Knowledge: Students have been studying the history of flight and have engaged in hands-on activities like making paper airplanes and launching model rockets.

Objectives: By the end of this lesson, students will be able to:

1. Explain the significance of the Apollo 11 mission in the context of space exploration.
2. Describe the steps involved in the Apollo 11 mission.
3. Analyze the impact of the Apollo 11 mission on technology and society.

Procedure:

1. Warm-up activity (10 min): - Begin the class by asking students what they know about the Apollo 11 mission. Encourage them to share any facts or prior knowledge they have. This will help activate their prior knowledge and set the stage for the lesson.
2. Introduction to the Apollo 11 mission (15 min):

   - Show the 10-min YouTube video on the Apollo program and the moon landing. This video will provide an overview of the mission and the significance of the moon landing. Pause at key points to allow for class discussion and clarification of any questions or misconceptions.

3. Lecture and discussion (20 min):

   - Using the textbook chapter on space flight, provide a brief lecture on the Apollo 11 mission. Highlight key points such as the crew members, the spacecraft, the launch, the lunar landing, and the return to Earth. Encourage students to ask questions and engage in discussion throughout the lecture.

4. Hands-on activity: Lunar module design challenge (15 min):

   - Divide the class into small groups and provide each group with materials such as paper, tape, scissors, and straws.
   - Explain that they will be designing and building their own lunar modules that can safely land on the moon. Encourage creativity and problem-solving skills.
   - After the groups have completed their designs, invite them to present their lunar modules and explain their design choices to the class.

5. Summary and reflection (5 min):

   - Ask students to reflect on what they have learned about the Apollo 11 mission and its significance. Allow them to share their thoughts and any new insights they gained during the lesson.
   - Provide a brief summary of the key points covered in the lesson, emphasizing the impact of the Apollo 11 mission on technology and society.

Assessment:

- Assessment can be conducted through class participation and engagement during the discussion and hands-on activity.
- Additionally, students can be given a short-written assignment or quiz to test their understanding of the key concepts covered in the lesson.

Extension activities:

- If time permits, students can research and present on other significant space missions, exploring the scientific and technological advancements made in those missions.
- Students can also create posters or multimedia presentations highlighting the key events and achievements of the Apollo 11 mission.

Note: If additional time is available, the lesson plan can be extended or revised accordingly.

References

1. D'Amour, A., et al.: Underspecification presents challenges for credibility in modern machine learning. J. Mach. Learn. Res. **23**(226), 10237–226:10297 (2022)
2. Kuhn, L., Gal, Y., Farquhar, S.: CLAM: selective clarification for ambiguous questions with generative language models. In: ICML 2023 Workshop on Deployment Challenges for Generative AI. (2023)
3. Park, J., et al.: CLARA: Classifying and Disambiguating User Commands for Reliable Interactive Robotic Agents (2023). http://arxiv.org/abs/2306.10376, https://doi.org/10.48550/arXiv.2306.10376
4. Fillmore, C.J.: Some problems for case grammar. In: Shuy, R.W., Fasold, R.W. (eds.) Report Of The Twenty-Second Annual Round Table Meeting on Linguistics and Language Studies. Georgetown Univ. Press, Washington, DC (1973)
5. Pollard, C., Sag, I.A.: Head-Driven Phrase Structure Grammar. University of Chicago Press, Chicago (1994)
6. Valin, R.D.V.: Role and reference grammar. Work Papers of the Summer Institute of Linguistics, vol. 37, p. 12 (1993)
7. Cui, L., Wu, Y., Liu, J., Yang, S., Zhang, Y.: Template-Based Named Entity Recognition Using BART (2021). http://arxiv.org/abs/2106.01760, https://doi.org/10.48550/arXiv.2106.01760
8. Krishnan, V., Manning, C.D.: An effective two-stage model for exploiting non-local dependencies in named entity recognition. In: Proceedings of the 21st International Conference on Computational Linguistics and 44th Annual Meeting of the Association for Computational Linguistics, pp. 1121–1128. Association for Computational Linguistics, Sydney, Australia (2006). https://doi.org/10.3115/1220175.1220316
9. Lample, G., Ballesteros, M., Subramanian, S., Kawakami, K., Dyer, C.: Neural architectures for named entity recognition. In: Proceedings of NAACL 2016. (2016)
10. Choi, S., et al.: DramaQA: character-centered video story understanding with hierarchical QA. In: Proceedings of the AAAI Conference on Artificial Intelligence, vol. 35, pp. 1166–1174 (2021)
11. Farrell, R., Robertson, S., Ware, S.G.: Asking hypothetical questions about stories using QUEST. In: Nack, F. and Gordon, A.S. (eds.) Interactive Storytelling. ICIDS 2016. LNCS, vol. 10045, pp. 136–146. Springer, Cham (2016). https://doi.org/10.1007/978-3-319-48279-8_12

12. Mueller, E.T.: Story understanding through multi-representation model construction. In: Proceedings of the HLT-NAACL 2003 Workshop on Text Meaning - Volume 9, pp. 46–53. Association for Computational Linguistics, USA (2003). https://doi.org/10.3115/1119239.1119246
13. Schwartz, R., Sap, M., Konstas, I., Zilles, L., Choi, Y., Smith, N.A.: Story cloze task: UW NLP system. In: Proceedings of the 2nd Workshop on Linking Models of Lexical, Sentential and Discourse-level Semantics, pp. 52–55. Association for Computational Linguistics, Valencia, Spain (2017). https://doi.org/10.18653/v1/W17-0907
14. Das, S., Giles, C., Sun, G.: Learning Context-free Grammars: Capabilities and Limitations of a Recurrent Neural Network with an External Stack Memory (1992)
15. Mikolov, T., Zweig, G.: Context dependent recurrent neural network language model. In: 2012 IEEE Spoken Language Technology Workshop (SLT), pp. 234–239. IEEE, Miami, FL, USA (2012). https://doi.org/10.1109/SLT.2012.6424228
16. Boughoula, A., San, A., Zhai, C.: Leveraging book indexes for automatic extraction of concepts in MOOCs. In: Proceedings of the Seventh ACM Conference on Learning @ Scale, pp. 381–384. Association for Computing Machinery, New York, NY, USA (2020). https://doi.org/10.1145/3386527.3406749
17. Cheng, J., Dong, L., Lapata, M.: Long Short-Term Memory-Networks for Machine Reading (2016). http://arxiv.org/abs/1601.06733, https://doi.org/10.48550/arXiv.1601.06733
18. Jozefowicz, R., Vinyals, O., Schuster, M., Shazeer, N., Wu, Y.: Exploring the Limits of Language Modeling (2016). http://arxiv.org/abs/1602.02410
19. Brown, T., et al.: Language models are few-shot learners. Adv. Neural Inf. Process. Syst. 1877–1901. Curran Associates, Inc. (2020)
20. Radford, A., Narasimhan, K., Salimans, T., Sutskever, I.: Improving Language Understanding by Generative Pre-Training (2018)
21. Radford, A., Wu, J., Child, R., Luan, D., Amodei, D., Sutskever, I.: Language Models are Unsupervised Multitask Learners. OpenAI blog. 1.8, (2019)
22. Hill, F., Bordes, A., Chopra, S., Weston, J.: The Goldilocks Principle: Reading Children's Books with Explicit Memory Representations. arXiv:1511.02301 [cs]. (2016)
23. Levesque, H., Davis, E., Morgenstern, L.: The Winograd Schema Challenge
24. Reddy, S., Chen, D., Manning, C.D.: CoQA: a conversational question answering challenge. Trans. Assoc. Comput. Linguist. 7, 249–266 (2019). https://doi.org/10.1162/tacl_a_00266
25. Wei, J., et al.: Chain-of-Thought Prompting Elicits Reasoning in Large Language Models (2023). http://arxiv.org/abs/2201.11903. https://doi.org/10.48550/arXiv.2201.11903
26. Lenat, D.: Not Good As Gold: Today's AI's Are Dangerously Lacking In AU (Artificial Understanding). https://www.forbes.com/sites/cognitiveworld/2019/02/18/not-good-as-gold-todays-ais-are-dangerously-lacking-in-au-artificial-understanding/. Accessed 05 Dec 2022
27. Lenat, D.: Getting from Generative AI to Trustworthy AI: What LLMs might learn from Cyc. (2023)
28. Moore, J.M., Shipman, F.M.: A comparison of questionnaire-based and GUI-based requirements gathering. In: Proceedings ASE 2000. Fifteenth IEEE International Conference on Automated Software Engineering, pp. 35–43 (2000). https://doi.org/10.1109/ASE.2000.873648
29. Pandey, D., Suman, U., Ramani, A.K.: An effective requirement engineering process model for software development and requirements management. In: 2010 International Conference on Advances in Recent Technologies in Communication and Computing, pp. 287–291. IEEE, Kottayam, India (2010). https://doi.org/10.1109/ARTCom.2010.24
30. Tabalba, R., et al.: Articulate+ : an always-listening natural language interface for creating data visualizations. In: Proceedings of the 4th Conference on Conversational User Interfaces,

pp. 1–6. Association for Computing Machinery, New York, NY, USA (2022). https://doi.org/
10.1145/3543829.3544534

31. Pyatkin, V., et al.: ClarifyDelphi: Reinforced Clarification Questions with Defeasibility
Rewards for Social and Moral Situations (2023). http://arxiv.org/abs/2212.10409. https://
doi.org/10.48550/arXiv.2212.10409

32. Zhang, S., Pan, L., Zhao, J., Wang, W.Y.: Mitigating Language Model Hallucination with
Interactive Question-Knowledge Alignment (2023). http://arxiv.org/abs/2305.13669, https://
doi.org/10.48550/arXiv.2305.13669

33. Mu, F., et al.: ClarifyGPT: Empowering LLM-based Code Generation with Intention
Clarification (2023). http://arxiv.org/abs/2310.10996

34. Ge, Y., Xiao, Z., Diesner, J., Ji, H., Karahalios, K., Sundaram, H.: What should I Ask: A
Knowledge-driven Approach for Follow-up Questions Generation in Conversational Surveys
(2023). http://arxiv.org/abs/2205.10977. https://doi.org/10.48550/arXiv.2205.10977

35. Papineni, K., Roukos, S., Ward, T., Zhu, W.-J.: Bleu: a method for automatic evaluation of
machine translation. In: Proceedings of the 40th Annual Meeting of the Association for Computational Linguistics, pp. 311–318. Association for Computational Linguistics, Philadelphia,
Pennsylvania, USA (2002). https://doi.org/10.3115/1073083.1073135

36. Zhang, T., Kishore, V., Wu, F., Weinberger, K.Q., Artzi, Y.: BERTScore: evaluating text
generation with BERT. Presented at the International Conference on Learning Representations
September 25 (2019)

37. Rogers, A., Gardner, M., Augenstein, I.: QA dataset explosion: A taxonomy of NLP resources
for question answering and reading comprehension. ACM Comput. Surv. **55**, 1–45 (2023).
https://doi.org/10.1145/3560260

38. Lin, S., Hilton, J., Evans, O.: TruthfulQA: Measuring How Models Mimic Human Falsehoods
(2022). http://arxiv.org/abs/2109.07958. https://doi.org/10.48550/arXiv.2109.07958

39. Wang, B., Zhu, Y., Chen, L., Liu, J., Sun, L., Childs, P.: A study of the evaluation metrics for
generative images containing combinational creativity. AIEDAM. **37**, e11 (2023). https://doi.
org/10.1017/S0890060423000069

40. Yang, L.-C., Lerch, A.: On the evaluation of generative models in music. Neural Comput.
Appl. **32**, 4773–4784 (2020). https://doi.org/10.1007/s00521-018-3849-7

41. Ramesh, A., et al.: Zero-shot text-to-image generation. In: Proceedings of the 38th International Conference on Machine Learning, pp. 8821–8831. PMLR (2021)

42. Webson, A., Loo, A.M., Yu, Q., Pavlick, E.: Are Language Models Worse than Humans at
Following Prompts? It's Complicated (2023). http://arxiv.org/abs/2301.07085 https://doi.org/
10.48550/arXiv.2301.07085

Enhancing Representation Learning of EEG Data with Masked Autoencoders

Yifei Zhou[✉] and Sitong Liu

George Washington University, Washington, DC 20052, USA
{yzhou87,sitong.liu}@gwmail.gwu.edu

Abstract. Self-supervised learning has been a powerful training paradigm to facilitate representation learning. In this study, we design a masked autoencoder (MAE) to guide deep learning models to learn electroencephalography (EEG) signal representation. Our MAE includes an encoder and a decoder. A certain proportion of input EEG signals are randomly masked and sent to our MAE. The goal is to recover these masked signals. After this self-supervised pre-training, the encoder is fine-tuned on downstream tasks. We evaluate our MAE on EEGEyeNet gaze estimation task. We find that the MAE is an effective brain signal learner. It also significantly improves learning efficiency. Compared to the model without MAE pre-training, the pre-trained one achieves equal performance with 1/3 the time of training and outperforms it in half the training time. Our study shows that self-supervised learning is a promising research direction for EEG-based applications as other fields (natural language processing, computer vision, robotics, etc.), and thus we expect foundation models to be successful in EEG domain.

Keywords: EEG · Gaze estimation · Self-supervised pre-training · Masked autoencoders

1 Introduction

Electroencephalogram (EEG) data, with its rich multidimensional structure, offers unique insights into various neurological phenomena [20]. Understanding the complexities of human brain activity through EEG signals has long been a focal point in neuroscience. EEG-based research holds immense potential of decoding cognitive processes, mental states, and various spatial and temporal aspects of brain functioning. The EEGEyeNet dataset [13], specifically designed for diverse neurocognitive studies, presents a valuable repository for exploring and analyzing EEG data in the context of predictive modeling tasks.

Among the numerous EEG-based tasks, gaze position estimation is a significant challenge due to its relevance in spatial cognition. This task is performed based on the *Large Grid Paradigm* where participants are instructed to focus on a succession of dots that appear one after another, with each dot appearing at one of 25 distinct positions on the screen [13]. The task is to

D. D. Schmorrow and C. M. Fidopiastis (Eds.): HCII 2024, LNAI 14695, pp. 88–100, 2024.
https://doi.org/10.1007/978-3-031-61572-6_7

predict the XY-coordinate of the participant's gaze position. Accurate decoding of absolute positions from EEG signals holds implications for neurorehabilitation, brain-computer interfaces, and understanding fundamental aspects of spatial awareness.

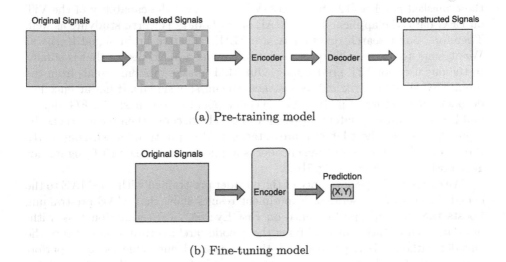

(a) Pre-training model

(b) Fine-tuning model

Fig. 1. Pre-training and fine-tuning model architectures. EEG signals collected from multiple channels are arranged into a matrix. **(a)** We mask random elements from the input EEG signal matrix. Our MAE learns to recover these missing signals. **(b)** Our main purpose is to measure the encoder's performance change after MAE pre-training, so we remove the decoder and fine-tune the encoder to predict gaze positions.

Deep learning methodologies have shown remarkable promise in unraveling intricate patterns within EEG data [1,26]. Recently, the widely-used Vision Transformer (ViT) model [10] has been proven to be able to significantly improve the accuracy of absolute position prediction [29]. The model proposed by this study, EEGViT, provides further evidence that EEG-based tasks could benefit from computer vision models. EEGViT leverages ViT model weights pre-trained on the ImageNet dataset [9] to achieve state-of-the-art performance, demonstrating that pre-training can contribute to the success of the model in addition to the model architecture [29]. Our study further explores the potential of pre-training to boost the model performance without data augmentation or modifying the model architecture.

Self-supervised pre-training is a prevailing practice to facilitate the representation learning of deep learning models. It helps the models learn useful patterns and representation from the data and thus the models achieve better performance on downstream tasks. In natural language processing (NLP), self-supervised pre-training has been employed to guide large language models to learn contextual information from text corpora [5,14,21,24,25]. Inspired by

BERT [14], masked autoencoder (MAE) is applied to computer vision models and shown to be successful and scalable vision learners [2, 10, 12].

As a self-supervised pre-training technique, MAE removes certain ratios of content from inputs and tries to reconstruct them. When it is applied in ViT, a certain ratio of input image patches are masked, and the goal is to recover these masked patches [12]. Since EEGViT has shown the capability of the ViT on EEG data, the applicability of MAE on EEG data is worth studying as well. Therefore, our research question is: are MAEs effective brain signal learners? We attempt to answer this question by employing a MAE design that is similar to the one used for ViT pre-training. Our MAE masks random signals from the input EEG signal matrix and reconstructs the missing signals. It has an encoder-decoder architecture (Fig. 1a). The encoder operates on masked EEG signals and learns meaningful latent representations. The decoder then reconstructs the input signals from these latent representations. After pre-training with our MAE, the decoder is removed and the encoder is applied to unmasked EEG signals for gaze position prediction (Fig. 1b).

We compare the performance of the encoder pre-trained with our MAE to the encoder trained from scratch. Experiment results show that MAE pre-training boosts the encoder's performance on EEGEyeNet gaze estimation task without data augmentation or modifying the encoder architecture. Compared to the encoder without MAE pre-training, the pre-trained one achieves equal performance with 1/3 the time of training and outperforms it in half the training time (Fig. 3). We anticipate that EEG-based applications will benefit more from self-supervised pre-trained deep learning models just as other fields (NLP, computer vision, robotics, etc.), and this even suggests the promising research on foundation models [4, 11, 18, 30, 32] in the EEG domain.

2   Related Work

2.1   Masked Modeling in Language and Vision

Self-supervised pre-training by masked modeling has brought huge progress to natural language processing (NLP). The masking mechanism in BERT [14] is to randomly mask a certain percentage of the input tokens, and train the model to predict the original token that has been masked out. GPT [5, 21, 24, 25] adopts an autoregressive training approach that predicts the next word in a sentence given all the previous words, which means that during training, the model looks at a part of a sentence and learns to predict the word that comes next. Inspired by the practices in NLP, masked encoding has been applied to visual representation learning [2, 6, 10, 12].

2.2   Masked Autoencoder for EEG Data

Various deep learning models such as convolutional neural network (CNN), recurrent neural network (RNN) and Transformer have been applied to EEG data [3,8,16,19,26–29,31]. While supervised learning has been a dominant paradigm of training large deep learning models for a decade, in recent years, self-supervised pre-training by masked modeling has been a great performance booster. A deep learning model pre-trained with masked autoencoders (MAE) often outperforms the same model solely trained with supervised learning. The success of MAE in NLP and computer vision suggests that it is an effective representation learner for both temporal and spatial data. Therefore, it is a natural idea to apply MAE to EEG data.

Previous work has demonstrated the advantage of MAE on EEG-based sleep stage classification [7], seizure sub-type classification [22] and cognitive load classification [23]. The MAEs in these studies reconstruct original features or raw signals from masked *features*. Our study, however, employs a simple approach that reconstructs original EEG signals from masked *signals*. The input EEG signals are directly masked and fed to our MAE without further preprocessing and feature extraction. Experiments have shown that this simple design can still guide our MAE to learn signal representation that is useful for downstream tasks.

2.3   EEG-Based Gaze Estimation

EEG-based gaze estimation aims at combining EEG signals with computational techniques to predict the direction or position of a person's gaze. This approach leverages the fact that certain patterns in brain activity, as captured by EEG, correlate with where a person is looking.

The EEGEyeNet dataset [13] is a comprehensive collection of high-density, 128-channel EEG data synchronized with eye-tracking recordings from 356 healthy adults. This dataset is unique due to its large scale and precise annotation, encompassing over 47 h of recording. The third task in the associated benchmark involves determining the absolute position of the subject's gaze on a screen, described in terms of XY-coordinates. This task is performed using data from the Large Grid paradigm, where participants fixate on a series of dots at different screen positions. It is the most challenging task in the benchmark, aiming to simulate a purely EEG-based eye-tracker. The performance is measured as the euclidean distance in millimeters between the actual and the estimated gaze position. Current performance of deep learning models on this task is presented in Table 4 of [29].

3   Methods

We design a masked autoencoder (MAE) that randomly masks signals from the input EEG signal matrix and recovers these missing signals. As shown in Fig. 1, our MAE has an encoder-decoder architecture. The encoder operates on masked EEG signals and learns meaningful latent representations. The decoder then reconstructs the input signals from these latent representations. As the overall goal is to enhance the encoder's capability to learn useful signal representations, after MAE pre-training, the decoder is removed and the encoder is applied to unmasked EEG signals to perform downstream tasks. By doing so, we are able to measure the encoder's performance change after MAE pre-training.

3.1 Masking Mechanism

The masking is applied based on the matrix representation of EEG signals. Raw EEG signals are collected from multiple channels. The signals from each channel can be stacked row by row to form a matrix that is suitable for being neural network input [29].

Before an EEG signal matrix is sent to our MAE encoder, a certain proportion of its elements are randomly selected to be set to zero. We implement a simple random selection. Suppose the dimension of EEG signal matrices is $m \times n$ and the masking ratio is r. First we generate a random permutation of integers from 0 to $m \times n - 1$. Then we select the first $m \times n \times r$ integers from this permutation as the indices to be masked. Next these selected indices are converted into 2D indices corresponding to the row and column dimensions of the EEG signal matrix. For index i in the selected indices, its corresponding row index is $\lfloor \frac{i}{n} \rfloor$ and column index is $i \bmod n$. The corresponding elements in the EEG signal matrix will be set to 0.

During training, a mask is generated for each batch and epoch, which means that none of the previously used masks is directly reapplied to the current batch. This will avoid overfitting by ensuring that our MAE can learn as rich local and global patterns as possible. The MAE cannot solve the reconstruction task by simply memorizing the signal values.

3.2 Encoder Design

Our MAE encoder is EEGViT [29], a hybrid Vision Transformer (ViT) architecture designed for EEG data. It combines a two-step convolution block [17] with the ViT layers. When the ViT layers are initialized with the model weights pre-trained on ImageNet dataset [9], EEGViT achieves state-of-the-art performance (Table 4 of [29]).

The visual knowledge that ViT learns from large image datasets is beneficial to EEG data as well. However, EEGViT utilizes pre-trained ViT model weights directly for supervised training. We believe that the ViT model can first learn some general EEG signal knowledge before it is applied to a specific task at hand, by which the model can experience a milder transfer from vision domain to EEG. We bridge this gap by using pre-trained ViT weights for MAE pre-training. The ViT layers in our encoder are initialized with the model weights pre-trained on ImageNet dataset. After the encoder learns general EEG signal representation, it will be fine-tuned on downstream tasks.

3.3 Decoder Design

Following the MAE for ViT [12], our MAE decoder is a series of Transformer blocks. The reason for this choice resembles the one for vision MAE. Our reconstruction task is at *signal* level. It requires a low-level understanding of EEG raw signals. A low-level reconstruction task like pixels, or in our case, signals, needs a non-trivial decoder architecture. As described in [12], the decoder design determines the semantic level of learned information. Different decoder structures drive the encoder to extract different levels of signal patterns.

As introduced before, in the fine-tuning stage, only the encoder is kept for supervised training. The MAE decoder assists the encoder with efficient signal encoding, but since our main purpose is to compare the encoder's performance before and after MAE pre-training, the decoder is not used for downstream tasks.

3.4   Reconstruction Task

Our MAE takes in masked EEG raw signals and outputs reconstructed signals. Note that we aim to recover the missing signals, but for implementation simplicity the unmasked signals are also "reconstructed". That is, our MAE output has the same dimension as the input. Since we only care about the recovery of missing signals, the reconstruction loss is computed on the masked elements of an EEG signal matrix. This practice is similar to previous work [12,14].

Following MAEEG [7], we adopt a similarity loss function[1]:

$$\mathcal{L} = 1 - \frac{\hat{\mathbf{x}} \cdot \mathbf{x}}{\|\hat{\mathbf{x}}\|\|\mathbf{x}\|} \tag{1}$$

where $\mathbf{x}$ is the original signals and $\hat{\mathbf{x}}$ is the reconstructed signals. $\frac{\hat{\mathbf{x}} \cdot \mathbf{x}}{\|\hat{\mathbf{x}}\|\|\mathbf{x}\|}$ computes cosine similarity. Subtracting it from 1 ensures that our MAE learns to minimize the reconstruction loss. Cosine similarity encourages our MAE to capture the intrinsic characteristics of EEG signals. We apply a reversed mask to both the MAE output and full input, so that previously masked positions are now retained and unmasked positions are now set to zero. Then we flatten these two matrices to compute the loss.

4   Experiment Setting

We use the EEGEyeNet dataset [13] for MAE pre-training. Then we fine-tune all layers of the MAE encoder on the same dataset.

4.1   EEG Data

The EEG data for training our model are from "Large Grid Paradigm" in EEGEyeNet dataset which involves participants fixating on 25 different positions on a screen [13]. EEGEyeNet provides both minimally and maximally pre-processed data. We focus on the minimally pre-processed data. This data includes trials from 27 participants and a total of 21464 samples. Following EEGViT [29], we split 70% of these samples into the training set, 15% into the validation set, and 15% into the test set.

---

[1] We also experiment with mean squared error (MSE) loss function, the performance increase brought by it is not obvious.

4.2 Training

We train our models on Google Colaboratory with 1 NVIDIA A100 GPU. Table 1 shows our training settings. For pre-training, we employ a larger learning rate decay step size and train for more epochs than during fine-tuning. This is because the reconstruction task is more complicated than the downstream gaze estimation task. For fine-tuning, our settings are consistent with EEGViT. The reason is that we use EEGViT model as our MAE encoder, and the goal is to evaluate the encoder's performance increase solely brought by MAE pre-training. This consistent approach ensures that we are making a fair comparison.

Table 1. Pre-training and fine-tuning settings.

	Pre-training	Fine-tuning
optimizer	Adam [15]	Adam
base learning rate (lr)	1e–4	1e–4
batch size	64	64
lr decay step size	10	6
lr decay factor	0.1	0.1
epochs	30	15

5 Results

We study the effects of masking ratio and decoder architecture, and report the root mean squared error (RMSE) on the test set. The RMSE is in millimeters (mm). See Sect. 2.3 for details of the gaze estimation task.

Each pre-training epoch takes approximately 2.4 to 2.6 min. A higher masking ratio takes slightly more time. Each fine-tuning epoch takes approximately 2 min.

5.1 Encoder's Performance

For MAE pre-training, we experiment with different masking ratios (10%–90%). The MAE decoder has 1 or 2 Transformer blocks. In Sect. 3.3, we hypothesize that our reconstruction task needs a non-trivial decoder architecture. Here, we also use a simple multilayer perceptron (MLP) decoder as a baseline. Table 2 shows the mean and standard deviation over 5 fine-tuning runs. EEGViT's result is from our experiment[2]. For each decoder architecture, the best result among all the masking ratios is presented in the table. See Fig. 2 for the full results.

---

[2] Here "EEGViT" is equivalent to "EEGViT Pre-trained" in Table 4 of [29]. This applies to the following mentions as well.

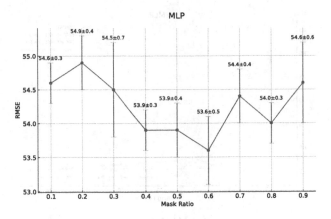

(a) MLP decoder

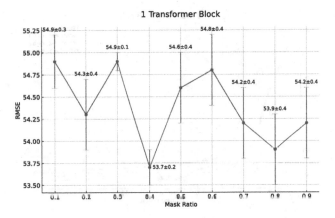

(b) 1 Transformer block decoder

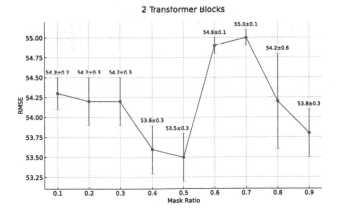

(c) 2 Transformer blocks decoder

Fig. 2. Fine-tuning results under different settings.

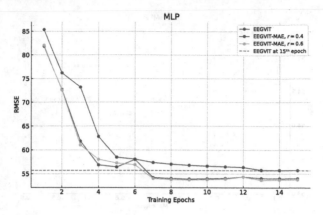

(a) MLP decoder

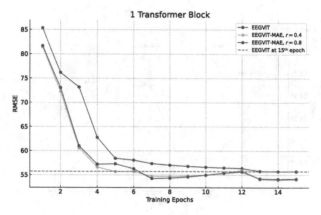

(b) 1 Transformer block decoder

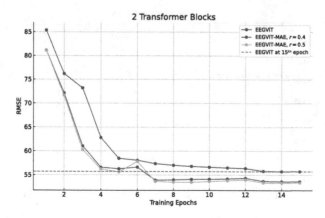

(c) 2 Transformer blocks decoder

Fig. 3. Fine-tuning loss curves. For each decoder setting, top two results among all the masking ratios (r) are presented.

We find that MAE pre-training reduces the encoder's prediction error without extra hyperparameter tuning. MAE decoder with 2 Transformer blocks achieves the lowest average RMSE. However, the best results of these three decoder architectures are fairly close. From Fig. 2, we see that the encoder's variance on the gaze estimation task tends to be lower when pre-trained along with more complex decoders, indicating that non-trivial decoder architectures help stabilize the fine-tuning. We also notice that masking 40% of the input signal gives relatively good results in all these three decoder settings. We infer that a masking ratio between 40% and 50% is the optimal choice for our MAE.

Table 2. Results from 5 fine-tuning runs.

Model	RMSE (mm)
EEGViT	55.9 ± 0.7
EEGViT-MAE, MLP	53.6 ± 0.5
EEGViT-MAE, 1 Transformer Block	53.7 ± 0.2
EEGViT-MAE, 2 Transformer Blocks	$\mathbf{53.5 \pm 0.3}$

5.2 Encoder's Efficiency

As discussed in Sect. 4.2, our supervised fine-tuning setting is consistent with EEGViT supervised training. We have shown that EEGViT pre-trained with our MAE achieves better results within the same training epochs. This suggests that it adapts faster to the gaze estimation task after MAE pre-training. Figure 3 shows the fine-tuning loss curves. For each decoder setting, top two results among all the masking ratios are presented.

We find that after MAE pre-training, EEGViT achieves better performance with half the training epochs. For masking ratio $r = 0.4$ in the 1 Transformer block setting and $r = 0.5$ in the 2 Transformer blocks setting, EEGViT achieves equal performance with 1/3 of training epochs. This demonstrates a significant improvement in learning efficiency. We also observe mild overfitting in EEGViT-MAE models, but it is mitigated in the 2 Transformer blocks setting.

6 Discussion and Conclusion

Visual knowledge that is learned from large image datasets like ImageNet can be transferred to the EEG domain, which indicates that these two different signals share some common underlying characteristics. Masked autoencoders (MAEs) are capable of learning useful visual representations. We show that MAEs are effective brain signal learners as well. MAE pre-training is beneficial to downstream tasks in terms of prediction precision and learning efficiency. In this work, we use the EEGViT model as the MAE encoder. However, we expect MAE pre-training to be a generalizable approach to learn EEG signal representations. The encoder model's choice is flexible. In our future work, we plan to explore alternative encoder models beyond EEGViT to evaluate the generalizability of MAE pre-training. Additionally, we plan to extend the experiments to cover more EEG datasets.

Self-supervised pre-training has been widely explored in NLP and computer vision. Similarly, EEG signal research could take this path by building large and diverse EEG datasets to pre-train deep learning models. These pre-trained models can serve as foundation models [4,11,18,30,32] for EEG-based applications. They can be fine-tuned on downstream tasks and are expected to obtain superior performance and efficiency compared to models trained solely with supervised learning.

Disclosure of Interests. The authors have no competing interests to declare that are relevant to the content of this article.

References

1. Altaheri, H., et al.: Deep learning techniques for classification of electroencephalogram (eeg) motor imagery (mi) signals: a review. Neural Comput. Appl. **35**(20), 14681–14722 (2023)
2. Bao, H., Dong, L., Piao, S., Wei, F.: Beit: bert pre-training of image transformers. arXiv preprint arXiv:2106.08254 (2021)
3. Bashivan, P., Rish, I., Yeasin, M., Codella, N.: Learning representations from EEG with deep recurrent-convolutional neural networks. arXiv preprint arXiv:1511.06448 (2015)
4. Bommasani, R., et al.: On the opportunities and risks of foundation models. arXiv preprint arXiv:2108.07258 (2021)
5. Brown, T., et al.: Language models are few-shot learners. Adv. Neural. Inf. Process. Syst. **33**, 1877–1901 (2020)
6. Chen, M., et al.: Generative pretraining from pixels. In: International Conference on Machine Learning. pp. 1691–1703. PMLR (2020)
7. Chien, H.Y.S., Goh, H., Sandino, C.M., Cheng, J.Y.: Maeeg: masked auto-encoder for EEG representation learning. arXiv preprint arXiv:2211.02625 (2022)
8. Craik, A., He, Y., Contreras-Vidal, J.L.: Deep learning for electroencephalogram (EEG) classification tasks: a review. J. Neural Eng. **16**(3), 031001 (2019)
9. Deng, J., Dong, W., Socher, R., Li, L.J., Li, K., Fei-Fei, L.: Imagenet: a large-scale hierarchical image database. In: 2009 IEEE Conference on Computer Vision and Pattern Recognition, pp. 248–255. IEEE (2009)
10. Dosovitskiy, A., et al.: An image is worth 16×16 words: transformers for image recognition at scale. arXiv preprint arXiv:2010.11929 (2020)
11. Firoozi, R., et al.: Foundation models in robotics: applications, challenges, and the future. arXiv preprint arXiv:2312.07843 (2023)
12. He, K., Chen, X., Xie, S., Li, Y., Dollár, P., Girshick, R.: Masked autoencoders are scalable vision learners. In: Proceedings of the IEEE/CVF Conference on Computer Vision and Pattern Recognition, pp. 16000–16009 (2022)

13. Kastrati, A., et al.: EEGEyenet: a simultaneous electroencephalography and eye-tracking dataset and benchmark for eye movement prediction. In: Thirty-fifth Conference on Neural Information Processing Systems Datasets and Benchmarks Track (Round 1) (2021)
14. Kenton, J.D.M.W.C., Toutanova, L.K.: Bert: pre-training of deep bidirectional transformers for language understanding. In: Proceedings of naacl-HLT, vol. 1, p. 2 (2019)
15. Kingma, D.P., Ba, J.: Adam: a method for stochastic optimization. arXiv preprint arXiv:1412.6980 (2014)
16. Kostas, D., Aroca-Ouellette, S., Rudzicz, F.: Bendr: using transformers and a contrastive self-supervised learning task to learn from massive amounts of eeg data. Front. Hum. Neurosci. **15**, 653659 (2021)
17. Lawhern, V.J., Solon, A.J., Waytowich, N.R., Gordon, S.M., Hung, C.P., Lance, B.J.: Eegnet: a compact convolutional neural network for EEG-based brain-computer interfaces. J. Neural Eng. **15**(5), 056013 (2018)
18. Li, C., et al.: Multimodal foundation models: from specialists to general-purpose assistants, vol. 1, no. 2, p. 2 (2023). arXiv preprint arXiv:2309.10020
19. Mao, W., Fathurrahman, H., Lee, Y., Chang, T.: EEG dataset classification using CNN method. In: Journal of Physics: Conference Series, vol. 1456, p. 012017. IOP Publishing (2020)
20. Murungi, N.K., Pham, M.V., Dai, X.C., Qu, X.: Empowering computer science students in electroencephalography (EEG) analysis: a review of machine learning algorithms for EEG datasets (2023)
21. OpenAI, R.: Gpt-4 technical report. arXiv, pp. 2303–08774 (2023)
22. Peng, R., et al.: Wavelet2vec: a filter bank masked autoencoder for EEG-based seizure subtype classification. In: ICASSP 2023-2023 IEEE International Conference on Acoustics, Speech and Signal Processing (ICASSP), pp. 1–5. IEEE (2023)
23. Pulver, D., Angkan, P., Hungler, P., Etemad, A.: EEG-based cognitive load classification using feature masked autoencoding and emotion transfer learning. In: Proceedings of the 25th International Conference on Multimodal Interaction, pp. 190–197 (2023)
24. Radford, A., Narasimhan, K., Salimans, T., Sutskever, I., et al.: Improving language understanding by generative pre-training (2018)
25. Radford, A., Wu, J., Child, R., Luan, D., Amodei, D., Sutskever, I., et al.: Language models are unsupervised multitask learners. OpenAI blog **1**(8), 9 (2019)
26. Roy, Y., Banville, H., Albuquerque, I., Gramfort, A., Falk, T.H., Faubert, J.: Deep learning-based electroencephalography analysis: a systematic review. J. Neural Eng. **16**(5), 051001 (2019)
27. Weng, N., Płomecka, M.B., Kaufmann, M., Kastrati, A., Wattenhofer, R., Langer, N.: An interpretable attention-based method for gaze estimation using electroencephalography (2023)
28. Xiao, G., Shi, M., Ye, M., Xu, B., Chen, Z., Ren, Q.: 4d attention-based neural network for EEG emotion recognition. Cogn. Neurodyn. 1–14 (2022)
29. Yang, R., Modesitt, E.: Vit2eeg: leveraging hybrid pretrained vision transformers for eeg data. arXiv preprint arXiv:2308.00454 (2023)
30. Yang, S., Nachum, O., Du, Y., Wei, J., Abbeel, P., Schuurmans, D.: Foundation models for decision making: problems, methods, and opportunities. arXiv preprint arXiv:2303.04129 (2023)

31. Yi, L., Qu, X.: Attention-based CNN capturing EEG recording's average voltage and local change. In: Degen, H., Ntoa, S. (eds.) HCII 2022. LNCS, vol. 13336, pp. 448–459. Springer, Heidelberg (2022). https://doi.org/10.1007/978-3-031-05643-7_29

32. Zhou, C., et al.: A comprehensive survey on pretrained foundation models: a history from bert to chatGPT. arXiv preprint arXiv:2302.09419 (2023)

Applications of Augmented Cognition
in Various Contexts

Small Languages and Big Models: Using ML to Generate Norwegian Language Social Media Content for Training Purposes

Ole Joachim Arnesen Aasen[1]([✉]), Ricardo G. Lugo[2,3],
and Benjamin J. Knox[1,3,4]

[1] Department of Information Security and Communication Technology,
Norwegian University of Science and Technology, Gjøvik, Norway
`ole.joachim@hotmail.com`
[2] Center for Digital Forensics and Cyber Security, TalTech, Tallinn, Estonia
[3] Faculty of Health, Welfare and Organisation, Østfold University College,
Halden, Norway
[4] Norwegian Armed Forces Cyber Defence, Jørstadmoen, Norway

Abstract. The advancement of language models has showcased their tremendous potential for both good purposes, and harmful misuse. However, the majority of research have been concentrated on high-resource languages, leaving much to be desired in low-resource languages. This article focuses on exploring the use of language models in Norwegian, a low-resource language. Addressing the threats these models pose in the context of influence operations in social media.

The methodology uses a mixed-methods approach, combining quantitative analysis and qualitative investigations. The quantitative analysis entails evaluating the performance of language models across various contexts, assessing their ability to generate perceived authentic content, and analyzing user responses to such generated content. The qualitative investigations involve conducting interviews and surveys to gather insights from participants, aiming to understand their experiences, perceptions, and concerns regarding the use of language models.

By investigating the use of language models in a low-resource language, this thesis aims to contribute to the advancement of natural language processing research in an underrepresented linguistic context. As well as exploring the use of these language models for training purposes in isolated social networks.

Keywords: Machine Learning · Misinformation · Social Media

1 Introduction

This research explores the implications of language models, particularly in the Norwegian context, leveraging a mixed-methods approach to address the rising concerns of misinformation and influence operations. Propelled by the transformative capabilities of models like GPT-3, the study delves into the challenges of discerning between human and machine-generated content. The work was a collaborative effort involving the Norwegian Defense Research Establishment (FFI), the Norwegian University of Science and Technology (NTNU), and the Norwegian Armed Forces Cyber Defence (CYFOR). By applying a social media [cyber]-range, built to train Norwegian total-defense entities in for example, identifying and countering malign influence operations, the range allowed for researchers to emphasize the role and effect of machine learning models' in generating Norwegian-language content.

The project focused on disinformation through the use of targeted short texts akin to social media posts that can be generated and applied by language models to potentially sway opinions or damage reputations. As GPT-3 blurs the lines between human and machine-generated content, the study poses crucial questions about the accessibility and use of such powerful models, especially in educational settings.

In the social media context, language models present a potential tool for malicious manipulation, exploiting the inadequacies of traditional identification methods. This study investigates the model's ability to generate credible disinformation in Norwegian, a language with limited prior research. The primary focus is on determining if a machine learning model can effectively simulate human-authored Norwegian text, suggesting a vulnerability in Norway where individuals may struggle to discern targeted and general disinformation on social media.

The research scrutinizes the authenticity of machine-generated texts and explores factors influencing perceived authenticity. Additionally, it assesses the language model's applicability in a cyber-social media context for training purposes, evaluating its ability for independent operation and specific tasks.

Anticipated outcomes include insights into the model's effectiveness in the Norwegian language, contributing to the training of individuals and organizations in Norwegian total defense for detecting online influence. This research uniquely examines the active role of the model in producing disinformation, a form intended to influence populations, contrasting with existing studies primarily focused on detection. Ultimately, the study contributes to the development of the cyber-social media range for enhanced education and training purposes.

2   Theory

2.1   Influence Operations

Although the term information warfare or information operations are relatively new, the actions of using information as a weapon in warfare is not novel. Traditionally it encompassed misinforming, propaganda, and deception. In later years, as radio transmission entered the battlespace, methods such as electronic warfare become prevalent and fell under the term information warfare [11].

As social media connected the world in a greater way than ever before, it brought with it changes in how people interact with brands, states, and politicians [22]. One example is 'echo chambers' that arise as existing views circulate without encountering opposing views. The result is a confirmation bias as people are more inclined to believing and spreading disinformation when information comes from people who share the view [12,20–22]. As presented information gains 'likes' or similar approving signs, this further entrenches ideas, beliefs, and enhances legitimacy. Countering this effect requires awareness, and to a greater extent, cognitive skills training. In a study by Helkala and Rønnfeldt that described how physiological and psychological resilience increases a soldier's cognitive performance [6], one of the key features they present as important for a person's resilience towards influence operations is awareness of the constant effect information around us can have. The awareness of self as much as the information system you are part of, is key to building resilience.

Examining the operations of the Internet Research Agency (IRA), commonly known as the Russian troll factory, reveals a noteworthy alignment of certain tactics with findings from existing research on the heightened susceptibility of individuals to disinformation. As articulated by Linvill and Warren, the tweets disseminated and the corresponding accounts exhibit discernible categorizations, aligning with distinct political affiliations and other thematic classifications [10]. Given the substantial resource investment required to rigorously verify the accuracy of the text generated by these models, an alternative methodology is proposed. This involves adopting an approach akin to that employed by the IRA, wherein text production spans topics of varying sentiments to assess the capacity of these models to navigate diverse ideological domains, mirroring the versatile engagement observed in the IRA's activities [10].

2.2 AI and Influence Operations

In their inquiry into the transformative impact of language models on information dissemination strategies, Kreps, McCain, and Brundage [8] conducted a comprehensive examination of pivotal determinants. The efficacy of individuals in discerning machine-generated text from human-generated text, the potential influence of partisanship on perceived credibility, and the consequential alterations in individuals' policy perspectives upon exposure to such text constituted focal points of their investigation. The outcomes of their research indicate that individuals exhibit an inherent incapacity to differentiate between machine-generated and human-generated text. Furthermore, the study underscores the significant role of an individual's partisanship in shaping their perception of credibility. However, in terms of the impact of exposure on individuals' policy views, the findings suggest a marginal effect with limited substantive change

In investigating the capacity of artificial intelligence (AI) to produce persuasive propaganda, Goldstein et al. ascertained that large language models, exemplified by GPT-3, exhibit the capability to generate propaganda of comparable effectiveness to that produced by adversarial foreign entities [5]. Employing news articles involved in covert propaganda campaigns as the foundation for their study, the researchers leveraged GPT-3 to generate articles addressing the same thematic content. The research discerned that both the original propaganda and that generated by GPT-3 proved highly efficacious in influencing the perspectives of respondents. The implications of their findings suggest that the utilization of language models can render propaganda campaigns more economically feasible and scalable, requiring minimal human intervention.

2.3   Fake News in Social Media

In the realm of news consumption, social media has emerged as a predominant source [14]. Platforms like Twitter (now X), for instance, attract a substantial portion of American users, with over fifty percent relying on the platform for news dissemination. This stands in stark contrast to the pre-social media era, where news primarily emanated from newspapers or traditional news channels. The contemporary landscape signifies a departure from the conventional tethering of news distribution to media establishments. The transformative impact of the Internet on these dynamics has not only facilitated global interconnectedness but has also augmented accessibility [22]. However, this enhanced accessibility has concurrently heightened the propensity for the dissemination of misinformation.

In their investigation, Talwar et al. discerned that users' intrinsic urgency to expeditiously disseminate information for the purpose of raising awareness had a favorable correlation with the proliferation of misinformation, or fake news [21]. Supplementary studies in the field substantiate that individuals on social media platforms are inclined to endorse and propagate false information when their trust in the content originator is pronounced, particularly when the source aligns with their personal affiliations [12,20]. These psychological phenomena, coupled with cognitive biases such as the bandwagon effect and confirmation bias, are delineated by researchers at the Norwegian Defence Research Establishment (FFI) as social attributes susceptible to exploitation in influence operations [18].

Amidst the concurrent backdrop of the global pandemic and the United States elections, heightened attention has been directed toward the efficacy of social media platforms in mitigating the dissemination of misinformation. Researchers have systematically assessed the impact of moderation mechanisms, including warning labels and the removal of social endorsement cues (e.g., likes, retweets), on the propagation of content [7,16,17]. The outcomes of these evaluations, focusing on both soft moderation, represented by warning labels, and hard moderation, exemplified by the blocking of content, have yielded nuanced results. An intriguing observation emerged during the analysis of tweets authored by former President Trump between November 2020 and January 2021, where the enforced blocking on Twitter corresponded with an augmented dissemination on alternative social media platforms [16]. Additionally, the placement of warning labels on tweets was associated with an increased spread. However, the data remains inconclusive regarding whether Twitter's intervention causally influenced the content's spread or if the marked or blocked content would have proliferated even in the absence of such intervention [16]. Noteworthy considerations also arise from research indicating potential backfiring effects of warning labels, wherein recipients may exhibit an increased inclination to adhere to their initial beliefs [17]. An online experiment conducted in Germany provides insights into the perceptual impact of warning labels on the credibility of fake news pertaining to climate change [7]. This investigation revealed analogous patterns of motivated reasoning, akin to confirmation bias, with left-leaning individuals perceiving the falsified information as more credible and displaying a higher proclivity for content amplification [7]. Furthermore, the study identified correlations between lower educational attainment, less analytical thinking styles, and an elevated likelihood of content amplification.

An additional strategy employed to counteract the proliferation of misinformation involves the application of machine learning models for content classification on social media platforms [1]. Given the voluminous content generated on these platforms, reliance on automated tools for detection is inevitable, albeit accompanied by inherent drawbacks. Notably, research focusing on tweets labeled in the context of the Covid-19 pandemic revealed instances of mislabeling, engendering skepticism regarding the efficacy of Twitter's soft moderation approach [17]. This consideration assumes significance in the development of countermeasures against misinformation on social media platforms.

The current state of the art in classification models exhibits considerable variability, reflecting the disparate datasets employed across studies [1,4,15]. Notably, a study evaluating detection models for low-resource languages, exemplified by Amharic, reported a remarkable 99% accuracy with high precision. However, this result was contingent upon evaluation solely on the dataset used for training, owing to the scarcity of diverse datasets for the language in question [4]. This trend is observed across other low-resource languages, underscoring the dearth of dedicated resources in this domain.

In the realm of fact-checking and fake news detection, models have achieved commendable accuracies surpassing 96% [1]. However, considerations arise regarding factors such as article structure, which can exert a substantial impact on accuracy [15].

Recognizing the inherent limitations of these models, coupled with the variable effects of the labels they apply, necessitates a broader examination of machine learning's role in the social media context. FFI underscores the critical imperative of cultivating a resilient populace in the face of influence operations and misinformation on social media [18]. Drawing from the Finnish model, which emphasizes training and educating the population on identifying fake news, valuable insights emerge. The deployment of language models, as explored in this research, contributes to a nuanced understanding of how social media platforms must adapt to the evolving threat landscape of influence operations augmented with language models. Furthermore, these models serve as effective tools for training the populace, bolstering their resilience in the context of influence operations and disinformation.

2.4   Intersection of Fake News and Language Models

This research article investigates the dual applications of language models, assessing their potential for malicious use and training purposes. To contextualize the research, a review of existing studies exploring language models' utilization in generating fake news or social media content was essential. OpenAI's GPT-3, in particular, was examined to gauge its proficiency in crafting news articles deemed authentic by humans. The results revealed that the largest model achieved a recognition accuracy of only 52%, marginally surpassing chance [2]. Subsequently, OpenAI and other researchers have intensified their scrutiny of the societal threats posed by language models when wielded for nefarious purposes.

2.5 Different Strategies

In "Truth, Lies, and Automation," Buchanan et al. assess GPT-3's efficacy in various influence operation strategies on social media [3]. The study delves into multiple facets of disinformation creation, including the model's performance in reiterating existing narratives, generating new ones, and executing more targeted influence operations. The findings underscore the model's potential for malicious use. Given the scale of our model and the experimental scope, this project will predominantly focus on the domain of narrative reiteration.

3 Methodology

The methodology for this research was split into two main parts. The first part involved achieving a proper comparison between an English model and a Norwegian model. The second part was an experiment to evaluate the Norwegian model in a more naturalistic environment.

Prior to this, a pilot study was conducted. The pilot study involved testing two language models on various topics before fine-tuning them on political datasets. An iterative within-subject design was employed, ensuring each participant evaluated every text, preventing bias. Evaluators, presented with texts from humans and models, identified the model-generated ones. Initial findings from this work laid the foundation for subsequent adjustments to enhance internal validity.

To refine models and tests, an extended literature review was conducted to understand how misinformation spreads. The goal was to adapt the model to mimic propaganda and disinformation on social media. The review delved into language models in low-resource languages, influence operations on social media, and the impact of language models on such operations.

The initial work provided insights into the impact of different datasets and domains on perceived authenticity. However, limitations in data validity prompted a 2×2 factorial within-subject design. This design aimed to understand how language and domain specificity influence the perceived human-likeness of generated text. The test matrix considered language (English or Norwegian) and domain (General or Domain-specific) variables.

An embedded research design was implemented to gain a deeper understanding of how language models can fit into a purpose built cyber-social media training environment, or 'range'. This design aimed to support and build greater understanding relating to language models that can be used for the purpose of training and preparing people to be more aware of the challenges they face when attempting to differentiate between machine and human made content. The experiment involved 3rd-year bachelor students from the Norwegian Defence Cyber Academy, who were presented with model-generated tweets through the cyber-social media range. Supporting data, including verbal literacy assessments and self-assessment manikin evaluations, were collected to explore factors affecting participant performance.

To complement quantitative data, semi-structured group interviews were conducted with participants. The interviews aimed to capture participants' perspectives on the experiment, identifying strengths, weaknesses, and the alignment of theory with their experiences. This qualitative data supported the interpretation of quantitative results.

3.1   Language Model Preparation

Prior to this research two language models were fine tuned and evaluated based on an iterative testing process. The models were based on the current largest models available for the Norwegian language. That model was a fine tuned version of the GPT-J6B [9,13,23]. These models were fine tuned on datasets intended to increase their capabilities in generating political content for both sides of the political spectrum.

3.2   Cyber-Social Media Simulator: Somulator

To enhance ecological validity in this experiment, it was conducted using the Somulator, a social media simulator developed by FFI, NTNU and the Norwegian Cyber Defence for exercise and research purposes. The Somulator comprises various open-source social media platforms mimicking well-known counterparts like Twitter, Facebook, Instagram, YouTube, and a platform for news article po sting [1]. The content in the news feeds of the different clones is distributed using an exercise control panel, through which content, profiles and the overall information ecology can be staged and managed. Experiment participants can navigate in and interact with the social media clones as they would on "real life" social media, which enhances the authenticity of the experimental environment. For this experiment, the Twitter clone, Mastodon, was applied. The participants were exposed to the material in their news feeds before answering the questionnaires. The Somulator operates as an isolated platform, ensuring restricted access and separation between administrative and participant-accessible sites. The Somulator employs a lightweight setup, utilizing Docker containers to segregate components and minimize computing power usage. The structured container approach facilitates data collection post-experiment by separating the databases into separate containers. The results were extracted using SSH access and SQL statements.

3.3 Supplementary Tests

The experiment incorporated a comprehensive research design involving participants undergoing verbal literacy tests before the main testing phase. This preliminary assessment aimed to gauge participants' proficiency in verbal comprehension and expression. The verbal literacy tests were carefully curated to assess participants' language skills and their ability to understand and interpret written and spoken language.

Following the verbal literacy assessment, participants engaged in the primary testing phase, during which they were presented with various stimuli, such as texts and prompts generated by language models. To better understand the participants' emotional responses and engagement during this phase, the Self-Assessment Manikin (SAM) tool was employed. At specific intervals throughout the testing session, participants used SAM to self-report their emotional states, providing valuable insights into their subjective experiences.

SAM, a widely used tool in psychological research, employs graphical representations of affective states, allowing participants to express their emotional responses on dimensions like valence, arousal, and dominance. Participants self-evaluated their emotional experiences by selecting the corresponding figures on the SAM scale.

By incorporating both verbal literacy tests and SAM assessments, the experiment aimed to explore the interplay between participants' language comprehension skills and their emotional responses during language model-generated content evaluation. This multifaceted approach provided a nuanced understanding of the cognitive and affective aspects influencing participants' interactions with the generated texts. The integration of these assessments enhanced the experiment's robustness and contributed to a comprehensive analysis of participants' experiences and responses.

4 Results

4.1 2 × 2 Factorial Within-Subject Design

The 2×2 factorial within-subject design aimed to give a comparison between an English models and the Norwegian models performance. The text produced was both general and domain-specific. There were 23 participants, **12** female and **11** male. For each group 4 tweets were presented, 2 human-written and 2 machine-generated.

The comparison of male and female participants regarding the identification of machine-generated and human-written texts reveals notable differences. On average, male participants correctly identify 0.7 more machine-generated tweets than females but incorrectly mark human-written texts 1.386 more times. This trend persists for both Norwegian and English texts. Male participants consistently outperform females in correctly identifying machine-generated texts and incorrectly marking human-written ones. Specifically, males score 0.310 higher in identifying Norwegian machine-generated texts and 0.833 higher in incorrectly

Table 1. Comparison of rightly identified and incorrectly identified texts between genders

Category	correct	wrong
Norwegian (male)	1.727	2
Norwegian (female)	1.417	1.167
Norwegian (Average)	1.565	1.565
English (male)	1.273	1.636
English (female)	0.917	1.083
English (Average)	1.087	1.348
Total (male)	3	3.636
Total (female)	2.333	2.25
Total (Average)	2.652	2.913

marking Norwegian human-written texts compared to females. In English texts, males score 0.356 higher in identifying machine-generated texts and 0.553 higher in incorrectly marking human-written texts than females.

Analyzing Table 1 further, females tend to correctly identify machine-generated texts slightly more than they incorrectly mark human-written ones. However, males exhibit the opposite trend, marking human-written texts incorrectly more often than correctly identifying machine-generated ones. Both genders' scores remain relatively low, falling below 50% for both languages and overall. A perfect score would entail correctly identifying four machine-generated texts for each language, totaling eight, indicating that both male and female participants' results fall below this threshold.

Descriptive Statistics										
	correct cat 1	wrong cat 1	wrong cat 2	correct cat 2	correct cat 3	wrong cat 3	correct cat 4	wrong cat 4	How sure are you of your answers?	Surveytime (minutes)
Valid	23	23	23	23	23	23	23	23	23	23
Mean	0.809	0.826	0.739	0.957	0.565	0.783	0.522	0.565	2.130	7.073
Std. Deviation	0.722	0.650	0.619	0.706	0.590	0.518	0.511	0.507	1.058	5.431
95% CI Std. Dev. Upper	0.825	0.778	0.736	0.884	0.717	0.650	0.511	0.511	1.242	7.219
95% CI Std. Dev. Lower	0.518	0.470	0.470	0.507	0.470	0.344	0.449	0.422	0.736	2.702
Minimum	0.000	0.000	0.000	0.000	0.000	0.000	0.000	0.000	1.000	1.283
Maximum	2.000	2.000	2.000	2.000	2.000	2.000	1.000	1.000	4.000	22.233

Fig. 1. Descriptive statistics 2×2 factorial design

When looking at the overall results from the 2×2 factorial testing, one can see that there is a noticeable decrease in the mean score of correct answers, going from generic Norwegian to domain-specific Norwegian. However, the mean score of wrong answers rises slightly.

The English categories, on the other hand, stay relatively equal between the categories, with the main changes being in the mean score of wrong answers. From Fig. 1 it can be seen that there is no one that had 2 correct or 2 wrong answers in the category domain-specific English.

4.2   Embedded Research Design

The participants in the case study consisted of 35 students, 26 male and 9 female. Of these 35 students, only 10 participated in both the testing with the Somulator tweets and the group-interview.

Experiment in Somulator On average, the students identified **51.3%** of the tweets correctly. The lowest accuracy was at **33%**, while the highest was at **67%**, with the CI Mean being [48.279, 54.349]. In Table 2 you can see the variance in the average between the genders, as well as between each set of 25 tweets (Fig. 2).

Table 2. Average correct identified tweets

	male avg	female avg	total avg
first 25 tweets	11.96	13.88	12.45
second 25 tweets	13.26	14	13.45
third 25 tweets	12.23	14.22	12.74
fourth 25 tweets	12.76	12.33	12.65
total	50.23	54.44	51.31

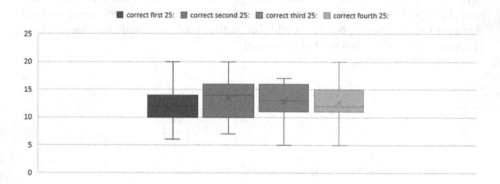

Fig. 2. Box and whisker plot for correct answers per 25 tweets

Only marking tweets as human or only machine would give an accuracy of 50%, meaning the precision of the students' evaluation of tweets needed to be investigated. In Table 3 the students' precision when identifying machine generated tweets is presented. As there was a varying amount of machine-tweets in each round of tweets, there are different baselines for the different groups.

Similar to the score of 50% that could be used as a baseline when looking at the total score, the baseline when looking at precision is as follows:

$$Precision\ Baseline = \frac{Amount\ of\ machine\ tweets\ in\ round}{Total\ amount\ of\ tweets\ in\ round}$$

Each round has 25 tweets, while the amount of machine generated tweets vary. For the first three rounds, there were 11 machine generated tweets in each, giving a baseline of 0.44. Meaning that only answering machine would give a precision of 0.44. For the last round, the amount of machine generated tweets were 16, giving a baseline of 0.64. For the total, a precision of 0.5 is the baseline. When looking over the data, it was identified that some students had answered machine on every tweet in a specific category (Fig. 3).

Table 3. Average precision identifying machine generated tweets

	male avg	female avg	total avg
first 25 tweets	0.4795	0.5189	0.4896
second 25 tweets	0.5810	0.5714	0.5785
third 25 tweets	0.4848	0.5186	0.4935
fourth 25 tweets	0.6492	0.6638	0.6530
total	0.5536	0.5701	0.5579

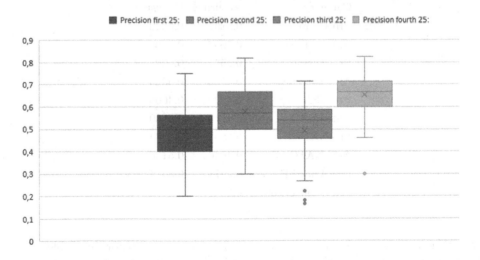

Fig. 3. Box and whisker plot for precision per 25 tweets

Looking at the tables describing the average correct identified tweets, Table 2 and the precision Table 3 there are slightly better results among the female

participants. There is however not a large enough sample size to draw any conclusions to the larger population. The average correctly identified tweets stay
roughly at 50% for each round, with the biggest variance being the second round,
which sits at 53.8%. When observing the Table showing the precision, there is a
bigger variance in the second round, however, with a precision of **0.5785**.

Table 4. Paired Samples T-Test

Measure 1		Measure 2	t	df	p
correct first 25:	−	correct second 25:	−1.311	34	0.199
correct first 25	−	correct fourth 25:	−0.255	34	0.800
correct second 25:	−	correct fourth 25:	1.169	34	0.251

Note. Student's t-test.

A paired samples T-test was also performed to see how well students perform
between the different rounds. This could potentially indicate whether fatigue had
any impact on their ability to perform. The third round was removed from the
comparison, due to its low scores when testing for normal distribution.

As can be seen from Table 4 there are no strong indications of fatigue having
an impact between the rounds.

Table 5. Accuracy and Precision in categories

Category	Accuracy	Precision
Pro-Ukraine	0.5857	0.6342
Anti-Ukraine	0.5057	0.4939
Pro-Russian	0.5571	0.6091
Anti-Russian	0.4886	0.5325
Pro-USA	0.4229	0.4608
Anti-USA	0.4714	0.5130
Pro-NATO	0.5857	0.6484
Anti-NATO	0.4686	0.5106
Pro-Armed Forces	0.4971	0.5474
Anti-Armed Forces	0.5457	0.5973

When analysing the accuracy and precision in each category in Table 5 one
can see that most stay close to 0.5. This is the baseline described earlier. For
most of the categories, the students score better at identifying the pro-category
compared to the counterpart. The exceptions are for the categories on the USA
and Armed Forces. Here, the students score lower on the pro, compared to the
anti-category.

The categories that can be reckoned as slight outliers are; Pro-Ukraine, Pro-NATO and Pro-USA. Closer inspection of these tweets revealed no explanatory factors were found in the data. To see if there were any traits that could have an impact on the outcome, some analysis of the individual tweets was conducted.

The length of each tweet was analyzed, as well as how many correct answers there were for each tweet, to see for correlations. The result was **0.00507**, showing no sign of a correlation between the two variables. When looking at the correlation between the students' evaluation of how well they did in the prior round, with how well they actually did, there was a correlation of **-0.06024**. When looking at the same correlation, but factoring in how sure they were of their own evaluation, the correlation still remained low, at **-0.0516**. Showing no signs of correlation between their own evaluation and performance.

When looking at the students' confidence before a round, and their own results, a slightly higher correlation can be seen, at **0.1376**. This correlation is still not high enough however, to claim any correlation between the two variables.

In their research on how an IT-background impacts participants' meta-cognitive accuracy, confidence and overestimation in ability to identify deep fakes, Sütterlin et al. used what they called the Overconfidence Score (OCS) [19]. The research found that the results from the OCS was a good indicator of participants in need of more follow-up training. As the data collected in this present study was collected via self-assessment mannequins, the same as Sütterlin et al. used on their participants for self evaluation, it was decided to calculate the same variable in this thesis. The purpose was to see if their findings were in any way visible in this research. The variable, OCS, is calculated with the following formula:

$$OCS = \frac{(\frac{Pre-CIA*100}{11}) + 1}{\% \ of \ correct \ ratings \ | \ 1}$$

Pre-CIA (Confidence in Abilities) is the participants' confidence in how well they think they will perform in the following round. That is divided by 11, as that is the degree of freedom the participants have when answering that question. The score calculated from the formula will describe how the participants' self-evaluation aligns with their accomplishment. A score below 1 means the participants underestimate their own performance, while a score above 1 means the participants overestimate their own abilities. The OCS was calculated for each round, as well as plotting the scores for how the students' confidence changed throughout.

Looking at the correlation matrix, Fig. 4, and the heatmap, Fig. 5 we can see a moderate negative correlation between the OCS from the first round and the % of correct answers in the first round. There is also a moderate negative correlation between the total OCS and the total % of correct answers. For the pre-tests, there was a low correlation between the semantics and the total score.

The tweets were analyzed by groupings based on the generic nature of the text. Tweets were split into two groups: generic and concrete. The deciding factor for whether a tweet was put in the generic group or the concrete group was if the tweet could actually be connected to a concrete event or action.

Spearman's Correlations

Variable		Phonetical 1	Phonetical 2	Phonetical 3	Semantics 1	Semantics 2	OCS1	correct first 25:	OCS total	total correct
1. Phonetical 1	Spearman's rho	—								
	p-value	—								
2. Phonetical 2	Spearman's rho	0.615***	—							
	p-value	< .001	—							
3. Phonetical 3	Spearman's rho	0.575***	0.635***	—						
	p-value	< .001	< .001	—						
4. Semantics 1	Spearman's rho	0.171	0.226	0.481**	—					
	p-value	0.326	0.192	0.003	—					
5. Semantics 2	Spearman's rho	0.427*	0.454**	0.635***	0.426*	—				
	p-value	0.011	0.006	< .001	0.011	—				
6. OCS1	Spearman's rho	−0.018	−0.131	−0.067	−0.035	−0.038	—			
	p-value	0.917	0.452	0.704	0.841	0.828	—			
7. correct first 25:	Spearman's rho	0.347*	0.256	0.232	0.170	0.252	−0.636***	—		
	p-value	0.041	0.137	0.179	0.329	0.143	< .001	—		
8. OCS total	Spearman's rho	0.098	−0.149	−0.071	−0.105	-2.129×10^{-4}	0.795***	−0.257	—	
	p-value	0.577	0.392	0.686	0.547	0.999	< .001	0.136	—	
9. total correct	Spearman's rho	0.147	0.332	0.284	0.416*	0.308	−0.327	0.466**	−0.555***	—
	p-value	0.398	0.052	0.099	0.013	0.071	0.055	0.005	< .001	—

$* p < .05, ** p < .01, *** p < .001$

Fig. 4. Correlation matrix

As can be seen in the Fig. 6, there were a slightly bigger group of generic tweets than there were of concrete tweets. There is also a big difference between the confidence interval of the generic tweets and the concrete tweets. When doing a one-tailed independent t-test, testing for the hypothesis that concrete texts are more easily detected than the generic tweets, the following score 7 is the result. Showing a significant difference between the groups.

When looking specifically at machine-tweets, there is a higher p-value at 0.154. Yet still the same trend, indicating that the generic tweets are harder to spot.

4.3 Group Interview

The group interview initially aimed to involve 16 participants. However, due to dropouts, only 10 students participated. Prior to the experiment the participants received lectures in information and influence operations. They were then tasked with creating their own influence operations. Split into 8 teams, each group received different tasks relating to a central topic that could be used in an online influence operation. The groups had freedom in their approach, utilizing tactics such as creating false profiles or generating large numbers of accounts to manipulate perceptions. Their reflections highlighted the importance of education on the topic and the perceived threats posed by influence operations, particularly those augmented by language models.

Regarding influence operations, participants discussed their concealment and techniques like overloading platforms to suppress opposing opinions. They noted shifts in their confidence in detecting machine-generated tweets during the experiment, realizing biases in their judgements. Suggestions to counter these challenges included increased awareness, critical thinking campaigns, and algorithmic detection of manipulation attempts.

Concerning AI-enhanced operations, participants highlighted the accessibility and ease of use of tools like ChatGPT. While some gained insights into

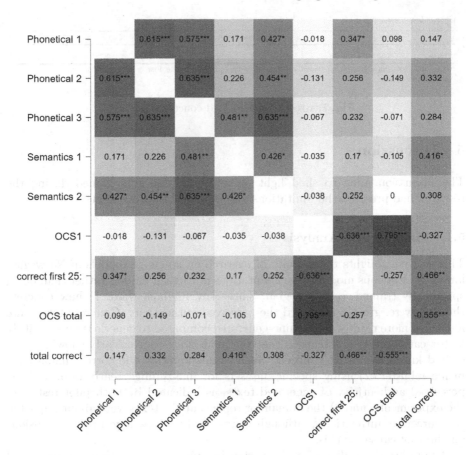

Fig. 5. Heatmap

Group Descriptives

	Group	N	Mean	SD	SE	Coefficient of variation
correct	concrete	42	19.095	4.563	0.704	0.239
	superficial	58	17.121	5.585	0.733	0.326

Fig. 6. Descriptive statistics of generic and concrete tweets

language model responses, they struggled to differentiate between human and AI-generated content. They expressed concerns about AI's ability to scale operations, echoing concerns raised by Goldstein et al. about AI-driven propaganda's reach and impact [5].

Independent Samples T-Test

	t	df	p	Mean Difference	SE Difference	Cohen's d	SE Cohen's d
correct	1.881	98	0.031	1.975	1.050	0.381	0.207

Note. For all tests, the alternative hypothesis specifies that group *concrete* is greater than group *superficial*.
Note. Student's t-test.

Fig. 7. t-test of generic and concrete tweets

5   Discussion

The discussion aims to shed light on additional insights gained during the research and presents the limitations and potential improvements.

5.1   Findings and Analysis

This study highlights the scarcity of research on language models in Norwegian language. Previous models were adaptations of English models rather than being specifically trained for Norwegian. Three key findings were: 1) how concrete the text were, greatly impacted the perceived authenticity. Concrete tweets are identified more readily as machine-generated compared to generic tweets. A likely factor causing this difference is that the models are more clearly showing signs of bad knowledge on the subject. Such as not knowing the correct name for a prime minister. 2) using specific datasets for fine-tuning greatly improved the perceived authenticity of generated texts, as indicated by both pilot tests and the experiments, and 3) the domain or topic that the texts were about impacted the perceived authenticity, although it was hard to draw any direct conclusions on the root cause for this.

Exploring the utility of a Norwegian language model within a cyber-social media range for education and training purposes led the inquiry into the model's potential efficiency in reducing the resource and time costs associated with exercises in the Somulator.

The study showed that such a language model can facilitate influence operations. By exploring various techniques, including narrative reiteration, and focusing on how well the model can replicate existing narratives, the results suggest that the language model performs best when participants select machine-written texts without individually evaluating each one.

The model's ability to operate independently was examined. The study minimized human intervention in output generation to assess the model's performance. The results indicate that while the model can produce generic content effectively, it requires human intervention, especially when dealing with named entities.

The study sought to understand the concrete tasks within the purview of the language model, particularly in content generation for training purposes. The findings indicate that the model exhibits proficiency in generating authentic texts applicable to the Somulator; however, its contextual relevance necessitates human intervention for assurance.

Overall, the language model demonstrates potential for automating tasks in a cyber-social media range. With the potential to make content with both innocuous and potentially influencing content. However, the study identifies limitations such as the model's dependence on human intervention and challenges related to recent dataset availability. Although this problem is solved by newer models, there is currently no system in place to keep a model up to date with knowledge of current events.

The research gives insight into participants' performance, the correlation between confidence and performance, and the impact of machine-generated texts on the perceived authenticity of human-written ones. Moreover, the study highlights biases in evaluating machine-generated content that can result in negative outcomes should the intention behind the machine tweet be malicious or subversive. Also, limitations in the experimental design, such as the timing constraints imposed on participants and the granularity of tweet analysis was a factor that would need to be rectified in future studies. Despite these limitations, the research offers valuable insights into the use of language models in low-resource languages and the lack of available cognitive defences we have to identify and differentiate them from human made tweets. This has implications for how develop training and education tools, such as cyber-social media ranges.

5.2 Further Considerations

Future research should explore the impact of participant biases and knowledge on evaluation accuracy. Testing with different datasets and domains can provide deeper insights into model performance. The study hints at users scrutinizing human-written texts more closely in the presence of language models.

6 Conclusion

This research explores the performance of language models in generating short texts in the Norwegian language, akin to the length of tweets, and their utility for training in an isolated social network. The research focused on factors influencing perceived text authenticity and the Norwegian language model's application in a cyber-social media range built for training total defence actors in Norway. Two pipelines, implementing Norwegian and English transformer-based models, were developed and evaluated through within-subject design, 2×2 factorial within-subject design, and an experiment with pre-test data collection and a subsequent group interview.

The within-subject design identified the Norwegian model as superior, leading to its use in subsequent tests. The 2×2 factorial design suggested the language models' texts could go undetected when participants were not required to give conclusive answers. The case study, conducted in the Somulator, revealed the impact of text domain on perceived authenticity, highlighting challenges in handling domain-specific content. The study also found a correlation between participants' semantic performance and outcomes. Correcting named entities post-generation improved the models' capabilities, indicating potential for various training tasks. However, the study emphasizes the need for human intervention to achieve optimal results.

6.1 Funding

This research was conducted as part of the Advancing Cyber Defense by Improved Communication of Recognized Cyber Threat Situations (ACDICOM; #302941) project. ACDICOM is funded by the Norwegian Research Council.

References

1. Ahmed, A.A.A., Aljabouh, A., Donepudi, P.K., Choi, M.S.: Detecting fake news using machine learning: a systematic literature review (2021)
2. Brown, T.B., et al.: Language models are few-shot learners. CoRR https://arxiv.org/abs/2005.14165(2020)
3. Buchanan, B., Lohn, A., Musser, M., Sedova, K.: Truth, lies, and automation. Technical report. Center for Security and Emerging Technology (2021)
4. Gereme, F., Zhu, W., Ayall, T., Alemu, D.: Combating fake news in "low-resource" languages: amharic fake news detection accompanied by resource crafting. Information (Basel) **12**(1), 20 (2021)
5. Goldstein, J.A., Chao, J., Grossman, S., Stamos, A., Tomz, M.: Can AI write persuasive propaganda? (2023). https://osf.io/preprints/socarxiv/fp87b/
6. Helkala, K.M., Rønnfeldt, C.F.: Understanding and gaining human resilience against negative effects of digitalization. In: Lehto, M., Neittaanmaki, P. (eds.) Cyber Security, vol. 56, pp. 79–91. Springer, Cham (2022). https://doi.org/10.1007/978-3-030-91293-2_4
7. Koch, T.K., Frischlich, L., Lermer, E.: Effects of fact-checking warning labels and social endorsement cues on climate change fake news credibility and engagement on social media. J. Appl. Social Psychol. (2023). https://doi.org/10.1111/jasp.12959
8. Kreps, S., McCain, R.M., Brundage, M.: All the news that's fit to fabricate: Ai-generated text as a tool of media misinformation. J. Exp. Polit. Sci. **9**(1), 104–117 (2022). https://doi.org/10.1017/XPS.2020.37
9. Kummervold, P.E., De la Rosa, J., Wetjen, F., Brygfjeld, S.A.: Operationalizing a national digital library: the case for a Norwegian transformer model. In: Proceedings of the 23rd Nordic Conference on Computational Linguistics (NoDaLiDa), pp. 20–29 (2021). https://aclanthology.org/2021.nodalida-main.3/
10. Linvill, D.L., Warren, P.L.: Troll factories: manufacturing specialized disinformation on twitter. Polit. Commun. **37**(4), 447–467 (2020)
11. Mackey, R.R.: Information warfare (2014). https://www.oxfordbibliographies.com/view/document/obo-9780199791279/obo-9780199791279-0024.xml. Accessed 26 Apr 2022
12. Moravec, P.L., Minas, R.K., Dennis, A.R.: Fake news on social media: people believe what they want to believe when it makes no sense at all. MIS Q. **43**(4) (2019)
13. of Norway, N.L.: Nbailab/nb-gpt-j-6b - huggingface. https://huggingface.co/NbAiLab/nb-gpt-j-6B. Accessed 15 Feb 2024
14. Pew Research Center: Social media and news fact sheet. Technical report, Washington, D.C. (2022). https://www.pewresearch.org/journalism/fact-sheet/social-media-and-news-fact-sheet/

15. Riedel, B., Augenstein, I., Spithourakis, G.P., Riedel, S.: A simple but tough-to-beat baseline for the fake news challenge stance detection task (2018)
16. Sanderson, Z., Brown, M.A., Bonneau, R., Nagler, J., Tucker, T.J.: Twitter flagged donald trump's tweets with election misinformation: they continued to spread both on and off the platform (2021). https://doi.org/10.37016/mr-2020-77. https://misinforeview.hks.harvard.edu/article/twitter-flagged-donald-trumps-tweets-with-election-misinformation-they-continued-to-spread-both-on-and-off-the-platform/
17. Sharevski, F., Alsaadi, R., Jachim, P., Pieroni, E.: Misinformation warning labels: twitter's soft moderation effects on covid-19 vaccine belief echoes (2021)
18. Sivertsen, E.G., Hellum, N., A., B., Bjørnstad, L.B.: Hvordan gjøre samfunnet mer robust mot uønsket påvirkning i sosiale medier (2021). https://www.ffi.no/publikasjoner/arkiv/hvordan-gjore-samfunnet-mer-robust-mot-uonsket-pavirkning-i-sosiale-medier
19. Sütterlin, S., et al.: The role of it background for metacognitive accuracy, confidence and overestimation of deep fake recognition skills. Lect. Notes Comput. Sci. **13310**, 103–119 (2022)
20. Talwar, S., Dhir, A., Kaur, P., Zafar, N., Alrasheedy, M.: Why do people share fake news? associations between the dark side of social media use and fake news sharing behavior. J. Retail. Cons. Serv. **51** (2019)
21. Talwar, S., Dhir, A., Singh, D., Virk, G.S., Salo, J.: Sharing of fake news on social media: application of the honeycomb framework and the third-person effect hypothesis. J. Retail. Consum. Serv. **57**, 102197 (2020)
22. Tarman, B., Yigit, M.F.: The impact of social media on globalization, democratization and participative citizenship. J. Soc. Sci. Educ. **12**(1) (2012)
23. Wang, B., Komatsuzaki, A.: GPT-J-6B: A 6 Billion Parameter Autoregressive Language Model (2021). https://github.com/kingoflolz/mesh-transformer-jax

Early Use of Augmented Cognition for Online Learning Games in Hawai'i

Martha E. Crosby$^{(\boxtimes)}$, Marie K. Iding, and Thanh Trúc T. Nguyễn

University of Hawai'i at Mānoa, Honolulu, HI 96822, USA
{crosby,miding,nguyen}@hawaii.edu

Abstract. This paper provides a historical and regional perspective on the adoption of technologies in online learning, focusing on gamification as an aspect of technological innovation and research in Hawai'i. The paper also addresses transitions in technology uses and instructors' opportunities for adopting new technologies for online learning, specifically gaming and its potential contribution to augmented cognition's goal of increasing task performance by directly addressing the motivation of the user to remain engaged in the learning activity. An extended example is provided from research involving language learning in an online instructional collaboration between Hawai'i and Japan. Further, we discuss how gamifying instruction in online learning and technology has transitioned, empowering both instructors and learners to create content with learning driven strongly by them. We show how historically gaming in online learning has help foster the flow of ideas, connection, and relevance for students.

Keywords: augmented cognition · gaming · simulations · online instruction

1 Introduction

This paper examines serious online games used for educational purposes in schools and universities. Given the popularity of online games and applications (apps) among children, adolescents, and young adults, there is enthusiasm for their implementation as instructional tools, especially as much of the world's instruction has moved online in the Covid-19 era. However, is this enthusiasm warranted? What specific gamification features are effectively and easily adopted by instructors in online instruction? What are the challenges to incorporating gamification aspects in instruction? To address these questions, we first examine relevant research that empirically examines aspects of educational games that have been demonstrated to be effective. Then we present, as a case study from a historical perspective, the development of aspects of gamification in online instruction Hawai'i. As the 50th state in the US, Hawai'i's demographics – its cultural milieu - and geographic isolation have created a unique environment for technological innovation including online instruction and gamification in educational contexts.

D. D. Schmorrow and C. M. Fidopiastis (Eds.): HCII 2024, LNAI 14695, pp. 122–141, 2024.
https://doi.org/10.1007/978-3-031-61572-6_9

1.1   Games, Gamification, and Serious Games

For purposes of this paper, we begin by describing a serious game as one with a purpose beyond mere entertainment. As computer science and education professors, in this paper, we focus on serious games that help students learn some content.

However, what is a game? Defining "game," and "gamification" is no simple task and could be the focus of the entire paper. However, as Plass, Homer, and Kinzer [48] described, "What exactly is meant by gamification varies widely, but one of its defining qualities is that it involves the use of game elements, such as incentive systems to motivate players to engage in a task they otherwise would not find attractive" (p. 259). Further, they quote Salen and Zimmerman's [54] definition of game, as "a system in which players engage in an artificial conflict, defined by rules, that results in a quantifiable outcome" (p. 80).

In considering serious educational games, we note that although most definitions of games such as the ones above focus on incentives, Plass, Homer, and Kinzer [48] also mentioned the importance of "play" in games and the potential social and participatory aspects of games. We would emphasize these aspects in our conceptualizations of instructional games. Furthermore, although reward structures often imply competitive elements, we include simulations, role play, and social/collaborative aspects within immersive environments as elements of gamification in online settings. Such elements do not always involve clear reward structures, competitive aspects, or winner/loser outcomes beyond the intrinsic motivation inherent in participation. For example, students can work together to create or participate in an immersive environment. Additionally, we recognize that not all online learning environments employing elements of gamification are fully gamified. Realistically, a teacher or instructor incorporates aspects of gamification when those are determined to facilitate instructional goals, are within the instructor's (and students') technological expertise and are available for use. Thus, costs and benefits are assessed. One way to begin to assess potential costs and benefits is to evaluate research on serious games. In the next sections, we review research on Internet and game use generally, then we focus on empirical research on serious games for instructional purposes.

1.2   Internet and Game Research

Anderson and Rainie [1] of the PEW Research Center described the results of an online survey in which "53% agreed…[that] 'By 2020 there will have been significant advances in the adoption and use of gamification. It will be making waves on the communications scene and will have been implemented in many new ways for education, health, work, and other aspects of human connection and it will play a role in the everyday activities of many of the people who are actively using communications networks in their daily lives" (p. 3). Several respondents also objected to the term "gamification", and predicted it would soon be outmoded, and others elaborated on the potential contributions and detriments of games.

More recently, Perrin [45] of Pew Research Center described five trends in American gaming culture. A survey study by Parker et al. [43] found that a majority (72% ages 18–29 and 58% ages 30–49) of young men often or sometimes play video games. About

48–49% of women ages 18–49 often or sometimes play video games. Overall, about 43% of adults play video games. Of the types of games that were most popular, strategy (62%) and puzzle games (62%) were most played followed by adventure (49%) and shooter (42%) games. Among teenagers, 82% reported having a game console at home and 90% reported they played games on their computer, game console, or cell phone [17]. About 41% of teen boys and 11% of teen girls reported that they spent too much time playing games. Another 41% of teen boys and 42% of teen girls reported that they spent about the right amount of time playing video games [17]. The last major trend was that many adults, 82% of those 65 years or older and 42% of those 18–29 years of age, thought video games were a contributing factor to violence [43].

Over the years these authors have observed and assessed technological innovations and their inclusion in instructional contexts, we note some common trends: Hyper-enthusiasm of some convinced that a new technology will be an instructional panacea (e.g., instructional television American Samoa in the 1960's and 1970's) contrasted to fears and resistance exhibited by those convinced we are on a road to instructional and social ruin. For example, Gershenfeld [19] pointed out with respect to today's computer games, "On the one hand [some authors] are making the case that games and 'gamification'…can save the planet. On the other hand, parents struggle with the amount of time their kids spend on digital media – roughly eight hours a day…. And it is hard for parents to watch their children gleefully annihilating virtual humans with heavy artillery and not be concerned" (p. 56).

In contrast, one of the strongest claims in favor of the contribution of games in education is the example Anderson and Rainie [1] who described the University of Washington's game Foldit. In 2011, 46,000 gamers on Foldit participated in generating a solution for how a particular protein might advance a cure for HIV. Most notably, the gamers' solution was generated in 10 days in contrast to the 15 years that scientists had invested in this work. Indeed, it appeared that the potential for serious gaming contributions had only been touched upon. Even before Foldit, the Sony PlayStation was used by the Stanford Folding@Home program [26, 65], where Sony and PlayStation reported more than 15 million users donated over 100 million computation hours from their home console, the PlayStation 3 from 2007 to 2012.

However, these prognosticators, both optimistic and pessimistic, certainly did not count on the rapid and ubiquitous move to online instruction as a response to the COVID-19 pandemic – a factor that has pushed serious games, and their related potentials into the forefront. However as dramatic the COVID-19 pandemic reaction seems; we predict this surge will be surpassed by an extensive use of AI and LLM software that gamify educational online games to augment a learner's cognition. Although in a Pew report on the state of the internet, Anderson, Rainie, and Vogels [2] consulted various innovators, experts, and researchers on their views of social change and technology considering the aftermath of the 2020 pandemic and with an eye toward 2025. Amidst the many themes described changes in education prompted by the mass movement to online instruction as a driver for instructional innovation is relevant to the present discussion. Clearly any teacher or instructor (or parent) knows the strongly motivational aspect of games. As Theodor Geisel [20] stated in a children's book, "Oh the places you'll go! There is fun to be done! There are points to be scored. There are games to be won!" The contention that underlies this paper is that if employed in ways that facilitate learning, "serious" or educational games, in contrast to merely entertaining ones (of the sort we presume Suess described), valuable contributions to learning can be made.

1.3 Game Research

Given that games have been highly touted in educational contexts and considering given the presence of high degrees of optimism regarding these and other technological advancements, it is imperative to examine the genuine empirical effects of games as documented in the research. Mayer [32] quotes his own earlier determination, "Many strong claims are made for the educational value of computer games, but there is little strong evidence to back up those claims" [31, p. 281].

In 2013, Wouters, van Nimwegen, Oostendorp and van der Spek [69] conducted a meta-analysis of serious games. They concluded that games facilitated learning over conventional teaching strategies, particularly when accompanied by additional instruction and involving group activities. Contrary to popular expectation, serious games alone did not increase motivation. However, Ikehara et al. [25] reported a gamified activity in which the instructor's goal of the child learning fractions and the child's goal of participating in an engaging activity were mutually satisfied. Evaluating the value of a fraction can increasingly be a challenging task for children and adults alike, as the numerator and denominator of the fraction increase in size. The goal of teaching fractions is normally accomplished by asking children to repetitively practice fraction problems of increasing difficulty. A typical fraction exercise may consist of a set of problems varying from an easy example such as "Is $1/2 > 1/3$?" to "Is $11/18 > 1/3$?" which can be more difficult. In a project initially designed to use the physiological sensors of augmented cognition to determine cognitive load, the fraction exercise, known as "The Moving Targets Fractions (MTF) task was gamified by Ikehara and his colleagues. MFT presented a fixed number of oval targets containing fractions on a computer screen. These fractions floated across the screen from left to right. The cognitive load was controlled by adjusting fraction values, speed of the fractions across the screen, and how many fractions were presented. The primary goal of the user is to maximize the score by selecting the fractions greater than 1/3 before they reached the right edge of the screen. This engaging activity also gave the instructors the ability to determine if individual students found the level of difficulty to be easy or hard.

Since streaming video games became popular, an activity emerged where spectators (streamers) watch players engaging in video games. Twitch is one of these popular sites viewed by millions of viewers who visit it each day to watch other players compete in popular online games. Biometric data is used to enhance the spectator experience. Software such as "All the Feels" [52], developed by Robinson et al. in 2017, provides an overlay of biometric and webcam-derived data onto the screen to reveal the biometrics of the streamers to the spectating audience. A dashboard provides a visualization of the streamer's heart rate, skin conductance, and emotions. The researchers found that this additional layer of data enhanced the viewers' experience and improved the connectivity between the streamer and spectator.

A systematic review by Manzano-León et al. [30] of studies from 2016 through 2020 that sorted through 750 articles from Web of Science, Scopus, and Dialnet, found that

227 were duplicates. From 198 of these studies that were further analyzed, 184 were further excluded because they were not about formal education environments, not about gamification in education, or did not specify gamification. The reviewers' final fourteen experimental and quasi-experimental studies of educational games indicated that games can improve students' academic performance and motivation [30]. Additionally, the commitment of students to persevere through the learning experience provided by the games was elevated.

An additional recent review is provided by Mayer [31] who reviewed empirical research on educational games and developed a useful tri-fold typology or trifecta for this research including: "(a) value-added research, which compares the learning outcomes of groups that learn academic material from playing a base version of the game to the outcomes of those playing the same game with one feature added; (b) cognitive consequences research, which compares improvements in cognitive skills of groups that play [a]… game to the skills improvement of those who engage in a control activity; and (C) media comparison research which compares the learning outcomes of groups that learn academic material in a game…to those who learn with conventional media" (p. 531).

In the value-added category are features of games that can render them useful. He described the following as having positive effects in the value-added research: the use of "spoken text," language that is "conversational," pretraining on a game, "coaching" throughout and prompts requiring participants "to explain or reflect" (p. 538). Unexpectedly, Mayer [31] described his own finding that virtual reality was not a feature that improved learning over simple computer depictions. For cognitive consequences studies, games were found to improve perceptual attention and aspects of mental rotation. Finally, media comparisons indicated games facilitate learning in math, science, and second-language studies.

In addition to typologies and empirical research reviews, the present authors contend that case studies of the development and implementation of educational games in specific cultural and historical milieus can be valuable for understanding the processes, developments, and instructional factors that contribute to instructional success with games. Thus, we focus on the Hawai'i context.

2 Hawai'i Background

To provide some geographic/demographic background, Hawai'i comprises eight major islands in the central Pacific and other uninhabited islands, atolls, and seamounts across 1,500 miles. The annual estimate of the population in Hawai'i is 1,407,006, 21% of which are age 17 or under according to U.S. 2020 census data [62]. The larger ethnic groups are white (25.5%), Asian (37.6%), two or more races (24.2%), Native Hawaiian and other Pacific Islander groups (10.1%). Hawai'i's state (public) university system consists of 3 universities and 7 community colleges and there is a single statewide department of education (DOE) that administers public schools and complexes at the elementary and secondary levels.

Although Hawai'i's cultural/ethnic mix is different from the rest of the US, many technological and educational needs are the same. Further, by virtue of geographic isolation and distribution of the population over an island chain, there is a pressing need to be at the forefront of technological innovation particularly with innovations regarding distance education. A further and central consideration is accommodating learners from a range of linguistic and cultural backgrounds in the broader Asia-Pacific region, making Hawai'i the ideal "test bed" for 21st century technologies in educational contexts.

In the next section, we focus on several seminal developments that took place in Hawai'i to describe its long history of gamification.

2.1 Past Online Instruction in Hawai'i with Simulations

Returning to the Hawai'i situation, we illustrate with examples from the past the continuing cycle of challenges and successes in implementing games in online instruction. Then, we describe more recent examples and contrast the early enthusiasm and optimism regarding these technologies' instructional potentials with a perspective tempered by instructional use in different contexts. We as authors draw upon our different disciplinary and teaching perspectives in computer science, educational psychology, and high school teaching.

We integrated a wide variety of platforms and social technologies with collaborative learning approaches into courses taught at the University of Hawai'i by different instructors to address educational trends to increase engagement in college courses. The courses spanned educational psychology, computer science, and language learning. Students made use of a variety of free interactive technologies to meet synchronously online in small teams of three or four to carry out collaborative tasks and projects assigned in a particular course.

The advent of the Internet provided fertile ground for improving the design of learning. Networks made it possible to use simulations of natural social settings, even using somewhat primitive technology. The success of the improved curriculum design, however, should be attributed more to the pedagogy that provides the stimulus, than the technology. If technology is used in ways that make sense for the curriculum to the students and teachers, the projects are likely to succeed.

For example, UH researchers were able to use primitive tools such as experimental computers and teletypes to provide online education to high school students from the neighbor islands and other areas of Oahu in the early 1970's. This was accomplished by using an innovative system of networked computers called ALOHAnet, a precursor to the Ethernet and Wi-Fi systems [24]. Almost thirty years later, in 1999, cross-cultural content was made possible also using relatively primitive Web technologies that allowed language learners to interact with other learners and native speakers of the second language in role-playing and problem-solving games.

An example of the early possibilities of a language learning game was Kanji City, begun in 1988 [4]. This game utilized hypermedia (HyperCard) to create as fully an immersive experience for language learning as was possible at the time. As the authors explained, "It employs the metaphor of navigating an urban environment (Tokyo) by reading and reacting to the signs occurring there – a special problem in the case of Japanese and Chinese Orthography" (p. 28). Actual signs in the city, stops on the train, were used in participants' navigation. Participants exchanged money, bought tickets for the train, interpreted maps, planned, and "went" on excursions to restaurants, used menus and placed orders, went to casinos, school, a disco, a bank, and a coffee house. In the school they could pass tests to earn currency, calculate using an abacus. In the casino, they could "play" a slot machine to earn currency. At the disco, they could listen to popular music. Even at this writing, over 30 years later, one can imagine the students' excitement and enthusiasm in participating in such an environment.

Another early example of a learning environment that began in 1997 [67] involved the collaborative and cross-institutional development of virtual team projects by students and instructors of Japanese working together from the University of Hawai'i in Honolulu, Hawai'i, USA, Seiryo Commercial High School in Nagoya, Japan, and Haverford University in Philadelphia, Pennsylvania, USA (three very geographically-dispersed locations) [23]. Students conducted Internet-based synchronous and asynchronous sessions using the following tools: eWeb Chat and Forum, Microsoft Chat-2 and Net Meeting, WebCrossing, CUSeeMe, CoolTalk, and email. Teams created an "ideal town" via MUD/MOO-like team rooms. Designing the town required intensive imagination, negotiation, and design - a clearly gamified and immersive aspect that capitalized upon the tools that were available at that time. The town included a bookstore, restaurant, educational and recreational facilities, and a hot spring. Thus, in this virtual town teams visited and completed business dealings involving the use of more specialized and advanced language and conversational skills than would be used in many Japanese-language courses. The USA-based students also produced a Web-based magazine with the Japan-based students acting as reviewers. Additional socialization among groups took place during brainstorming activities, interviews, and presentations.

These socializations and conversational exchanges exceeded typical language-learning dialogues with other language learners that occur in face-to-face classes. Situations were created that simulated a range of genuine social interactions with Japanese native speakers. Students' conversations were in Japanese language and computer-based interaction involved using Romanji (Roman characters). For instructional planning, faculty members utilized groupware technology that then existed. Other interactions and introductions between the groups of students involved the early uses of chat rooms. Technologies that were used at this time involved CUSeeMe enabling video-based interactions, and CoolTalk, an Internet telephony program.

The first author of the present paper and other researchers involved in this project noted that students' involvement in gamified aspects of this project, particularly the "design a town" task seemed truly immersive and appeared to parallel game designer Jane McGonigal's work [33, 34]. Specifically, she identified four "powers or abilities" inherent in computer games [35, 36] that facilitate the progress of a game for players resulting in a "flow" state. According to Csikszentmihalyi [9, 10, p.74], "Flow tends to occur when a person's skills are fully involved in overcoming a challenge that is just about manageable". Murphy [35] identified the affective current essential to flow states in the discussion of the laws of learning and game design, "flow is entirely about motivation, our first law of learning for games. Specifically, flow is about intrinsic motivation – the joy of doing." The first game power McGonigal [33] described was termed "urgent optimism" and represents an ability and desire to enthusiastically re-assess the environment to find the next challenge. The second power, "blissful productivity" enables one to continue the quest by evaluating progress through benchmarks and feedback. Third is "social fabric" that enables one to experience the pleasures of community belonging. Lastly, "sense of epic meaning" involves efforts directed toward large-scale rather than solely individual goals.

1. Urgent Optimism
2. Blissful Productivity
3. Social Fabric
4. Sense of Epic Meaning

Results from analyses of chats showed various approaches to teaching and indicated challenges inherent at that time in using an Internet-based learning environment. The sample analysis shown in Table 1 shows a sample of chat transcripts coded to indicate McGonigal's [33] four "powers or abilities" associated with aspects of gamification that were speculated to be associated with flow states.

This type of early virtual classroom allowed students to practice and develop second language and cross-cultural communication and collaboration skills in as highly realistic yet simulated environments as were possible given the technologies at the time. Developing a town involved the kinds of creativity and imagination one employs when interacting in imagined, virtual worlds that typify the contextual aspects of online games that were emerging and would follow. Early uses and recognition of aspects of gamification and how they might effectively be employed in serious learning contexts depended upon implementations such as these, mostly developed by Computer Science faculty members. However, adoption and use of such aspects of gamification for online learning was slower among instructors, lecturers, and professors not as adept with Computer Science, aspects of gamification, or online learning.

These approaches to gamification in online learning demonstrated early use of augmented cognition in these systems. When evaluating gamification implementations, measures such as time-to-respond were considered but not deeply rooted in the design and development of the learning environments.

Fifteen years later, the initial optimism regarding online learning and gamification had dampened a bit and focused on instructional and pedagogical issues rather than on the online technologies themselves. The rapid development of online technologies to improve online teaching and learning experiences has improved the veridical nature of the instruction so that in many ways early criticisms of lack of face-to-face contact among students and instructors is no longer an issue. However, the inclusion of gaming as an instructional strategy in online environments appears to have been adopted initially by the most technologically adept instructors, such as those in computer science, educational technology (with a professor using Second Life) and learning technology.

2.2   The U.S. and Hawai'i in the Present Context

The Pew Research Center [46] estimates that 90% of people in the U.S. use the Internet. The 2019 United States Census revealed that of the 121,520,200 households in the U.S., 91.8% had a computer and 85.4% had Internet access in 2018. Hawai'i households were very similar. Of 455,300 Hawai'i households, 91.8% had a computer and 85.9% had Internet access in 2018. In 2016, Hawai'i already had slightly higher broadband

Table 1. Powers of gamification example (translated from Romanji into English)

Threaded Discussion Posts	Game Power
Well then…shall we send everything that we decide to Nagoya? Then, getting feedback from them…how about it? Without waiting for time	Urgent Optimism
Why don't we make up the list of things to decide right now…I'm a bit confuse…sorry about that	Urgent Optimism
It may be a better idea to send a compilation of things about how the town is shaping up	Urgent Optimism
On the roof, why don't we just put some kind of bench up there like they have in the park?	Blissful Productivity
In any case I think the first floor will end up being pretty noisy because there are comics and cartoons there	Blissful Productivity
And on the roof, you can even talk in a quiet voice because it is outside	Blissful Productivity
Did you read the email from Nagoya people? She recommended dokudamiburo and the sakeburo. What do you think?	Social Fabric
Don't you know about dokudami tea? It's a variety of tea that is bitter and, to tell you the truth, it tastes really bad but it's good for the health apparently. They say that it's good if you put the leaves into the bath and it's apparently very effective in relieving back pain	Social Fabric
I think that having a sake bath would attract a lot of customers but if you enter a sake bath you will smell of alcohol and people will mistake you for being drunk	Epic Sense of Meaning
A sake bath means that you put sake into the bath. Wouldn't you get drubk from the aroma?!	Epic Sense of Meaning
Yeah, let's continue with the discussion of the hot springs	Epic Sense of Meaning

subscriptions such as cable, fiber optic or digital subscriber lines/DSL at 73% and the U.S. at 67% [21].

As seen in Table 2, about 77.7% of the population in 2017 used the Internet from anywhere, with 25–29 years olds reporting the highest use at 85.6% followed by 20- to 24-year-olds then 15- to 19-year-olds. The largest fluctuation was seen in the 3- and 4-year-olds who jumped from 19.9% in 2003 to 86.9% in 2010 then back to 31.6% in 2012 then up again to 51.0% in 2017 (see Fig. 1). But the largest growth has been among those age 70 and older, increasing by 37%. In general, the adult population increased about 22 percentage points between 2003 and 2017. Should there be alarm that so many young people are using Internet technologies so early in life? Perhaps not since access to those technologies would likely not be possible without adults giving them access. But the impression remains that these children will be growing up into a world where the Internet will have more influence than not.

Table 2. Number and percentage of persons 3 years old and over who use the Internet

Age	2003 U.S. Census		2010 U.S. Census		2012 U.S. Census		2017 U.S. Census		Between 2003 and 2017
	# (in thousands)	% of population	# (in thousands)	% of population	# (in thousands)	% of population	# (in thousands)a	% of population	% change
3 and 4	1,662 (62.5)	19.9 (0.67)	7,693 (80.9)	86.9 (0.73)	2,534 (81.9)	31.6 (0.93)	8,003	51.0 (1.18)	+31.1
5 to 9	8,259 (137.2)	42 (0.54)	18,753 (109.3)	89.9 (0.50)	11,961 (148.95)	58.3 (0.65)	20,434[a]	69.3 (0.68)	+27.3
10 to 14	14,570 (179.4)	68.9 (0.49)	18,640 (90.2)	93.1 (0.39)	16,720 (152.83)	81.1 (0.64)	20,699[a]	77.0 (0.71)	+8.1
15 to 19	15,768 (186.1)	77.7 (0.45)	19,410 (81.3)	93.3 (0.37)	18,785 (200.46)	89.3 (0.47)	21,042[a]	84.9 (0.58)	+7.2
20 to 24	13,800 (174.9)	69.4 (0.50)	18,986 (93.3)	89.9 (0.44)	18,846 (258.24)	86.1 (0.50)	22.066[a]	85.3 (0.55)	+15.9
25 to 29	12,492 (167)	66.7 (0.53)	18,781 (95.6)	88.9 (0.45)	17,721 (185.24)	85.7 (0.51)	23,336[a]	85.6 (0.52)	+18.9
30 to 39	28,580 (242.3)	69.2 (0.35)	35,792 (133.5)	90.8 (0.34)	33,493 (199.96)	84.8 (0.41)	43,876[a]	85.5 (0.42)	+16.3
40 to 49	29,978 (247.3)	67.5 (0.34)	38,582 (123.5)	90.1 (0.29)	34,526 (162.92)	82.6 (0.35)		84.9 (0.43)	+17.4
50 to 59	21,911 (215.9)	62.7 (0.40)	35,171 (165.3)	84.7 (0.38)	32,890 (221.95)	76.4 (0.42)		79.7 (0.40)	+17.0
60 to 69	9,677 (148)	43.9 (0.51)	22,622 (158)	78.1 (0.45)	22,171 (176.46)	69.6 (0.49)		75.8 (0.43)	+31.9
70 or older	4,940 (106.9)	20.1 (0.39)	14,603 (158.3)	54.6 (0.60)	12,391 (233.25)	43.7 (0.54)		57.1 (0.52)	+37.0
All	161,636 (309.1)	58.7 (0.14)	249,031 (580.7)	85.2 (0.20)	222,032 (673.6)	74.7 (0.21)		77.7 (0.24)	+19.0

[a] Numbers were no longer reported with percentages in age groups. Age groupings were reported as 3 and 4, 5 and 6, 7 to 13, 14 to 17, 18 and 19, 20 and 21, 22 to 24, 25 to 29, and 30–34. Numbers are estimated. Data yet available for 35 and over

Note: Standard errors appear in parentheses

SOURCE: U.S. Department of Commerce, Census Bureau, Current Population Survey, October 2003, unpublished data, [57, 58]; U.S. Department of Commerce, Census Bureau, Current Population Survey (CPS), October 2010, (U.S. Census Bureau, 2018); U.S. Department of Commerce, Census Bureau, Current Population Survey (CPS), October 2012 [60]; U.S. Department of Commerce, Census Bureau, Current Population Survey (CPS), July 2011 and November 2017 [61]; U.S. Department of Commerce, Census Bureau, Current Population Reports, Series P-25, Nos. 1000, 1022, 1045, 1057, 1059, 1092, and 1095; 2000 through 2009 Population Estimates, retrieved August 14, 2012, from https://www.census.gov/popest/data/national/asrh/2011/index.html; and 2010 through 2019 Population Estimates, retrieved November 29, 2019, from https://www.census.gov/data/datasets/time-series/demo/popest/2010s-national-detail.html#par_textimage_57373479 [36, 37]

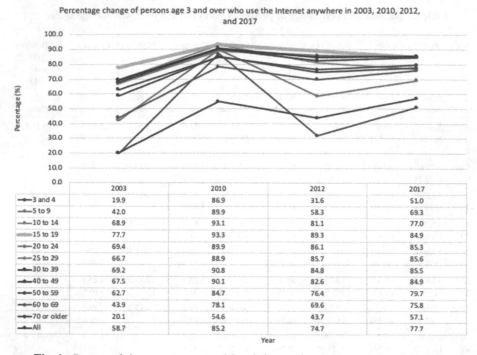

Fig. 1. Percent of change, persons aged 3 and above using the Internet anywhere [59].

In highlights of the 2019 American Community Survey for Hawai'i, the number of households with one or more computing devices was 465,299 or 93%, 28.9% of which have people under the age of 18 [14]. Interestingly, though the category of smartphone and tablet or portable device were only added during the 2016 survey, they were more present than the traditional laptop or desktop. Hawai'i households reported that the most prevalent type of computer in their homes were a smartphone, tablet or other portable wireless computer (82.8%) followed by a desktop or laptop computer (81.5%). 9.6% reported having only a smartphone, tablet, or other portable wireless computer. Those numbers varied by county also as seen in Table 3. Of the four major counties, Kauai County (94.0%) had the highest percentage of households that had a computer, followed by Honolulu County (93.7%), Hawai'i county (91.9%), and Maui County (90.9%).

So where there were concerns that many students did not have access to devices, it seems from Census data that the devices are present in a good number of Hawai'i households. However, more detail is needed to investigate if those households with devices are available to children, are perhaps too few for the number of users in the household, or have the capacities needed for schoolwork. Further, closer review of the 7–8% of households that do not have any computer devices is needed so that those families in households with school-aged children are provided as much support as possible so that the children have high quality opportunities to learn and thrive.

Table 3. Computers and broadband presence in households in Hawai'i by county, 2019.

		Total households	With a computer	With broadband Internet
State of Hawai'i	Estimate	465,299 (5,012)	432,658 (5,351)	409,577 (5,448)
	Percentage		93 (0.5)	88 (0.8)
Hawai'i County	Estimate	71,193 (2,209)	64,872 (2,505)	60,573 (2,594)
	Percentage		91.1 (1.9)	85.1 (2.6)
Honolulu County	Estimate	316,456 (3,394)	296,525 (4,072)	282,366 (4,360)
	Percentage		93.7 (0.7)	89.2 (0.9)
Kauai County	Estimate	22,898 (1,313)	21,521 (1,414)	21,012 (1,413)
	Percentage		94 (2.3)	91.8 (2.7)
Maui County	Estimate	54,744 (2,300)	49,732 (2,612)	45,618 (2,600)
	Percent		90.8 (2.3)	83.3 (2.8)

Note: 1-year dataset includes geographic areas with populations of 65,000 or more
Source: U.S. Census Bureau, 2019 American Community Survey 1-Year Estimates, Table DP-02, released September 17, 2020 [14]. Table modified from the Department of Business, Economic Development & Tourism, Research and Economic Analysis Division, Hawaii State Data Center

We note that hundreds of millions of children across the globe between 8–15 years old represent the largest online age group, spending hours weekly in hundreds of immersive animated virtual worlds, playing with near and distant friends and family [27], acquiring virtual skills. Hawai'i is likely not very different. Some studies identify some problematic areas of internet use by adolescents such as stress [28] and sleep [18], as well cautions to universities that these youth will enter college expecting digital environments to be virtual and immersive [6, 12]). According to the 2010 MacArthur Foundation report on Digital Media and Learning [11, p. 37] "Not only is educational gaming starting to be perceived as a viable alternative to formal education, other types of virtual environments and massively multiplayer online games are being recognized for their educational components".

2.3   K–12 Online Instruction in Hawai'i's K-12 Schools

The K–12 public school system in Hawai'i offers E-School for its students, which is described as distance- and online-learning opportunities. These 148 courses, 20 of which are advanced placement courses, are available through online charter schools or partnership programs with local community colleges and universities (see http://hawaiipub licschools.org/). In findings reported by Nguyen [39], establishing an understanding of youth perspectives and their habits was critical as K–12 teachers grappled with the advent of more computer use in face-to-face classes and gaming into formal classroom environments. Curriculum that use gaming approaches like Scratch, Makey Makey, and Dash and Dot Robots were reported as used by Hawai'i computer science teachers [41]. Youths considered gaming to be "their online world" and questioned if adults knew how to effectively engage them through gaming. Teachers had their initial foray into augmented cognition-based instructional design. With many of these technologies being hosted on servers rather than personal computers, they were able to identify time spent on different tasks to determine challenge level and were able to adjust support and instruction based on personalized student needs. Several researchers have urged teachers to help youth develop strategies to uphold responsible behaviors using computers and to view computers as not only as gaming tools but learning tools [5, 29, 38, 70]. Prensky [47] has long seen gaming as a positive strategy for engagement and Yee [71] advocated for game play's positive motivating influences by drawing upon social interaction, a sense of achievement, and immersive experiences. Moreover, the reward structures of games [49] sustain interest and interaction.

The shift from being consumers of technology to producers of information that lead towards mastery of knowledge is seen clearly in the revisions of the International Society for Technology in Education's (ISTE). Originally written in 1998 as the National Educational Technology Standards with a focus on operations [36], a major reformulation to information fluency occurred in 2007 [37] and to digital collaboration and creativity in 2015 [8]. Since 2016, the focus continues to strive to empower student voice and ensure that learning is a student-driven process. Overall, there are now 29 ISTE standards for more than just students. In addition to student standards, there are teacher, administrator, coaches, and computer educator standards too.

The ISTE students standards state that educators should strive to enable empowered learners, digital citizens, knowledge constructors, innovative designers, computational thinkers, creative communicators, and global collaborators. The need has moved from simply teaching students and instructors how to use technologies to how to be effective stewards of technologies, including instruction in ethics [40]. Fostering learning in inclusive classrooms that support culturally and linguistically diverse needs for learners can benefit from implementation of the Universal Design for Learning (UDL) framework, designed to help educators to "improve and optimize teaching and learning for all people based on scientific insights into how humans learn". The UDL framework can be used to address the different students' needs to engage with the learning, understand the through various representations, and express their learning in various ways [44, 50, 51, 64]. Furthermore, supporting students to demonstrate their learning in novel ways has included gaming. And gaming has been an integral part of innovative designs from the students as well as the teachers in K–12 education.

2.4 Moving to Online Instruction During Covid-19

In March and April, 2020, all public K–12 instruction and university-level instruction moved online in Hawai'i, as a precautionary measure for protecting its students, families, instructors and others. Since the use of distance education had previously begun out of necessity, as we have described earlier, due to inter-island geographic isolation, the current transition, at least at the university level was seamless for many units already operating with online classes, or hybrid courses (both face-to-face and online components). For example, in the University of Hawai'i at Mānoa's College of Education, many courses were already offered online and the college has a separate unit solely devoted to assisting faculty with instructional support for teaching online. The Department of Information and Computer Sciences started 20 years ago online when the department received a Sloan Foundation grant to develop an inexpensive online learning environment. A professor who used the system twenty years ago and has continued online instruction since then transitioned seamlessly to COVID instruction. In a Fall 2020 semesters' evaluation, a student commented the following:

"He is one of my favorite professors of all time. His style of collaboration and constant questioning and reasoning made me not only excited for this class, but it has been contagious in all my classes. Additionally, he is the only teacher that did not seem to have an emotional breakdown over the changes in the teaching format (in person to online). He seemed to embrace it and used it to motivate me to be a better student. He is my favorite teacher at UH so far!!"

At the University of Hawaiʻi at Mānoa campus, a report was released in August 2020 by a Student Learning Working Team that identified the changes to academic programs and educational activities [56]. Overall, no instructional rooms allowed for enough social distancing for courses with more than 71 students. Three rooms could have been used for courses with 50–70 students, 15 rooms for courses with 30–49 students, 18 rooms for courses with 20–29 students, 106 rooms for courses with 10–19 students, and 21 rooms for courses with 4–9 students. About 86% of courses transitioned to online, 10% to hybrid (a combination of in-person and online instruction), and 4% in-person either in a classroom or in an alternate education space. Instructional design support and professional development sessions were offered by the university, with engagement strategies that supported student voice and choice as well as increased relevance garnering high interest [56]. These sessions presented many strategies that incorporated gaming features to increase motivation in student learning.

In the Hawaiʻi Department of Education (HIDOE), which serves about 84% of Hawaiʻi's approximately 210,000 school-aged children [63], all public schools transitioned to online learning. Some small private, independent schools were able to maintain face-to-face teaching by adjusting their schedules. In the HIDOE, teachers incorporated choice boards to support at-home learning [22]. The activities were designed to serve as reinforcement and enrichment rather than meeting specific learning outcomes. Many of these enrichment activities incorporated games for younger children, with the word "play," for example, appearing in 13 of 60 activities across five days. In a survey of K–12 teachers in March 2021, 65 (13.9%) respondents (n = 468) indicated in early results that a positive aspect of teaching online was becoming more confident with technology and being able to incorporate more interactive games as formative assessment or temperature checks during instruction [42]. The sudden transition to online learning due to COVID-19 has brought forward game-like instructional and assessment tools such as Kahoot [13, 68], Socrative [15, 34], Quizlet [16], Poll Everywhere [55], Mentimeter [53, 66], and Flippity.net, which have all gained traction during the pandemic with K–12 teachers. Additionally, teachers are supporting students in developing immersive gaming experiences in Minecraft (see Minecraft.net) and Scratch (see https://scratch.mit.edu/) that allow for students to program their own paths and play.

In the swift emergency transition, both K–12 and higher education had similar tests in instruction, access, engagement, and equity concerns for the students. Challenges in domains such as physical education, music, art, or dance included not just providing video-based instruction, but in observing and assessing students' performances. Other problems in teaching sciences, fashion and design-related courses, sciences involving labs and other work with realia and actual specimens needed to be reasonably met.

Additional personal challenges were faced by students and faculty with the stay-at-home orders. Some students did not have dedicated effective WiFi or computer equipment as they had been accustomed to using on-campus computers at libraries and elsewhere. Many students were faced with job-loss and economic hardship. Graduate students described challenges of working at home or in healthcare or education-related work, while educating their own children at home (some with special needs), and sometimes taking care of older parents and grandparents; in Hawai'i, many families lived together as larger 'ohana (families) that typify Pacific Island communities rather than nuclear family units that are prevalent in much of the continental US.

In Fall, 2020, the second author taught an online course on university teaching to graduate students. The transition to fully online teaching when the shelter-in-place order was enacted in Hawai'i had been relatively seamless as she was experienced in online instruction and had anticipated that all instruction would go fully online as the pandemic accelerated. In sharing technologies for learning, the graduate students eagerly took the lead and shared online games that they successfully used with their own students, such as Kahoot quizzes for reviewing material, Canva, and Mural for brainstorming and visual design, and simulations of the Jeopardy television show that students created online themselves. In her own instruction for future professors and teachers-in-training, she emphasizes that the inclusion of games in instruction should have clear instructional goals related to content learning. A good metric for inclusion of games could be comparisons to Bloom's Taxonomy [7], subsequently revised in 2001 [3]. The taxonomy relates to aspects of learning in the cognitive domain from remembering (the lower, more rote level), to understanding, applying, analyzing, evaluating, and creating (the highest level). Many of the games her students employ (e.g., Kahoot, Jeopardy) involve testing for information retrieval at the lower levels, while brainstorming and visual design aspects involve higher cognitive skills. These approaches aligned well with initial teaching training for the use of augmented cognition in instructional settings. Many of these games included tracking of students' accuracy and time (effort) to identify individual differences in learning through gamification. Many were able to use this information to diagnose the difference between confidence (speed) and accuracy (correctness). These games gave educators on a larger scale the ability to use augmented cognition-based approaches to refine learning opportunities which would have been more difficult to implement without the use of gamification approaches to learning. It is noteworthy that students enjoy taking on teaching or leading roles in facilitating games for review purposes with their classmates. Instructors working on improving their technology skills in online instruction can profitably incorporate students' leadership and collaboration in adopting aspects of serious games into their classes.

At this writing, we completed the 2019–2022 COVID-19 academic years (celebrated with online graduations) and are approaching the completion of the 2023–2024 academic year. Although we cannot foretell what the future holds in this rapidly changing era, we are optimistic about the further adoption of aspects of gamification into our online classes, particularly with the availability of open-source AI software, both for serious learning about instructional content and for supporting students as they navigate their educational progress.

3 Discussion

We see online instruction that leverages gaming models for engagement with critical analysis with augmented cognition-based approaches towards their intended effectiveness as growing. As game platforms improve, Gaming has been reviewed as an effective educational approach for instruction and assessment because it increases motivation, and commitment of students [30], particularly with use of spoken text and conversational prompts [32] and perceptual attention and mental rotation in math, science, and second-language studies [32]. As we work to develop instructional approaches that incorporate game play for serious learning, we have the following recommendations.

Instructors: should:

- Use AI-inspired virtual resources, and games with high quality content that serve central, rather than peripheral roles in instruction. These resources should be incorporated gradually, often with students' assistance, as they become adept using them.
- Be trained to use augmented cognition-based approaches to analyzing game-based learning data, such as time on task and accuracy depending on the challenge level. This data can complement other approaches to learning and while giving instructors the ability to adapt their instruction.
- Develop ways to leverage students' high levels of interest in gaming by incorporating appropriate aspects of gaming for content learning rather than viewing games as merely entertainment and online distraction.
- Facilitate learning online through games and social and cultural collaborations across geographic and other boundaries. Games and simulations offer ways to bridge and unite participants with mutual educational goals such as science and language learning.
- Be made aware of various crowdsourced, governmental, and scientific ventures that enable students as gamers to contribute to genuine scientific advances using gaming skills, as in the Foldit game described by Anderson and Rainie [1].
- Become aware of and use game-play strategies in the classroom that increase interactions of students with each other, with the content, and with the instructors.
- Facilitate learning online through games and social and cultural collaborations across geographic and other boundaries. Games and simulations offer ways to bridge and unite participants with mutual educational goals such as science and language learning.
- Seek ways to foster a safe space for play to occur as they challenge students with content and design experiences to pique additional curiosity.

Students should:

- Learn to be productive participants in gaming and online gaming communities by skillfully evaluating their own and others' contributions as well as by evaluating the information accuracy, views, and potential biases that the games may be convey.

- Create collaborative instructional games online to review course content, as test preparation, and to teach each other.

Acknowledgements. This material is based on work that was partially supported by Grant No. 1662487 from the National Science Foundation (NSF) and by Grant No. H98230-22-1-0329 from the National Security Agency (NSA), National Centers of Academic Excellence in Cybersecurity.

References

1. Anderson, J., Rainie, L.: Gamification: experts expect 'game layers' to expand in the future, with positive and negative results. Pew Research Center's Internet & American Life Project, Washington, D.C. (2012)
2. Anderson, J., Rainie, L., Vogels, E.A.: Experts say the 'new normal' in 2025 will be far more tech-driven, presenting more big challenges. Pew Research Center, Washington, D.C. (2021)
3. Anderson, L. W., Krathwohl, D.R.: A Taxonomy for Learning, Teaching and Assessing: A Revision of Bloom's Taxonomy of Educational Objectives: Complete Edition. Longman, New York (2001)
4. Ashworth, D., Stelovsky, J.: Kanji City an exploration of hypermedia applications for CALL. CALICO J. **6**, 27–39 (1989)
5. Berson, M., Berson, I., Desai, S., Falls, D.: The role of electronic media in decision-making and risk assessment skill development in young children. In: 2008 the Society for Information Technology and Teacher Education International Conference (SITE), Las Vegas, NV (2008)
6. Blascovich, J., Bailenson, J.: Infinite Reality: Avatars, Eternal Life, New Worlds, and the Dawn of the Virtual Revolution. HarperCollins e-books, New York City (2011)
7. Bloom, B.S.: Taxonomy of Educational Objectives Book 1: The Cognitive Domain, 2nd edn. Addison Wesley Longman, New York (1956)
8. Brooks-Young, S.: ISTE Standards for Students: A Practical Guide for Learning with Technology. International Society for Technology in Education (2015)
9. Csikszentmihalyi, M.: Flow: The Psychology of Optimal Experience. Harper Perennial, New York City (1990)
10. Csikszentmihalyi, M.: Finding Flow: The Psychology of Engagement with Everyday Life. Basic Books, New York City (1997)
11. Davidson, C.N., Goldberg, D.T.: The Future of Thinking: Learning Institutions in a Digital Age, p. 37. MIT Press, Cambridge (2010)
12. de Freitas, S.: Serious Virtual Worlds: A Scoping Study. JISC e-Learning Programme (2018). http://www.jisc.ac.uk/media/documents/publications/seriousvirtualworldsv1.pdf
13. Dellos, R.: Kahoot! A digital game resource for learning. Int. J. Instruct. Technol. Dist. Learn. **12**, 49–52 (2015)
14. Department of Business, Economic Development & Tourism, State of Hawai'i. American Community Survey 2019, Hawai'i. State of Hawai'i (2019). https://census.hawaii.gov/acs/acs-2019/
15. Dervan, P.: Increasing in-class student engagement using Socrative (an online student response system). Ireland J. Teach. Learn. High. Educ. **6** (2014)
16. Dizon, G.: Quizlet in the EFL classroom: enhancing academic vocabulary acquisition of Japanese university students. Teach. Engl. Technol. **16**, 40–56 (2016)
17. Duggan, M.: Gaming and gamers. Pew Research Center, Washington, D.C. (2015). http://www.pewinternet.org/2015/12/15/_gaming-and-gamers/

18. Ekinci, Ö., Çelik, T., Savaş, N., Toros, F.: Association between internet use and sleep problems in adolescents. Noro Psikiyatr Ars **51**, 122–128 (2014). https://doi.org/10.4274/npa.y6751

19. Gershenfeld, A.: Mind games. Sci. Am. **310**, 54–59 (2014)

20. Geisel, T.S.: Oh, The Places You'll Go. Random House, New York (1990)

21. Hawaii State Data Center. Highlights of the 2016 American Community Survey 1-year data for Hawaii. Research Economic & Analysis Division, Hawaii State Data Center (2016). https://files.hawaii.gov/dbedt/census/acs/ACS2016/ACS2016_1_Year/Other_Files/ACS_2016_Analysis_DBEDT_final.pdf

22. HIDOE Choice Boards (2021). https://sites.google.com/k12.hi.us/resources-student-parent/parents-caregivers/choice-boards. Accessed 15 Jan 2021

23. Iding, M., Vick, R., Crosby, M.E., Auernheimer, B.: Metacognition knowing about knowing in synchronous on-line chats. In: Proceedings of 8th World Conference on Computers in Education (WCCE). Document Transformation Technologies, Cape Town, South Africa (2005). [CD ROM - Document 194, 1–8]

24. Iding, M., Crosby, M.: Hawaii: a pacific crossroads for distance education. In:, Barton, S.-M., Hedberg, J., Suzuki, K. (eds.) Proceedings of Global Learn Asia Pacific 2011 International Conference, AACE, pp. 1814–1818. Association for the Advancement of Computing in Education, Chesapeake (2011)

25. Ikehara, C., Crosby, M., Silva, P.: Combining augmented cognition and gamification. In: Schmorrow, D.D., Fidopiastis, C.M. (eds.) AC 2013. LNCS, vol. 8027, pp. 676–684. Springer, Heidelberg (2013). https://doi.org/10.1007/978-3-642-39454-6_72

26. Isanders. PS3 System Software Update (v4.30): View PS vita trophies on your PS3. PlayStation.Blog (2012). https://blog.playstation.com/archive/2012/10/22/ps3-system-software-update-v4-30-view-ps-vita-trophies-on-your-ps3/

27. Kids and Tween Worlds. KZERO Worldswide. http://www.kzero.co.uk/blog/category/kidstween-worlds/

28. Lam, L.L., Wong, E.M.Y.: Stress moderates the relationship between problematic internet use by parents and problematic internet use by adolescents. J. Adolesc. Health. **56**, 300–306 (2015). https://doi.org/10.1016/j.jadohealth.2014.10.263

29. LaRose, R., Rifon, N.J., Enbody, R.: Promoting personal responsibility for internet safety. Urban Sens.: Out Woods **51**, 71–76 (2008)

30. Manzano-León, A., et al.: Between level up and game over: a systematic literature review of gamification in education. Sustainability **13**, 2247 (2021). https://doi.org/10.3390/su13042247

31. Mayer, R.E.: Multimedia learning and games. In: Tobias, S., Fletcher, J.D. (eds.) Computer Games and Instruction, pp. 281–306. Information Age Publishers, Charlotte (2011)

32. Mayer, R.E.: Computer games in education. Annu. Rev. Psychol. **70**, 531–549 (2019)

33. McGonigal, J.: Reality is Broken. Penguin Books, New York City (2011)

34. Méndez Coca, D.M., Slisko, J.: Software "Socrative" and smartphones as tools for implementation of basic processes of active physics learning in classroom: an initial feasibility study with prospective teachers. Eur. J. Phys. Educ. **4**, 17–24 (2013)

35. Murphy, C.: Why games work and the science of learning. In: Interservice, Interagency Training, Simulations, and Education Conference, pp. 260–272 (2011)

36. National educational technology standards for students 1998. International Society for Technology in Education (1998). https://www.iste.org/standards

37. National educational technology standards for students 2007. International Society for Technology in Education (2007). https://www.iste.org/standards

38. Nguyen, T.T.T.: An experimental computer literacy course: is it needed? University of Hawai'i at Mānoa, Honolulu (2008)

39. Nguyen, T.T.: Internet safety: implications for teacher education. In: Gibson, I., Weber, R., McFerrin, K., Carlsen, R., Willis, D. (eds.) 2009 Proceedings of Society for Information Technology & Teacher Education International Conference, pp. 1660–1665. Association for the Advancement of Computing in Education, Charleston (2009). http://www.editlib.org/p/30854

40. Nguyen, T.T.: Multimedia juvenile victimization: helping teachers understand youth behavior. In: Gibson, D., Dodge, B. (eds.) Proceedings of Society for Information Technology & Teacher Education International Conference 2010, p. 3174. Advancement of Computing in Education, Chesapeake (2010). http://www.editlib.org/p/33858

41. Nguyen, T.T.T., Mordecai, M.: Catching up to move forward: a computer science landscape report of Hawai'i public schools, 2017–2020, p.169. University of Hawai'i, Honolulu (2020). http://hdl.handle.net/10125/69382

42. Nguyen, T.T.T., Serna, A.K., Smith, K., Breckenridge, J., Ho, K.: Teaching during COVID in Hawai'i: the K–12 teacher experiences. Presented at Teaching, Colleges, and Community Conference, Online, USA (2021)

43. Parker, K., Horowitz, J., Igielnik, R., Oliphant, B., Brown, A.: America's complex relationship with guns. Pew Research Center, Washington, D.C. (2017). https://www.pewresearch.org/social-trends/wp-content/uploads/sites/3/2017/06/Guns-Report-FOR-WEBSITE-PDF-6-21.pdf

44. Ok, M.W., Rao, K.: Digital tools for the inclusive classroom: Google Chrome as assistive and instructional technology. J. Spec. Educ. Technol. **34**, 204–211 (2019). https://doi.org/10.1177/0162643419841546

45. Perrin, A.: 5 facts about Americans and video games. Pew Research Center, Washington, D.C. (2018). https://pewrsr.ch/2vbbMxD

46. Pew Research Center. Internet/Broadband fact sheet. Pew Research Center (2019). https://www.pewresearch.org/internet/fact-sheet/internet-broadband/

47. Prensky, M.: Digital game-based learning. Comput. Entertain. **1**, 21 (2003). https://doi.org/10.1145/950566.950596

48. Plass, J.L., Homer, B.D., Kinzer, C.K.: Foundations of game-based learning. Educ. Psychol. 258–283 (2015). https://doi.org/10.1080/00461520.2015.1122533

49. Przybylski, A., Rigby, C.S., Ryan, R.M.: A motivational model of video game engagement. Rev. Gener. Psychol. **14**, 154–166 (2010). https://doi.org/10.1037/a0019440

50. Rao, K., Meo, G.J.: Using universal design for learning to design standards-based lessons. SAGE Open **6**, 1–12 (2016). https://doi.org/10.1177/2158244016680688

51. Rao, K., Skouge, J.: Using multimedia technologies to support culturally and linguistically diverse learners and young children with disabilities. In: Heider, K.L., Renck Jalongo, M. (eds.) Young Children and Families in the Information Age. EYC, vol. 10, pp. 101–115. Springer, Dordrecht (2015). https://doi.org/10.1007/978-94-017-9184-7_6

52. Robinson, R., Rubin, Z., Márquez Segura, E., Isbister, K.: All the feels: designing a tool that reveals streamers' biometrics to spectators. In: Proceedings of the 12th International Conference on the Foundations of Digital Games (FDG 2017). ACM, New York (2017). Article 36

53. Rudolph, J.: A brief review of mentimeter – a student response system. J. Appl. Learn. Teach. **1**, 35–37 (2018)

54. Salen, K., Zimmerman, E.: Rules of Play: Game Design Fundamentals. MIT Press, Cambridge (2004)

55. Shon, H., Smith, L.: A review of poll everywhere audience response system. J. Technol. Hum. Serv. **29**(3), 236–245 (2011)

56. Student Learning Working Team. Educational Activities & COVID-19 at UH Mānoa, p. 27. University of Hawai'i at Mānoa, Honolulu (2020). https://manoa.hawaii.edu/wp/wp-content/uploads/2020/07/fall-2020-student-learning-plan.pdf

57. U.S. Census Bureau. Number and percentage of persons 3 years old and over using the Internet and percentage distribution by means of internet access from home and main reason for not having high-speed access, by selected characteristics of students and other users: 2010 (2012). https://nces.ed.gov/programs/digest/d12/tables/dt12_018.asp

58. U.S. Census Bureau. Number and percentage of persons 3 years old and over using the Internet and percentage distribution by means of internet access from home and main reason for not having high-speed access, by selected characteristics of students and other users: 2012 (2013). https://nces.ed.gov/programs/digest/d13/tables/dt13_702.10.asp

59. U.S. Census Bureau. Percentage of persons age 3 and over who use the Internet anywhere and who use the Internet at selected locations, by selected characteristics: 2011 and 2017 (2018). https://nces.ed.gov/programs/digest/d18/tables/dt18_702.30.asp

60. U.S. Census Bureau. Estimates of resident population, by age group: 1970 through 2019 (2019). https://nces.ed.gov/programs/digest/d19/tables/dt19_101.10.asp

61. U.S. Census Bureau. Number and percentage of households with computer and internet access, by state: 2018 (2019). https://nces.ed.gov/programs/digest/d19/tables/dt19_702.60.asp

62. U.S. Census Bureau. QuickFacts: Hawaii (2020). https://www.census.gov/quickfacts/HI

63. U.S. Department of Education, National Center for Education Statistics. Common Core of Data (CCD). Private School Universe Survey (PSS), 2017–18. Public Elementary/Secondary School Universe Survey, 2017–18 v.1a. State Nonfiscal Public Elementary/Secondary Education Survey, 2017–18 v.1a (2018)

64. Universal Design for Learning Guidelines version 2.2. https://udlguidelines.cast.org/

65. Vande, D.: Folding@home. Distributed computing (2010). http://pinus.ptkpt.net/_lain.php?_lain=8630

66. Vallely, K., Gibson, P.: Engaging students on their devices with Mentimeter. Compass: J. Learn. Teach. **11** (2018)

67. Vick, R.M., Crosby, M.E., Ashworth, D.E.: Japanese and American students meet on the web: collaborative language learning through everyday dialogue with peers. Comput. Assist. Lang. Learn. **13**, 199–219 (2000). https://doi.org/10.1076/0958-8221(200007)13:3;1-3;FT199

68. Wang, A.I., Tahir, R.: The effect of using Kahoot! for learning – a literature review. Comput. Educ. **149**, 103818 (2020). https://doi.org/10.1016/j.compedu.2020.103818

69. Wouters, P., van Nimwegen, C., van Oostendorp, H., van der Spek, E.D.: A meta-analysis of the cognitive and motivational effects of serious games. J. Educ. Psychol. **105**, 249–265 (2013). https://doi.org/10.1037/a0031311

70. Ybarra, M.L., Mitchell, K.J., Finkelhor, D., Wolak, J.: Internet prevention messages: targeting the right online behaviors. Arch. Pediatr. Adolesc. Med. **161**, 138–145 (2007)

71. Yee, N.: Motivations for play in online games. J. CyberPsychol. Behav. **9**, 772–775 (2006). https://doi.org/10.1089/cpb.2006.9.772

Collaborative Game: Using Explicit Biofeedback to Enhance Empathy Loop

Fang Fang and Jie Wu[✉]

College of Design and Innovation, Tongji University, Fu Xin Road, Shanghai 200092, China
cpacol@psu.edu.ph

Abstract. This article discusses an interactive system that strengthens emotional cycles through collaborative interaction mechanisms and explicit biofeedback. The study collected data using the Muse device and utilized Mind Monitor software for transmission and recording of EEG data, along with Python-based programming software for crafting the interactive device. It explores whether explicit biofeedback can enhance empathy in a multi-user system within a collaborative environment. Employing a design science research methodology and analyzing reactions from 10 participants, the study confirms the correlation between EEG information and emotional experience, offering new perspectives on multi-person emotional communication.

Keywords: Collaborative Game · Explicit Biofeedback · Empathy Loop · Biological Data · EEG

1 Introduction

Explicit biofeedback effectively conveys an individual's physiological data, allowing participants to exert direct and conscious control. Physiological data are categorized into two types: indirect control, such as EEG, heart rate, and GSR, which are not entirely controllable, and direct control, such as breathing and facial expressions, which users can fully control [1]. EEG is a non-invasive method for monitoring brain activity through electrodes placed on the scalp, recording spontaneous electrical activity over a period. Commercial EEG devices commonly used in interactive experiments include Muse, Emotiv, and NeuroSky [2].

Emotions, rooted in biological action tendencies, play a crucial role in determining behavior [3]. Most theorists agree that emotions comprise three components: subjective experience (e.g., feeling happy), expressive behavior (e.g., smiling), and physiological arousal (e.g., sympathetic nervous system activation) [4]. Physiological signals can be effectively used in automatic human emotion recognition systems [5]. Thus, by gathering and processing relevant physiological signal data from participants through various measurement methods and feeding this information into a system loop, it's possible to enhance the emotional experience of interactive systems, aiding in emotional self-recognition and facilitating communication among multiple participants [6].

D. D. Schmorrow and C. M. Fidopiastis (Eds.): HCII 2024, LNAI 14695, pp. 142–151, 2024.
https://doi.org/10.1007/978-3-031-61572-6_10

In the current field of human-computer interaction, numerous studies and practices have applied biofeedback technology to solo experiential works to enhance emotional experiences and understanding of the work's theme. However, the use of biofeedback technology to increase empathy among participants in multi-person collaborative systems remains relatively rare.

This paper designs an interactive device that delves into the role of explicit biofeedback in the emotional connection between experiencers and the system through collaborative interaction mechanisms. By sharing physiological data (such as EEG) among participants, the study promotes mutual understanding and emotional resonance, deepening the perception and empathy towards others' emotional states. This not only offers a new perspective for innovative interactive design but also opens new avenues for exploring interpersonal relationships and emotional communication.

2   Materials and Methods

The Mind Monitor software was employed to record EEG data, complemented by a device interaction designed with Python-based programming software. The research was developed through Design Science Research (DSR) [7], a methodology legitimizing the creation of artifacts as a means to generate technological knowledge, particularly after identifying gaps in the audio-visual system's technical and scientific production. DSR's critical element involves understanding the external and internal environment surrounding the artifact to be created [8]. Recent findings show a lack of models, methods, or structures mentioned in human-computer interaction or media studies to support multi-person emotional communication in collaborative systems through biofeedback and direct or indirect control. The method's phases include problem identification, objective determination, design and development, demonstration, evaluation, and conclusion.

Dominant Color

Fig. 1. "NeuroBrush" enhances interaction and competition among players with real-time shared drawing processes and dynamic background color changes.

In the literature, the use of EEG for emotional recognition research has proven effective, achieving a 86.97% accuracy rate through data fusion with fuzzy integration. Researchers also explored how displaying biofeedback affects the user experience in multiplayer interaction systems. "Bacteria Hunt," a multiplayer EEG-based game, utilizes alpha waves and SSVEP for scoring points by controlling bacteria, examining the impact of relaxation and attention-driven brainwave bands in competitive environments, underscoring collective participation and experiential value [9]. "BrainBall" allows players to control a ball race using EEG and EMG [10], while "NeuroBrush," a web application (see Fig. 1), facilitates competitive post-modern art creation through BCI, enhancing interaction and competition among players with real-time shared drawing processes and dynamic background color changes, highlighting social collaboration and creative experience [11].

3   Goal Setting and Experiment Development

This study investigates if explicit biofeedback in a collaborative setting can enhance empathy within a multi-user system. Key features of the experiment include:

1. A dual-user wearable device for simultaneous experience.
2. Capturing participants' EEG waves.
3. Employing existing software for real-time, aesthetic data visualization.
4. Data storage for future analysis.
5. Collecting user feedback through surveys and interviews.

We detail the system's design, implementation, and testing processes, along with insights and conclusions.

The hardware utilized is the Muse headband for EEG. Data transmission involves WiFi LAN and OSC communication via Mind Monitor software, with data processing on a website developed using the Google Charts API, and interaction and visualization through touch designer software based on Python (see Fig. 2).

Muse is an advanced commercial EEG device designed for real-time brain activity feedback via wireless Bluetooth, enhancing focus and relaxation through meditation practices [12]. It features multiple reading channels primarily located in the frontal areas, like the FP1 and FP2 positions, and uses specific ear clips as reference points for accuracy and stability [13]. High sampling rates capture EEG data, which are then filtered by built-in algorithms for real-time feedback and converted into an easily understandable format. Data, stored in Excel format via Mind Monitor software to Dropbox, facilitates further analysis, including EEG readings, event markers, and other physiological indicators [14].

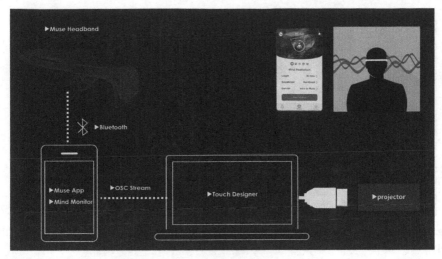

Fig. 2. Software and hardware of the system.

4   Experiment Description

Against the backdrop mentioned, we designed a multi-person, multimodal biometric data collaborative interaction system. Following the DSR method, 10 users were tested, comprising five males and five females, within the media lab at Tongji University. To mitigate external experimental influences, a pre-experiment survey based on the Likert scale was conducted [15], gathering data on emotions, physical condition, sleep levels, hunger, caffeine intake, and prescription medication usage to identify potential noise and variances in EEG data.

The interaction and feedback process involved two participants, "the questioner" and "the respondent", both equipped with EEG devices, headphones, and cameras, without direct interaction (see Fig. 3). The questioner's interface displayed the respondent's facial expressions, an emotion-triggering question selector, EEG visual effects, and guidelines, while the respondent saw the questioner's image and their EEG graphics. EEG visualizations showcased alpha (blue spheres), beta (purple pentagons), and theta (yellow triangles) waves, with sounds from the International Affective Digitized Sounds (IADS) library inducing emotions [16].

Fig. 3. The interaction and feedback process involved two participants, "the questioner" and "the respondent".

When the questioner clicks a question on the screen, the respondent hears the question and ambient sounds, eliciting an emotional response. For example, the "turtle" question triggers a calm emotion, indicated by the enlargement of a blue sphere representing calm emotions (α waves), showing the respondent's pleasure. Excessive tension triggers an auditory alarm. Ten triggering questions are divided into five positive and five negative emotional questions (see Fig. 4).

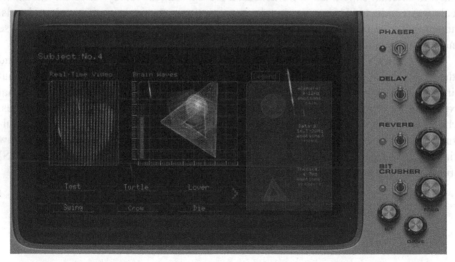

Fig. 4. The system's interface, including brainwave visualization, the other person's facial data, and questions to stimulate emotions.

After a 20-min experience, a post-experience survey with five questions based on the Social Presence Scale theory assesses emotional fluctuations, perception of others' emotions, the impact of others' behaviors, and emotional interaction [17]. Participants rate their experience on a Likert scale from "strongly disagree" to "strongly agree".

5   Analysis of Experimental Results

During the experience process, when the questioner selects the "death" option, the respondent hears unsettling sounds and sees frightening scenes on the screen. The combination of scenes and sounds can somewhat affect the viewer, causing short-term emotional fluctuations. These can be identified by reading specific EEG data bands. For example, in the frontal lobe areas represented by the A73 and AF8 electrodes, an increase in beta waves, indicating a significant amount of scare-related information processing accompanied by fear and anxiety, is noticeable (see Fig. 5). Additionally, larger peaks of alpha waves, associated with relaxation, suggest a reduced level of relaxation after being scared (see Fig. 6).

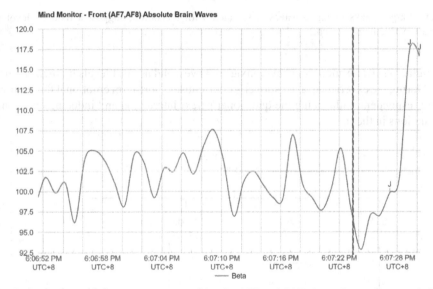

Fig. 5. In the frontal lobe areas represented by the A73 and AF8 electrodes, an increase in beta waves, indicating a significant amount of scare-related information processing accompanied by fear and anxiety, is noticeable.

Emotional stimuli result from cognitive mechanisms processing sensory input. When an event occurs, this mechanism processes the stimulus and generates emotional stimuli for each affected emotion [18] (see Fig. 7). The Valence-Arousal model explains this [19], where valence represents the positive or negative nature of emotions, and arousal describes the level of emotional stimulation (see Fig. 8). Assessing emotional experience requires analyzing emotional valence (positive and negative) and arousal levels (intensity) related to stimuli (images, sounds, etc.). This study measures emotional levels

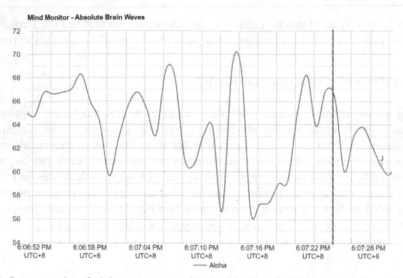

Fig. 6. Larger peaks of alpha waves, associated with relaxation, suggest a reduced level of relaxation after being scared.

through alpha (relaxation) and beta (anxiety) waves, and arousal levels by their intensities. During the experience, a questioner's click causes short-term emotional fluctuations in the respondent, influencing the questioner's next interaction and inducing emotional fluctuations in them.

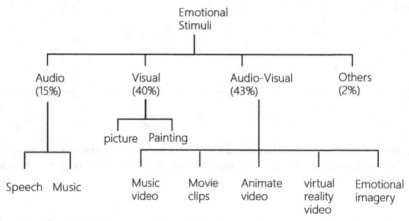

Fig. 7. Emotional stimuli result from cognitive mechanisms processing sensory input. When an event occurs, this mechanism processes the stimulus and generates emotional stimuli for each affected emotion.

At a specific moment, it was observed that a few seconds after the questioner clicked, the respondent's emotional data showed significant changes. Subsequently, after some time, the questioner also exhibited similar emotional fluctuations (see Fig. 9). This

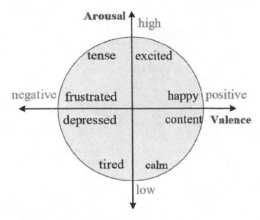

Fig. 8. The Valence-Arousal model explains this, where valence represents the positive or negative nature of emotions, and arousal describes the level of emotional stimulation.

sequence of emotional responses suggests complex information processing and emotional interaction are taking place. Specifically, it indicates that in an interactive environment, one participant's actions may initially trigger an emotional response in another, leading to their own emotional change (see Fig. 10). This pattern of alternating fluctuations reflects the dynamics and interdependence of emotional interaction from a macro perspective.

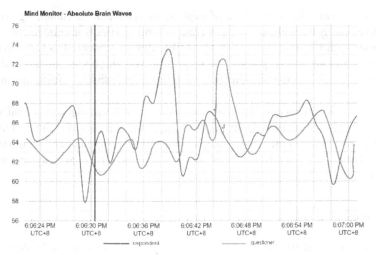

Fig. 9. After the interaction point, it was observed that a few seconds after the questioner clicked, the respondent's emotional data showed significant changes. Subsequently, after some time, the questioner also exhibited similar emotional fluctuations.

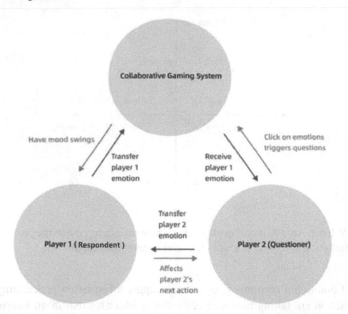

Fig. 10. One participant's actions may initially trigger an emotional response in another, leading to their own emotional change.

6 Conclusion

This study explores the application of explicit biofeedback in enhancing emotional cycles and empathy through designing and implementing a multi-user interactive system. Experiments with 10 participants using Muse EEG devices collected and analyzed brainwave data and emotional responses, showing improved emotional communication and understanding, highlighting the potential of explicit biofeedback in fostering emotional resonance.

Despite insightful results, limitations include a small sample size, signal stability issues of Muse devices under certain conditions, and the complexity of interpreting EEG data. Future research requires larger samples, improved equipment and algorithms, and more detailed emotion and biofeedback analysis methods to enhance system accuracy and user experience.

References

1. Rosenboom, D.: Biofeedback and the arts: Results of early experiments. J. Aesthetics Art Criticism **35**(3) (1977)
2. Mourão, A., Magalhães, J.: Competitive affective gaming: winning with a smile. In: Proceedings of the 21st ACM International Conference on Multimedia (2013)
3. Kamiya, J.: Conditioned discrimination of the EEG alpha rhythm in humans. Western Psychological Association, San Francisco (1962)
4. Vidal, J.J.: Toward direct brain-computer communication. Annu. Rev. Biophys. Bioeng. **2**(1), 157–180 (1973)

 5. Sra, M., Xu, X., Maes, P.: BreathVR: leveraging breathing as a directly controlled interface for virtual reality games. In: Proceedings of the Proceedings of the 2018 CHI Conference on Human Factors in Computing Systems (2018)
 6. Crawford, C., Cioli, N., Holloman, A.: NeuroBrush: a competitive, artistic multi modal BCI application. In: Proceedings of the CHI: Artistic BCI Workshop (2018)
 7. Kim, D., Kim, H.: Biosensor interface: interactive media art using biometric data. Int. J. Bio-Sci. Bio-Technol. **6**(1), 129–136 (2014)
 8. Krol, L., Andreessen, L., Podgorska, A., et al.: Passive brain computer interfacing in the museum of stillness. In: Proceedings of the Artistic BCI Workshop at the SIGCHI Conference on Human Factors in Computing Systems (CHI), 2018,
 9. Schöffern, N., Habasque, G.: Éditions du Griffon (1963)
10. Cornock, S., Edmonds, E.: The creative process where the artist is amplified or superseded by the computer. Leonardo **6**(1), 11–16 (1973)
11. Edmonds, E.: The man—computer interface: a note on concepts and design. Int. J. Man-Mach. Stud. **16**(3), 231–236 (1982)
12. Chen, W., Shidujaman, M., Jin, J., Ahmed, S.U.: A methodological approach to create interactive art in artificial intelligence. In: Stephanidis, C., et al. (eds.) HCII 2020. LNCS, vol. 12425, pp. 13–31. Springer, Cham (2020). https://doi.org/10.1007/978-3-030-60128-7_2
13. Kluszczynski, R.: Strategies of interactive art. J. Aesthetics Cult. **2**(1), 5525 (2010)
14. Kuikkaniemi, K., Laitinen, T., Turpeinen, M., et al.: The influence of implicit and explicit biofeedback in first-person shooter games. In: Proceedings of the SIGCHI Conference on Human Factors in Computing Systems (2010)
15. Nacke, L.E., Kalyn, M., Lough, C., et al.: Biofeedback game design: using direct and indirect physiological control to enhance game interaction. In: Proceedings of the SIGCHI Conference on Human Factors in Computing Systems, pp. 103–112. Association for Computing Machinery, Vancouver (2011)
16. Wadeson, A., Nijholt, A., Nam, C.S.: Artistic brain-computer interfaces: state-of-the-art control mechanisms. Brain-Comput. Interfaces **2**(2–3), 70–75 (2015)
17. Kim, J., André, E.: Four-channel biosignal analysis and feature extraction for automatic emotion recognition. In: Fred, A., Filipe, J., Gamboa, H. (eds.) BIOSTEC 2008. CCIS, vol. 25, pp. 265–277. Springer, Heidelberg (2008). https://doi.org/10.1007/978-3-540-92219-3_20
18. Ravaja, N., Saari, T., Salminen, M., et al.: Phasic emotional reactions to video game events: a psychophysiological investigation. Media Psychol. **8**(4), 343–367 (2006)
19. Gonsalve, S., Tin, A.: Empathy and interactivity. Comput. Entertain. **8**(1), 1–14 (2010)

Reflection of Individual Differences on Emotion Map for Kansei Evaluation of Packaging Design with Physiological Indexes

Naoya Kumagai, Yuri Nakagawa, Chen Feng, and Midori Sugaya[✉]

Shibaura Institute of Technology, 3-7-5 Toyosu, Koto-ku, Tokyo 135-8548, Japan
{ma23074,nb23112,feng.chen.i9,doly}@shibaura-it.ac.jp

Abstract. Kansei evaluation is a method that quantitatively assesses human sensibilities and emotions using numerical values. It enhances the temporal efficiency of product exterior design decisions and other applications by objectively evaluating human sensibilities and emotions. Using sensory evaluation methods with physiological indexes quantitatively captures individuals' unconscious reactions, reducing the influence of subjective biases. A method has been proposed to compare and evaluate such assessments corresponding to Arousal-Valence space (A-V space), which is known as the Emotion Map. This method, capable of displaying human sensory values on a two-dimensional coordinate system, is effective for intuitively discussing the impact of stimuli on sensibilities based on their positions. However, a challenge in creating the Emotion Map lies in the significant individual differences in physiological reactions due to bodily characteristics. Therefore, to address this challenge, it is desirable to normalize or standardize all values before mapping them onto the coordinates. However, it is not thoroughly discussed which of these methods is most suitable for evaluation in the Emotion Map. Hence, this study aims to compare and examine these methods, wherein actual emotional responses of individuals when viewing product packages are acquired through physiological indexes, normalized and standardized using appropriate methods, and evaluated in the Emotion Map. Furthermore, comparisons will be made with the results of the Self-Assessment Manikin (SAM) method to discuss which normalization method is most appropriate.

Keywords: Emotion · EEG · HRV · Packaging design

1 Introduction

Kansei evaluation plays an important role in both design and industry [1]. Specifically, in the exterior design of products, it quantifies people's sensibilities and emotions. Then, based on the quantified values, consideration is given to new designs. In this way, the efficiency of design consideration can be achieved. Additionally, by providing more attractive products, it contributes to the industry.

Traditionally, Kansei evaluation of products has relied mainly on self-reported methods such as surveys and interviews [2]. These methods are effective means of quantitatively capturing individuals' sensibilities and emotions towards products. However, there

© The Author(s), under exclusive license to Springer Nature Switzerland AG 2024
D. D. Schmorrow and C. M. Fidopiastis (Eds.): HCII 2024, LNAI 14695, pp. 152–165, 2024.
https://doi.org/10.1007/978-3-031-61572-6_11

are several challenges. For example, there are issues such as the social desirability bias, where individuals may excessively express or suppress their responses to specific products due to factors like expectations from others. Additionally, there are issues related to self-awareness of responses. Specifically, there are concerns about the evaluation of scale items, such as in surveys. Evaluating scale items requires a large amount of cognitive processing, and there is a risk that participants may become aware of their emotions, hindering the true unconscious measurement of sensibilities and emotions [3].

On the other hand, there is an evaluation method that does not rely on self-reporting, which utilizes physiological indexes. The use of physiological indexes for evaluation is a method that can address some of the challenges associated with self-reporting [4]. In evaluations using physiological indexes, metrics such as heart rate variability and brainwave activity are employed to assess the emotional states of experimental participants. With this approach, participants do not need to consciously report on their emotions. In other words, it is possible to evaluate emotions based on bodily responses independently of the emotions that participants consciously experience. As a result, compared to methods relying on self-reporting, biases can be minimized, and results can be obtained from individuals' unconscious responses.

2 Related Work

In the field of Kansei, there has been discussion regarding the emotional responses evoked by product design [5]. Emotional responses are considered important in the field of purchasing. To evaluate emotional responses evoked by product design, some methods using physiological indexes have been proposed [5]. Among them, a method has been proposed to visualize emotions on a 2D coordinate system that is easily interpretable by individuals, using Russell's circumplex model [6] to represent emotional responses [7]. This method is called the "Emotion Map." The Emotion Map is a technique for measuring emotional responses by positioning physiological indicator values based on Russell's circumplex model commonly used in psychology. Russell's circumplex model [5] applies arousal to the vertical axis and valence to the horizontal axis, enabling the expression of basic emotions on two axes (A-V space). Due to its fundamental scales on two axes, it is used in various fields [8]. The physiological indexes used in the Emotion Map are EEG and HRV. Brainwave indexes collected from EEG are plotted on the arousal axis, while indexes related to parasympathetic nervous activity collected from HRV are plotted on the valence axis. From the coordinates plotted on the A-V space, emotions in response to stimuli can be visualized in an understandable manner. Hereafter, in this study, the method of plotting physiological indexes on the A-V space and evaluating emotional responses will be referred to as the "Emotion Map."

The Emotion Map methodology has the advantage of being able to be conducted in various experimental environments due to the predominant use of inexpensive and simple EEG and pulse wave meters (or heart rate monitors). From such ease of use, many attempts have been made. For example, evaluations of emotions in car interiors [7] and emotion assessments of elderly individuals for whom self-reporting is difficult [9] have been conducted. Thus, methods using inexpensive EEG and HRV can be conducted in various experimental environments. It is anticipated that they will be useful for measuring emotional reactions to product design as they can be implemented with minimal burden on participants. Therefore, the Emotion Map, which can display human sensibility values on a two-dimensional coordinate system, is effective for intuitively discussing the impact of stimuli on sensibilities based on their positions. However, a challenge in creating the Emotion Map lies in the significant individual differences in physiological reactions due to bodily characteristics. Therefore, it is desirable to normalize or standardize all values before mapping them onto the coordinates to address this challenge. However, it is not thoroughly discussed which of these methods is most suitable for evaluation in the Emotion Map.

3 Methods

To address this challenge, this study aims to compare and evaluate normalization or standardization methods for the acquired physiological measurements. In achieving this goal, emotional responses of individuals when viewing product packages are acquired through physiological indexes, and the indexes are normalized or standardized, followed by evaluation using the Emotion Map. Furthermore, comparisons will be made with the results of the Self-Assessment Manikin (SAM) method to discuss which normalization method is most appropriate.

In this section, we first describe the two physiological indexes used in the Emotion Map visualization of the A-V space, namely, heart rate variability index and brainwave index, in Sects. 3.1 and 3.2. Next, in Sect. 3.3, we discuss the visualization method of the Emotion Map. Finally, in Sect. 3.4, we address the normalization and standardization methods for the data.

3.1 HRV Index

Heart Rate Variability (HRV) is an index that measures the degree of variation in consecutive heartbeats and is associated with the activity of the Autonomic Nervous System (ANS) [10]. The autonomic nervous system controls the body's involuntary functions and adjusts to both external circumstances and internal states. The autonomic nervous system is broadly classified into the parasympathetic nervous system and the sympathetic nervous system. One classification of the ANS, the parasympathetic nervous system, induces relaxation and promotes digestion and rest when activated. Therefore, in this study, we use pNN50 [10] to represent the X-axis (Valence axis) on the Emotion Map. A higher value of pNN50 indicates a more dominant parasympathetic nervous system activity. In this study, a higher pNN50 value is interpreted as a higher Valence value (a relaxed state). The details of pNN50 are shown in Table 1.

Table 1. HRV indexes and related psychological states [10]

Parameter	Description	Related
pNN50[%]	Percentage of successive RR intervals that differ by more than 50 ms	Parasympathetic nerves

3.2 EEG Index

EEG index is a metric used to analyze brainwave activity. Among these indexes, the ratio of alpha waves to beta waves (β/α) is commonly used to represent aspects such as thought and concentration. Therefore, in this study, we utilize β/α waves as the Y-axis (Arousal axis) of the Emotion Map. Specifically, in this study, we use Low β waves and Low α waves obtained from the EEG device described later [12] as the Arousal axis. A higher value of Lowβ/Lowα indicates a higher proportion of beta waves compared to alpha waves, indicating increased arousal. The frequency bands of brainwave indexes used in the Emotion Map of this study and their corresponding psychological states are shown in Table 2.

Table 2. Frequency bands of EEG indexes and psychological states [11, 12]

EEG Index	Frequency Band (Hz)	Related mental states
Lowα	8–9	Relaxed but not drowsy, calm, eyes closed
Lowβ	13–17	Relaxed yet focused, integrated

We'll use these indexes to work with the Emotion Map. Then, we'll discuss how to create the Emotion Map.

3.3 Visualization Steps for Emotion Map

To apply the visualization of emotional responses using physiological indexes to product evaluation, the Emotion Map in this study considered the following aspects:

- Reflection of appropriate trends in emotional responses

There are few precedents for applying the visualization of emotional responses using physiological indexes to product evaluation. Therefore, there is a possibility of significant differences between the results obtained from physiological indexes and those from surveys. For example, stimuli that yield High Arousal, High Valence (HAHV) results in surveys may result in Low Arousal, Low Valence (LALV) according to physiological indexes. In this study, the main objective is to understand the trends of the Emotion Map coordinates that are expected to address these points.

- Improvement of Applicability to Classifiers

To understand the trends in emotional responses, we aimed to standardize the scale and range of the data, enhancing their applicability for future analyses, including classifiers.

In this study, the Emotion Map was created through the following steps: verifying the data and removing any data that may not have been accurately measured during the experiment.

1. Extraction of visualization intervals:

   • Extraction of evaluation target intervals
   • Extract the necessary intervals for analysis from all experimental data.
   • Extraction of reference intervals (baseline resting intervals)
   • Establish baseline resting intervals to confirm emotional displacements.

2. Calculation of representative values in evaluation intervals and resting intervals:

Lowβ/Lowα, EEG index, calculates the average value within the evaluation interval as the representative value. The brainwave indicator Lowβ/Lowα may produce extremely large values when the ratio of α waves is small. Therefore, clipping of outliers was performed for brainwave indexes.

We applied the IQR method to clip outliers within all experiment participants. The IQR method sets the upper and lower limits for data as 1.5 times the interquartile range, serving as an outlier detection technique. Data detected beyond these limits are not removed but set as the maximum or minimum value. The advantage of the IQR method is its applicability to non-parametric data, without the need for normality [13]. The reason for clipping outliers instead of removing them is to maintain the total amount of data and minimize the loss of information related to the magnitude of values.

The heart rate variability index pNN50 is calculated based on the values of the previous 30 s at a given time point; therefore, the representative value is calculated from the data 30 s after the start of the evaluation interval.

3. Calculation of evaluation interval - resting interval:

In calculating the coordinates in the Emotion Map, after computing the representative values for the evaluation and rest periods as described in 2., the difference between each evaluation period and the rest period is calculated. This difference represents the change in emotional response from rest to activity, treated as coordinates in the A-V space. This allows for individual consideration of changes from rest for each person.

4. Implementation of normalization processing:

Normalize the coordinates calculated in step 3."

3.4 Normalization Methods

The normalization of data is important for two reasons:

1. **Consideration of individual differences:** Physiological indicators exhibit significant individual variability, necessitating consideration of these differences.

2. **Improved handling of indicators with different units:** Data normalization is a preprocessing technique that involves scaling or transforming data to ensure that each feature with different units has equal influence [14]. For example, extreme outliers may exist in the brainwave indicators of Arousal, potentially biasing evaluations towards these values. Therefore, it is advisable to avoid such cases whenever possible.

In the next sections, we will discuss the normalization methods to be applied to the coordinates of the Emotion Map for comparative analysis.

1. Non-Normalization

Without performing normalization of coordinates conducted in Step 4 of Sect. 3.1, we directly utilize the physiological indicator values calculated in Step 4 of Sect. 3.1. While calculating the difference from the baseline for the values can be interpreted as normalization itself, this section focuses on normalization methods for coordinates in the A-V space and does not address the issue of that interpretation.

2. Min-Max Normalization

Min-Max Normalization is a method that typically converts the values of features into a range from 0 to 1 [14]. In this study, as information regarding positive and negative values from the baseline is crucial, scaling was conducted with a maximum value of 1 and a minimum value of -1. The calculation method is shown in Eq. (1). Min-Max Normalization is susceptible to outliers because it is heavily influenced by the maximum and minimum values. Therefore, in this study, outlier detection, as described in Sect. 3.2, is conducted.

$$x' = \frac{x - x_{min}}{x_{max} - x_{min}} \tag{1}$$

1. Z-Score (Standardization)

Z-Score allows data to be represented in terms of the number of standard deviations from the mean, independent of the original data units [14]. The calculation method is shown in Eq. (2). Scaling is performed so that the data has a mean (μ) of 0 and a standard deviation (σ) of 1. This enables easy comparison of distributions from different datasets by assuming that the data follows a normal distribution.

$$x' = \frac{x - \mu}{\sigma} \tag{2}$$

2. Robust Z-score

Z-Score standardizes data points using the mean and standard deviation, but these statistics are susceptible to the influence of outliers. Therefore, when the data distribution deviates significantly from a normal distribution, it may lead to incorrect results. The Robust Z-Score addresses this issue by standardizing data points using robust statistics less affected by outliers, such as the median and interquartile range (IQR) [15]. The calculation method is shown in Eq. (3)

$$x' = \frac{x - median(x)}{IQR} \tag{3}$$

4 Experiment

4.1 Experiment Overview

To quantify emotional responses when people view products, we conducted an experiment comparing images with altered elements of package design. The participants included 30 men and women aged 20–30. One participant who potentially did not accurately measure brainwave indicators was excluded, leaving data from 29 participants. The images used were product package images from S&B Foods INC. The package images used are shown in Fig. 1. During the experiment, images with specific elements such as color or shape were displayed. Multiple images consisting of the same comparison elements were defined as image groups, and the order between image groups was fixed. To prevent order effects, the display order of images within each image group was randomized. This paper only addresses the comparison results of package images with varied background colors.

Package images were used to compare images with different elements of package design to quantify emotional responses when viewing products. The reactions to each package image were evaluated, using physiological indicators of brainwaves (EEG) and heart rate variability (HRV) as evaluation metrics. In the experimental setup, participants viewed the display screen while wearing EEG sensors [12] and pulse sensors [16].

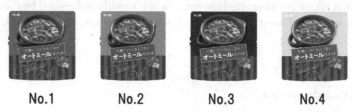

No.1   No.2   No.3   No.4

Fig. 1. Packaging design with different background colors (Color figure online)

4.2 Experimental Procedure

The experimental procedure is depicted in Fig. 2. Initially, a questionnaire survey regarding the experimenter's information is conducted before attaching the experimental apparatus. Subsequently, the EEG and PPG sensors are affixed, as illustrated in Fig. 3. Following the experiment's commencement, there is a 1-min rest period (extended to 2 min only for the initial session), followed by image presentation and the SAM questionnaire. This sequence is then repeated for the images of the packages being compared. Out of the 20 images compared in this study, 4 are selected for discussion.

SAM (Self-Assessment Manikin) is a visual scale utilized for emotional evaluation, measuring subjective emotional experiences [17]. It assesses two dimensions: Arousal and Valence. Valence measures the range from happiness to unpleasantness, while Arousal evaluates levels from calmness to excitement.

Fig. 2. Experimental procedure

Fig. 3. Experimental scene

5 Results

5.1 Comparison Evaluation Results of Physiological Indexes

First, we conducted inter-image comparisons of the effects of package images used in the experiment on physiological indicators using baseline-corrected averages. The baseline-corrected average refers to the mean value obtained by subtracting the baseline value from the measured data. This allows for evaluating the variability of the data as relative changes from the baseline. In this study, the baseline for each individual was calculated as the average value of the final 30-s interval of the initial resting period, considered emotionally "neutral".

We conducted stimulus-by-stimulus comparisons using the baseline-corrected average of the initial resting period, presumed to be emotionally "neutral," for the brainwave indicator Lowβ/Lowα (Fig. 4). A repeated measures ANOVA revealed no significant differences.

We also conducted stimulus-by-stimulus comparisons for the heart rate variability index pNN50 using the baseline-corrected average (Fig. 5). A repeated measures ANOVA revealed no significant differences.

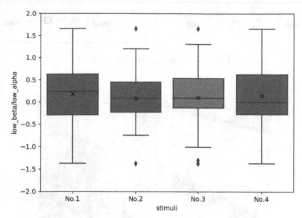

Fig. 4. Comparison between stimuli based on the baseline-corrected average of EEG index Lowβ/Lowα across all participants.

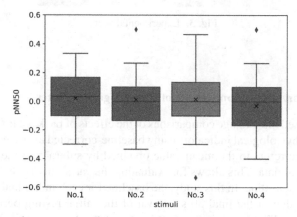

Fig. 5. Comparison between stimuli based on the baseline-corrected average of HRV index pNN50 across all participants.

The lack of significant differences in both EEG and HRV indexes could be attributed to the significant individual differences in physiological indicators among the participants. Additionally, it may be possible that the emotional responses elicited by the stimulus images used in this experiment were minimal.

5.2 Comparison Results of Normalization Methods for Evaluation Using Emotion Map

To assess individual emotional responses among participants, we visualized and compared emotional responses using an Emotion Map.

Figure 6 shows (a) Non-normalization, (b) Min-Max, (c) Z-Score, and (d) Robust Z-Score from the top left. The scale is set to [−3, 3], except for the pNN50 plot in Non-normalization (a) and the Min-Max method (b).

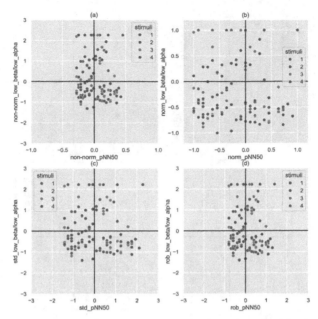

Fig. 6. Comparison of normalization methods for evaluations plotted in Emotion Map by physiological indexes. From left to right: (a) Non-normalization, (b) Min-Max, (c) Z-Score, (d) Robust Z-Score.

Referring to the graph of Non-normalization (a), a bias in the plot is observed around $Y = 2.3$ on the Arousal axis (Y-axis), which is presumed to be the maximum value clipped by the IQR method.

Looking at the graph with Min-Max applied (b), scaling is adjusted to match the clipped maximum value in (a). Min-Max scales based on the maximum and minimum values, making it susceptible to the influence of outliers. Performing outlier clipping can mitigate quadrant shifts from (a).

Examining the graph with Z-Score standardization applied (c), it can be observed that the scales on the x-axis and y-axis are aligned, and the distribution has spread.

Observing the graph with Robust Z-Score applied (d), the scale varies significantly between the brainwave and heart rate variability indices, suggesting its effectiveness when the influence on the coordinates differs drastically.

Next, we will use the averaged values, which exclude individual differences, to confirm the overall trends among all experiment participants. We calculated the average values for all experiment participants using the values after normalization processing applied to individual results.

We conducted a comparison of graphs scaled using three different methods of physiological indices for the average of all experiment participants. In contrast to the previous Fig. 7, where the maximum and minimum absolute values were used, here all units have been standardized to the same value (0.5).

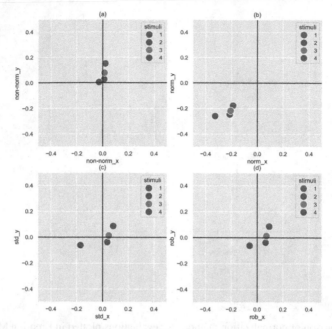

Fig. 7. Comparison of normalization methods for evaluations plotted in Emotion Map by physiological indexes using the average of all participants. From the top left: (a) Non-normalization, (b) Min-Max, (c) Z-Score, (d) Robust Z-Score.

Looking at Fig. 7, we noticed slight variations in the quadrants where the averages of each image are positioned depending on the normalization method used. Overall, there was a tendency for No.4 (yellow) to be closer to Low Arousal, Low Valence (LALV), while No.1 (red) tended to plot closer to High Arousal, High Valence (HAHV).

Examining Fig. 7(a), representing HAHV physiological indicators, the x-axis (Valence) appears compressed, indicating the use of different units for brainwave and heart rate variability indicators.

In Fig. 7(b) with Min-Max, we observed that all averages clustered towards the LALV quadrant, suggesting susceptibility to outlier influence due to the calculation based on maximum and minimum values.

Next, examining the standardization using z-score and robust z-score, depicted in Fig. 7(c) and (d), respectively, it is evident that the distributions are similar in both the X-axis (Arousal axis) and Y-axis (Valence axis). Additionally, there were no noticeable differences observed in the positions of the quadrants for each image between (c) and (d).

Based on this observation, we opt for methods aligned with the objectives of this study. As a general trend in the experiment, techniques such as Z-Score and Robust Z-score, which maintain information about the positions of Arousal and Valence while aligning the units between Arousal and Valence, are deemed appropriate.

5.3 Comparison Results of SAM

Next, the average of SAM (Self-Assessment Manikin) emotional evaluations for all experiment participants was calculated. In Fig. 8, it was noticed that the image with a pink background (No.2) fell into the LALV quadrant, while the other images fell into the HAHV quadrant. When comparing this to the average results of the physiological indices shown in Fig. 7, it was observed that while the image with yellow background (No.4, indicated by purple in the graph) leaned towards LALV in the physiological indices' results, the image with a pink background (No.2, indicated by blue in the graph) leaned towards LALV in the SAM results. The graphs illustrating this trend in the physiological indices (Fig. 7) were those standardized using Z-score (Fig. 7(c)) and Robust Z-score (Fig. 7(d)). Moreover, in the SAM results (Fig. 8), although Image No. 2 appeared to have a lower Valence, its position was closer to a neutral rating of 5. The graph representing this trend in the physiological indices was the one standardized by Robust Z-score (Fig. 7(d)).

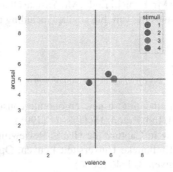

Fig. 8. Self-reported evaluation on the A-V space using the average SAM values of all participants

Therefore, in terms of evaluation on the Emotion Map, Robust Z-score is considered most appropriate for assessing emotional responses. Following closely, Z-score is also deemed suitable. Standardizing using Z-score may facilitate easier comparisons in the future with subjective evaluations and other metrics.

5.4 Discussion

When normalizing data on the Emotion Map, caution is required in handling the results as there is a risk of altering quadrant positions and the positional relationships between images. It is crucial to choose an appropriate data processing method based on the intended use.

Furthermore, discrepancies between physiological and self-reported emotional evaluations were observed in some images. This suggests that the psychological effects of color may have influenced the results of physiological indicators. Further discussion is needed regarding the differences between physiological and self-reported emotional evaluations.

In this study, visual inspection was conducted for the comparison between physiological indicators and SAM. However, for a more quantitative evaluation, there is a need to discuss the handling of distances on the Emotion Map.

6 Conclusion

In this study, the aim was to enhance the versatility of the Emotion Map, which significantly reflects individual differences in results. We compared and examined normalization methods for physiological indicators. From the positional relationships on the Emotion Map concerning individual differences in emotional responses, it was inferred that methods utilizing Z-Score or Robust Z-score best reflected emotional responses based on physiological indicators. Additionally, using these methods makes it easier to handle physiological indicators with different units.

Acknowledgments. We would like to thank you for the valuable cooperation from Mr. Taketo Sagawa and Mr. Shunsaku Isaji, Mr. Kenichi Endo, Mr. Yusuke Okada, and Mr. Masayuki Omachi of SB Foods Co., Ltd. They give us the variable advices including providing packaging design.

References

1. Nagamachi, M.: Kansei engineering: a new ergonomic consumer-oriented technology for product development. Int. J. Ind. Ergon. **15**(1), 3–11 (1995)
2. Poels, K., Dewitte, S.: How to Capture the Heart? Reviewing 20 Years of Emotion Measurement in Advertising. Katholieke Universiteit Leuven, Open Access publications from Katholieke Universiteit Leuven, vol. 46 (2006)
3. King, S.C., Meiselman, H.L., Thomas Carr, B.: Measuring emotions associated with foods: Important elements of questionnaire and test design. Food Qual. Prefer. **28**(1), 8–16 (2013)
4. Beyts, C., Chaya, C., Dehrmann, F., James, S., Smart, K., Hort, J.: A comparison of self-reported emotional and implicit responses to aromas in beer. Food Qual. Prefer. **59**, 68–80 (2017)
5. Songsamoe, S., Saengwong-ngam, R., Koomhin, P., Matan, N.: Understanding consumer physiological and emotional responses to food products using electroencephalography (EEG). Trends Food Sci. Technol. **93**, 167–173 (2019)
6. Russell, J.A.: A circumplex model of affect. J. Pers. Soc. Psychol. **39**(6), 1161–1178 (1980)
7. Ueno, S., Zhang, R., Laohakangvalvit, T., Sugaya, M.: Evaluating comfort in fully autonomous vehicle using biological emotion map. In: Stanton, N. (eds.) AHFE 2021. LNNS, vol. 270, pp. 323–330. Springer, Cham (2021). https://doi.org/10.1007/978-3-030-80012-3_38
8. Alarcão, S.M., Fonseca, M.J.: Emotions recognition using EEG signals: a survey. IEEE Trans. Affect. Comput. **10**(3), 374–393 (2019)
9. Nakagawa, Y., Sugaya, M.: Emotion estimation for elderly people with dementia using EEG and HRV. In: Gao, Q., Zhou, J., Duffy, V.G., Antona, M., Stephanidis, C. (eds.) AHFE 2021. LNCS, vol. 270, pp. 140–149. Springer, Cham (2023). https://doi.org/10.1007/978-3-031-48041-6_11
10. Shaffer, F., Ginsberg, J.P.: An overview of heart rate variability metrics and norms. Front. Public Health **5** (2017)

11. Khosla, A., Khandnor, P., Chand, T.: A comparative analysis of signal processing and classification methods for different applications based on EEG signals. Biocybern. Biomed. Eng. **40**(2), 649–690 (2020)
12. NeuroSky. https://neurosky.com/. Accessed 26 Oct 2023
13. Jones, P.R.: A note on detecting statistical outliers in psychophysical data. Atten. Percept. Psychophys. **81**(5), 1189–1196 (2019)
14. Jain, A., Nandakumar, K., Ross, A.: Score normalization in multimodal biometric systems. Pattern Recogn. **38**(12), 2270–2285 (2005)
15. En, X., Ma, Y.-Z., Xiao, T., Park, C.: The Robustified Z Score with its Application to Robust Design. SSRN Electron. J. (2022)
16. S&B FOODS INC. https://www.sbfoods.co.jp/. Accessed 26 Oct 2023. (in Japanese)
17. World Famous Electronics llc. https://pulsesensor.com/. Accessed 27 Oct 2023
18. Bradley, M.M., Lang, P.J.: Measuring emotion: the self-assessment manikin and the semantic differential. J. Behav. Ther. Exp. Psychiatry **25**(1), 49–59 (1994)

Tabletop Exercise for Ransomware Negotiations

Lea Müller[✉]

Albstadt-Sigmaringen University, Albstadt, Germany
muellele@hs-albsig.de

Abstract. Ransomware has grown to become one of the most significant cyber threats to organizations worldwide. In the event of an attack,
many victims choose to pay in order to restore their systems or prevent
stolen data from being published or sold. If this decision is made, organizations should consider entering into negotiations with the attackers,
as ransoms are often negotiable. It is important that relevant personnel
are prepared for such negotiations. The aim of this work is to evaluate
how Tabletop Exercises can be used to prepare for possible Ransomware
Negotiations. A concept for Tabletop Exercises is developed, which is
slightly adapted to the requirements of Ransomware Negotiation Training. The main modification involves the inclusion of an adversarial team
in the exercise, representing the attackers or ransomware operators. This
will provide participants with the opportunity to negotiate with an opponent who will react to their actions in a spontaneous and unpredictable
manner. A basic model for designing a Tabletop Exercise in this format
is provided, supplemented by an exemplary scenario for a Ransomware
Negotiation Tabletop Exercise.

Keywords: Ransomware Negotiation · Tabletop Exercise

1 Introduction

Ransomware is a type of malware that is designed to restrict or prevent its victim
from accessing systems or data, primarily through encryption. In order to regain
access, the victim must pay a ransom demanded by the attackers. In addition,
attackers often threaten to publish or sell stolen data to press the victim to
pay rather than recover systems from backups. This is known as the double
extortion model [5]. Consequently, many victims pay the demanded ransom,
hoping to quickly recover from the attack and prevent stolen data from being
published [8]. In some cases, paying causes the victim less loss than experiencing
temporary system unavailability and the laborious process of recovery [7].

The effectiveness of ransomware attacks lies in their immediate impact and
the high pressure they exert on those affected. Recent developments show that
ransomware is increasingly being targeted at large organizations. This approach
is known as Targeted Ransomware [17]. Attacks are often targeting companies

D. D. Schmorrow and C. M. Fidopiastis (Eds.): HCII 2024, LNAI 14695, pp. 166–184, 2024.
https://doi.org/10.1007/978-3-031-61572-6_12

in order to demand higher ransoms [7], but critical infrastructure [12] and government institutions are also frequently affected [7]. Attackers using Targeted Ransomware invest considerable time and effort in attacking large organizations, expecting high profits. As a result, perpetrators are willing to negotiate ransom demands, as they too have large amounts of money at stake [17].

Although government institutions such as the FBI do not recommend paying ransoms or negotiating with attackers [8,12], many of those affected still choose to pay in the hope of quickly recovering their systems and returning to normal operation [7]. In 2023, nearly 73% of businesses being attacked by ransomware paid [2]. Once an organization has made the decision to pay, negotiations regarding the ransom amount may be considered. Negotiating ransom demands has been successful in various cases [11], with negotiated discounts ranging from 20% up to 90%, and in most cases, victims have been able to negotiate discounts of over 50% [2].

The purpose of this work is to elucidate the principles and strategies that can be employed to negotiate ransoms demanded by ransomware operators, as well as how organizations can prepare for such negotiations. To this end, a slightly adapted format of Tabletop Exercise is selected as the medium for preparation, and a basic model of a Tabletop Exercise for Ransomware Negotiations is designed.

2   Preparation

When organizations choose to pay a ransom or enter into negotiations with attackers, legal considerations may arise. Although government institutions strongly advise against it [8,12], paying the demanded ransom is not illegal in principle. However, paying a ransom could lead to legal liabilities if the ransomware group or the country they work for are subject to sanctions [14]. In addition, the publication of sensitive data can have legal implications, which may make victims more willing to pay or negotiate to mitigate the consequences of a potential data breach [6]. Attackers are also aware of the legal consequences of breaches and may use the threat of notifying regulators as leverage in negotiations [8].

One major concern regarding ransomware attacks is that paying the ransom supports criminal activity. Therefore, government institutions, such as the FBI, strongly advise against paying the demanded ransom [8,12]. If criminals continue to achieve their primary goal of financial gain, attacks will persist. The decision to pay may fuel further attacks, ultimately weakening the overall security of cyberspace [7]. However, organizations may face situations where refusing to pay could cause harm to stakeholders for whom the organization bears responsibility, such as employees or customers [14]. If the sensitive data of these stakeholders is at risk, those responsible may decide that paying or negotiating is the ethically better decision [6].

Before or in the event of a ransomware attack, organizations should consider certain issues before entering into negotiations. This can prevent them from making hasty decisions under stress that they might not have made if they had more time, and which may be contrary to their real objectives. To be able to respond adequately in the event of a ransomware attack, organizations should include ransomware attacks and potential negotiations in their incident response plan [14]. To prepare effectively, it is also advisable to consider setting a maximum ransom that the organization is willing to pay [18], keeping abreast of potential threats and monitoring criminal behaviour [13], and conducting exercises to train individuals on their roles and responsibilities [10].

3 Ransomware Negotiations

3.1 Conditions

When an organization falls victim to a ransomware attack, the impacts are both immediate and far-reaching. For example, access to systems or data may be restricted or completely prevented, resulting in lost productivity. This sets ransomware attacks apart from other types of malware and places significant pressure on the victim to limit the damage. As victims seek to minimise the time of business interruption and payment is seen as the quickest solution, many victims comply with the attackers' demands [8].

Targeted Ransomware attacks have become increasingly prevalent in recent years [7]. Attackers invest significant effort in these attacks, resulting in higher ransoms being demanded from victims [17]. To maximize the ransom amount, attackers calculate it on an individual basis [2,5], taking into account the victim's financial status or publicly available reports [5]. They are also willing to negotiate the final amount to avoid receiving no ransom at all [17].

One of the things organizations should consider before entering into negotiations is the reliability of the ransomware used in the attack, or the group responsible for the attack. As the outcome of the negotiation is crucial not only for the victim but also for the attacker, it is in the interest of both parties that the ransomware is highly reliable in terms of data restoration after payment. The victim's decision to pay the demanded ransom is influenced by the likelihood of data recovery. Only if it is probable that the data can be restored will the affected organization be willing to pay. Attackers or ransomware developers invest in improving the reliability of their ransomware because a high level of willingness to pay on part of the victim supports their financial motives [17].

When it comes to negotiating the amount of the ransom, the lack of trust between the attacker and the victim is of crucial importance. Even after paying the ransom, the victim cannot be completely certain that their data will be recovered. In general, the attacker may delete the files irrespective of whether a ransom was paid [3]. Additionally, during the negotiation, the attacker aims to conceal the minimum ransom amount they are willing to accept in exchange for the decryption tool. The attacker, on the other hand, does not know whether the victim is being honest about the amount of ransom they are willing to pay [18]. Since trust and cooperation are essential to achieving a solution, a lack of trust is not beneficial to the negotiation process [19].

Another significant factor in Targeted Ransomware attacks is the uneven distribution of information between the negotiating parties. This means that both parties lack information that is relevant for the outcome of the negotiation. For instance, the attacker does not know the exact value of the files to the victim, which is an important factor in estimating the amount of ransom to be demanded. However, attackers have access to the victim's data and systems, providing a reasonable basis for calculation [17]. Conversely, the victim generally has little information about the attacker, such as the minimum amount of ransom for which the attacker is willing to restore the data [18] or the reliability of the decryptor [8].

In addition to the uneven distribution of information about the other party, the negotiation process also suffers from an uneven distribution of levers. This is particularly evident in the double extortion model, where attackers exert additional pressure on the victim by threatening to publish or sell the victim's data if the ransom is not paid [7]. Sometimes attackers even threaten to inform regulatory authorities about possible regulation violations, which represents another lever in the negotiation process [8]. This asymmetry arises in the initial infection of systems and the subsequent demand for a ransom. From this point on, the attacker can aim to maximize gain, while the victim can only aim to minimize loss [3]. It is important to note that even if the victim chooses not to pay the ransom, there will still be losses due to downtime and the recovery of systems [18]. Therefore, the attacker holds an advantageous position throughout the negotiation process [3].

Unlike most other cyber attacks, ransomware creates a hostage-like situation and forces the victim into negotiating [3], as attackers invest heavily in ensuring that data can only be recovered by paying a ransom [17]. Furthermore, using double extortion makes victims more likely to pay, even if they have backups from which to restore their systems [8]. Consequently, the amount of ransom paid by the victim depends on the likelihood of being able to recover from backups and the sensitivity of the data being held hostage [3]. Many organizations are forced into Ransomware Negotiations for various reasons, so it is important to be prepared for this eventuality.

3.2   Strategies

This section outlines strategies for Ransomware Negotiations. The suggested strategies, gathered from various sources [2,5,11,19], can be summarised as follows:

1. Asking attackers to set up different means of communication
2. Maintaining professionalism
3. Buying and leveraging time
4. Gathering information
5. Requesting decryption of a test file
6. Offering a smaller, but immediate payment
7. Convincing the attackers that the ransom is too high

8. Omitting mention of cyber insurance
9. Requesting proof of deletion
10. Asking for an explanation of how one was hacked

Different Means of Communication

At the start of a Ransomware Negotiation, it is advisable to request an alternative means of communication from the attackers. This is due to the fact that chat platforms used for negotiations can be easily accessed by third parties [11]. In the case of CONTI ransomware, possessing a victim ID, which is typically provided after an attack, allows anyone to access the negotiation chats. These IDs can be found online and are sometimes reused by CONTI [5]. Switching to another medium will not only prevent unwanted parties from reading the chat but also from interfering. In several cases, third parties accessed the chats and disturbed or trolled the negotiation [5,11].

Maintaining Professionalism

During negotiations, victims should maintain a professional and respectful demeanor. This can be difficult as ransomware attacks can cause major losses or threaten livelihoods. It is important to note that being friendly can lead to a lower ransom, whereas acting frustrated or angry can lead to the perpetrators withdrawing from the negotiation [11]. Organizations should aim to treat interactions with attackers as business transactions and remain calm without showing signs of desperation [2]. In [19], Wade suggests going even further by acknowledging the attacker's effort and praising their skill to build rapport and mitigate escalation [19].

Buying and Leveraging Time

Attackers may attempt to coerce victims by threatening to leak data and imposing deadlines [11]. However, victims are advised to request additional time as this will enable them to consider all available recovery options [2], devise strategies or make necessary arrangements, such as purchasing cryptocurrency [11].

Time can be used as a tool against attackers, as it is of great importance to them [2]. To buy time, Wade suggests delaying responses or pretending to have encountered issues, such as with purchasing cryptocurrency [19]. However, organizations should also consider that extended periods of downtime can result in significant losses and may not be in their best interest [18].

Gathering Information

Ideally, the affected organization should have gathered information about the attacker prior to the attack or before the ransom notice was opened [11]. If this is not the case, information gathering should be done during the negotiation to identify the impact of the attack and obtain more information about the attacker. Section 3.1 outlines how knowledge of a ransomware group's reliability can influence an organization's negotiation behaviour. Understanding a group's past negotiation behaviour can aid victims in determining a strategy. Furthermore, if a ransomware group has compromised multiple organizations simultaneously and has more options for receiving payment, this may influence the attacker's negotiation behaviour to be less patient [2].

Decryption of a Test File
Organizations should always verify that the ransomware group has the decryption key and that it functions correctly before paying any ransom. If organizations do not request proof, they cannot be certain that the perpetrators will be able to recover their data [5]. While knowledge of the attacker's reliability may provide some insight, it is still advisable for organizations to make sure that the decryption works [11]. Often, to demonstrate their reliability and gain the victim's trust, attackers will suggest this themselves and offer a few files [19].

Small Early or Large Late Payments
Ransomware attackers aim to make a quick profit and therefore prefer early payment [2,11]. As a result, they may offer discounts for immediate payment [5] to allow them to move on to the next target. In some cases, when given the choice of receiving a small ransom immediately or a larger ransom later, attackers have offered large discounts for early payment [11]. This not only reduces the loss for the affected organization but also minimizes downtime.

Convincing that Ransom is too High
An effective strategy in Ransomware Negotiations is to convince the attacker that payment of the ransom amount is not possible. This approach has proven successful for several organizations by emphasizing it throughout multiple rounds of negotiation [11]. However, attackers may calculate the ransom on an individual basis [5], and may know if the victim is trying to deceive them and be unwilling to lower their demands [11]. Even so, the basis of calculation used by the attackers may not be a good reflection of the organization's true financial position. If this is the case, negotiators should consider providing the attackers with information about their true financial situation in order to convince them that they are truly unable to pay the amount demanded [?]

Omitting Mention of Cyber Insurance
If an organization has cyber insurance, it should not mention this during negotiations, and it is advisable to keep relevant documents in a secure location so that attackers do not have access to them. If the attacker is aware of the victim's insurance coverage, they may be less willing to negotiate as they know the maximum amount that will be covered [11].

Proof of Deletion
Once the ransom amount has been agreed upon and paid by the victim, they should request proof of their files' deletion [11]. However, it is important to note that even if attackers agree to provide proof of deletion, there is no guarantee that they will actually do so. Therefore, organizations should prepare for the possibility of their files being leaked [11]. In some cases, negotiators have also requested that the attackers delete the negotiation chat. As mentioned above, these chats can be easily accessed by third parties, and deletion can prevent unauthorised access to the conversation [5].

Explanation of Attack
In addition, affected organizations should ask the attackers how they were able to gain access to the systems [11]. While in most cases attackers do not provide

much information [5], in some cases they are willing to share details about the attack and even suggest improvements or recommend security solutions [5,11]. This information can help organizations improve their security and prevent future attacks.

4   Tabletop Exercise for Ransomware Negotiations

4.1   Tabletop Exercise

Tabletop Exercises (TTXs) are a type of Serious Games [1], which are games designed not only for entertainment, but primarily to support the training of knowledge, skills and behaviour. As such, TTXs must have clearly established rules, end with a score, and provide interactivity to be engaging for participants. This helps to develop intrinsic motivation among participants, in addition to any existing extrinsic motivations [9].

Tabletop Exercises are commonly used to train individuals in incident or emergency response, including cybersecurity incident response. This interactive and experiential training format can improve participants' understanding of a specific process or plan [1]. The National Institute of Standards and Technology (NIST) defines TTXs as 'discussion-based events where personnel with roles and responsibilities in a particular IT plan meet in a classroom setting or in break-out groups to discuss their roles during an emergency and their responses to a particular emergency situation' [10]. The purpose of TTXs is to confirm that staff members are familiar with their entrusted responsibilities and the contents of the plan being exercised [10]. Another central goal of a TTX is to build a functioning team in a threat-free environment [4]. TTXs also provide an opportunity to review the applicability and effectiveness of IT plans and enhance them if necessary [10]. For negotiations with attackers, the IT plans exercised may be incident response plans or, if available, any procedures specifically designed for Ransomware Negotiations.

TTXs are conducted using hypothetical scenarios based on the plan exercised and are led by a facilitator who guides the discussion [10] and may also take on minor roles in the chosen scenario [16]. According to [4], there are four different roles in a TTX: participants play an active role, usually representing the roles or responsibilities they have within the organization. If gaps exist in the scenario, they may fulfill other roles. Observers do not take an active role but can support the discussion by asking questions or providing relevant expertise. The facilitator moderates the exercise, provides updates to the scenario, and resolves ambiguities. Additionally, a note-taker observes the activities within the exercise and assesses whether they conform to the plan exercised [4]. Both the facilitator and the note-taker should have a good understanding of the IT plan being exercised and the objectives of the exercise [10].

The scenario is presented to participants through a guide provided at the beginning of the exercise, as well as through further explanations given by the facilitator. Participants are selected based on the roles relevant to the scenario [10] and may include personnel from various fields within an organization [1]. Following the introduction of the scenario and the exercise's scope, the facilitator initiates a discussion among the participants by posing a question related to the scenario. During the discussion, the facilitator may ask questions to enhance the conversation or ensure that the exercise's objectives are met [10]. The facilitator may also introduce changes to the scenario, referred to as injects [1]. Following the discussion, the exercise is analysed to identify any further training requirements or areas for improvement in the IT plan [10].

TTXs are most useful when conducted after recent training of participants. This ensures that they are aware of their roles and responsibilities in the specific plan. According to NIST, TTXs should be conducted periodically, after organizational changes or when an IT plan is updated [10]. This will ensure that all personnel are made aware of potential changes within their role, and to determine if there are any improvements to be made to the newly established changes or plans.

Advantages of Tabletop Exercises. In [1], the advantages of TTXs in comparison to traditional methods, such as lectures or quizzes, are highlighted by reviewing various academic research and literature on TTXs for cybersecurity incident response training. These advantages include the promotion of a better understanding of processes and plans, the encouragement of collaboration, the development of practical skills, the teaching of skills for incident prevention, and the flexibility of TTXs. With the exception of incident prevention skills, all of these chracteristics are useful for preparing for Ransomware Negotiations.

The TTX format enhances participants' comprehension of processes and plans by discussing and evaluating the steps involved. Participants make strategic decisions within the scenario, leading to a better understanding and coordination of processes to be applied in case of an incident. This improved understanding of procedures will allow participants to develop confidence and situational awareness. It also provides an opportunity to review and update the plans exercised, ensuring that processes and procedures are in line with the organization's objectives [1].

One of the primary goals of a TTX is to improve the way participants work together to create a team that will function well in the event of a real incident [4]. This is accomplished by promoting communication and the exchange of knowledge and skills among participants. Collaboratively developing problem-solving strategies is facilitated by a non-threatening environment, where participants can learn from the decisions of others and receive feedback on their own actions. Another benefit of fostering collaboration through TTXs is that individuals become familiar with whom they can turn to in the event of an actual incident [1].

During a TTX, participants typically simulate their own roles and choose actions that they would take in a real incident [4]. Immediate feedback is provided during the TTX, allowing participants to reflect on their decisions and identify potential gaps in their skills and knowledge [1]. By engaging in this process, individuals can gain an understanding of specific procedures, become familiar with their responsibilities within the organization, and test solutions without causing any harm [16]. This approach allows for the development of skills relevant to specific roles and enables players to adapt to changing scenarios through a learning-by-doing approach [1].

One further advantage of TTXs is that they are very flexible, as they can be adapted during the exercise by adding injects or unexpected changes to the scenario. This enables the facilitator to easily tailor the exercise to the participants' individual needs and emphasize important objectives [1]. Due to its high flexibility, this approach teaches participants how to deal with situations of high uncertainty and ambiguous or missing information - a level of information that is well-suited to real-life incident response situations [16]. The flexibility of TTXs applies not only to the scenario and range of possible responses, but also to the time allotted, which can range from 10 min [4] to 8 h [10].

Light Weight Tabletop Exercise. Tabletop Exercises are already highly flexible and require moderate effort to design and conduct [1]. In [16], Rain Ottis aims to reduce the workload and time needed to prepare the exercise even further. Ottis calls this concept the 'Light Weight Tabletop Exercise'. Furthermore, the light-weight version of the TTX offers more opportunities for active decision-making compared to the traditional format mentioned above. In Light Weight TTXs, the scenario is not as clearly defined, but rather left up to the participants and potential injects. Participants are given a few basic conditions around which the situation is built, which is then further developed throughout the exercise [16].

The main difference with the Light Weight TTX is the inclusion of a Red Team, which creates an adaptable opponent that introduces injects to the scenario instead of the facilitator. As a result, the facilitator's role is no longer to explain and update the scenario, but rather to introduce and enforce exercise rules throughout the discussion. During the exercise, the attacking Red Team and the defending Blue Team take turns making and responding to injects. The facilitator may play minor roles or pause the discussion to emphasize specific lessons to be learned [16].

4.2   Concept

Adapted TTX Format. In order to improve the adaptation of Tabletop Exercises to the specific requirements of Ransomware Negotiations, certain changes, similar to those suggested by Ottis in [16], are made to the exercise format. The primary modification is to introduce a Red Team to the scenario, which will represent the adversary of the organization. Unlike the Light Weight TTX format proposed by Ottis, which includes multiple Blue Teams, the format proposed here consists of only one Blue Team and one Red Team. The Blue Team represents the organization affected by a ransomware attack, while the Red Team represents the attacking ransomware group. Other entities, such as media or law enforcement, do not directly influence the negotiation and therefore do not need to be actively represented in the TTX. The TTX for Ransomware Negotiatons focuses on the negotiation itself, which takes place exclusively between the organization (Blue Team) and the attackers (Red Team). Therefore, the exercise is limited to two teams. If the selected scenario involves additional entities, the relevant information may be included in the scenario description or provided by the facilitator during the discussion.

Although Ottis presents the Light Weight Tabletop Exercise format as a means of Cybersecurity Education for students [16], it may also be applied to incident response training in an organization. To achieve this, some adaptions may be necessary, such as providing more detailed specifications for the Blue Team's conditions. In Ottis' concept, the Blue Team can in most ways freely develop the scenario [16], but in the context of an organization, the plans and procedures to be followed in the event of an incident can be very clearly specified. Allowing participants to set up the scenario could result in an insufficient description of the organization, which would prevent the exercise from meeting its objectives. Therefore, it is essential to precisely specify the fundamental requirements for the Blue Team and ensure that the participants represent their roles within the organization and the incident response plan being exercised. This means that the conditions provided by the organization's infrastructure, management, etc. should be adequately represented in the exercise scenario.

While the terms and conditions for the Blue Team, representing the organization itself, may be very clearly defined, the Red Team may have more freedom in its choice of actions and preconditions. In particular, when practicing Ransomware Negotiations, incorporating active opponents into a TTX, as suggested by Ottis, allows participants to interact with an adversary who will react to their actions in a spontaneous and unpredictable manner. Creating a static scenario with pre-planned injects does not align with the dynamic nature of Ransomware Negotiations. Traditional TTXs focus on team communication and collaboration, but in Ransomware Negotiations, communication with attackers may play an even more critical role in the resolution than communication with other employees.

The Red Team has a certain amount of freedom in its actions, but its conditions and characteristics may be specified in a more concrete way. This means that an organization may need to exercise a particular type of attacker or scenario. This could include, but is not limited to, the percentage of the attacker's previous victims who have been provided with working decryption keys (attacker's reputation), the risk of the decryption tool not working properly, if sensitive data has been extracted, the cost of the attack to the attacker, and the like. If any special conditions are required for the exercise, these should be made known to the Red Team during the introduction of the scenario.

The exercise format assumes that the organization has already been infected with ransomware and is unable, or only limitedly able, to access its systems or files. It is also assumed that the attackers have provided a means of communication and that the organization has decided to negotiate. The proposed format does not include other aspects of the incident response to a ransomware attack, such as deciding whether or not to negotiate with the attackers. This approach ensures that participants can start negotiating immediately, and can concentrate solely on the negotiation process.

Basic Model. When designing a Tabletop Exercise using the above format, different instructions must be prepared. These include a guide for the facilitator and instructions for each team. The facilitator guide should contain the scenario, possible injects, and debrief questions. It should also provide additional information about the exercise setup and rules. The team instructions outline the exercise objectives, scenario, team tasks, and considerations for the negotiation.

The exercise scenario assumes that the organization has already fallen victim to a ransomware attack and that the attackers have provided a means of communication, such as email chat or a dedicated portal. It is assumed that the affected organization has already made the decision to negotiate with the attackers, and therefore, the scenario should provide a credible reason for this decision. In Ransomware Negotiations, it is common for the affected organization to initiate communication through the means provided by the attackers. Therefore, the Blue Team will initiate the negotiation.

The scenario is presented to both teams in the instructions they receive. The scenario is described from each team's individual perspective and provides only the information that would be available to that party in an actual Ransomware Negotiation. As a result, the two teams have different levels of information about each other and the scenario, which is a common occurence in such situations. The facilitator has complete information about the scenario.

Depending on the scenario, the two teams can be given varying degrees of autonomy over certain terms of the scenario. As mentioned above, it is important to specify the terms for the Blue Team precisely, so that they can adequately represent the organization. However, they may have some flexibility in terms of their negotiation behaviour or the amount of ransom they are willing to pay. The conditions for the Red Team may be less precisely specified, providing participants with more opportunities to make their own decisions. This could include deciding on the amount of ransom demanded or the reliability of the malware used.

When creating a scenario for the exercise, the following aspects should be considered:

Number of participants per team and roles of the participants.
It is recommended that the Red Team comprises of two participants. While in a real incident, the organization may negotiate with a single negotiator, having two participants representing the attackers enables them to discuss their actions and strategies. The size of the Blue Team may be chosen according to specific requirements given by the organization or the selected scenario. The members of the Blue Team should represent the roles and responsibilities they have within the organization.
Data Extraction and Data Sensitivity
The scenario should clearly indicate whether or not the attackers extracted data. This information may be provided in the initial description given to both

teams or left to the discretion of the Red Team to reveal to the Blue Team during the negotiation. If the scenario involves data extraction, it should also specify the sensitivity level of the extracted data.

Backups

The existence of backups depends on the organization's backup plan and is not defined in the scenario. However, in the selected scenario, it is possible that backups were stored on an infected server and have been encrypted. The scenario may also include an inject where data recovery from backups was unsuccessful.

Reliability

The scenario should specify the reliability of the ransomware or ransomware group in decrypting data after payment. This decision may be left to the Red Team, but it is recommended to avoid choosing an overly optimistic value.

Ransom Amount

The ransom amount demanded by the attackers may either be specified in the scenario or left to the judgment of the Red Team. Depending on the scenario, the Red Team may be provided with some information about the financial situation of the organization as a basis for calculating the ransom amount.

Availability of information

The scenario should specify the extent of information available to the teams about the other party. For instance, the Blue Team may be provided with information on the reliability of the ransomware group, while the Red Team may be given details on the financial situation of the organization or the sensitivity of its data. It is not necessary to include all of this information in the initial scenario description, but it may become available to the teams during the negotiation. For instance, the Blue Team could conduct research on the ransomware group and discover their reliability.

Prior to the start of the Tabletop Exercise, participants should be seated in such a way that allows them to discuss within their group without being overheard by the other team. The only way to communicate with the other team is to write on a board placed in a central location of the room. To ensure that both teams' messages can be distinguished, it is recommended to use pencils in two different colours.

During the exercise, the facilitator may introduce modifications to the scenario through injects. These injects can be predefined or created during the exercise. Possible injects to a scenario are:

- The organization is unable to restore data from backups, for example because the backups are damaged.
- The extracted data was lost during transfer by the attackers. Therefore, they can no longer threaten to publish it and can only negotiate the price of the decryption key.
- To simulate the unavailability of a team member, the facilitator may choose to (temporarily) exclude one member of the Blue Team from the negotiation.
- The extracted data is partially published by the attackers on their website.

Example Scenario - Beverage Producer. This section provides an example scenario for a Ransomware Negotiation Tabletop Exercise. It involves a fictitious beverage producer and a fictitious ransomware group. The company has been targeted by the ransomware group, and while the company has backups of its data, the attackers are threatening to publish stolen data, including a secret recipe for the company's most popular product.

Participants:

Blue Team: 3–5 participants
Red Team: 2 participants

Facilitator Guide In this Tabletop Exercise, two teams will represent an organization (Blue Team) and a ransomware group that has attacked the organization (Red Team). The teams will negotiate with each other to come to an agreement regarding the ransom amount. A Tabletop Exercise is an activity that presents a hypothetical scenario to which participants must respond. You will act as the facilitator of the Tabletop Exercise. As the facilitator, your role is to explain the rules to the participants and ensure compliance. You may modify the scenario through injects. Participants are permitted to ask questions during the exercise, but answers should only be given if the information would be available in a real negotiation. Additionally, you may take on minor roles in the scenario if necessary.

Agenda:
1. Introduction
2. Scenario Discussion
3. Debrief

Introduction:
Setup:
Allocate seats to the two teams so that they can discuss within their own group without being overheard by the other team.
Rules:
Explain the rules of the exercise to the participants.
   – The aim of the exercise is to reach an agreement regarding the ransom amount.
   – Communication between the two teams will occur through messages.
   – During the negotiation, the two teams are not allowed to communicate with each other except through negotiation messages.
   – A team is not obligated to answer to a message sent by the other team. They can choose to wait instead.
   – Participants are permitted to conduct research, such as asking questions or gathering information from the internet.
Start of the Exercise:
The Blue Team will initiate the negotiation by delivering its initial message to the Red Team.

Scenario:
The scenario comprises a Blue Team and a Red Team.

The Blue Team represents a medium-sized beverage producer with an average revenue of EUR 15 million and an average profit of EUR 1.8 million. The company's cash position is EUR 500,000. Its most popular product is made according to a secret recipe that is only available in digital form. The company has fallen victim to ransomware and has received the following notice on their systems: 'All your data has been encrypted by ransomware and you are no longer able to access it. But there is help: We offer you the decryption key which is the only way to regain access to your important data. Do not try to ignore us: Before encrypting your data, we secured some of your files and are ready to publish them on our website. So it will be better for you to contact us asap.' The attackers also provide a link to a portal through which the affected company can contact them. The company has backups available and can thus resume production within one day.

The Red Team represents the ransomware group that has attacked the company, extracted some of its data and encrypted all of its systems. They are aware of the potential value of the secret recipe and may search for a buyer. The attackers have built a reputation for keeping their promise and providing the decryption key after the victim has paid the ransom. Their decryptor is reliable, and 90% of the businesses that paid the ransom successfully recovered their data. The attackers know the company's financial situation and will calculate the ransom accordingly.

Possible injects:

- *Blue Team:* Your backups are damaged and only 70% of your data can be recovered. The file containing your secret recipe is not included in that 70%. Does this affect your negotiation strategy?
- *Red Team:* An operator informs you that two more companies have been compromised and you are to lead the negotiations. This provides you with more options for receiving payment. Will this affect your behaviour towards the company?
- *Red Team:* As the negotiation process is not progressing as quickly as desired, you publish 10% of the stolen data on your website. The secret recipe is not included in the published data. Inform the company about this action.
- *Facilitator:* If the Red Team decides to sell the recipe, you can determine whether or not they find a buyer and the amount the buyer is willing to pay.

Debrief:

During the debrief, both teams should review successful and unsuccessful strategies and identify potential areas for improvement.

- What strategies and actions of the Blue Team contributed to reaching an agreement?
- What strategies and actions of the Blue Team hindered reaching an agreement?
- What improvements could be made to the procedure?
- Are there events that the Blue Team should be better prepared for?

Blue Team Instruction In this Tabletop Exercise, you will represent an organization and work as a team to negotiate with another team representing a
ransomware group. The goal is to come to an agreement regarding the ransom
amount. A Tabletop Exercise is an activity that presents a hypothetical scenario to which participants must respond. The scenario in this case involves
a Blue Team, the organization you represent, and a Red Team, the attackers.
Communication with the Red Team will occur solely through messages. You
are not allowed to discuss with the other team during the exercise.

Agenda:

1. Introduction
2. Scenario Discussion
3. Debrief

Objectives:

The objectives of the exercise are:

- Identify strategies and actions that support reaching an agreement.
- Identify strategies and actions that hinder reaching an agreement.
- Identify areas for improvement by reflecting on your strategies and
  actions.

Scenario:

You will represent a medium-sized beverage producer. Your most popular
product is a drink made according to a secret recipe, which is stored in digital
form only on your systems. Your average annual revenue is EUR 15 million,
with an average profit of EUR 1.8 million, and a cash position of EUR 500,000.
You do not own any cryptocurrency.

Upon entering your production hall on Monday morning, you discover that
you no longer have access to any of the data on your systems. Instead, you
find a notice with the following text: 'All your data has been encrypted by
ransomware and you are no longer able to access it. But there is help: We
offer you the decryption key which is the only way to regain access to your
important data. Do not try to ignore us: Before encrypting your data, we
secured some of your files and are ready to publish them on our website. So
it will be better for you to contact us asap.' They also provide a link to a
portal for contacting them.

Fortunately, backups exist for your systems. This means, that you can resume
production within one day. However, restoring data from backups will not
prevent your files from being published. As you are concerned that the secret
recipe may be among the stolen data, you decide to contact the attackers and
enter into negotiations with them.

Your task:

1. Determine the roles within the company. Assign one person to represent
   the CEO and another to represent the IT department. The remaining
   participants are free to choose their role.
2. Think about a strategy for the negotiation.
3. Decide on your initial message and communicate it to the attackers.
4. Try to reach an agreement through negotiation.

During the negotiation, consider the following:

- What is the maximum amount that you are willing to pay?
- You can research how likely the attackers are to keep their promises after payment.
- It is advisable to reach an agreement quickly as negotiating can extend downtime and result in losses.
- Who is responsible for making the final decision?
- What strategies and tactics exist and how can they be used?

Red Team Instruction In this Tabletop Exercise, you will represent a ransomware group and work as a team to negotiate with another team representing an organization you have attacked. The goal is to come to an agreement regarding the ransom amount. A Tabletop Exercise is an activity that presents a hypothetical scenario to which participants must respond. The scenario in this case involves a Blue Team, the organization, and a Red Team, the attackers you represent. Communication with the Blue Team will occur solely through messages. You are not allowed to discuss with the other team during the exercise.

Agenda:
1. Introduction
2. Scenario Discussion
3. Debrief

Objectives:

The objectives of the exercise are:
- Identify the strategies and actions of the opposing team that support reaching an agreement.
- Identify the strategies and actions of the opposing team that hinder reaching an agreement.
- Identify areas for improvement by evaluating the strategies and actions of the opposing team.

Scenario:

You will represent a ransomware group that has just compromised a medium-sized beverage producer and is waiting for their initial message to be delivered via a dedicated portal. Before encrypting the company's systems, you extracted some of the company's most valuable files and left a notice on its systems: 'All your data has been encrypted by ransomware and you are no longer able to access it. But there is help: We offer you the decryption key which is the only way to regain access to your important data. Do not try to ignore us: Before encrypting your data, we secured some of your files and are ready to publish them on our website. So it will be better for you to contact us asap.' The extracted data includes the secret recipe for the company's most popular drink, which has considerable value and may be of interest to a buyer.

However, you have put a lot of effort into building a reputation for reliability in data recovery after companies have paid the ransom. In about 90% of cases where those affected paid, their data was successfully recovered.

Before encrypting the company's systems, you searched its data for valuable information to calculate the ransom demand. Your research revealed that the company has an average annual revenue of EUR 15 million and an average annual profit of EUR 1.8 million.

Your task:

1. Decide on the amount of ransom you will demand from the company, taking into account the information provided about their financial situation.
2. Think about a strategy for the negotiation.
3. Wait for the company's first message.
4. In your reply, state your demand. You may also want to remind them of the value of the data you have extracted.
5. Try to reach an agreement through negotiation.

During the negotiation, consider the following:

- What is the minimum amount for which you will provide the decryption key?
- You can try to estimate the value of the secret recipe and find potential buyers.
- You can give the company a deadline for when you will start publishing data.
- You can publish data on your website to increase the pressure on the company.

5   Conclusion

A Tabletop Exercise format slightly adapted to the requirements of Ransomware Negotiation Training has been developed. The format includes an adversarial team representing the ransomware operators. It is assumed that negotiating with an actual opponent during the exercise will allow participants to adequately prepare for possible Ransomware Negotiations. To assess the applicability of the adapted Tabletop Exercise format and its effectiveness in improving negotiation skills for Ransomware Negotiations, a Tabletop Exercise was conducted using the proposed format. The participants evaluated the exercise to determine whether organizations can enhance their incident response capabilities by incorporating Ransomware Negotiation Tabletop Exercises into their incident response training. The practical implementation and evaluation as well as further recommendations have been published as a thesis and can be found here: Lea Müller (researchgate.net)

Acknowledgement. The project funded under Grant Agreement No. 101127970 is supported by the European Cybersecurity Competence Centre.

This research resembles part of a thesis [15].

References

1. Angafor, G.N., Yevseyeva, I., He, Y.: Game-based learning: a review of table-top exercises for cybersecurity incident response training. Secur. Priv. **3**(6), e126 (2020). https://doi.org/10.1002/spy2.126. https://onlinelibrary.wiley.com/doi/abs/10.1002/spy2.126
2. Boticiu, S., Teichmann, F.: How does one negotiate with ransomware attackers? Int. Cybersecur. Law Rev. (2023). https://doi.org/10.1365/s43439-023-00106-w
3. Caporusso, N., Chea, S., Abukhaled, R.: A game-theoretical model of ransomware. In: Ahram, T.Z., Nicholson, D. (eds.) AHFE 2018, vol. 782, pp. 69–78. Springer, Heidelberg (2019). https://doi.org/10.1007/978-3-319-94782-2_7
4. Cybersecurity & Infrastructure Security Agency: Cybersecurity tabletop exercise tips (2022). https://www.cisa.gov/sites/default/files/publications/Cybersecurity-Tabletop-Exercise-Tips_508c.pdf
5. DFIR Research Group, Team Cymru: Analyzing ransomware negotiations with conti: an in-depth analysis (2022)
6. Formosa, P., Wilson, M., Richards, D.: A principlist framework for cybersecurity ethics. Comput. Secur. **109** (2021). https://doi.org/10.1016/j.cose.2021.102382. https://www.sciencedirect.com/science/article/pii/S0167404821002066
7. German Federal Office for Information Security: Ransomware bedrohungslage 2022 (german) [ransomware threat situation 2022] (2022). https://www.bsi.bund.de/SharedDocs/Downloads/DE/BSI/Cyber-Sicherheit/Themen/Ransomware.pdf?__blob=publicationFile&v=5
8. German Federal Office for Information Security: The state of it security in Germany in 2023 (2023). https://www.bsi.bund.de/SharedDocs/Downloads/EN/BSI/Publications/Securitysituation/IT-Security-Situation-in-Germany-2023.pdf?__blob=publicationFile&v=8
9. Gobron, S.: Gamification & serious game. In: Symposium 2016, 4–5 July 2016 (2016). https://doi.org/10.26039/JHCK-PK54. http://arodes.hes-so.ch/record/4270
10. Grance, T., Nolan, T., Burke, K., Dudley, R., White, G., Good, T.: Sp 800-84. guide to test, training, and exercise programs for it plans and capabilities (2006)
11. Hack, P., Wu, Z.Y.: "we wait, because we know you." inside the ransomware negotiation economics (2021). https://research.nccgroup.com/2021/11/12/we-wait-because-we-know-you-inside-the-ransomware-negotiation-economics/
12. Internet Crime Complaint Center (IC3): Internet crime report 2022 (2022). https://www.ic3.gov/Media/PDF/AnnualReport/2022_IC3Report.pdf
13. Kremez, V., Farral, T.: How ransomware has become an 'ethical' dilemma in the eastern European underground (2017). https://flashpoint.io/blog/ransomware-ethical-dilemma-eastern-european-underground/
14. Mierzwa, S., Drylie, J., Bogdan, D.: Ransomware incident preparations with ethical considerations and command system framework proposal. J. Leadership Accountabil. Ethics **19**(2), 110–120 (2022). https://doi.org/10.33423/jlae.v19i2.5112
15. Müller, L.: Tabletop exercise for ransomware negotiations (bachelor's thesis, albstadt-sigmaringen university) (2024). https://www.researchgate.net/profile/Lea-Mueller-25
16. Ottis, R.: Light weight tabletop exercise for cybersecurity education. J. Homel. Secur. Emerg. Manag. **11**(4), 579–592 (2014). https://doi.org/10.1515/jhsem-2014-0031

17. Ryan, P., Fokker, J., Healy, S., Amann, A.: Dynamics of targeted ransomware negotiation. IEEE Access **10**, 32836–32844 (2022). https://doi.org/10.1109/ACCESS.2022.3160748
18. Vakilinia, I., Khalili, M.M., Li, M.: A mechanism design approach to solve ransomware dilemmas. In: Bošanský, B., Gonzalez, C., Rass, S., Sinha, A. (eds.) Decision and Game Theory for Security, pp. 181–194. Springer, Cham (2021)
19. Wade, M.: Digital hostages: leveraging ransomware attacks in cyberspace. Bus. Horizons **64**(6), 787–797 (2021). https://doi.org/10.1016/j.bushor.2021.07.014. https://www.sciencedirect.com/science/article/pii/S0007681321001373

The Role of Cognition in Developing Successful Cybersecurity Training Programs – Passive vs. Active Engagement

Julia Prümmer(✉) (iD)

Leiden University, Turfmarkt 99, 2511 DP The Hague, The Netherlands
j.prummer@fgga.leidenuniv.nl

Abstract. End-user cybersecurity, and the risks associated with it, are receiving more and more attention, particularly in organizational settings. This increase in attention has led to a growing body of research on how to mitigate end-user error through cybersecurity training, as well as the implementation of training programs in many organisations across the world. Unfortunately, training programs currently found in the academic landscape and within organisations fail to adequately specify the mechanisms of behaviour that are required of the end-user. This article outlines an alternative approach that differentiates between different kinds of cybersecurity behaviours – those requiring continuous active engagement from the user, and those that can become more passive and habitual over time. To this end, current cybersecurity training approaches and their limitations will be outlined, followed by a brief exploration of habit theory and habit creation. Subsequently, the level of engagement needed for specific cybersecurity behaviours is analysed. In addition, practical approaches to training design, as well as areas for future research are highlighted.

Keywords: Human Factor · Behaviour Change · Training

1 Introduction

In 2022, 83% of organisations were affected by a data breach on more than one occasion. These incidents have led to declines in stock valuation and a mean market loss that has reached the 5 billion $ mark [1]. While media reporting on large security incidents has become more and more frequent, small means of attacks, through phishing, inadequate passwords, or others, are utilized every day without adequate recognition. Many of these methods exploit human vulnerabilities by targeting users' lack of knowledge and attention or utilizing visual deception to mimic legitimate sources [2]. While technological advances regarding incident prevention continue to grow, human actors still play an essential role in achieving security in cyberspace. However, end-users, particularly in organizational settings, are often faced with a multitude of demands and pressures in relation to their organizational responsibilities, leading to cybersecurity falling by the wayside. Still, many training programs utilized today are attempting to shift end-users'

© The Author(s), under exclusive license to Springer Nature Switzerland AG 2024
D. D. Schmorrow and C. M. Fidopiastis (Eds.): HCII 2024, LNAI 14695, pp. 185–199, 2024.
https://doi.org/10.1007/978-3-031-61572-6_13

focus to become more security-conscious. Unfortunately, training programs currently found in the academic landscape and within organisations often do not place a specific focus on what is required of the end-user to behave securely. This is emphasized by the lack of differentiation between different cybersecurity behaviours within existing training programs. While behaviours such as screen locking, strong password use and phishing resilience can all be summarized under the umbrella of cybersecurity, they involve different mechanisms of action required of the end user. This is currently not what the focus is placed on in existing training programs, also with regard to the methods that are used to train, as identified through a systematic literature review conducted by Prümmer et al. [3]. Serious games, presentations and simulations have all been suggested and evaluated as training methods for the variety of behaviours outlined above [4–6]. Based on the findings of these studies, no single training method appears to be outperforming another, not just when it comes to effectiveness [7, 8], but also regarding which methods end-users prefer [6, 9]. Studies have also shown that while current approaches to cybersecurity training are successful in changing end-users' attitudes or knowledge, a change in behaviour is often much harder to achieve [4, 9, 10]. A potential explanation for these observations could be the lack of differentiation between cybersecurity behaviours outlined previously, and the skills and level of engagement they require from the end-user.

Adding to this, training programs often constitute an additional task that needs to be performed alongside end-users' responsibilities, thereby increasing the pressures they are often faced with. Instead of the benefits end-users are supposed to gain from training programs, the consequences are often negative, leading to depletions in compliance budgets and in some cases to security fatigue. Security fatigue occurs primarily when end-users become disillusioned with their ability to perform the security behaviours demanded of them. Consequently, despite being conscious of the consequences that can occur when not adhering to security guidelines, they engage in insecure behaviour [11, 12]. In a study conducted by Cram et al. [12] "quantity of security policy communications and activities" was highlighted as one factor leading to security fatigue. Included in this category were security reminders and training programs, illustrating that these activities currently being undertaken to educate users are actively dissuading from secure behaviour. They also found that the way requirements are communicated, such as the length or style of communication, can have a negative effect as well.

Research conducted on concepts such as training effectiveness, but particularly security fatigue can provide a variety of insights for the field of cybersecurity training. Knowledge of mechanisms leading to security fatigue, as well as the effects of it on end-user behaviour with regard to cybersecurity constitute a unique opportunity to inform training programs in the future. Many of the concepts highlighted in Cram et al. [12] indicate that end-users wish to minimize the amount of time they have to engage with security practices. This is underlined by the observation that end-users experiencing security fatigue actively try to minimize the effort they expend to comply with security guidelines. Rather than chastising end-users for such measures, researchers and creators of training programs should take advantage of this knowledge. One way to do so is to provide employees with behavioural shortcuts that would minimize the level of active engagement needed to achieve an adequate level of cybersecurity. By drawing on information found in the field of habit theory and habit creation, a possible approach to cybersecurity training of specific types of behaviours will be outlined in this article. First, in Sect. 2 current approaches to cybersecurity training, as well as their limitations, will be analysed, followed by an introduction to habit theory in Sect. 3. Section 4 will highlight under what category of behaviour (i.e. passive vs. active) different cybersecurity behaviours may fall. Lastly, Sect. 5 will discuss how habit theory approaches can be applied to the cybersecurity landscape by outlining potential practical applications with regard to training design.

2 Cybersecurity Training

Cybersecurity training programs have been a topic of debate for many years. While initially deemed as a small-scale problem demanding technical solutions, the growing and continued targeting of end-users and the large-scale implications of cyberattacks that emerged in the 2000s [13] have since placed at least some of the focus on the end-users themselves. Particularly in organisations, cybersecurity has become an important focus for management, as employees often constitute the first line of defence for malicious software or hackers to enter the organizational systems [13]. Since the rise of the concept of cybersecurity education, awareness campaigns have been at the forefront of practical applications. These awareness campaigns often involve educating the user through newsletters and pamphlets, as well as posters and sometimes campaign stationary (i.e. pens, notebooks). While research has since shown that the effect of these awareness campaigns is either not evaluated [14] or not sufficient to change behaviour [15], they are still utilized in a variety of governmental and organizational cybersecurity initiatives.

Since the 2010s, researchers have shifted their focus from awareness campaigns to in-depth cybersecurity training. This type of training often requires direct involvement from the end-user, beyond a cursory glance at a poster or e-mail. Rather, end-users are instructed to engage with content, often for several hours depending on their occupation. The methods with which end-users are trained are varied, ranging from more traditional techniques such as video-based [16] and presentation-based interventions [17] to novel methodologies such as serious games [4] or simulations [18]. Particularly serious games have gained popularity in recent years. These games often attempt to simplify cybersecurity behaviours and enhance engagement through unique imagery, storylines or rewards. 'Anti-Phishing Phil', a game developed by Sheng et al. [19] and used in Abawajy [20] involves players distinguishing legitimate URLs from fake ones by having the protagonist of the game, a fish named Phil, consume legitimate URLs in order to grow. Other examples include a 'password protector game' where users are instructed to create strong passwords based on visual cues and game rules and are awarded points if successful [21]. As evidenced here, these training programs are often extensive. In addition, the same training methods are used to educate users on cybersecurity behaviours that appear to involve different behavioural mechanisms from the end-user.

While a variety of topics are addressed in training programs, some appear much more frequently than others. Social engineering, and phishing in particular, is often chosen as a training focus [22], while insider threat [23] and malware issues [24] are addressed much less frequently. Considering the popularity of phishing as an attack vector [25] this is not surprising. Many articles also choose to address cybersecurity in general, rather than targeting a specific behaviour [26, 27]. Again, in these cases, the same training program is used to educate users on a variety of behaviours.

2.1 Limitations of Current Training Approaches

While the positive effects of training programs are shown in a variety of studies [9, 28, 29], there are several limitations to be found in common practices. Due to the increasingly detrimental effects cyberattacks have on organisations, more and more focus is placed on end-user education. While this is, in principle, a good development, it appears as if current practices are often more burdensome for end-users than they are helpful [12]. As discussed previously, training programs are often treated as an additional task employees need to complete on top of their other responsibilities. Consequently, the programs are either completed in a rush, leading to a lack of information absorption, or the amount of effort required from employees goes beyond their compliance budget and in turn leads to security fatigue.

Additional limitations primarily pertain to training content. For example, the use of sanctions and rewards to dissuade or incentivize end-users to behave a certain way has not been found to be effective [30] but is still actively used in many training programs today. In addition, many programs are focused on the distribution of knowledge on cybersecurity and why it is an issue that end-users should care about. While knowledge and perception of cybersecurity can act as potential precursors to changes in cybersecurity behaviour, this transfer is not guaranteed [31]. In fact, studies that investigate the effectiveness of interventions on behaviour, often report lower effects than those that focus on changes in knowledge, intention or other precursors to behaviour [4, 9].

Lastly, a lack of differentiation between outcome behaviours with regard to training methods can also be observed. This, as well as the lack of theoretical underpinnings considered before training creation, lends to the impression that many training programs are being created based on common-sense determinations and novelty, rather than a clear exploration of goals and needs. Not all cybersecurity behaviours require the same thought processes and actions. While not engaging with a phishing e-mail may require active cognitive engagement throughout the process of checking senders, links, and attachments, other behaviours, such as screen locking and the use of password managers, could potentially become much more passive with time. Instead of knowledge as a defining factor to success, these types of behaviours could become much more reliant on skill, as posited by Pfleeger et al. [32]. The methods currently investigated in the field are not designed in a way that addresses these potential discrepancies. I posit that potential solutions can be found in the field of habit theory.

3 Habits

As stated by Verplanken & Orbell [33], "a habit is formed when someone repeatedly and automatically responds in a specific way to a specific cue in a recurrent, stable, context" (p. 66). A cue, in this case, may not just be a physical object, but a variety of other things, such as a specific time of day, a location, an activity, a psychological state or even another person. For example, buying a specific type of coffee when visiting a specific café could constitute a habit tied to a location. Listening to podcasts when taking a walk could constitute a habit tied to an activity. And biting your nails when feeling anxious may be an example of a habit tied to a psychological state. As illustrated here, a variety of influences in our environment and within ourselves can cue a habit to take place. In fact, research has found that humans spend nearly half of their day engaging in activities that are habitual and require little attention and focus and are instead influenced by automatic mental processes [34]. Automaticity, in many cases, can be classified as a difficulty to control or stop a process, as well as a lack of awareness and a lack of intentionality, but also mental efficiency [33, 35]. This mental efficiency may be particularly useful in the context of cybersecurity. It has also been found that the connection between the cue, in whatever form it comes, and the associated behaviour strengthens when repeated consistently. Once the connection has led to changes in procedural memory [36], the behaviour will no longer be performed intentionally. Instead, executive control is no longer needed, and the behaviour will turn into an automatic and unconscious association between a cue and a response.

The lack of active cognitive engagement required of the individual when performing a habit is one of many benefits. Particularly in a cybersecurity context, where end-users are overburdened with information and task requirements, a singular focus on performing a secure action without deliberate thought could provide much-needed mental relief. Similarly, the development of habits can also lead to a lack of attention being paid to alternative courses of action or other information on the context within which the behaviour is being performed. Individuals engaging in a habit take on something often referred to as an 'action-oriented mindset', rather than a 'deliberate mindset'. In other words, habits can lead to 'tunnel vision' that blocks out other important information within the environment [33]. While this can be desirable in many instances, e.g. locking the computer screen even when distracted by something else, this is not always the case. The habit of connecting to a public Wi-Fi network when entering a specific location may be a good example of an action-oriented mindset overriding a deliberate analysis of whether this could potentially expose sensitive personal information to others. From this, it becomes apparent that not all behaviours that occur in a cybersecurity context will benefit from habituation. In those instances, the goal should instead be to discourage and prevent habitual behaviour.

3.1 Habit Creation

One way to create new habits is by employing so-called 'implementation intentions. Implementation intentions [37] are intentions to behave a certain way when a specific circumstance occurs. For example, an implementation intention to promote screen locking could look like this: "When I stand up from my chair, I will lock my screen.". With implementation intentions, the cue that is to trigger the new habit is explicitly identified and specified. When this 'if-then' pattern is repeated sufficiently, a new habit will form [33]. A similar idea is iterated in Wood & Neal [38] who posit that habits can arise through purposeful goal setting. Once habits are created through frequent repetition of behaviour, this link between the goal and the behaviour diminishes, and habits become goal-independent.

In order to be successful, the identification of an appropriate cue to trigger the response needs to be considered carefully. Similarly, the formulated intention needs to be specific, as well as strong enough to be transformed into action. Sufficient motivation also plays an important role. While an intention to floss after brushing one's teeth is specific and does not require a lot of motivation, running a 5k after returning from work does. While the cue of 'coming home from work' may initially seem sensible, it is often not specific enough. In addition, running five kilometres every day requires tremendous amounts of motivation. Based on this, one of the most important aspects of habit creation is therefore the context in which it occurs. This also implies that as soon as contextual cues change repeatedly, the necessary mental processes that create and strengthen habits do not occur. Stable situational contexts, in whichever form they come, are a necessary condition for habit creation to occur. According to Wood & Neal [38], habits cued through context can happen in two ways. One is through 'direct cueing', which involves the formation of a direct association between the cue/context and the response/behaviour. Repeated coactivation of the cue and response leads to neural changes that make the behaviour more and more likely to occur in the future when the cue is encountered. In contrast, 'motivated cueing' is mediated by the reward value of a specific response, which is then transferred onto the context in which the response occurred. With frequent repetition, the cue/context will soon become associated with the reward, in turn prompting a specific behaviour to occur. Unfortunately, this form of cueing has only been analysed in non-human research [39].

According to the Fogg Behavior Model [40], habits form through adequate motivation and ability, as well as an appropriate trigger. Similar to the methodologies outlined previously, a strong focus is placed on the importance of a carefully selected cue to trigger the response. In addition, the role of motivation and ability is outlined. Firstly, the model posits that motivation and ability can compensate for each other. This means that as long as the motivation to perform a behaviour is high, the ability to do so does not need to be. In turn, when a behaviour is easy to implement, a low level of motivation is often enough for the behaviour to occur. By influencing ability, as well as the level of motivation and finding an appropriate trigger to prompt the behaviour, habit formation will occur.

While the creation of new habits is a complex and often lengthy undertaking, changing existing habits can prove even more difficult. As stated by Verplanken & Orbell [33], existing habits are difficult to override and merely intending to behave differently is often not enough. Even when a conscious decision is made to behave differently, a lack of attention paid to the task that is being performed can lead to something called an 'action slip' [41]. When an action slip occurs, the intended behaviour is overridden by a habitual response that would normally be performed in the context one is in. This has practical implications, particularly for the dismantling of 'bad habits' that an individual has developed. Still, some methodologies and techniques are available to do so, one of which is, again, implementation intentions [33], which have been discussed previously. As outlined above, implementation intentions are most useful when attempting to override existing habits and replace them with new ones. Another technique to stop existing habits has been termed the 'habit discontinuity hypothesis' [42]. The general principle here is that the removal or disruption of the cue that triggers the habit will stop the habit from materializing. For example, when an employee is familiar with a specific operating system and has developed habits around it, moving to a new role in an organization where a different operating system is used can serve as a disruption. The previously relied-on cues are no longer applicable; hence the habit is no longer carried out.

4 Passive vs Active Engagement

Based on information gathered from the field of cybersecurity training, as well as habit theory, it becomes apparent that not all cybersecurity behaviours are the same. While some behaviours, such as phishing, seem to require a continuous level of engagement from the end-user in order to be performed correctly, others, such as screen locking, seem to bear a close resemblance to other habitual behaviours. By differentiating between these behaviours that require either active or passive engagement from the end-user and training them accordingly, training effectiveness, particularly in relation to objective behaviour change, could increase. Therefore, this section will outline how habits have been discussed so far in the cybersecurity literature, followed by an exploration of which behaviours can be classified as passive, and which can be classified as active.

4.1 Habits in Cybersecurity

Habits have been a frequent topic of discussion in other fields such as healthcare or nutrition. Unfortunately, this does not extend to the field of cybersecurity education. While a variety of articles have investigated the ability of existing habits to predict cybersecurity intention [30, 43–47], no significant exploration of how good security habits can be formed was found in the literature. A similar observation was made by Weickert et al. [48] who conducted a network-based analysis on the context within which habits are discussed in the cybersecurity literature. They found that habits are primarily discussed in relation to other models and theories of behaviour, rather than as an isolated concept. A notable exception to this is Vishwanath [49], who found that participants who had developed strong habits with regard to their e-mail behaviour (such as checking e-mails while commuting or before bed) were found to be increasingly likely to be susceptible to phishing, while those users engaging in systematic processing of clues were less likely. In addition, although habits are not frequently discussed within the field of cybersecurity education, website designers and software developers have identified a variety of techniques frequently used in habit creation and have implemented them in the form of dark patterns.

Dark Patterns. Dark patterns occur when interfaces are designed in such a way, that users are prompted or persuaded to select choices that are to their detriment. The design of these interfaces is often based on knowledge gained from psychology and end-users' desires for easy-to-access solutions and shortcuts [50]. Unfortunately, these dark patterns can cause negative habits to develop. A good illustration of this is the occurrence of Cookie Banners. By purposefully highlighting the 'accept cookies' button and minimizing the 'reject cookies' button, websites are purposefully steering their users to click accept, even when the sharing of cookies is something users wish to minimize. In some cases, the 'reject' button is not available entirely, and instead, users have the option to select 'further preferences', adding an additional barrier the user needs to overcome. This kind of dark pattern strategy has been termed "obstruction" [50] and has been shown to significantly increase the willingness of participants to sign up for something that they do not want [51]. By employing a design like this, users' motivation to proceed to the website they wish to visit, as well as their ability to click a button is exploited. The appropriate trigger, in this case, showing the cookie banner before any information contained on the website is shown, aids in getting users to make a choice that they would not make if the interface were designed differently. The fact that this behaviour is repeated frequently – often multiple times a day – has turned it into a habitual behaviour for many users.

Overall, while habit formation has not been a major topic of discussion within the cybersecurity literature so far, allowing end-users to more passively engage in at least some cybersecurity behaviours appears to be a viable topic to explore. Therefore, the following sections will outline which behaviours are conducive to habit formation, and which behaviours are not.

4.2 Passive Engagement

Screen Locking. Locking one's screen is a cybersecurity behaviour that is often overlooked within the literature. Compared to other attack vectors, particularly phishing, exploitations originating from an unlocked screen are relatively uncommon. Still, not locking one's screen, particularly when working in a location other than one's office, can have detrimental effects on the end-user, as well as the organisation they work for. An unlocked computer is often a blank canvas for attackers and can lead to the accessing and stealing of sensitive data or even the installation of malware that can give hackers access to the organizational network at a later time. Therefore, screen locking is a cybersecurity behaviour that should be actively encouraged by organisations. By nature, locking one's screen is easy to do, as it often takes only a handful of keystrokes. It is also a behaviour that remains stable, even in different contexts. Whether an end-user is at their office, in a café or at home, the act of locking one's screen is the same. Because it is such an easy behaviour to perform, the motivation to perform the behaviour, in turn, does not need to be high either. All these factors make screen locking an ideal behaviour to focus on when attempting to form cybersecurity habits.

Passwords. Authentication of one's identity through passwords is the most common method of authentication in use today. Passwords in organizational settings are often used to access a variety of sensitive information. That is why educating users on how to create safe passwords has been a strong focus of attention within the cybersecurity training literature. Users are instructed to create passwords that are appropriate in length, contain both upper- and lower-case letters, as well as numbers and other symbols, and differ significantly from previously created passwords. In addition, the password should be changed regularly. Unfortunately, the guidelines presented in these training programs are often burdensome to end-users. Remembering complex passwords without additional aid is nearly impossible, particularly when considering the number of passwords end-users need to remember [52]. This is why end-users often resort to easy-to-guess - and therefore easy-to-remember - passwords and reuse them throughout a variety of their accounts. One way to support end-users in generating and remembering secure passwords is through password managers [53]. By using a password manager, users are only required to remember a single password that unlocks the passwords for other websites or applications. This significantly decreases the cognitive load that is usually associated with password behaviour [54]. Since the motivation to generate/remember secure passwords appears to be low, this increase in ability could make it more likely for end-users to engage in the behaviour of using a password manager. Previous research has already shown that end-users view password managers as a useful and easy-to-use tool to enhance performance and reduce cognitive load [53]. Integrating habit-promoting tools into security training, particularly when addressing password behaviour, could therefore have tremendous benefits for both end-users and organisations.

Software Updates. The importance of software updates in protecting devices from malicious software and other attacks has been well-established [55, 56]. In fact, users are particularly at risk when updates with patches to system vulnerabilities are available, but not installed in a timely manner [57]. Unfortunately, the installation of updates usually takes up a considerable amount of time during which no work can be completed by the end-user. This often means that end-users delay updates until they have no choice but to install them, exposing them and their organisation to preventable attacks. By attempting to habituate update behaviour and finding appropriate moments during an employee's workday to let updates complete in the background, the strain on end-user productivity could be minimized. By encouraging employees to find pockets of time within their day when they are away from their devices and finding appropriate cues to trigger the behaviour, a habit to check for updates consistently and run them if available could be developed.

4.3 Active Engagement

Checking E-mails/Links. Contrary to the behaviours outlined above, cybersecurity behaviours where the attack mechanisms rely on social engineering may not benefit from habituation and a reduction of active engagement. By nature, the success of social engineering is dependent on exploiting end-users' lack of attention on the task they are performing. For example, the imitation of company logos or e-mail addresses in phishing attempts deliberately exploits users who are not careful enough when looking through their e-mail. In turn, end-users who have developed strong e-mail habits, such as reacting or responding to e-mails instinctively and/or in specific moments, are much more likely to become victimized as a result of social engineering [49]. By comparison, Vishwanath [49] found that end-users who did not display strong e-mail habits, and instead engaged in conscious processing, were less likely to fall for social engineering/phishing attacks. Therefore, building habits with regard to e-mail/link checking should be actively discouraged during cybersecurity training programs. Instead, the programs should give practical guidelines and examples on how to spot social engineering and steps of action that end-users can take next.

Wi-Fi. It is well established within the cybersecurity landscape that connecting to open-access Wi-Fi networks can have detrimental consequences to end-users, as data transmitted over public Wi-Fi can be intercepted and therefore stolen. Unfortunately, connecting to public Wi-Fi is a behaviour that a lot of end-users engage in [58]. Similar to e-mail behaviour, connecting to Wi-Fi networks outside of the home or work environment does not seem to lend itself to habit building, as habitually connecting to the most convenient network available could put end-user and organizational data at risk. Instead, training programs should, again, provide users with necessary practical guidelines that aid in identifying networks that are safe to connect to.

5 Practical Applicability

In order to allow end-users to engage more passively with their cybersecurity, a variety of techniques, particularly from research on habit creation, can be utilized. Utilizing these techniques, in combination with the previously discussed implementation intentions, may aid in changing end-user behaviour.

5.1 Ability

Previous approaches to cybersecurity have focused largely on increasing end-user ability by having them learn how to do new things. What they are asked to do is often complicated and time-consuming, depleting compliance budgets and leading to frustration. Taking inspiration from research on habit creation tells us that the fostering of habits is often brought about by simplifying behaviours instead [40]. While not all techniques encountered in the habit literature are applicable to a cybersecurity context, a substantial number are. One of them is the time factor [40]. One of the potential reasons preventing employees from further engaging with their cybersecurity is the lack of time they have at their disposal to do so. Updates are delayed because tasks need to be completed right away, passwords are kept simple and easy to guess to prevent time-consuming resets when stronger passwords get inevitably forgotten, and so on. By offering end-users solutions that decrease the amount of time they spend on these tasks, they may be more willing to engage with them. And as discussed previously, when ability is high, motivation does not need to be. A practical way to do so could be the use of password managers within organizational contexts, as outlined above. By using a password manager, employees do not need to come up with complicated passwords themselves and, more importantly, they do not need to remember them because it is all done automatically. This could also be a potential way to target an additional technique of increasing ability, namely routine integration [40]. Behaviours are usually easier to perform when they fit into our routines seamlessly. Running lengthy updates in the middle of the day when other things need to be accomplished is often a big disturbance to a normal workday routine. Instead, finding pockets of time within the day when completing this task is no longer a nuisance might enhance an end-users' willingness to run the updates. Inquiring about end-users' routines and advising them on where certain cybersecurity behaviours may fit within them, could significantly increase ability.

5.2 Motivation

Increasing end-user motivation is more in line with traditional awareness-raising techniques that outline the harmful consequences of inadequate cybersecurity and attempt to change end-user perception. While this change in perception has been successful in a variety of studies [9, 59], this effect has unfortunately not translated to changes in behaviour. Still, techniques from the field of habit creation should at least be considered when designing programs that aim to create and strengthen more passive end-user engagement. In particular, social acceptance/rejection could be a motivating factor [40]. From an evolutionary perspective, being rejected from a group is something we often wish to avoid. By creating a culture of security in which secure behaviours are normalized among the majority of employees, others may be more willing to adhere in order to avoid rejection from the group. It may also lead to structural changes within the organization that could afford end-users more time to complete security-related tasks. While this is not necessarily easy to accomplish through targeted training programs, security culture should still be considered in future research.

5.3 Triggers/Cues

Due to the portability of technological devices, creating a stable contextual environment for automatic processes to form can be difficult. Relying solely on cues dependent on the physical environment may therefore not be an adequate approach in cybersecurity [60]. Rather, the device itself, the operating system being used, as well as the physical environment should all act as triggers and cues for a behaviour to occur. Adequately specifying all potential instances in which an end-user engages in a specific behaviour is therefore important. Only then can adequate implementation intentions involving all possible instances be specified. In addition, finding appropriate spots within existing routines for a new habit to take place (see routine integration above) and specifying/creating a trigger around it could aid in initial habit formation. By using 'signals' [40], such as strategically placed post-it notes or timed reminders, end-users may be more likely to perform a behaviour. As outlined by Fogg [40], this type of trigger works best when the behaviour has previously been simplified to lower the barrier of performance.

5.4 Interface Design

While dark patterns themselves are often harmful to end-users, their success in guiding human behaviour could aid in creating interfaces that have a positive impact. Using interface design to promote a secure behaviour, e.g. locking the screen by merely moving the mouse to the corner of the screen, can aid significantly in increasing end-user ability. Taking inspiration from the field of nudging, which involves making changes to interfaces in order to steer users to a safer option, could be of particular use here [61, 62]. This idea is supported by Garaialde et al. [63], who have shown that when interface habits are formed, the selection of a desired option occurs much quicker and more accurately than when these habits are not created. Still, caution needs to be taken here, as changes to the interface can significantly disrupt the effectiveness of previously established habits, as formerly utilised cues for behaviour are no longer accessible (Garaialde et al., 2020). If or when changes to the interface are made, appropriate educational programs that retrain the habitual behaviour according to the new interface may need to be implemented alongside.

6 Conclusion

Overall, the main conclusion that can be drawn from this article is that not all cyber-security behaviours are the same and therefore should also not be trained that way. By integrating knowledge gained from the field of habit creation, I hypothesize that some cybersecurity behaviours are akin to habitual behaviour and should therefore be treated that way when designing a security training. To this end, a variety of techniques are available to foster security habits in relation to these behaviours, such as increasing ability through simplification or finding appropriate cues to trigger a behaviour. From the information gathered for this article, it also becomes apparent that not all cyberse-curity behaviours are conducive to habit creation. It is therefore imperative that future research determines which cybersecurity behaviours could indeed benefit from more passive engagement, and which could not. In addition, the exact mechanisms to train passive vs active cybersecurity behaviours need to be explored and specified. In general, recognising the fundamental differences that exist between cybersecurity behaviours and designing training programs accordingly, must be the way forward.

Disclosure of Interests. The author has no competing interests to declare that are relevant to the content of this article.

References

1. Huang, K., Wang, X., Wei, W., Madnick, S.: The Devastating Business Impacts of a Cyber Breach. https://hbr.org/2023/05/the-devastating-business-impacts-of-a-cyber-breach
2. Dhamija, R., Tygar, J.D., Hearst, M.: Why phishing works. In: Proceedings of the SIGCHI Conference on Human Factors in Computing Systems, pp. 581–590 (2006)
3. Prümmer, J., van Steen, T., van den Berg, B.: A systematic review of current cybersecurity training methods. Comput. Secur. **136**, 103585 (2024). https://doi.org/10.1016/j.cose.2023.103585
4. van Steen, T., Deeleman, J.R.A.: Successful gamification of cybersecurity training. Cyberpsychology Behav. Soc. Netw. (2021). https://doi.org/10.1089/cyber.2020.0526
5. Adinolf, S., Wyeth, P., Brown, R., Altizer, R.: Towards designing agent based virtual reality applications for cybersecurity training. In: Proceedings of the 31st Australian Conference on Human-Computer-Interaction, pp. 452–456. Association for Computing Machinery (2019)
6. Cook, A., Smith, R.G., Maglaras, L., Janicke, H.: SCIPS: using experiential learning to raise cyber situational awareness in industrial control system. Int. J. Cyber Warf. Terror. **7**, 1–15 (2017). https://doi.org/10.4018/IJCWT.2017040101
7. Baillon, A., de Bruin, J., Emirmahmutoglu, A., van de Veer, E., van Dijk, B.: Informing, simulating experience, or both: a field experiment on phishing risks. PLoS ONE **14** (2019). https://doi.org/10.1371/journal.pone.0224216
8. Chin, A.G., Etudo, U., Harris, M.A.: On mobile device security practices and training efficacy: an empirical study. Inform. Educ. **15**, 235–252 (2016). https://doi.org/10.15388/infedu.2016.12
9. Chen, T., Stewart, M., Bai, Z., Chen, E., Dabbish, L., Hammer, J.: Hacked time: design and evaluation of a self-efficacy based cybersecurity game. In: Proceedings of the 2020 ACM Designing Interactive Systems Conference, pp. 1737–1749. Association for Computing Machinery (2020)

10. Albrechtsen, E., Hovden, J.: Improving information security awareness and behaviour through dialogue, participation and collective reflection. An intervention study. Comput. Secur. **29**, 432–445 (2010). https://doi.org/10.1016/j.cose.2009.12.005
11. Furnell, S., Thomson, K.-L.: Recognising and addressing 'security fatigue.' Comput. Fraud Secur. **2009**, 7–11 (2009). https://doi.org/10.1016/S1361-3723(09)70139-3
12. Cram, W.A., Proudfoot, J.G., D'Arcy, J.: When enough is enough: investigating the antecedents and consequences of information security fatigue (2021)
13. Ganapati, S., Ahn, M., Reddick, C.: Evolution of cybersecurity concerns: a systematic literature review. In: Proceedings of the 24th Annual International Conference on Digital Government Research, pp. 90–97. Association for Computing Machinery, New York (2023)
14. van Steen, T., Norris, E., Atha, K., Joinson, A.: What (if any) behaviour change techniques do government-led cybersecurity awareness campaigns use? J. Cybersecur. **6** (2020). https://doi.org/10.1093/cybsec/tyaa019
15. Bada, M., Sasse, A.M., Nurse, J.R.C.: Cyber Security Awareness Campaigns: Why do they fail to change behaviour? CoRR. abs/1901.02672 (2019)
16. Jenkins, J.L., Durcikova, A., Burns, M.B.: Simplicity is bliss: controlling extraneous cognitive load in online security training to promote secure behavior. J. Organ. End User Comput. **25**, 52–66 (2013). https://doi.org/10.4018/joeuc.2013070104
17. Sykosch, A., Doll, C., Wübbeling, M., Meier, M.: Generalizing the phishing principle: analyzing user behavior in response to controlled stimuli for IT security awareness assessment. In: Proceedings of the 15th International Conference on Availability, Reliability and Security. Association for Computing Machinery (2020)
18. Loffler, E., Schneider, B., Asprion, P.M., Zanwar, T.: CySecEscape 2.0-a virtual escape room to raise cybersecurity awareness. Int. J. Serious Games **8**, 59–70 (2021). https://doi.org/10. 17083/ijsg.v8i1.413
19. Sheng, S., et al.: Anti-phishing phil: the design and evaluation of a game that teaches people not to fall for phish (2007). https://doi.org/10.1145/1280680.1280692
20. Abawajy, J.: User preference of cyber security awareness delivery methods. Behav. Inf. Technol. **33**, 237–248 (2014). https://doi.org/10.1080/0144929X.2012.708787
21. Alotaibi, F.F.G.: Evaluation and enhancement of public cyber security awareness (2019)
22. Gordon, W.J., et al.: Evaluation of a mandatory phishing training program for high-risk employees at a US healthcare system. J. Am. Med. Inform. Assoc. **26**, 547–552 (2019). https://doi.org/10.1093/jamia/ocz005
23. Carlson, A.: Combating Insider Threat with Proper Training (2020)
24. Ikhalia, E., Serrano, A., Bell, D., Louvieris, P.: Online social network security awareness: mass interpersonal persuasion using a Facebook app. Inf. Technol. People **32**, 1276–1300 (2019). https://doi.org/10.1108/ITP-06-2018-0278
25. gov.uk: Educational institutions findings annex - Cyber Security Breaches Survey 2022. https://www.gov.uk/government/statistics/cyber-security-breaches-survey-2022/educat ional-institutions-findings-annex-cyber-security-breaches-survey-2022#chapter-2-key-fin dings
26. Hepp, S.L., Tarraf, R.C., Birney, A., Arain, M.A.: Evaluation of the awareness and effectiveness of IT security programs in a large publicly funded health care system. Health Inf. Manag. J. **47**, 116–124 (2018). https://doi.org/10.1177/1833358317722038
27. Kletenik, D., Butbul, A., Chan, D., Kwok, D., LaSpina, M.: Game on: teaching cybersecurity to novices through the use of a serious game. J. Comput. Sci. Coll. **36**, 11–21 (2021)
28. Alzahrani, A., Johnson, C.: Autonomy motivators, serious games, and intention toward ISP compliance. Int. J. Serious Games **6**, 67–85 (2019). https://doi.org/10.17083/ijsg.v6i4.315
29. Curry, M., Marshall, B., Correia, J., Crossler, R.E.: InfoSec process action model (IPAM): targeting insiders' weak password behavior. J. Inf. Syst. **33**, 201–225 (2019). https://doi.org/ 10.2308/isys-52381

30. Pahnila, S., Siponen, M., Mahmood, A.: Employees' behavior towards IS security policy compliance. In: 2007 40th Annual Hawaii International Conference on System Sciences (HICSS 2007), p. 156b (2007)
31. Scott, J., Ophoff, J.: Investigating the knowledge-behaviour gap in mitigating personal information compromise. In: HAISA, pp. 236–245 (2018)
32. Pfleeger, S.L., Sasse, M.A., Furnham, A.: From weakest link to security hero: transforming staff security behavior. J. Homel. Secur. Emerg. Manag. **11**, 489–510 (2014). https://doi.org/10.1515/jhsem-2014-0035
33. Verplanken, B., Orbell, S.: Habit and behavior change. In: Sassenberg, K., Vliek, M.L.W. (eds.) Social Psychology in Action: Evidence-Based Interventions from Theory to Practice, pp. 65–78. Springer, Cham (2019). https://doi.org/10.1007/978-3-030-13788-5_5
34. Wood, W., Quinn, J.M., Kashy, D.A.: Habits in everyday life: thought, emotion, and action. J. Pers. Soc. Psychol. **83**, 1281 (2002)
35. Bargh, J.A.: The four horsemen of automaticity: awareness, intention, efficiency, and control in social cognition. In: Handbook of Social Cognition, pp. 1–40. Psychology Press (2014)
36. Wood, W., Rünger, D.: Psychology of habit. Annu. Rev. Psychol. **67**, 289–314 (2016). https://doi.org/10.1146/annurev-psych-122414-033417
37. Gollwitzer, P.M.: Implementation intentions: strong effects of simple plans. Am. Psychol. **54**, 493–503 (1999). https://doi.org/10.1037/0003-066X.54.7.493
38. Wood, W., Neal, D.T.: A new look at habits and the habit-goal interface. Psychol. Rev. **114**, 843–863 (2007). https://doi.org/10.1037/0033-295X.114.4.843
39. Mirenowicz, J., Schultz, W.: Preferential activation of midbrain dopamine neurons by appetitive rather than aversive stimuli. Nature **379**, 449–451 (1996). https://doi.org/10.1038/379449a0
40. Fogg, B.: A behavior model for persuasive design. In: Proceedings of the 4th International Conference on Persuasive Technology. Association for Computing Machinery, New York (2009)
41. Heckhausen, H., Beckmann, J.: Intentional action and action slips. Psychol. Rev. **97**, 36 (1990)
42. Verplanken, B., Roy, D., Whitmarsh, L.: Cracks in the wall: habit discontinuities as vehicles for behaviour change. In: Verplanken, B. (ed.) The Psychology of Habit: Theory, Mechanisms, Change, and Contexts, pp. 189–205. Springer, Cham (2018). https://doi.org/10.1007/978-3-319-97529-0_11
43. Vance, A., Siponen, M., Pahnila, S.: Motivating IS security compliance: insights from habit and protection motivation theory. Inf. Manage. **49**, 190–198 (2012). https://doi.org/10.1016/j.im.2012.04.002
44. Tsai, H.S., Jiang, M., Alhabash, S., LaRose, R., Rifon, N.J., Cotten, S.R.: Understanding online safety behaviors: a protection motivation theory perspective. Comput. Secur. **59**, 138–150 (2016). https://doi.org/10.1016/j.cose.2016.02.009
45. Aigbefo, Q.A., Blount, Y., Marrone, M.: The influence of hardiness and habit on security behaviour intention. Behav. Inf. Technol. **41**, 1151–1170 (2022). https://doi.org/10.1080/0144929X.2020.1856928
46. Moody, G.D., Siponen, M., Pahnila, S.: Toward a unified model of information security policy compliance. MIS Q. **42**, 285–311 (2018). https://doi.org/10.25300/MISQ/2018/13853
47. Sommestad, T., Karlzén, H., Hallberg, J.: The theory of planned behavior and information security policy compliance. J. Comput. Inf. Syst. **59**, 344–353 (2019). https://doi.org/10.1080/08874417.2017.1368421
48. Weickert, T.D., Joinson, A., Craggs, B.: Is cybersecurity research missing a trick? Integrating insights from the psychology of habit into research and practice. Comput. Secur. **128**, 103130 (2023). https://doi.org/10.1016/j.cose.2023.103130

49. Vishwanath, A.: Examining the distinct antecedents of e-mail habits and its influence on the outcomes of a phishing attack. J. Comput.-Mediat. Commun. **20**, 570–584 (2015). https://doi.org/10.1111/jcc4.12126
50. Gray, C.M., Kou, Y., Battles, B., Hoggatt, J., Toombs, A.L.: The dark (patterns) side of UX design. In: Proceedings of the 2018 CHI Conference on Human Factors in Computing Systems, pp. 1–14. Association for Computing Machinery, New York (2018)
51. Luguri, J., Strahilevitz, L.J.: Shining a light on dark patterns. J. Leg. Anal. **13**, 43–109 (2021). https://doi.org/10.1093/jla/laaa006
52. Spadafora, A.: Struggling with password overload? You're not alone. https://www.techradar.com/news/most-people-have-25-more-passwords-than-at-the-start-of-the-pandemic
53. Maclean, R., Ophoff, J.: Determining key factors that lead to the adoption of password managers. In: 2018 International Conference on Intelligent and Innovative Computing Applications (ICONIC), pp. 1–7 (2018)
54. Li, Z., He, W., Akhawe, D., Song, D.: The emperor's new password manager: security analysis of web-based password managers. In: 23rd USENIX Security Symposium (USENIX Security 2014), pp. 465–479. USENIX Association, San Diego, CA (2014)
55. Microsoft: Microsoft Digital Defense Report 2021 (2021)
56. Khan, M., Bi, Z., Copeland, J.A.: Software updates as a security metric: passive identification of update trends and effect on machine infection. In: MILCOM 2012 - 2012 IEEE Military Communications Conference, pp. 1–6 (2012)
57. Bilge, L., Dumitraş, T.: Before we knew it: an empirical study of zero-day attacks in the real world. In: Proceedings of the 2012 ACM Conference on Computer and Communications Security, pp. 833–844. Association for Computing Machinery, New York (2012)
58. Ahmmed, N.M.A.: An evaluation of targeted security awareness for end users (2019)
59. Bauer, S., Bernroider, E.W.N., Chudzikowski, K.: Prevention is better than cure! Designing information security awareness programs to overcome users' non-compliance with information security policies in banks. Comput. Secur. **68**, 145–159 (2017). https://doi.org/10.1016/j.cose.2017.04.009
60. Bayer, J.B., Campbell, S.W.: Texting while driving on automatic: considering the frequency-independent side of habit. Comput. Hum. Behav. **28**, 2083–2090 (2012). https://doi.org/10.1016/j.chb.2012.06.012
61. Thaler, R.H., Sunstein, C.R.: Nudge: Improving Decisions about Health, Wealth, and Happiness. Yale University Press (2008)
62. van Steen, T.: When choice is (not) an option: nudging and techno-regulation approaches to behavioural cybersecurity. In: Schmorrow, D.D., Fidopiastis, C.M. (eds.) Augmented Cognition, pp. 120–130. Springer, Cham (2022). https://doi.org/10.1007/978-3-031-05457-0_10
63. Garaialde, D., et al.: Quantifying the impact of making and breaking interface habits. Int. J. Hum.-Comput. Stud. **142**, 102461 (2020). https://doi.org/10.1016/j.ijhcs.2020.102461

Health Informatics Associations Between Mindfulness Traits and Health Outcomes in Veterans with Chronic Multi-symptom Illness

Immanuel Babu Henry Samuel[1,2,3]($\boxtimes$), Calvin Lu[1,2,3], Timothy Chun[2], Nathaniel Allen[2], Lucas Crock[2], Kyle Jaquess[2], MaryAnn Dutton[4], Matthew J. Reinhard[1,2], and Michelle E. Costanzo[1,2]

[1] Complex Exposure Threats Center, Veterans Health Affairs, 50 Irving St NW, Washington, DC, USA
immanuel.samuel@va.gov

[2] War Related Illness and Injury Study Center, Veterans Health Affairs, 50 Irving St NW, Washington, DC, USA

[3] The Henry M. Jackson Foundation for the Advancement of Military Medicine Inc., 6720A Rockledge Drive, Suite 100, Bethesda, MD, USA

[4] Department of Psychiatry, Georgetown University School of Medicine, Washington, DC, USA

Abstract. Behavioral health interventions and lifestyle medicine intended to augment wellness and resilience, offer promising solutions to chronic disease management for Veterans. We aimed to test the broad-spectrum benefits of trait mindfulness and identify facets of mindfulness with the most profound effect on Veteran's overall health and neuropsychological performance, and to identify neural markers of mindfulness facets. Veteran participants (n = 145, age = 44–77; male = 117) who were: (a) U.S. Gulf War Veteran and (b) meet CDC CMI criteria and assessed using a cross-modal design. Nineteen participants (age = 52–71, gender = 17M, 2F) underwent EEG session. We measured trait mindfulness using the Five Facet Mindfulness questionnaire and looked at associations with multi-modal health outcomes using standard health questionnaires, neuropsychological performance and electroencephalography (EEG). Factor analysis revealed that trait mindfulness dimensions support a dual-factor framework: (a) Proactive factor comprised of Awareness, Describing and Non-Judging loaded; (b) Reactive factor comprised of Observing and Non-Reactivity. Structural modeling was applied to the highest loaded FFMQ dimensions for each factor and outcome variables. Proactive factor was significantly associated with higher scores on self-reported health and psychological performance measures. The two factors of mindfulness showed preliminary associations with distinct EEG spatial-temporal features of alpha rhythm suggesting distinct neuronal sources of proactive and reactive factors of mindfulness. Higher trait mindfulness specifically the proactive factor promotes resiliency to adverse health outcomes and higher cognitive performance with quantifiable neural representations. These findings suggest that mindfulness programs targeting the proactive factor could maximize mindfulness related improvement in health outcomes.

Keywords: Mindfulness · EEG · Cognitive Performance

© The Author(s), under exclusive license to Springer Nature Switzerland AG 2024
D. D. Schmorrow and C. M. Fidopiastis (Eds.): HCII 2024, LNAI 14695, pp. 200–212, 2024.
https://doi.org/10.1007/978-3-031-61572-6_14

1 Introduction

Behavioral health interventions and lifestyle medicine intended to augment wellness and resilience, offer promising solutions to chronic disease management. Such holistic models of care are particularly interesting for individuals with chronic illness whose etiology is poorly understood as treatment is focused on isolated symptoms rather than addressing the underlying mechanism maintaining the illness. The practice of mindfulness meditation has garnered significant attention and has been found to benefit multiple biological systems simultaneously and improving overall health. Specifically, studies have shown that mindfulness is associated with physical and mental changes such as reduced anxiety (Lang, 2013; Cernetic, 2016), stress (Creswell et al., 2014; Tang, 2015), negative emotions (Eberth & Sedlmeier, 2012; Eberth & Schäfer, 2019; Khusid & Vythilingam, 2016; Wu et al., 2019), body pain (Creswell et al., 2014; Zeidan et al., 2011), depression (Chambers et al., 2008; Hofmann et al., 2010; Ma & Teasdale, 2004), improvements in cognitive performance (Creswell, 2017; Hölzel et al., 2011; Larson et al., 2013;), attention (Eberth & Schäfer, 2019; Hölzel et al., 2011; Jensen et al., 2012; Jha et al., 2015; Lindsay & Creswell, 2017) and emotional state (Eberth & Schäfer, 2019; Eberth & Sedlmeier, 2012; Gibson, 2019; Goyal et al., 2014;). Mindfulness has also been associated with changes in EEG brain rhythms such as alpha power which are posited to enhance relaxed alertness which improves mental health (Ahani et al., 2013; Chiesa & Serretti, 2010; Lazar et al., 2000). Assessing the impact of trait mindfulness on health outcomes is important for understanding its implications for those who have endured significant stressful life events such as combat Veterans, since the trait and cultivated aspects of mindfulness influence each other (Duan & Li, 2016). Therefore, evaluating how facets of trait mindfulness relate to post-deployment health factors (such as depression, stress, sleep quality, fatigue and overall health), cognitive function and cortical dynamics may be of particular importance in Veterans since it would reveal mindfulness facets that have the most beneficial effect on complex symptoms. In this study, we look at the relationship between trait mindfulness using the Five Facet Mindfulness Questionnaire (FFMQ) which measures disposition across five distinct dimensions: Awareness, Describing, Non-judging, Observing and Non-reactivity (Baer et al., 2006) and clinical symptom profiles, objective cognitive performance, and resting brain activity in previously-deployed Veterans with Chronic Multi-symptom Illness (CMI).

While mindfulness has been posited to have distinct facets, prior studies have shown differential modulation characteristics and associations with health outcomes (Bruin et al., 2012; Baer et al., 2012; Brown et al, 2015; Lykins & Baer, 2009; Petrocchi & Ottaviani, 2016). However, a prior study suggests the presence of a higher order mindfulness structure comprising of two dimensions (Tran et al., 2013) which is in alignment with existing theories such as two meta-traits of the Big Five personality theory (Digman, 1997), assessments of personality (Blackburn et al., 2005), mindfulness-based cognitive therapy 'bring' and 'doing' phases and Dual Modes of Control (DMC) framework in cognitive control theory which categorizes control processes into "proactive" and "reactive" processes (Braver, 2012; Braver et al., 2007). Hence, in this study we also looked at the relationship between such higher order factors of mindfulness and cross-modal health measures.

1.1 Study Summary

While associations with specific health measures and mindfulness have limited explanatory power, multi-modal analysis of mindfulness associations across multiple domains of health measures helps connect subjective improvements in health and objective changes in performance. In this report, we used a two-pronged approach to test the relationship between mindfulness dimensions and (1) self-reported behavioral health measures which included well-established general health related questionnaires and (2) Cognitive performance using Repeatable Battery for the Assessment of Neuropsychological Status (RBANS) and (3) Electroencephalography (EEG) with a focus on the alpha rhythm (8 Hz–12 Hz) which has been shown to be associated with mindfulness (Lardone et al., 2018; Lee et al., 2018).

2 Materials and Methods

Veteran participants (n = 145, age = 44–77; male = 117 and female = 28) were enrolled in baseline assessments as part of a clinical trial. The eligibility criteria were: (a) U.S. Veteran deployed in the 1990–1991 Gulf War and (b) meet CDC (Fukuda et al., 1998) criteria for CMI. Questions regarding symptoms were taken from the "National Health Survey of Gulf War Era Veterans and Their Families" item pool. Three participants withdrew from the study after their baseline appointments due to scheduling conflicts. One more participant was removed from analysis due to not fully completing the questionnaires and surveys. Resting state EEG was recorded for a subset of the participants (N = 21). One participant didn't complete EEG data collection and another didn't complete FFMQ leaving 19 participants (age = 52–71, gender = 17M, 2F) used in the analysis relating EEG and mindfulness facets.

2.1 Self-report and Cognitive Measures

Mindfulness facets were assessed using the Five-Factor Mindfulness Questionnaire (FFMQ): Observing, Describing, Awareness, Non-judgment, and Non-reactivity (Lilja et al., 2012). We used commonly administered measures of general health to get an estimate of overall health across multiple domains: RAND-36, Multidimensional Fatigue Symptom Inventory-Short Form (MFSI-SF), Pittsburgh Sleep Quality Index (PSQI), Patient Health Questionnaire-Depression Scale (PHQ), Posttraumatic Symptom Checklist (PCL), Perceived Stress Scale (PSS), Brief Symptom Inventory (BSI), Quality of Life in Neurological Disorders (Neuro-QoL) and Patient Reported Outcomes Measurement Information System (PROMIS). The total score calculated by these assessments were chosen for inclusion in the analysis. If an assessment does not provide a single total score, the global/general health sub-score was used (SF-36 and PROMIS). Similarly, we used an examiner-administered Repeatable Battery for the Assessment of Neuropsychological Status (RBANS) to estimate cognitive performance across multiple domains such as attention, language, visuospatial/constructional abilities, and memory to determine an overall estimate of cognitive functioning (Randolph et al., 1998).

2.2 Electroencephalography (EEG)

Our third hypothesis involved neural biomarkers influenced by inter-individual variations in trait mindfulness. This line of inquiry is important as it helps test direct associations between mindfulness and neural biomarkers in order to understand the mechanistic underpinnings of mindfulness. EEG signals of the participants were recorded using a 64 channel BrainVision system and shared a single ground to minimize noise through the actiCHamp amplifier. Subjects were asked to sit in a chair and relax before EEG was recorded under two conditions: eyes opened and then with their eyes closed, each for a duration of five minutes. EEG was preprocessed using a standard pipeline bad channels were interpolated, bandpass filtered from 1 Hz to 30 Hz, ICA was used to decompose data to 30 component, artifact ICA components were rejected and the data was reconstructed with the remaining components. The EEG measure of interest in this report is the alpha power which is associated with cortical inhibitory control (Barry et al., 2004; Barry et al., 2005; Lorenz et al., 2009). Specifically, we looked at the difference between eyes closed condition and eyes open condition during resting state. Alpha power difference was calculated by first obtaining the power spectral density at each channel and then obtaining the difference between eyes opened and eyes closed conditions. This alpha power difference value was then reduced to five components accounting for >99% of the variability in the data using principal component analysis. These five components were then used to identify relationships between EEG and mindfulness scores.

2.3 Analysis

First, factor analysis was performed to identify predominant mindfulness factors since prior studies have shown the existence of a higher order mindfulness structure (Tran et al., 2013). Factors with eigen values close to zero were rejected. Additionally, FA was performed on shuffled data to identify factors with greater eigen values for the original data compared to the shuffled data (Reise et al., 2000). These two methods were used to identify the most significant factors in the data and the corresponding most loaded measures. Pearson correlations were performed between mindfulness dimensions associated with each factor and the outcome variables: self-reported behavioral health scores, cognitive test scores and EEG features. False Discovery Rate (FDR) correction was done to control for multiple comparisons (Benjamini & Hochberg, 1995). Structural modeling (SEM) was applied to the highest loaded FFMQ dimensions for each factor and outcome variables. The following model goodness of fit measures are reported based on recommendations from prior studies (Hoe, 2008): (1) $X2/df$ = Chi-square/degrees of freedom is a normalized goodness of fit measure less affected by sample size (fit acceptable if $X2/df < 3$), (2) Comparative Fit Index (cfi) tests whether the model is different from a null/independence model where variables are uncorrelated (fit acceptable if cfi > 0.90) and (3) Root Mean Square Error of Approximation (rmsea) is related to covariance residuals in model (fit acceptable if rmsea < 0.08).

3 Results

To identify the predominant FFMQ sub-scores (Fig. 1A), factor analysis was performed. The resultant scree plot (Fig. 1B) revealed two factors having large eigen values (>1), while the remaining 3 factor loading were close to zero. Factor 1 with the largest eigen value primarily loaded on 'Awareness', 'Describing' and 'Nonjudging' dimensions of mindfulness whereas factor 2 primarily loaded on 'Nonreactivity' and 'Observing' (Fig. 1C). This two-factor model of FFMQ facets has already been identified in prior studies (Tran et al, 2013). Factor 1 facets are derived mostly from mindfulness questions that pro[be individual's propensity to stay alert, describe feelings, and inhibition of judgmental thoughts (Baer et al., 2006; Baer et al., 2008). Whereas factor 2 facets are derived mostly from mindfulness questions that assess the disposition to notice, sense, and feel thoughts (Kalill et al., 2014; Lykins, 2006). For concise presentation of findings and interpretability with regards to dual modes of control theory [refer 1.2 and 4.3], we term factor 1 as "proactive mindfulness" and factor 2 as "reactive mindfulness".

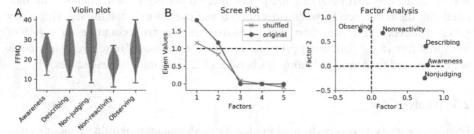

Fig. 1. Trait mindfulness factor analysis: (A) Violin plot showing distribution of trait mindfulness dimensions obtained from FFMQ. (B) Scree plot showing two predominant factors representing the mindfulness dimensions. (C) Factor loadings for the two factors with large eigen values (>1)

3.1 Association Between Mindfulness and Self-reported Symptoms

We observed that mindfulness dimension obtained from the FFMQ were in general negatively associated with symptom severity. Specifically, the mindfulness dimensions representing proactive mindfulness (factor 1) were more negatively associated (negative r-values) with symptoms than the dimensions representing reactive mindfulness (Nonreactivity and Observing) as shown in Fig. 1A and 1B. Next, we tested whether composite measures of proactive and reactive mindfulness differed in their association with subjective symptoms using structural equation models (SEM). Since factor analysis suggested that there were two latent factors, we tested two SEMs one for each factor representing proactive and reactive mindfulness. While the model fit parameters were acceptable, we observed that proactive mindfulness was in general negatively associated with symptoms measures (Fig. 2C, X2/df = 1.737, cfi = 0.989, rmsea = 0.071), whereas, the reactive mindfulness was not (Fig. 2D, X2/df = 1.699, cfi = 0.994, rmsea = 0.069).

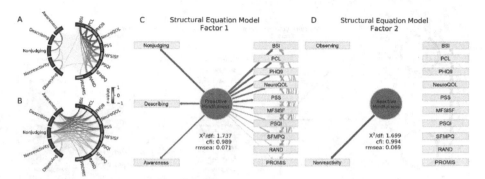

Fig. 2. Relationship between trait mindfulness and adverse self-reported health outcomes: (A) Positive and (B) negative circular correlation plot between mindfulness dimensions and self-reported health outcomes (C) Structural Equation Model (SEM) showing proactive mindfulness associated with reduction of adverse self-reported symptoms. (D) SEM showing reactive mindfulness not associated with self-reported measures. Note: Blue lines indicate negative r-values and SEM model coefficients and red lines indicate positive r-values and SEM model coefficients (Color figure online)

3.2 Association Between Mindfulness and Cognitive Assessment

We tested for associations between mindfulness and scores from the RBANS using the same approach as that used for the self-reported symptoms. Similar to the approach in previous analysis, we tested whether latent measures of proactive and reactive trait mindfulness differed in their association with objective measures of cognitive function. The SEM model fit parameters were mostly acceptable and shows that proactive mindfulness variable was positively associated with most neuropsychological performance scores (Fig. 1C, X2/df = 2.221, cfi = 0.960, rmsea = 0.092: marginal). The reactive mindfulness variable was not associated with any of the cognitive measures (Fig. 1D, X2/df = 0.880, cfi = 1, rmsea = 0) (Fig. 3).

3.3 Association Between Mindfulness and EEG

Direct neural associations with mindfulness were analyzed using EEG data. Alpha power difference between eyes open and closed conditions (Fig. 4A) was obtained at each channel (Fig. 4B) and then correlated with each of the mindfulness dimensions which resulted in distinct topographic patterns for proactive and reactive mindfulness (Fig. 4C). For consistency with previous analysis on symptom measures, we explored SEM models with the EEG measures as well. First, the alpha power difference across the channels were reduced to five components accounting for >99% of the variance using principle component analysis (Fig. 1D) in order to reduce the number of variables in the model. Proactive trait mindfulness dimensions (Awareness, Describing and Nonjudging) were most associated with Component 4 of the PCA which has a prominent medial central-parietal contribution as seen in the circular correlation plots (Fig. 4F) and in the SEM (Fig. 4G, X2/df = 2.229, cfi = 0.678, rmsea = 0.254). Reactive mindfulness dimensions (Observing and Nonreactivity) were most associated with components 1 and 2 with

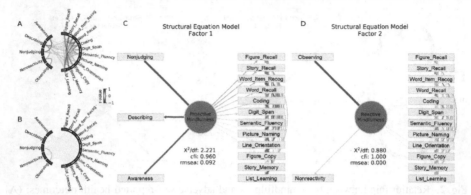

Fig. 3. Relationship between trait mindfulness and quantitative neuropsychological measures: (A) Positive and (B) negative circular correlation plot between Mindfulness dimensions and RBANS test scores. Structural Equation Models showing (C) positive association between proactive mindfulness and RBANS scores and (D) no association between reactive mindfulness and RBANS scores.

significant bilateral occipital contribution (Fig. 4E, 4H, X2/df = 1.533, cfi = 0.578, rmsea = 0.168). The only acceptable model fit parameter was X2/df whereas cfi and rmsea which are known to be dependent on sample size and require higher sample sizes to be meaningfully interpreted.

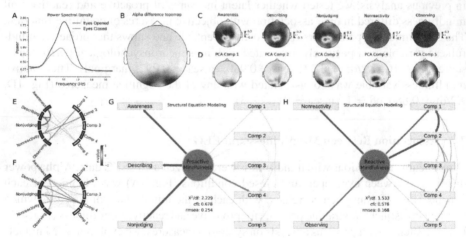

Fig. 4. EEG and mindfulness analysis: (A) Average power spectrum for eyes open and closed conditions. (B) Alpha power (8 Hz–12 Hz) difference at each channel. (C) Alpha power difference correlation with mindfulness dimensions at each channel. (D) Alpha power difference reduced to 5 principal components using PCA. (E) Positive and (F) negative circular correlation plots between mindfulness dimensions and the PCA components. SEM model of (G) proactive and (H) reactive mindfulness dimensions with the PCA components.

4 Discussion

Due to the wide spectrum of adverse health outcomes in CMI, compounded with age-related health decline, GW Veterans face challenging medical concerns that impact quality of life. This study examined the relationship between trait mindfulness and overall health (symptom severity) in GW Veterans with CMI with the contention that the broad-spectrum benefits of mindfulness could act as an effective countermeasure to CMI symptoms. Therefore, analyzing the psychometric properties of mindfulness and its relationship to a variety of health outcomes becomes crucial and was explored in this report. Our findings suggest that: (1) trait mindfulness dimensions obtained using FFMQ consisted of two higher-order factors. Awareness, Describing and Nonjudging loaded on the largest factor, termed proactive trait mindfulness due to its similarity with "proactive control" in Dual Modes of Control framework (DMC) in cognitive control theory (Braver, 2012; Braver et al., 2007). The questions associated with these facets probe individual's propensity to actively engage in describing feelings, staying alert and inhibiting judgmental thoughts (Baer et al., 2006; Baer et al., 2008). Observing and Nonreactivity loaded on the second largest factor, termed reactive trait mindfulness due to its similarity with "reactive control" in the DMC framework. The questions associated with these facets focus on disposition to react, notice, sense, and feel thoughts (Kalill et al., 2014; Lykins, 2006). (2) Proactive trait mindfulness was significantly associated with better self-reported health and psychological performance measures. (3) The two factors of mindfulness were associated with distinct EEG alpha difference metrics which reflects inhibitory control. Together, these findings suggest that proactive mindfulness may have more beneficial effects on mental health possibly due to different underlying mechanisms.

4.1 Dual Modes of Cognitive Control, Personality Meta-traits, and Dual Mode Mindfulness

While factor analysis seems to suggest a two-dimensional structure of mindfulness (Fig. 1B), it does not provide the theoretical, behavioral, or neural underpinnings of the different aspects of mindfulness. However, due to its similarity with the Dual Modes of Control (DMC) framework in cognitive control theory which categorizes control processes into "proactive" and "reactive" cognitive control (Braver, 2012; Braver et al., 2007), we termed the two higher order factors of FFMQ into "proactive" and "reactive" mindfulness. However, we note here that in current literature the dual mode framework has been proposed in multiple subdomains with varying labels such as 'Cognitive/Experiential' (Grecucci et al., 2020), 'Awareness/Action' (Watershoot et al., 2021) and 'Propositional/Non-propositional' (Dunne et al., 2019). We chose the cognitive control framework's labels as it best reflected the cognitive process underlying these psychological constructs.

The proactive factor comprising of Awareness, Describing and Nonjudging facets is associated with 'action' oriented questions that evaluate focused attention during daily activities and selective inhibition of bad thoughts which are top-down mediated (Wang et al., 2016; Nigg, 2017). These questions include phrases such as "I stay alert" and "I tell myself" reflecting attention and rumination which engage higher order neural substrates

(Liu et al., 2016) and suggests that proactive mindfulness engages top-down control processes in the brain. The reactive factor comprising of Observing and Nonreactivity facets were associated with 'perception' oriented questions which engage bottom-up processes and resembles reactive cognitive control (Gonthier et al., 2016; Babu Henry Samuel et al, 2019). These facets evaluate reflect bottom-up or stimulus evoked response to sensory stimuli such as wind and sunlight as well as spontaneous thoughts and mental imagery.

4.2 Mindfulness for Veterans, Service Members and Civilians

Participants were GW Veterans who met criteria for CMI due to the presence of a spectrum of adverse health symptoms. Since these symptoms are compounded by general health decline due to age, higher scores of trait mindfulness could act as a potential remedial factor across a spectrum of health concerns. In this cohort, active trait mindfulness appears to be associated with several indicators of cognitive, emotional, and physical functioning (Fig. 2). It may be a worthwhile investment for Veterans with CMI to pursue mindfulness meditation practices to improve resiliency to adverse health outcomes and cognitive decline. Programs such as the mindfulness-based stress reduction (MBSR) program report improvement in the mindfulness facets (Carmody et al., 2009; Robins et al., 2012) and demonstrated overall better health outcomes in Veterans with chronic symptoms (Kearney et al., 2016). These prior findings along with the broad-spectrum beneficial effects of trait mindfulness as demonstrated in this report, suggests that trait mindfulness could also play a beneficial role for service members and civilians with similar broad-spectrum adverse health conditions and are potential directions for future research.

4.3 Limitations

We used the FFMQ as a measure of mindfulness, which although widely used, is still a subjective score and doesn't provide an objective measure of mindfulness. While the findings in this report suggests the presence of two higher-order factors of mindfulness, it is only an estimation of a latent mindfulness trait and not a direct measure. Although direct associations with EEG spectral features were explored, the observed relationship between EEG and mindfulness presented in this report is only preliminary since it is not sufficiently powered. A larger sample size would help address these issues and lead to identification of direct measures of mindfulness. While this report analyzed global measures of questionnaires, further analysis with the subscores of the questionnaires to identify relationships between mindfulness and domain-specific health symptoms are required but is outside the scope of this report.

5 Conclusion

In this report we observe mindfulness as a construct of proactive and reactive components similar to that observed in dual modes of cognitive control theory. Proactive mindfulness is associated with lower self-reported health symptoms and higher scores on neuropsychological measures. The proactive and reactive mindfulness factors may be reflective of distinct neuronal substrates of the alpha rhythm (EEG). These findings add to the notion of higher trait mindfulness as a factor promoting resiliency to adverse health outcomes and cognitive decline with quantifiable neural representations.

Mandatory Disclosure. The opinions and assertions contained herein are the private views of the authors and are not to be construed as official or as reflecting the views of the US Department of Veterans Affairs, the Henry M. Jackson Foundation for the Advancement of Military Medicine Inc or Georgetown University School of Medicine.

Disclosure of Interests. The authors have no competing interests to declare that are relevant to the content of this article.

References

Ahani, A., Wahbeh, H., Miller, M., Nezamfar, H., Erdogmus, D., Oken, B.: Change in physiological signals during mindfulness meditation. In: International IEEE/EMBS Conference on Neural Engineering: [proceedings]. International IEEE EMBS Conference on Neural Engineering, pp. 1738–1381 (2013). https://doi.org/10.1109/NER.2013.6696199

Babu Henry Samuel, I., Wang, C., Burke, S.E., Kluger, B., Ding, M.: Compensatory neural responses to cognitive fatigue in young and older adults. Front. Neural Circ. **13**, 12 (2019). https://doi.org/10.3389/fncir.2019.00012

Baer, R.A., Carmody, J., Hunsinger, M.: Weekly change in mindfulness and perceived stress in a mindfulness-based stress reduction program. J. Clin. Psychol. **68**, 755–765 (2012). https://doi.org/10.1002/jclp.21865

Baer, R.A., Smith, G.T., Hopkins, J., Krietemeyer, J., Toney, L.: Using self-report assessment methods to explore facets of mindfulness. Assessment **13**, 27–45 (2006). https://doi.org/10.1177/1073191105283504

Baer, R.A., et al.: Construct validity of the five-facet mindfulness questionnaire in meditating and nonmeditating samples. Assessment **15**, 329–342 (2008). https://doi.org/10.1177/1073191107313003

Barry, R.J., Clarke, A.R., McCarthy, R., Selikowitz, M., Rushby, J.A., Ploskova, E.: EEG differences in children as a function of resting-state arousal level. Clin. Neurophysiol. **115**, 402–408 (2004). https://doi.org/10.1016/S1388-2457(03)00343-2

Barry, R.J., Rushby, J.A., Wallace, M.J., Clarke, A.R., Johnstone, S.J., Zlojutro, I.: Caffeine effects on resting-state arousal. Clin. Neurophysiol. **116**, 2693–2700 (2005). https://doi.org/10.1016/j.clinph.2005.08.008

Benjamini, Y., Hochberg, Y.: Controlling the false discovery rate: a practical and powerful approach to multiple testing. J. Roy. Stat. Soc. **57**(1), 289–300 (1995). https://doi.org/10.1111/j.2517-6161.1995.tb02031.x

Blackburn, R., Logan, C., Renwick, S.J., Donnelly, J.P.: Higher-order dimensions of personality disorder: hierarchical structure and relationships with the five-factor model, the interpersonal circle, and psychopathy. J. Pers. Disord. **19**, 597–623 (2005). https://doi.org/10.1521/pedi.2005.19.6.597

Braver, T.S.: The variable nature of cognitive control: a dual mechanisms framework. Trends Cogn. Sci. **16**, 106–113 (2012). https://doi.org/10.1016/j.tics.2011.12.010

Braver, T.S., Gray, J.R., Burgess, G.C.: Explaining the many varieties of working memory variation: dual mechanisms of cognitive control. Var. Work. Mem. **75**, 106 (2007). https://doi.org/
10.1093/acprof:oso/9780195168648.003.0004

Brown, D.B., Bravo, A.J., Roos, C.R., Pearson, M.R.: Five facets of mindfulness and psychological
health: evaluating a psychological model of the mechanisms of mindfulness. Mindfulness **6**,
1021–1032 (2015). https://doi.org/10.1007/s12671-014-0349-4

Bruin, E.I., Topper, M., Muskens, J.G.A.M., Bogels, S.M., Kamphuis, J.H.: Psychometric properties of the five facets mindfulness questionnaire (FFMQ) in a meditating and a non-meditating
sample. Assessment **19**, 187–197 (2012). https://doi.org/10.1177/1073191112446654

Carmody, J., Baer, R.A., Lykins, L.B., E., & Olendzki, N.: An empirical study of the mechanisms
of mindfulness in a mindfulness-based stress reduction program. J. Clin. Psychol. **65**, 613–626
(2009). https://doi.org/10.1002/jclp.20579

Cernetic, M.: The relationship between anxiety and mindfulness: the role of mindfulness facets,
implicit anxiety, and the problem of measuring anxiety by self-report. Psihologija **49**, 169–183
(2016). https://doi.org/10.2298/PSI1602169C

Chambers, R., Lo, B.C.Y., Allen, N.B.: The impact of intensive mindfulness training on attentional
control, cognitive style, and affect. Cogn. Ther. Res. **32**, 303–322 (2008). https://doi.org/10.
1007/s10608-007-9119-0

Chiesa, A., Serretti, A.: A systematic review of neurobiological and clinical features of mindfulness meditations. Psychol. Med. **40**, 1239–1252 (2010). https://doi.org/10.1017/S00332917
09991747

Creswell, J.D.: Mindfulness interventions. Annu. Rev. Psychol. **68**, 491–516 (2017). https://doi.
org/10.1146/annurev-psych-042716-051139

Creswell, J.D., Pacilio, L.E., Lindsay, E.K., Brown, K.W.: Brief mindfulness meditation training
alters psychological and neuroendocrine responses to social evaluative stress. Psychoneuroen-
docrinology **44**, 1–12 (2014). https://doi.org/10.1016/j.psyneuen.2014.02.007

Digman, J.M.: Higher-order factors of the big five. J. Pers. Soc. Psychol. **73**, 1246 (1997). https://
doi.org/10.1037/0022-3514.73.6.1246

Duan, W., Li, J.: Distinguishing dispositional and cultivated forms of mindfulness: item-level
factor analysis of five-facet mindfulness questionnaire and construction of short inventory of
mindfulness capability. Front. Psychol. **7**, 1348 (2016). https://doi.org/10.3389/fpsyg.2016.
01348

Dunne, J.D., Thompson, E., Schooler, J.: Mindful meta-awareness: sustained and non-
propositional. Curr. Opin. Psychol. **28**, 307–311 (2019). https://doi.org/10.1016/j.copsyc.2019.
07.003

Eberth, J., Schäfer, T.: Promise: a model of insight and equanimity as the key effects of mindfulness
meditation. Front. Psychol. **10**, 472453 (2019). https://doi.org/10.3389/fpsyg.2019.02389

Eberth, J., Sedlmeier, P.: The effects of mindfulness meditation: a meta-analysis. Mindfulness **3**,
174–189 (2012)

Fukuda, K., et al.: Chronic multisymptom illness affecting air force veterans of the gulf war. JAMA
280, 981–988 (1998). https://doi.org/10.1001/jama.280.11.981

Gibson, J.: Mindfulness, interoception, and the body: a contemporary perspective. Front. Psychol.
10, 475917 (2019). https://doi.org/10.3389/fpsyg.2019.02012

Gonthier, C., Braver, T.S., Bugg, J.M.: Dissociating proactive and reactive control in the Stroop
task. Mem. Cognit. **44**, 778–788 (2016). https://doi.org/10.3758/s13421-016-0591-1

Goyal, M., et al.: Meditation programs for psychological stress and well-being: a systematic review
and meta-analysis. JAMA Intern. Med. **174**, 357–368 (2014). https://doi.org/10.1001/jamain
ternmed.2013.13018

Grecucci, A., et al.: A dual route model for regulating emotions: comparing models, techniques
and biological mechanisms. Front. Psychol. **11**, 930 (2020). https://doi.org/10.3389/fpsyg.
2020.00930

Hoe, S.L.: Issues and procedures in adopting structural equation modeling technique. J. Appl. Quant. Methods **3**, 8 (2008)

Hofmann, S.G., Sawyer, A.T., Witt, A.A., Oh, D.: The effect of mindfulness-based therapy on anxiety and depression: a meta-analytic review. J. Consult. Clin. Psychol. **78**, 169–183 (2010). https://doi.org/10.1037/a0018555

Hölzel, B.K., et al.: Mindfulness practice leads to increases in regional brain gray matter density. Psychiatry Res. **191**, 36–43 (2011). https://doi.org/10.1016/j.pscychresns.2010.08.006

Hölzel, B.K., Lazar, S.W., Gard, T., Schuman-Olivier, Z., Vago, D.R., Ott, U.: How does mindfulness meditation work? Proposing mechanisms of action from a conceptual and neural perspective. Perspect. Psychol. Sci. J. Assoc. Psychol. Sci. **6**, 537–559 (2011). https://doi.org/10.1177/1745691611419671

Jensen, C.G., Vangkilde, S., Frokjaer, V., Hasselbalch, S.G.: Mindfulness training affects attention–or is it attentional effort? J. Exp. Psychol. Gen. **141**, 106–123 (2012). https://doi.org/10.1037/a0024931

Jha, A.P., Morrison, A.B., Dainer-Best, J., Parker, S., Rostrup, N., Stanley, E.A.: Minds at attention: Mindfulness training curbs attentional lapses in military cohorts. PLoS ONE **10**, 0116889 (2015). https://doi.org/10.1371/journal.pone.0116889

Kalill, K.S., Treanor, M., Roemer, L.: The importance of non-reactivity to posttraumatic stress symptoms: a case for mindfulness. Mindfulness **5**, 314–321 (2014). https://doi.org/10.1007/s12671-012-0182-6

Kearney, D.J., Simpson, T.L., Malte, C.A., Felleman, B., Martinez, M.E., Hunt, S.C.: Mindfulness-based stress reduction in addition to usual care is associated with improvements in pain fatigue, and cognitive failures among veterans with gulf war illness. Am. J. Med. **129**(2), 204–214 (2016). https://doi.org/10.1016/j.amjmed.2015.09.015

Khusid, M.A., Vythilingam, M.: The emerging role of mindfulness meditation as effective self-management strategy, part 1: clinical implications for depression, post-traumatic stress disorder, and anxiety. Mil. Med. **181**, 961–968 (2016). https://doi.org/10.7205/MILMED-D-14-00677

Lang, A.J.: What mindfulness brings to psychotherapy for anxiety and depression. Depress. Anxiety **30**, 409–412 (2013). https://doi.org/10.1002/da.22081

Lardone, A., et al.: Mindfulness meditation is related to long-lasting changes in hippocampal functional topology during resting state: a magnetoencephalography study. Neural Plasticity 5340717 (2018). https://doi.org/10.1155/2018/5340717

Larson, M.J., Steffen, P.R., Primosch, M.: The impact of a brief mindfulness meditation intervention on cognitive control and error-related performance monitoring. Front. Hum. Neurosci. **7**, 308 (2013). https://doi.org/10.3389/fnhum.2013.00308

Lazar, S.W., Bush, G., Gollub, R.L., Fricchione, G.L., Khalsa, G., Benson, H.: Functional brain mapping of the relaxation response and meditation. NeuroReport **11**, 1581–1585 (2000). https://doi.org/10.1097/00001756-200005150-00041

Lee, D.J., Kulubya, E., Goldin, P., Goodarzi, A., Girgis, F.: Review of the neural oscillations underlying meditation. Front. Neurosci. **12**, 320145 (2018). https://doi.org/10.3389/fnins.2018.00178

Lilja, J., Lundh, L.-G., Josefsson, T., Falkenström, F.: Observing as an essential facet of mindfulness: a comparison of FFMQ patterns in meditating and non-meditating individuals. Mindfulness **4**, 1 (2012). https://doi.org/10.1007/S12671-012-0111-8

Lindsay, E.K., Creswell, J.D.: Mechanisms of mindfulness training: monitor and acceptance theory (MAT). Clin. Psychol. Rev. **51**, 48–59 (2017). https://doi.org/10.1016/j.cpr.2016.10.011

Liu, Y., Bengson, J., Huang, H., Mangun, G.R., Ding, M.: Top-down modulation of neural activity in anticipatory visual attention: control mechanisms revealed by simultaneous EEG-fMRI. In: Cerebral Cortex, vol. 26, pp. 517–529 (2016). https://doi.org/10.1093/cercor/bhu204

Lorenz, I., Müller, N., Schlee, W., Hartmann, T., Weisz, N.: Loss of alpha power is related to increased gamma synchronization. A marker of reduced inhibition in tinnitus? Neurosci. Lett. **453**, 225–228 (2009). https://doi.org/10.1016/j.neulet.2009.02.028

Lykins, E.L.B.: Exploring Facets Of Mindfulness In Experienced Meditators (Ph.D. thesis; p. 55). University of Kentucky (2006)

Lykins, E.L.B., Baer, R.A.: Psychological functioning in a sample of long-term practitioners of mindfulness meditation. J. Cogn. Psychother. **23**, 226–241 (2009). https://doi.org/10.1891/0889-8391.23.3.226

Ma, S.H., Teasdale, J.D.: Mindfulness-based cognitive therapy for depression: Replication and exploration of differential relapse prevention effects. J. Consult. Clin. Psychol. **72**, 31–40 (2004). https://doi.org/10.1037/0022-006X.72.1.31

Nigg, J.T.: Annual research review: on the relations among self-regulation, self-control, executive functioning, effortful control, cognitive control, impulsivity, risk-taking, and inhibition for developmental psychopathology. J. Child Psychol. Psychiatry **58**, 361–383 (2017). https://doi.org/10.1111/jcpp.12675

Petrocchi, N., Ottaviani, C.: Mindfulness facets distinctively predict depressive symptoms after two years: the mediating role of rumination. Pers. Individ. Differ. **93**, 92–96 (2016). https://doi.org/10.1016/j.paid.2015.08.017

Randolph, C., Tierney, M.C., Mohr, E., Chase, T.N.: The repeatable battery for the assessment of neuropsychological status (RBANS): preliminary clinical validity. J. Clin. Exp. Neuropsychol. **20**, 310–319 (1998). https://doi.org/10.1076/jcen.20.3.310.823

Reise, S.P., Waller, N.G., Comrey, A.L.: Factor analysis and scale revision. Psychol. Assess. **12**(3), 287 (2000). https://doi.org/10.1037//1040-3590.12.3.287

Robins, C.J., Keng, S.-L., Ekblad, A.G., Brantley, J.G.: Effects of mindfulness-based stress reduction on emotional experience and expression: a randomized controlled trial. J. Clin. Psychol. **68**, 117–131 (2012). https://doi.org/10.1002/jclp.20857

Tang, Y.-Y.: The neuroscience of mindfulness meditation. Nat. Rev. Neurosci. **16**, 213–215 (2015). https://doi.org/10.1038/nrn3916

Tran, U.S., Glück, T.M., Nader, I.W.: Investigating the five facet mindfulness questionnaire (FFMQ): construction of a short form and evidence of a two-factor higher order structure of mindfulness. J. Clin. Psychol. **69**, 951–965 (2013). https://doi.org/10.1002/jclp.21996

Wang, C., Rajagovindan, R., Han, S.-M., Ding, M.: Top-down control of visual alpha oscillations: sources of control signals and their mechanisms of action. Front. Hum. Neurosci. **10** (2016). J. Cogn. Neurosci. **25**, 1343–1357. https://doi.org/10.3389/fnhum.2016.00015

Waterschoot, J., Van der Kaap-Deeder, J., Morbée, S., Soenens, B., Vansteenkiste, M.: "How to unlock myself from boredom?" The role of mindfulness and a dual awareness- and action-oriented pathway during the COVID-19 lockdown. Personality Individ. Differ. **175**, 110729 (2021). https://doi.org/10.1016/j.paid.2021.110729

Wu, R., et al.: Brief mindfulness meditation improves emotion processing. Front. Neurosci. **13**, 1074 (2019). https://doi.org/10.3389/fnins.2019.01074

Zeidan, F., Martucci, K.T., Kraft, R.A., Gordon, N.S., McHaffie, J.G., Coghill, R.C.: Brain mechanisms supporting the modulation of pain by mindfulness meditation. J. Neurosci. **31**, 5540–5548 (2011). https://doi.org/10.1523/JNEUROSCI.5791-10.2011

The AugCog of Work

Suraj Sood[(⊠)]

The Sirius Project, Long Beach, USA
thesiriusproj@gmail.com

Abstract. The relative value of automation is debated. On one hand, it is lauded for making mundane work doable by machines. Not only can such machines carry out such work more efficiently than humans: the latter are then empowered and opened up to fulfill endeavors [57] (e.g., creative). Furthermore, automation can itself inspire innovations and the creation of work, such as in the creation of driverless vehicles (including software and hardware, as well as new regulatory practice). In an ideal scenario where work is fully automated, humans would be able to maximize leisure and not be bound by economic demands. Automation fits into a vision for societal AugCog where humans put machines to work so that the former can invest in more rewarding cognitive activities. Humans can do so by deepening their respective cultures with furthered devotion to art, philosophy, science, engineering, mathematics, humanities, politics, spirituality, and religion. In day-to-day life, automation can augment cognition via reduced stress and increased life satisfaction as people's lives become more centered on relationships and meaning. Automation of work should proceed in a manner sensitive to overall economic and human impacts.

Keywords: automation · work · artificial intelligence · remote work · future

"An action…may be said to be conformable to the principle of utility…when the tendency it has to augment the happiness of the community is greater than any it has to diminish it" ([38], p. 2). -Jeremy Bentham, "Happiness is the Greatest Good"

1 Introduction

The term "automagically" arose as a portmanteau of automatic and magically, evoking how automation can render processes amazingly instantaneous. Every evening, or at least most evenings, adult Americans drive on the freeway. In Los Angeles, they can be confronted with digital billboards advertising businesses. While business is a staple in capitalistic life, automation is relatively newer.

Botlr is an example of automation in the hospitality industry. Not much larger than a child and with a black bow-tie, Botlr navigates a hotel on its own but will send an alert if it encounters an obstacle [1].[1] According to Steven Cousins, CEO of Savioke—the Silicon

---

[1] [1] also discusses work ethic and working conditions.

D. D. Schmorrow and C. M. Fidopiastis (Eds.): HCII 2024, LNAI 14695, pp. 213–235, 2024.
https://doi.org/10.1007/978-3-031-61572-6_15

Valley company that created Botlr—"It's not going to replace butlers, or be used in a kind of (hotel) brand where you have very high expectation of human interaction" [2]. An important consideration is how the automation of jobs has affected human interaction, especially the degree of relevance of communication (Fig. 1).[2]

Fig. 1. Wizard riding a rug. "Automating" is used as a verb that Zapier's user could do.

---

[2] [20] is a journalistic book about interfacing with an organization's developers. It covers Super-Phone, which purportedly "lets artists engage directly with their audiences…. SuperPhone lets…[the product's creator] publish his phone number at concerts, on his website, and in his social media; when people call or text the number, Ryan adds them to his list of millions of fans" (p. 80). Also discussed is Breaker, "a seven-employee company that sells podcasting software" (p. 81).

Some benefits of automation are obvious. Namely, automating processes makes them more efficient and (in the long run) cost-effective. While automation appears to be on the rise, it is not without controversy: this state of affairs is comparable (and likely directly related to) artificial intelligence. A justification for furthering knowledge of automation is to transcend hype and speculation.

One example of a subject valuing automation in principle was found on LinkedIn, where an interviewee named Rizel described her "idea of the perfect [software] app": "My perfect app is performant, with cleanly structured data that makes retrieval simple, and with well-written, readable code that makes it easy to navigate, understand, and troubleshoot. Beyond that, as long as automation [emphasis added] and a strong CI/CD pipeline are present, I'm happy" [43]. In Rizel's answer, automation is directly tied to her potential happiness or product satisfaction. Automation is an important topic at both societal and individual levels (Fig. 2).

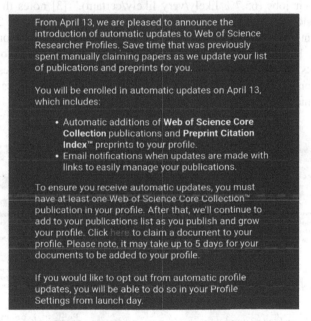

Fig. 2. Notification of automatic updates.

The following phenomena are now at least sometimes (if not often) automated:

- phone calls and texts from businesses
- grading submissions made by students
- external defibrillators
- pedestrian lights

The following processes are increasingly automatic:

- collection of web use(r) information (e.g., demographics and types of browsers used)
- login to online services
- rendering clinical sessions

2   Future of Work

It is good to "automate tedious tasks" and "augment creativity" [47]. According to a survey, "AI scientific experts express more positive attitudes about AI technology related to improving the economy and health than other applications. The majority of them think that AI will improve individuals' health (78.3% likely/very likely/certain) and strengthen the U.S. economy (72.6% likely/very likely/certain)" ([60], p. 2). In terms of A.I.'s riskiness, survey "respondents perceive[d] high likelihood of…AI displacing workers by automating their jobs (65.7% likely/very likely/certain)." [3] notes that "the market for personal and household service robots is already growing by about 20% annually" (p. 38). It distinguishes between low-, medium-, and high-risk professions with respect to replacement by computerization. The Millennium Project's Future Work/Technology 2050 represents a highly collaborative global forecasting effort also interested in automation's impact on the economy [4]. Future Work/Technology 2050 serves as an example of collective intelligence augmentation (Fig. 3).

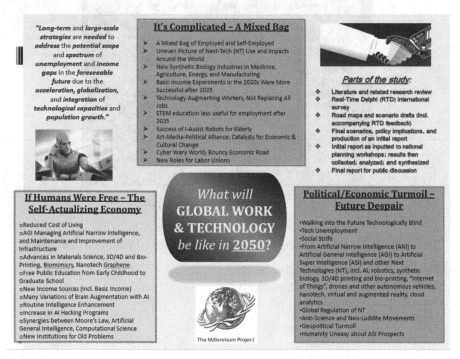

Fig. 3. Visual depiction of The Millennium Project's Future of Work and Tech 2050 "three scenarios" project.

In work, prevention without incidence is ideal. Optimal pairing between company and client or human and computer are worthwhile ends. With respect to recruitment, the science of information spread seems to suggest that half of new jobs are not posted online [5].

Recent years have seen the rise of remote presentations, including of doctoral dissertations and conference articles. A worthwhile consideration is the possible loss of affect experienced during tasks one completes automatically. Psychological safety—a trending topic—is important for cybersecurity, as a soft topic augmenting a hard (albeit, largely virtual) area.

3 Education

Learning style is a function of Pc (here, processing) and regulation strategies, M (here, mental) models, and orientations. Learning styles are a function of undirected, reproduction, and application- and meaning-directed styles. It would be useful to formalize learning style(s) as such, especially for training autonomous machine learning *a priori*: also, of course, for humans. With this latter case, it should be kept in mind that learning styles lie on a continuum from shallow to deep (with undirected being shallowness, reproduction being next shallowest, and meaning-directed being deepest).

Autism as defined in the DSM-V within special education is alleviated—and thus, augmented—via HCI apps like Proloquo2Go and N2Y. While the former app augments the user's communicative abilities, the latter informs them on a variety of topics ranging from purely educational (in the case of documentaries) to practical (e.g., daily living skills). Classes and courses have become increasingly virtualized.[3]

Work bringing out the best in humans is optimal. Hard work—i.e., perseverance—pays off. Success in life is defined by voice actress Sarah Natochenny as being the product of perseverance and friendship [53]. There are many factors important to success, and differing ways to define success. With respect to human evolutionary and economic success, [6] notes that the species' neurology invested into creating and processing comedy and art has been crucial, likely by enabling professional workers with distinct skillsets to cooperate (Fig. 4).

Attention paid in one domain can lead to insight and enacted wisdom in another. For instance, one could read the responses of others in a forum thread about relationships (in a VCoP like [7]), and have this translate into augmented performance at work. Related to this example, [31] teaches "strategies for building secure relationships in the remote and in person classroom." A computer intervention led to reduced substance use (including cigarette-smoking) in college students [28].

---

[3] See [19].

Fig. 4. Automatic water container-filler.

4 Industry

In [14], it is asserted that the methodology Agile—which originated in part from software development—is concerned with project management, as well as with how humans operate. [14] also states that most digitally-enabled businesses will include the following as goals: flexibility, the perpetual desire to learn and improve, and speed. This source presages that human resources could vanish given automation (possibly even before, e.g., call centers). It also discusses the future work scenario of humans competing against automation.

DevOps is defined as referring to a broad inclusion of what were previously separate organizational functions, like testing and development, and how automation can transform an organization [28]. [14] crucially poses the questions of whether empathy can: augment work productivity and speed, and preclude automation from rendering workers obsolete. [14] notes that multiple businesses (with keenness and curiosity) found that their workers were more collaborative and open while online during the COVID-19 pandemic (Fig. 5).

According to [17]: "There are more than forty thousand different jobs in the United States, each having a unique title and description as well as responsibilities and requirements. There are many more job openings than there are job types." [17] also discusses vocational psychology, as well as work and education.[4,5] Online job apps—especially for big tech—are discussed in ([8], p. 245).

---

[4] See [18] for coverage of work assignment and -breakdown structures, and of architect skills.

[5] [14] outlines a humanistic vision of work in the tech industry. It covers remote working, automation, work/life balance, affect, "Ways of Working" (pp. 63–8), pace, flexibility, parents, the

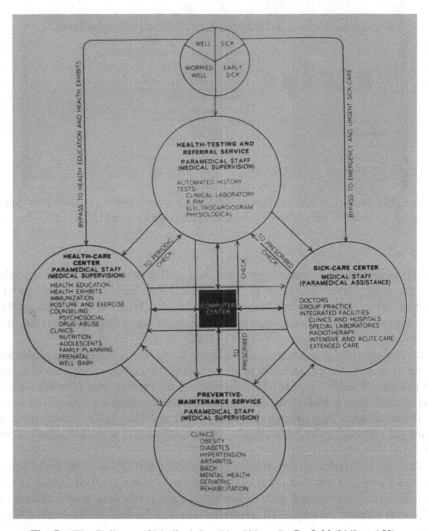

Fig. 5. "The Delivery of Medical Care" by Sidney R. Garfield ([44], p. 150).

Apps and computer accessory services provide useful automations. Rethink, a behavioral health app for data-recording, allows one to show a client's skill acquisition progression as a percentage. The mouse-distributing company Logitech notifies users of automatic software updates: "Logitech may from time to time provide bug fixes, updates, upgrades and other modifications to the Software ('Updates'). These may be automatically [emphasis added] installed without providing any additional notice or receiving any additional consent. You consent to these automatic Updates" [39] (Fig. 6).

Psychological Safety Works Team Solution, flexible/remote working practices, the four-day work week (and work weeks, in general), software timetables (e.g., Sprints), Ways of Work (WOWs), and WFH (work from home).

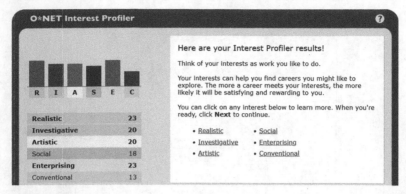

Fig. 6. O*NET Interest Profiler (computerized version). A computerized version of the Holland-type of occupational fit test is CIP, or Computerized Interest Profiler [12]. (Profiler accessed at [9][6].)

[21] advocates for a marriage between work skillset generalization and specialization. The combination of tech and professional coaching leads to a possible model for adapting and spreading evidence-based intervention [29]. Professional documents showing temporal data trends can be screen-shared through Zoom team meetings for all call participants to view and increase project understanding.

An example of augmenting cognition in the workplace is delivering a (behavioral) people styles presentation internally to a company, via PowerPoint and Zoom to augment said company's understandings of themselves and their teammates. *Hive-ish* organizations in which team players thrive and transformational leadership are discussed in ([40], Ch. 10). Behavioral programming is even described as a React.js (JavaScript) paradigm, including "b-threads", and event triggers (where events could be treated as behaviors B) [30].

The topic of "productive job creation" is mentioned in ([37], p. 4). Industrial automation could even be expressed to be its own industry. Patents are filed and approved to claim ownership over inventions; trademark (™) corresponds to legal or corporate ownership over identity; copyright (©) corresponds to legal ownership of a product (Figs. 7 and 8).

---

[6] O*NET has also been observed being used to prepare high school elective students in the K-12 special educational context for the workplace.

The difference between a patent, copyright, and trademark is 1 2 3 :

- A patent protects new inventions, processes, or scientific creations that are novel and useful.

- A trademark protects distinctive brand marks of a company that help the public identify its products and services, such as names, logos, and slogans.

- A copyright protects original works of authorship, such as books, music, art, and software.

Learn more: 1. investopedia.com   2. quickcompany.in   3. unitedcapitalsource.com   ⓘ

Fig. 7. Condensation of definitions of patent, ™, and © yielded by a Microsoft Bing search.

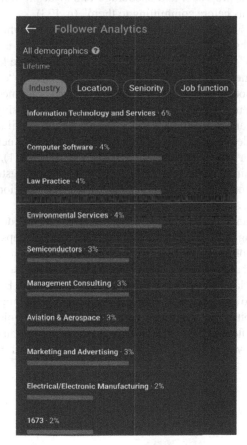

Fig. 8. LinkedIn business analytics.

5 Insight and Wisdom

[11] discusses e-commerce, and the "power of exponential growth". It uses the law of compounding as illustrated by early dotcom-era profit. According to [26], "satisfaction of the basic needs for competence, autonomy, and relatedness...predicted work engagement and well-being. Employees who reported greater need satisfaction on the job were more motivated and psychologically better adjusted" (p. 246). Team Zoom meeting calls can be ended insightfully with wisdom like, "Many hands make light work." [35] advises:

"An organization is encouraged to provide an environment conducive to positive behavior, by understanding the psychology of employees and the demands placed upon them. For example, establish success metrics that are relevant and appropriate to the work environment; encourage focusing on one thing at a time rather than multitasking; offer opportunities for employees to destress; routinely monitor employee workloads to ensure that they are appropriate; and encourage employees to think through projects, actions, and statements before committing to them" (p. 133).

How one decides to earn main income has "to do with who [one is] at [one's] core: [one's] strengths, weaknesses, and central interests.... It is a matter of [one's] core financial values" ([49], p. 19). In addition to discussing the knowledge asset and knowledge management system, [51] urges readers to have a "digital commonplace book": i.e., a study notebook, journal, and idea sketchpad combined.

[48] yielded several insights into customer preferences, raising revenue, advertising (e.g., branding), and marketing. It found marketing via email to outperform social media in terms of sales. The report emphasizes providing customers with deep, empathetic personalization and a "consistent user experience" (p. 11). The report defines "relationship marketing" as having a focus on "delighting customers for the long haul" (p. 14). Consumer values include businesses offering superior products, customer service, accessibility, and options.

Women fighters in anime are reflective of women's postmodern entrance into the workforce. Regarding behavioral economics (simply, but perhaps importantly): "The economy is the outcome of what we do" [54]. Advice has been read on a VCoP and implemented to build a strong work ethic. News relevant to forecasting futures of industry can be attained via sources like [52]. Amazon founder Jeff Bezos' held a faithful belief in low prices to gain consumer trust [10], possibly explaining his company's success more than any other singular factor (barring, perhaps, technological ingenuity and capacity). The basic flow of data visualization (in devoted programs like Power BI and the JavaScript framework d3.js, per [34]) is to load, format, and graphically represent data (Fig. 9).

Fig. 9. Several allusions to automation on one webpage [56].

Having more capital makes an entity likelier to outcompete its competition [44]. Is reductionism—viz., task analysis—necessarily or only contingently productive? One can attempt to discover their job-related values by inquiring into whether work is meaningful or comfortable, leaves room for leisure, generates cash, empowers the worker, and grants prestige or security [46]. Reactive affect A can lead to suboptimal B data-recording.

It was written that if one has trust, they can monetize it flexibly [58]. The same source philosophized that: "The...aim of science is power"; it further estimated that A.I. will outwork humans in 30–40 years. Academia.edu user analytics yield insight into trending work and ResearchGate enables one to send automated messages to other users alongside requested research.

6 Productivity

Productivity equals output divided by input. It can be defined as a characteristic of creating something valuable. Efficiency equals quantity of output divided by time t (Fig. 10).

Fig. 10. Example logo for the Peak Podcast on human transformation.

The "bounded automation perspective" emphasizes "how the networks and ambitions of power actors that craft technological development are based on calculated choices and vested interests to control labor, not simply to replace them with intelligent machines" ([63], p. 12). By this perspective, replacement by automation is not necessarily the goal. Instead, workforce control is prioritized (Fig. 11).

The software Trello can be used to facilitate collaborative e-workflow. One may learn about APIs (such as SOAP and RESTful) through participating in big tech job-screening. Automation of analytics tracking is often done for webpages using the Google Analytics service (Figs. 12 and 13).

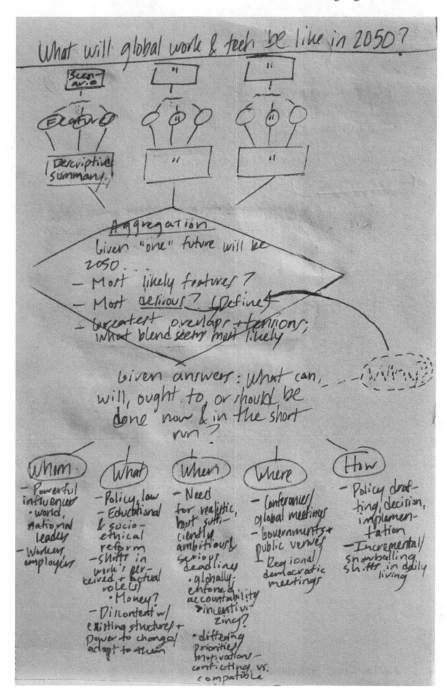

Fig. 11. Handwritten flowchart of global work and technology scenario(s).

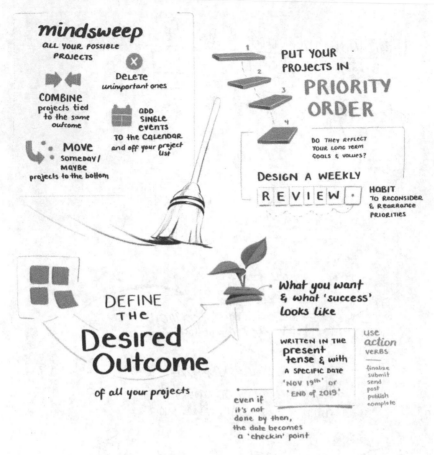

Fig. 12. Infographic for book on productivity [22]

```
<!-- Google Analytics -->
<script>
(function(i,s,o,g,r,a,m){i['GoogleAnalyticsObject']=r;i[r]=i[r]||function(){
(i[r].q=i[r].q||[]).push(arguments)},i[r].l=1*new Date();a=s.createElement(o),
m=s.getElementsByTagName(o)[0];a.async=1;a.src=g;m.parentNode.insertBefore(a,m)
})(window,document,'script','https://www.google-analytics.com/analytics.js','ga');

ga('create', 'UA-XXXXX-Y', 'auto');
ga('send', 'pageview');
</script>
<!-- End Google Analytics -->
```

Fig. 13. Google Analytics script implemented voluntarily into webpages.

6.1 Automation[7]

In the film 21, the character named Terry is conversed with about his group's loss of human work to facial recognition software. Google Docs Editors Suite products are the pinnacle of Web's original purpose: facilitating collaboration. Slack and cloud sharing services like Google Drive can facilitate project management and workflow [8] (Fig. 14).

Fig. 14. Automation implicated in the 2008 film *21*.

A computer network defense (CND) is "a joint human-machine collaborative task in which people depend on automated tools to perform their jobs but must remain in the loop as an information processor and decision maker" ([35], p. 107). Humans could outsource information-processing to their computers. Adaptive automation, which implicates user experience (UX), consists of "tools [that] can more effectively coordinate with users by providing the information users need at the time that they need" (p. 110) (Fig. 15).

[50] discusses leveraging "mobile technology to assist with clinical assessments, data collection, curricula development, billing and regulatory compliance increases clinician bandwidth while streamlining and improving operational efficiencies, and improving outcomes." This could be considered a kind of "automated decision support" ([62], p. xvii). Automation augments cognition by freeing it to concentrate on a different task (Fig. 16).

---

[7] [36] covers automation extensively in the cybersecurity context. Specific topics include adaptive automation, human-automation teaming components, the Automatic Certificate Management Environment (ACME), and the Automation-Induced Complacency Potential Rating Scale.

[8] Workflow is covered in [16]. Asana is another workflow augmentation software that allows for automated emailing and collaborator-tagging. This brings to light the phenomenon of hearing email mentally as one reads it. Also, analysis of workflow charts as structured systems that should be easily searchable, describable, and transparent to viewers is discussed.

Fig. 15. Automation of end-to-end testing across various application programming interfaces (APIs).

Fig. 16. Advertisement of batch record process automation (encountered on YouTube).

Downloads can start automatically, as can website redirections. Paperless workflow automation exists in industries such as law. The online marketplace for independent creators Etsy advertised a "fully automated dashboard" for project management, in the form of a Google Sheets-made template. In the role-playing game *Guild Wars 2*, automated game controls (such as for running and attacking enemies) are featured.

7   Current Directions

Logging in to various sites is often automated to the extent that one can do so using various social media accounts. In 2009, the company Velocity revolutionarily enabled automatic code deployment into production [27]. HCI at automated services like instant oil change (e.g., provided by Valvoline) and in automatic hybrid cars also exist.

Programming[9] itself is semi-automated: "IDEs provide interfaces for users to write code, organize text groups, and automate [emphasis added] programming redundancies" [32].[10] ChatGPT [33] is an example of how writers (including of software) have increasingly automated their work. The company LUV Systems' anti-viral fan augments cognition by allowing that underneath it to breathe more freely (e.g., while working in public spaces like Starbucks).

Computerized automation exists in car controls. Going farther back in time, cars came with two operative modes (and still do, but perhaps decreasingly): automatic versus shift. According to [15], "...knowledge in cognitive psychology...is sufficiently advanced to allow the analysis and improvement of common mental tasks, provided there is an understanding of how knowledge must be structured to be useful" (p. 91). Regarding psychology more broadly, [42] notes (Fig. 17):

"...a series of papers and special issues examining the details and ramifications of big data science [emphasis added] for the discipline of psychology have been published over the past 5 years in psychology journals...joining a broader community of scholars incognate disciplines (e.g., sociology, philosophy, science and technology studies [STS], and human–computer interaction [HCI]) committed to examining implications of the changes underway for the conception and practice of science..." (p. 11).

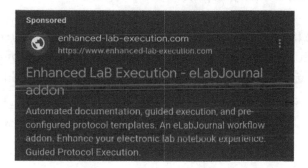

Fig. 17. "Automated documentation" as part of an online service.

---

[9] [23] is a worthwhile compilation of interviews with programming language creators. It covers productivity, teams, and programmer efficacy, as well as specialization of labor for programming. Innovation is a theme in the book, and even mathematical theorem work is discussed (p. 474).

[10] Python [13] has been used to program bots and the power-to-take game.

According to [41]:

"A large-scale study of more than 12,000 employees across 12 countries…[showed] that fulfilling employee recognition is associated with better employee wellbeing across four key dimensions:

- Increased overall life evaluations: Employees are as much as two times as likely to evaluate their lives and futures positively.
- Reduced levels of burnout: Employees are up to 90% less likely to report being burned out at work 'always' or 'very often.'
- Improved daily emotions: Employees are up to two times as likely to report having experienced a lot of gratitude the previous day and about 40% less likely to report having experienced a lot of stress, worry and sadness.
- Better social wellbeing: Employees are seven times as likely to strongly agree that they have meaningful connections or a best friend at work, and as much as 10 times as likely to strongly agree that they belong."

[41] further found that when "organizations create an environment in which employees consistently receive high-quality recognition…[stronger life evaluation, lower burnout, higher-quality emotionality, and improved social well-being]—and more—translate into clear ROI. To do this, leaders must first see recognition as a strategy that needs to be invested in and then scale it thoughtfully to change the culture of their workplaces—and, ultimately, employees' lives" (Fig. 18).

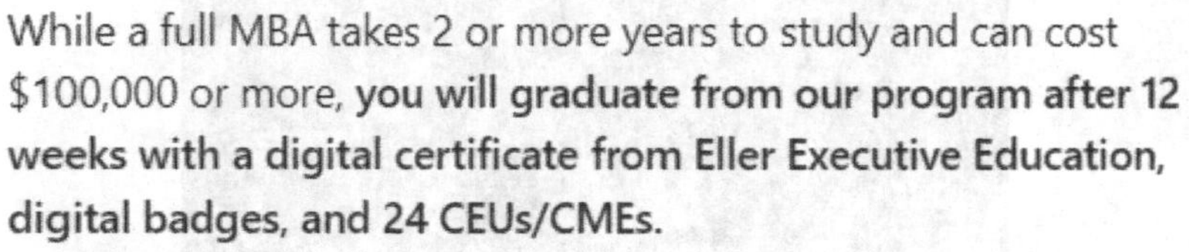

While a full MBA takes 2 or more years to study and can cost $100,000 or more, you will graduate from our program after 12 weeks with a digital certificate from Eller Executive Education, digital badges, and 24 CEUs/CMEs.

Fig. 18. LinkedIn-sponsored advertisement of digital certification program.

8 Conclusion

Can the relevance of automated messaging (e.g., via LinkedIn members) be increased through more personalized, targeted content? VG livestreaming (via YouTube, Twitch, and Facebook) is a new profession. A cornerstone of DevOps is "automation of deployment into production without any human intervention or checkpoints" [27]. In the context of software architecture, test automation is complex, ideally having a framework that automates large system tests. Also, "Poké Jobs" (in Pokémon Sword) automate Pokémon stat-training and encourage the player to keep clients happy (Fig. 19).

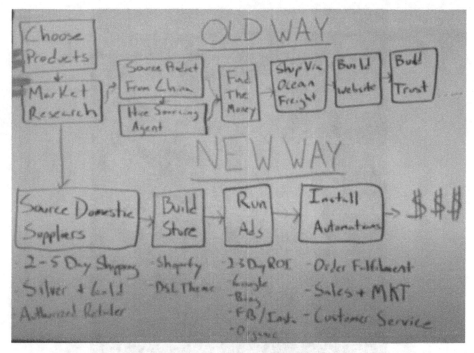

Fig. 19. The flow step "Install Automations" is included in the section, "New Way" [45].

"Alive Forever" [24] was an intriguing research project conducted at the University of California, Santa Barbara (UCSB). The goal was to build participants' avatars and allow them to have digital versions of their selves stored for posterity. The plan was to study reactions and how people were invested in digital "twins", i.e., counterparts (Fig. 20).

Seligman wrote of a work progression starting with a job, leading over time to a career, and finally crystallizing into a calling [25]. [55] notes that: "Social entrepreneurs worldwide are organizing strategic networks to help address complex challenges. These networks offer key advantages over conventional, centralized organizations, including the ability to accelerate change by aligning and activating large numbers of people." In terms of novelty, this chapter ends with the following pseudo-formula for artificial psychological intelligence:

$$A.\Psi I. = M + A.O.P. + B + M.I. + I.Q. + E.Q. \qquad (1)$$

where $A.\Psi I.$ equals "artificial psychological intelligence", M equals the Platonic-Freudian mind [61], A.O.P. equals agent-oriented programming (viz., SARL), B equals behavior and refers to data modeling (per recording and building, via apps like Rethink Behavioral Health), and M.I. equals multiple intelligences. I.Q. and E.Q. respectively refer to intelligence and emotional quotients.

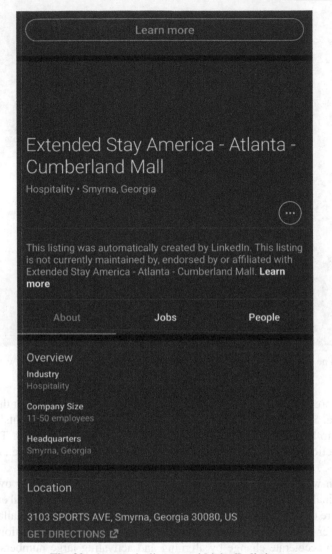

Fig. 20. Automatically-created LinkedIn listing.

A formula for artificial general intelligence $(A.G.I.)$ incorporating (1) is now offered:

$$A.G.I. = \{A.\Psi I. + automation + robotics + FHAI$$
$$+ narrowA.I. + learning \ldots\} \tag{2}$$

FHAI stands for fully-human A.I. Learning was addressed in a previous section in this chapter (in terms of learning styles) (Fig. 21).

Across the web and discussions of work, automation is ubiquitous. According to [59]: "To augment is a continuous journey…. addressing these 5 challenges [relating to technology, diversity, resilience, skills, and authenticity] allows for the balance required

Fig. 21. Bill Nye "the Science Guy" sitting in a control room [56].

for the successful integration of augmentation into our lives" (p. 3). Further, "building a foundation for augmentation means thinking about the organization as a whole and then finding use cases to run the new systems at the same time as keeping the traditional methods in place" (p. 7).

References

1. Havens, J.C.: Heartificial Intelligence: Embracing Our Humanity to Maximize Machines. Penguin Random House, New York (2016)
2. https://www.usatoday.com/story/news/nation/2014/10/28/low-skill-workers-face-mechanization-challenge/16392981/. Accessed 22 Jan 2022
3. Frey, C.B., Osborne, M.A.: The future of employment: how susceptible are jobs to computerization? https://enliza.es/SECCIONES_1/1_EL%20FUTURO%20DEL%20TRABAJO/RECURSOS/The_Future_of_Employment_OMS_Working_Paper.pdf. Accessed 22 Jan 2022
4. https://www.millennium-project.org/projects/workshops-on-future-of-worktechnology-2050-scenarios/. Accessed 22 Jan 2022
5. https://www.ted.com/talks/meg_jay_why_30_is_not_the_new_20. Accessed 27 Jan 2022
6. Sterling, P.: What is Health? Allostasis and the Evolution of Human Design. The MIT Press, Cambridge (2020)
7. https://intjforum.com/forums. Accessed 17 Aug 2022
8. Burnett, B., Evans, D.: Designing Your Work Life: How to Thrive and Change and Find Happiness at Work. Alfred A. Knopf, New York (2020)
9. https://www.mynextmove.org/explore/ip. Accessed 19 Sept 2022
10. Rossman, J.: The Amazon Way: 14 Leadership Principles Behind the World's Most Disruptive Company, 2nd edn. Clyde Hill Publishing (2016)
11. Quain, B.: Pro-sumer Power II! How to Create Wealth by Being Smarter, Not Cheaper, and Referring Others to Do the Same. INTI, Tampa (2008)
12. Eikleberry, C.: The Career Guide for Creative and Unconventional People, 3rd edn. Ten Speed Press, Berkeley (2007)

13. McGrath, M.: Python in Easy Steps. In Easy Steps Limited, U.K. (2016)
14. Blomstrom, D.: People Before Tech: The Importance of Psychological Safety and Teamwork in the Digital Age. Bloomsbury Business, Dublin (2021)
15. Card, S.K., Moran, T.P., Newell, A.: The Psychology of Human-Computer Interaction. Lawrence Erlbaum Associates, Hillsdale (1983)
16. Levitin, D.J.: The Organized Mind: Thinking Straight in the Age of Information Overload. Penguin, Ontario (2014)
17. Lowe, J., Lungrin, T.: CareerCode: Know Your Code, Find Your Fit. [Kindle DX]
18. Bass, L., Clements, P., Kazman, R.: Software Architecture in Practice, 3rd edn. Addison-Wesley, Upper Saddle River (2013)
19. Palloff, R.M., Pratt, K.: Building Learning Communities in Cyberspace: Effective Strategies for the Online Classroom. Jossey-Bass Publishers, San Francisco (1999)
20. Lawson, J.: Ask Your Developer: How to Harness the Power of Software Developers and Win in the 21st Century. Harper Business (2021). [Kindle DX]
21. https://youtu.be/XJsCM7xyETc?list=PLOiTiVAUx4bivjSs5J9dIp9JMOmlhvVPz. Accessed 14 Jan 2023
22. Untitleddesign_46_2000x.png (1100×1161) (shopify.com). Accessed 14 Jan 2023
23. Biancuzzi, F., Warden, S.: Masterminds of Programming: Conversations with the Creators of Major Programming Languages. O'Reilly, Beijing (2009)
24. Blascovich, J., Bailenson, J.: Infinite Reality: Avatars, Eternal Life, New Worlds, and the Dawn of the Virtual Revolution. William Morrow, New York (2011)
25. Seligman, M.: Learned Optimism: How to Change Your Mind and Your Life. Simon & Schuster Audio (2001)
26. Deci, E.L., Ryan, R.M.: The "what" and "why" of goal pursuits: human needs and the self-determination of behavior. Psychol. Inq. 11(4), 227–268 (2000)
27. https://www-theserverside-com.cdn.ampproject.org/v/s/www.theserverside.com/blog/Cof fee-Talk-Java-News-Stories-and-Opinions/Agile-vs-DevOps-differences-similarities-com pare-deployment-culture-silos?amp=1&amp_gsa=1&amp_js_v=a9&usqp=mq331AQKK AFQArABIIACAw%3D%3D#amp_tf=From%20%251%24s&aoh=16746046529288&ref errer=https%3A%2F%2Fwww.google.com&ampshare=https%3A%2F%2Fwww.theserver side.com%2Fblog%2FCoffee-Talk-Java-News-Stories-and-Opinions%2FAgile-vs-DevOps-differences-similarities-compare-deployment-culture-silos. Accessed 4 Feb 2023
28. ERIC - EJ952571 - Pilot of a Computer-Based Brief Multiple-Health Behavior Intervention for College Students. J. Amer. College Health (2012)
29. Computer-Based Intervention with Coaching: An Example Using the Incredible Years Program - PMC (nih.gov). Accessed 29 Aug 2023
30. An intro to Behavioral Programming with React: request, wait, and block (freecodecamp.org). Accessed 29 Aug 2023
31. https://www.youtube.com/watch?v=2_Tc9Sts_U0&t=1475s. Accessed 5 Feb 2023
32. https://www.g2.com/articles/ide#:~:text=An%20IDE%20or%20integrated%20developmen t,groups%2C%20and%20automate%20programming%20redundancies. Accessed 5 Feb 2023
33. Brown, T.B., et al.: Language models are few-shot learners. arXiv:2005.14165
34. Meeks, E.: D3.js in Action. Manning Publications, Shelter Island (2015)
35. Papadaki, M., Shiaeles, S.: Insider threat: the forgotten, yet formidable foe. In: Moallem, A. (ed.) Human-Computer Interaction and Cybersecurity Handbook, pp. 117–137. CRC Press, Florida (2019)
36. Moallem, A.: Human-Computer Interaction and Cybersecurity Handbook. CRC Press, Florida (2019)
37. Brown, J.D., Earle, J.S.: The Microeconomics of Creating Productive Jobs: A Synthesis of Firm-Level Studies in Transition Economies. World Bank Publications (2006)

38. https://philosophy.lander.edu/intro/articles/bentham-a.pdf. Accessed 22 Feb 2023
39. https://www.logitech.com/en-us/legal/eula.html. Accessed 1 Mar 2023
40. Haidt, J.: The Righteous Mind: Why Good People are Divided by Politics and Religion. Knopf Doubleday Publishing Group (2013)
41. Workhuman: Amplifying Wellbeing at Work and Beyond Through the Power of Recognition. Gallup, Washington, D.C. (2022)
42. Osbeck, L.: General psychology as common ground and point of view: enduring and evolving features. Rev. Gen. Psychol. **24**(1), 6–17 (2020)
43. https://www.linkedin.com/pulse/couples-counseling-front-back-end-developers-github/. Accessed 5 Mar 2023
44. Field, H.H.: Design implications of a changing health care system. In: Ittelson, W.H. (ed.) Environment and Cognition, pp. 127–156. Seminar Press, New York (1973)
45. dropshiftlifestyle.com. Accessed 11 Mar 2023
46. https://2012books.lardbucket.org/books/business-ethics/s09-employee-s-ethics-what-s-ther.html. Accessed 29 Mar 2023
47. https://www.notion.so/product/ai?utm_source=ads_youtube&utm_campaign=196980 46225&utm_medium=video&gclid=Cj0KCQjww4-hBhCtARIsAC9gR3a74XdFLWO rJhZEag5uBnU4r0yzEOBm2AXbEknM8gTlZKxWSANexFwaAiLlEALw_wcB. Accessed 28 Apr 2023
48. 2023 consumer trends index: global consumer attitudes and trends in personalization, privacy, messaging, advertising, brand loyalty and the rising cost of living. Marigold (2023)
49. Kiyosaki, R.T.: The Business of the 21st Century. Dreambuilders, Lake Dallas, TX (2010)
50. https://strategiccio360.com/demand-for-autism-care-is-at-an-all-time-high-technology-can-help/. Accessed 12 June 2023
51. Forte, T.: Building a Second Brain: A Proven Method to Organize Your Digital Life and Unlock Your Creative Potential. Simon & Schuster Audio, New York (2022)
52. https://www.millennium-project.org/tmp-news/?fbclid=IwAR0m_yDNH39Xxzr_ljAs7eO Rvyq6-HutZBB1fMYTWV3bIPeiCaxCbMXHWSM. Accessed 13 Jun 2023
53. https://youtu.be/x6WVCoOoyEA. Accessed 19 June 2023
54. https://www.youtube.com/watch?v=ycVBoWsGLJs. Accessed 28 June 2023
55. https://www.schusterman.org/resource/network-know-how-guides?utm_source=facebook& utm_medium=paid&utm_campaign=NKHG&fbclid=IwAR0ZOFd-AncCz6pQ9pbe45Z EfWeH6frjJuKPJEAt-CN96DpNGu85Chpdvng_aem_AYJY4AotIj_Kp_xY0Ppquvme g1PCmrodl401vCyDMTanB1lTwOtIH-ZMax1D_wZ4m58kJqTqc0izaXHky0QAbHBI. Accessed 1 July 2023
56. https://www.itape.com/product/perfect-packer/. Accessed 5 July 2023
57. Altman, E.J., Kiron, D., Schwartz, J., Jones, R.: Workforce Ecosystems: Reaching Strategic Goals with People, Partners, and Technologies. The MIT Press, Cambridge (2023)
58. https://youtu.be/UTchioiHM0U. Accessed 8 July 2023
59. Making work human: 5 challenges. Automation Anywhere (2019)
60. Bao, L., et al.: AI Scientists' Perspectives on AI. SCIMEP, Madison (2023)
61. Sood, S.: The platonic-freudian model of mind: defining "self" and "other" as psychoinformatic primitives. In: Schmorrow, D.D., Fidopiastis, C.M. (eds.) HCII 2020. LNCS (LNAI), vol. 12196, pp. 76–93. Springer, Cham (2020). https://doi.org/10.1007/978-3-030-50353-6_6
62. Hancock, M.F.: Practical Data Mining. CRC Press, Boca Raton (2013)
63. Cheong, P.H.: Bounded religious automation at work: communicating human authority in artificial intelligence networks. J. Commun. Inq. **45**(1), 5–23 (2021)

Distance-Based Lifestyle Medicine for Veterans with Chronic Multi-symptom Illness (CMI): Health Coaching as Behavioral Health Intervention for Clinical Adherence

Angela C. Summers[1](✉), Rebecca McCullers[1], Walter Jachimowicz[1,2],
Charity B. Breneman[1,2], Immanuel Babu Henry Samuel[1,2], Peter J. Bayley[3,4],
Lindsey Proctor[3], Leah Eizadi[3], Jeremy Chester[1], John Barrett[1,5],
Matthew J. Reinhard[1,6], and Michelle E. Costanzo[1,5]

[1] War Related Illness and Injury Study Center, Veterans Affairs Medical Center,
Washington, DC, USA
angela.summers@va.gov
[2] Henry M. Jackson Foundation for the Advancement of Military Medicine, Inc., Bethesda,
MD, USA
[3] War Related Illness and Injury Study Center, Veterans Affairs Medical Center, Palo Alto, CA,
USA
[4] Department of Psychiatry and Behavioral Sciences, Stanford University School of Medicine,
Stanford, CA, USA
[5] Uniformed Services University of the Health Services, Bethesda, MD, USA
[6] Department of Psychiatry, Georgetown University Medical School, Washington, DC, USA

Abstract. Chronic multi-symptom illness (CMI) is characterized by persistent, difficult to treat symptoms that interfere with daily functioning, affecting approximately 30% of post-deployment Veterans. Clinicians often provide many recommendations with limited patient adherence. Emerging research suggests health coaching may be an effective intervention for individuals with CMI. Importantly, Veterans often report barriers to health care, thus, telehealth may be a practical solution. Nevertheless, research is limited on the effectiveness of this intervention using telehealth. This preliminary pilot study aimed to assess the feasibility of remotely implementing health coaching to support Veterans' engagement with health goals. Following interdisciplinary medical evaluations, psychologically/medically stable participants were referred to the study. Health coaches incorporated clinical recommendations from the comprehensive evaluation, partnering with Veterans to create health goals, aligning clinical recommendations with Veterans' values. Coaching sessions were delivered via telehealth. The primary outcome of the present study was the status of health goals. Veterans (N = 39) were 50.2 ± 8.4 years old, 77% male, well-educated, and predominantly white (82%). They identified 60 health goals related to physical activity (35%), mindset (20%), and diet (17%). After eight sessions, 37% and 58% of Veterans fully met and partially met their goals, respectively. After 17 sessions, 56% and 44% fully met and partially met their goals, respectively. These findings demonstrate the feasibility of remotely delivered health coaching to increase Veterans' engagement in lifestyle changes. Use of telehealth to implement health coaching

© The Author(s), under exclusive license to Springer Nature Switzerland AG 2024
D. D. Schmorrow and C. M. Fidopiastis (Eds.): HCII 2024, LNAI 14695, pp. 236–249, 2024.
https://doi.org/10.1007/978-3-031-61572-6_16

may reduce barriers to care and increase treatment adherence for Veterans with chronic, medically unexplained symptoms.

Keywords: Health Coaching · Chronic Multi-symptom Illness · Telehealth · Whole Health · Veteran

1 Introduction

1.1 Whole Health for Veterans: Health Coaching for Complex Illness Care

The Department of Veterans Affairs (VA) has developed a Whole Health model of health care that takes a Veteran-centered approach by providing Veterans with tools and techniques to improve their overall health and well-being [1, 2]. The VA offers these services through Veteran-led courses, online materials, and Whole Health facility contacts (e.g., Veteran Peer-Facilitators and Whole Health Partners) that provide resources for Veterans interested in developing a personalized health plan [3, 4]. However, for Veterans seeking clinical care who report complex deployment histories and chronic multisymptom illness (CMI) and related disorders, additional support from VA trained health coaches, who guide Veteran's through self-discovery and explore personal values, develop personal health plans, and implement healthy lifestyle and behavior changes, may play an integral role in achieving improved health outcomes as identified through VA Whole Health [2, 3].

Health coaching incorporates aspects of motivational interviewing and positive psychology (i.e., evidenced-based models of health behavior change) to identify Veterans' personal values and guide them toward implementing lifestyle changes [2]. Central to health coaching is a shift in the providers' approach to promoting individual clinical goals: health coaches ask Veterans what is going well/right rather than focusing on what is going wrong in their lives and this insight guides alignment between the providers and Veterans by asking them "what matters most to you" and "what do you want your health for [2, 5, 6]?" Once these personal values are identified, Veterans develop a working alliance with their health coach to set long term goals and actionable steps to implement and achieve those goals. Early research into health coaching points towards improvements in multiple domains such as psychological well-being, mental and physical health, and activities of daily living, as well as increased engagement in enjoyable and rewarding activities [6–8]. Thus, health coaching that promotes adherence to clinical recommendations may be an important complementary, integrative-health intervention for those Veterans who experience CMI, but this has not been studied in a cohort of treatment-seeking Veterans receiving tertiary care. The capacity to improve care delivery for Veterans with complex deployment exposures provides critical insight into interventions for chronic illnesses that are difficult to treat and supports the broader VA Whole Health model of care [9].

1.2 Chronic Multisymptom Illness (CMI)

In military health care, CMI is defined as multiple, recurrent symptoms across more than one body system that persist for at least six months, interfere with daily activities, and are not better accounted for by another physical or mental health condition [10]. Fatigue, cognitive complaints, headache, gastrointestinal disorders, arthralgias, and/or myalgias are among the most common symptoms reported in individuals presenting with CMI [10]. These symptoms are often difficult to treat, creating a significant burden of illness and disability on patients, providers, and even caregivers [10, 11]. CMI is a broad diagnosis, which includes diagnoses such as Gulf War Illness (GWI), fibromyalgia (FMS), irritable bowel syndrome (IBS), and myalgic encephalomyelitis/chronic fatigue syndrome (ME/CFS) [12, 13].

Among Service Members and Veterans, CMI affects an estimated 29–50% of individuals who were deployed in combat zones, making it a significant health issue for providers serving this population [14, 15]. The VA/DoD Clinical Practice Guidelines outline a myriad of clinical recommendations for providers who are treating patients with CMI, including pharmacotherapy, behavioral health, and lifestyle changes, however, these are often focused on symptom management rather than holistic care [10]. Critically, patients with chronic illnesses frequently receive numerous recommendations from providers, with high rates of suboptimal adherence to these recommendations. One study found that when recommendations included sustained lifestyle changes, such as increased physical activity or dietary changes, nonadherence rates may be as high as 70% [16].

War Related Illness and Injury Study Center. The three War Related Illness and Injury Study Centers (WRIISC) provide tertiary care through the national referral program that focuses on evaluations of Veterans with post-deployment health concerns such as exposure-related illnesses [17]. WRIISC often receives referrals for Veterans who present with CMI, traumatic brain injuries, and/or posttraumatic stress disorder, among others with multifaceted exposure concerns. These Veterans present with unique clinical profiles that require high levels of specialized expertise and services due to the complexity of their symptoms. Veterans eligible for referral undergo a comprehensive week of evaluations with multiple providers, which may include a physician and/or psychiatrist, environmental exposure expert, social worker, neuropsychologist, and a health coach [17]. Evaluations are followed by an interdisciplinary team meeting to augment case conceptualization, then the physician and neuropsychologist each meet with Veterans for feedback to discuss results and clinical recommendations from the team of providers. Many of these comprehensive clinical recommendations include lifestyle changes for improved health, such as increasing physical exercise and align with the VA/DoD Clinical Practice Guidelines for CMI, when diagnostically relevant [10, 18].

Upon completing the WRIISC evaluation, Veterans are encouraged to meet with their primary care provider at their local VA to begin implementing recommendations. Historically, Veterans expressed gratitude for their experience at WRIISC, and were eager to work with their local VA providers. However, follow up interviews with WRIISC Veterans revealed poor adherence and a need for increased follow-up with this population was evident.

1.3 Barriers to Care

Across the VA, Veterans report multiple factors that prevent or reduce their engagement in health care, with one study reporting that over 62% of Veterans encountered at least one barrier to VA health care [19]. Among the most common barriers to care were wait times, concern about staff/reputations, stigma/embarrassment (particularly for mental health concerns), distance/location, paperwork, lack of information on available services, and limited hours of service [19]. Given that 25% of Veterans live in rural communities [20], one solution to reduce barriers was the VA's use of telehealth services that has successfully engaged Veterans who had difficulty accessing care due to complex medical and mental health concerns and/or geographical limitations [21]. A scoping review of telehealth services among patients with chronic illnesses found that availability of telehealth services increased both access to health care services and patient satisfaction with care [22]. However, for Veterans seeking tertiary care, like those referred to WRIISC, alleviating physical and administrative barriers may not be the only solution to improving clinical adherence. Given the variety of recommendations and detailed scope of WRIISC clinical evaluation, Veterans may leave their appointments without fully understanding the guidance provided, particularly if they are not able to prioritize these decisions to fit with their home life [23].

To support Veterans in their treatment plan following the WRIISC clinical encounters, the WRIISC providers determined that more follow-through was imperative and outcomes would need to be evaluated. Therefore, this pilot study aimed to assess the feasibility of remote health coaching through telehealth platforms to support Veterans' engagement with their health goals after receiving clinical care at WRIISC. There is limited research on the effectiveness of this intervention among Veterans with CMI using a telehealth platform, however, we predicted that health coaching via telehealth would increase continuity of care by supporting Veterans in completing clinical recommendations and creating a personal health plan that will achieve health goal(s) and improve overall physical and mental health.

2   Method

2.1 Participants

The current pilot study was approved by the Institutional Review Board at the Washington, DC Veterans Affairs Medical Center. All participants completed oral or written (via Docusign) informed consent using the Department of Veterans Affairs Video Connect (VVC) platform. Procedures for oral consent included Veterans' verbal confirmation that they consented to participate in the study in the presence of two study staff (consenting staff and a witness), who both signed the informed consent. Participants were referred to this study following a comprehensive medical evaluation through the DC and Palo Alto interdisciplinary WRIISC national referral programs. Eligible participants were former combat Veterans who were psychologically and medically stable (e.g., no active psychosis or unstable medical condition such as congestive heart failure). In this report we analyzed preliminary data collected through December 2023 as part of an ongoing pilot study.

2.2 Telehealth

All health coaching appointments were completed via the secure, HIPAA compliant VVC platform for virtual health care appointments [24]. Each appointment could only be accessed by individuals who were invited, included a list of all attendees present during the call, and was locked to prevent unauthorized users from accessing the meeting. Prior to beginning sessions, providers conducted the VA CAPS-Lock procedures, which required providers to obtain the Veteran's consent for video health care appointment, confirm Veteran's address and phone number during the appointment, survey the area to ensure Veteran is in a private space, and lock the meeting. Further, the VVC platform ensured Veteran privacy and security in several ways, including multiple encryption certifications and compliances[1].

VVC appointments could be accessed using almost any device with a camera, microphone, and speakers (e.g., computer or mobile device) by clicking on the VVC link provided or the VVC app (which was required only for those using an iOS device). Most Veterans found VVC easy to use, as it provides a reliable, face-to-face connection from the comfort of the Veteran's home, office, or other private location and offers a 24/7 Connected Care help desk for any Veterans experiencing difficulty with the system. VVC also sends reminders about the appointment, including resending the appointment link on the day of the appointment. Additionally, telehealth increased accessibility of the health coaching intervention to provide services to Veterans living across the United States.

2.3 WRIISC Health Coaching Intervention

As part of the WRIISC comprehensive medical evaluation, board-certified health coaches met with Veterans to review the Personal Health Inventory (PHI; described below), provided coaching on nutrition, and introduced the health coaching study. Veterans who consented to the study then completed the initial 60-min Wellness Vision session, at which time coaches and Veteran reviewed clinical recommendations from the WRIISC providers, identified the Veteran's Specific, Measurable, Attainable/Attractive, Realistic, and Time-bound (SMART) goals, and created an action plan for each goal. Next, the Veteran completed fifteen 30–60-min coaching intervention sessions followed by a program closeout session that explored the Veteran's plan moving forward (17 total coaching sessions).

---

[1] The platform uses encryption methods that have been certified by the Department of Defense Joint Interoperability Test Command and International Organization for Standardization/International Electrotechnical Commission (ISO/IEC) 270001 and is complaint with the European Union's General Data Protection Regulation (GDPR), Federal Information Processing Standard (FIPS) Publication 140–2, and Systems and Organization Controls 2 Statement on Standards for Attestation Engagements (SOC2/SSAE16) compliant.

Health coaches met with the Veteran once a week for the first month and then bi-weekly for the remaining sessions. At the beginning of each coaching appointment, the Veteran was invited to participate in a short mindfulness exercise. Next, the Veteran shared their wins, challenges, and learnings related to their last action steps/goals. The Veteran chose a specific focus for the coaching session and was provided with relevant health and wellness education, as appropriate. Then the SMART goals, stages of change, and progress towards goals were reviewed, with coaches incorporating support and accountability for Veterans' progress toward their goals. The status of the Veteran's medical symptoms and any clinical updates were also discussed during these sessions, as relevant. The Veteran was always given the opportunity to have the last word before scheduling the next coaching session. The final session consisted of a review of the baseline and post-intervention PHI, reflection on Veteran's progress, goal attainment, learnings, mindset shifts, and maintenance plan.

During sessions, Veterans also provided feedback regarding their health and status of completing their clinical recommendations. When a Veteran expressed frustration and/or other concerns that their local VA provider(s) was not engaged in implementation of WRIISC clinical recommendations, the health coaches served as the Veteran's advocate. The health coach often collaborated with social work and/or other WRIISC providers who could contact providers at the local VA to discuss the recommendations.

PHI. The PHI is a 15-item assessment tool developed by the VA for use during whole health coaching that guides Veterans on a self-reflection of their overall health [5, 25]. Using a 5-point Likert scale ($1 = $ low, $5 = $ high), Veterans first rate their current overall well-being in three domains (i.e., physical, mental/emotional, and day-to-day health). Next, Veterans rate their current ("where you are") and future goals ("where you would like to be") for each of the eight Whole Health "Circle of Health" self-care domains (i.e., moving the body; recharge; food and drink; personal development; family, friends, and co-workers; spirit and soul; surroundings; power of the mind). The PHI is administered at baseline and following the 8th and 17th coaching sessions.

The overall goal of the PHI is to help the Veteran determine how each area of self-care affects their health. Early studies have demonstrated that health coaching increases PHI ratings [26].

SMART Goals. After completing the PHI, Veterans selected one to three self-care domains in which they wanted to begin making changes (during or immediately follow-ing the Wellness Vision session). The Veteran and coach co-created a long-term (i.e., duration of health coaching intervention) goal for up to three domains. Importantly, as indicated by the name, SMART goals related to behavior change and were specific, mea-surable, attainable/attractive, realistic, and time-bound SMART. They also reflected the self-care domain(s) that were most important to the Veteran [3]. For example, a Veteran may identify a SMART goal to go for a 30-min walk with their partner five days a week, to increase plant-based dietary habits while assisting their partner in meal planning and preparation, or to commit to going to bed by 10 pm and wearing their CPAP each night. Additionally, the identified SMART goals aligned with clinical recommendations from the WRIISC comprehensive evaluation. SMART goals were designed to assist the Vet-eran with accountability and guide their progress as they worked toward their health goals and improving overall well-being. After the 8th and 17th health coaching session, Veterans were asked to assess the status of their SMART goals (i.e., fully met, partially met, or not met).

The goal was for the Veteran to create healthy habits and routines, moving toward sustainable change. As the Veteran went through the change process, they were coached towards expanding their circle of support and maintaining their new lifestyle behavior(s).

2.4 Statistical Analysis

In the current analyses, available data from the ongoing pilot study were examined for those Veterans who completed their mid and/or post-coaching sessions (8th and 17th sessions, respectively). Means and standard deviations were computed for continuous variables and sample size and percentages were computed for categorical variables. To compare change in scores over time, paired t tests were calculated, and were considered statistically significant if the one-tailed p-values were less than .05.

3 Results

3.1 Demographics

To date, 39 participants have completed at least three months of the study intervention. Table 1 characterizes study demographics. Briefly, Veterans were an average of 50.2 (SD = 8.4) years old and the majority were male (76.9%), well-educated (74.4% had a bachelor's degree or higher), and predominantly non-Latinx white. All Veterans in this study met criteria for CMI and/or a related disorder. Veterans were located throughout the United States, from the East Coast to the West Coast.

3.2 Mid-Intervention Evaluation

Preliminary results from the first 39 Veterans who completed at least half of the health coaching intervention (i.e., eight sessions) demonstrated that Veterans identified 60 SMART goals. As depicted in Table 2, Veteran-identified SMART goals related to the whole health self-care domains of moving the body (35%), power of the mind (20%), food and drink (17%), recharge (15%), and other domains (13%). After eight sessions, 37% of goals were fully met and another 58% were partially met (Fig. 1).

To determine if there was a change in Veteran's self-reported PHI ratings, using a paired t test, we analyzed the change from baseline to mid-intervention PHI score for the domain corresponding with the Veteran-identified SMART goal. On average, Veteran's PHI score improved between baseline ($M = 2.5 \pm 1.0$) and mid-intervention ($M = 2.8 \pm 1.0$, $t(44) = -1.7, p = .047$).

Table 1. Baseline demographic characteristics (N = 39)

Characteristic	n (%) or M ± SD
Age	50.2 ± 8.4
Gender	
Male	30 (76.9)
Female	9 (23.1)
Race	
White	32 (82.1)
Black or African American	3 (7.7)
Asian	1 (2.6)
Two or more races	3 (7.7)
Ethnicity	
Latinx/Hispanic	4 (10.3)
Non-Latinx/Hispanic	34 (87.2)
Marital Status	
Married	30 (76.9)
Separated/divorced	5 (12.8)
Single (never married)	3 (7.7)
Widowed	1 (2.6)
Education	
HS/GED	7 (17.9)
Technical/Trade School	2 (5.1)
Associate degree	1 (2.6)
Bachelor's degree	12 (30.8)
Master's degree or higher	17 (43.6)
Employment Status	
Unemployed	8 (20.5)
Receiving/applying for disability	4 (10.3)
Employed part time	3 (7.7)
Employed full time	17 (43.6)
Retired	7 (17.9)

Note: GED = General Education Development; HS = high school; M = mean; SD = standard deviation

Table 2. Veteran-Identified SMART Goals by Domain (N = 60)

Whole Health Self-Care Domain	n (%)
Moving the Body	21 (35.0)
Surroundings	1 (1.7)
Personal Development	5 (8.3)
Food and Drink	10 (16.7)
Recharge	9 (15.0)
Family, Friends, and Coworkers	1 (1.7)
Spirit and Soul	1 (1.7)
Power of the Mind	12 (20.0)

Note: SMART = specific, measurable, attainable/attractive, realistic, and time-bound

3.3 Immediate Post-intervention Evaluation

To date, 27 Veterans have completed the full 17 session of the health coaching intervention, representing 41 identified SMART goals. After 17 sessions, 56% of goals were fully met and another 44% were partially met (Fig. 1).

To determine if there was a change in Veteran's self-reported PHI ratings, using a paired t test, we analyzed the change from baseline to immediate post-intervention PHI score for the domain corresponding with the Veteran-identified SMART goal. On average, Veteran's PHI score improved between baseline ($M = 2.6 \pm 1.0$) and immediately post-intervention ($M = 3.2 \pm 1.4$, $t(33) = -3.2$, $p = .002$).

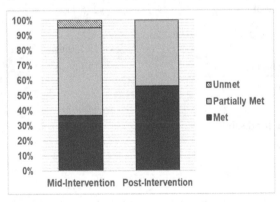

Fig. 1. SMART Goal Completion Rate at mid- and post-intervention evaluations. Participants self-reported whether they fully met, partially met, or did not meet their SMART goal at the time of the evaluation.

4 Discussion

Veterans who experience chronic, medically unexplained, and complex symptoms encounter limited treatment options that may be further compounded by barriers to care such as difficulty traveling for appointments due to distance, pain, fatigue, or other factors. This preliminary analysis of Veterans with chronic, complex medical symptoms demonstrated the feasibility of implementing a clinically-guided health coaching intervention among Veterans with CMI. Results indicated that Veterans both perceived sustained improvement in overall health and achieved health goals aligned with clinical recommendations following the WRIISC health coaching program.

Veterans who enrolled in this study had a high rate of completing the health coaching intervention, indicating strong engagement in telehealth as a delivery of care model. Importantly, Veterans often reported that they appreciated the personal connection they felt with their health coaches over video sessions. This is critical given a recent review that found that Veterans felt a loss of social connection and increased distractions during other remotely delivered Whole Health treatments (e.g., yoga, skills training groups) compared to those delivered in-person [27]. The one-on-one, Veteran-health coach telehealth model may be less impacted by these issues given the individual attention and engagement that health coaches were able to provide to Veterans. However, we are not aware of any studies that have directly compared differences in social connection between remote health coaching and other remotely delivered Whole Health treatments, and this remains an area for future investigation.

Further, telehealth enabled Veterans to participate in the study from across the United States, from various locations (e.g., home, work, vacation) and offered the advantages of individual health coaching without some of the costs of in-person visits, including long commutes to and from a VA health care facility. This enabled access for Veterans who had limited time (e.g., full-time job), lived far from locations where health coaching was offered, and/or were limited by other health-related factors.

In addition to strong attendance for virtual sessions, Veterans demonstrated progress related to their individual health goals and perceptions of their overall health. This progress is consistent with the emerging literature that suggests that health coaching interventions may provide services that improve management of other chronic diseases such as individuals with diabetes or heart disease, and those focusing on weight loss [2, 6, 27]. After completing half of the intervention, over a third of health goals had been achieved by Veterans who completed their mid-intervention evaluation as of December 2023. By mid-intervention, Veterans were working towards achieving most of the remaining goals. By the end of the intervention, Veterans who completed 17 sessions of health coaching had fully achieved more than half of their health goals and were working towards achieving all remaining goals. This suggests strong engagement with their goals throughout the coaching intervention.

Although the overall rate of fully achieving their goals slowed slightly between the mid- and post-intervention period, in the domains of food and drink and power of the mind, Veterans reported a high rate of fully achieving their goals following completion of the intervention compared to partially meeting them by mid-intervention. This may reflect perseverance by the Veteran to overcome long-standing habits (e.g., food selection, self-talk) and the gradual nature in achieving these types of changes. On the other hand, rate of completion for goals related to physical activity was similar between the mid- and post-intervention periods. Although not addressed in this analysis, Veterans' overall levels of pain, fatigue, and other transient illnesses (e.g., COVID, flu) or injuries may have continued to interfere with a Veteran's interest and/or ability to engage in their physical activity goals as fully as they planned. In fact, several Veterans reported to their health coaches that they had been sick or injured while completing the evaluations, and this was reflected in their scores.

Additionally, Veterans have historically reported being eager to engage with their local providers following WRIISC comprehensive evaluations. The vigor these Veterans felt immediately following WRIISC evaluations may have led to increased motivation for change during the initial phase of health coaching, which may have reduced slightly during the second half of the intervention, as Veterans were further removed from the evaluations and/or encountered obstacles when attempting to complete goals. Nevertheless, Veterans continued to work through these obstacles with the support of their health coaches, and made progress towards healthy lifestyle behavior changes, as evidenced by the high engagement in all goals and attainment of over half of their health goals.

Adequate dosing of health coaching for sustained change is still not clear, with one study assessing health coaching outcomes reporting that Veterans felt many health coaching programs (averaging 8–10 sessions) were not sufficient to achieve their desired health behavior changes [2]. Another review paper found that the ideal dose of health coaching varies by diagnosis and/or overall goal (i.e., diabetes and reduction of A1C versus weight loss) in both length, frequency, and total number of sessions, ranging from eleven 30–40-min sessions over 9–10 months (for diabetes) to 14 sessions 45-min sessions over 7–8 months [28]. In the present analysis, Veterans completed a total of seventeen 30–60-min health coaching sessions delivered over 7–9 months and this higher dose and frequency of sessions may be particularly important when providing care for Veterans diagnosed with CMI and multiple comorbid conditions. Thus, increasing the dose of health coaching sessions may support the completion of healthy lifestyle and behavior goals while equipping and empowering Veterans to take charge of their own health. These may be critical components to providing Veterans with the tools they need to continue making lifestyle changes to improve their health once health coaching is completed.

4.1 Study Limitations and Future Directions

Due to the nature of a pilot study, the sample size of this preliminary analysis was small. A larger study may have permitted further analysis of health goals to determine which goals were most associated with change in Veterans' perceptions of their overall health ratings. Nevertheless, the high completion rate of health goals and improved perceived health suggests that Veterans increased healthy lifestyle behaviors over the course of the intervention. We aim to expand our pilot study to include a larger sample size to further characterize health improvements across subgroups.

Given the nature of the study, the cohort included Veterans who completed comprehensive WRIISC evaluations, which entailed numerous appointments with providers across multiple specialties in a short period of time, these Veterans may represent a specific population of treatment-seeking Veterans who are more engaged with the health care system. Veterans self-selected to participate in this study, and thus may represent those Veterans who were ready to implement healthy lifestyle changes compared to those who declined to participate. Importantly, the Veterans enrolled in this study represented individuals with difficult to treat diagnoses, including CMI, and strong engagement with health coaching. While the study allowed for a wait-list control group, due to the high rate of self-selection into the intervention arm, a control group could not be defined. Future studies should include a non-intervention or wait-list control group to determine the extent that health coaching augmented implementation of clinical recommendations, particularly those requiring sustained behavior change (rather than time-limited treatment/medication). Additional control methods such as a general education or non-health related social interaction arm might further help dissociate the social interaction related psychosomatic improvements from health coaching.

4.2 Conclusions

In conclusion, health coaching delivered via telehealth platforms appears amenable to Veterans for several reasons, including flexibility in appointments, reduced commute times, and convenience of meeting from home/work. Further, Veterans engaged in health coaching demonstrated strong commitment to their health goals with successful completion of over half of their goals after six months of coaching. Therefore, this analysis provides preliminary evidence demonstrating the feasibility of telehealth as a delivery mechanism for health coaching to augment continuity of care with Veterans diagnosed with CMI, a traditionally difficult to treat population of Veterans who may benefit from health behavior change.

Acknowledgments. This study was supported by WRIISC.

Disclosure of Interests. The authors have no competing interests to declare that are relevant to the content of this article. The opinions presented in this article are those of the authors and do not reflect the views of any institution/agency of the U.S. government, Uniformed Ser-vices University of the Health Sciences, or the Henry M. Jackson Foundation for the Advancement of Military Medicine, Inc.

References

1. Whole Health Implementation - Designation_Framework_for_WH_Implementation.pdf - All Documents. https://dvagov.sharepoint.com/sites/VHAOPCC/WH-Implementation/Sha red%20Documents/Forms/AllItems.aspx?id=%2Fsites%2FVHAOPCC%2FWH%2DImpl ementation%2FShared%20Documents%2FDesignation%5FFramework%2FDesignation% 5FFramework%5Ffor%5FWH%5FImplementation%2Epdf&parent=%2Fsites%2FVHAO PCC%2FWH%2DImplementation%2FShared%20Documents%2FDesignation%5FFram ework. Accessed 14 Jan 2024
2. Purcell, N., Zamora, K., Bertenthal, D., Abadjian, L., Tighe, J., Seal, K.H.: How VA whole health coaching can impact veterans' health and quality of life: a mixed-methods pilot program evaluation. Glob. Adv. Health Med. **10** (2021). https://doi.org/10.1177/2164956121998283

3. U.S. Department of Veterans Affairs, Veterans Health Administration: Passport to Whole Health (2020)
4. Bokhour, B.G., et al.: From patient outcomes to system change: evaluating the impact of VHA's implementation of the Whole Health System of Care. Health Serv. Res. **57**, 53–65 (2022). https://doi.org/10.1111/1475-6773.13938
5. Bokhour, B.G., Haun, J.N., Hyde, J., Charns, M., Kligler, B.: Transforming the Veterans Affairs to a Whole Health System of Care Time for Action and Research (2020)
6. Gierisch, J.M., et al.: The Effectiveness of Health Coaching Evidence-based Synthesis Program (ESP) Durham VA Healthcare System Durham, NC Co-Investigators: Medical Editor (2017)
7. Denneson, L.M., Trevino, A.Y., Kenyon, E.A., Ono, S.S., Pfeiffer, P.N., Dobscha, S.K.: Health coaching to enhance psychological well-being among veterans with suicidal ideation: a pilot study. J. Gen. Intern. Med. **34**, 192–194 (2019). https://doi.org/10.1007/S11606-018-4677-2/TABLES/2
8. Rethorn, Z.D., Pettitt, R.W., Dykstra, E., Pettitt, C.D.: Health and wellness coaching positively impacts individuals with chronic pain and pain-related interference. PLoS One **15** (2020). https://doi.org/10.1371/journal.pone.0236734
9. Department of Veterans Affairs Fiscal Years 2022–28 Strategic Plan LETTER FROM THE SECRETARY
10. The Lewin Group: VA/DoD Clinical Practice Guideline for the Management of Chronic Multisymptom Illness The Management of Chronic Multisymptom Illness Work Group With support from (2021)
11. Afari, N., et al.: Psychological trauma and functional somatic syndromes: a systematic review and meta-analysis. Psychosom. Med. **76**, 2–11 (2014). https://doi.org/10.1097/PSY.0000000000000010
12. Clauw, D.: Fibromyalgia associated syndromes. J. Musculoskelet. Pain 201–214 (2002). https://doi.org/10.1300/J094v10n01_16
13. Mohanty, A.F., McAndrew, L.M., Helmer, D., Samore, M.H., Gundlapalli, A.V.: Chronic multisymptom illness among Iraq/Afghanistan-deployed US veterans and their healthcare utilization within the veterans health administration. J. Gen. Intern. Med. **33**, 1419–1422 (2018). https://doi.org/10.1007/s11606-018-4479-6
14. McAndrew, L.M., Helmer, D.A., Phillips, L.A., Chandler, H.K., Ray, K., Quigley, K.S.: Iraq and Afghanistan Veterans report symptoms consistent with chronic multisymptom illness one year after deployment. J. Rehabil. Res. Dev. **53**, 59–70 (2016). https://doi.org/10.1682/JRRD.2014.10.0255
15. Porter, B., Long, K., Rull, R.P., Dursa, E.K.: Prevalence of chronic multisymptom illness/gulf war illness over time among millennium cohort participants, 2001 to 2016. J. Occup. Environ. Med. **62**, 4 (2020). https://doi.org/10.1097/JOM.0000000000001716
16. Stonerock, G.L., Blumenthal, J.A.: Role of counseling to promote adherence in healthy lifestyle medicine: strategies to improve exercise adherence and enhance physical activity. Prog. Cardiovasc. Dis. **59**, 455 (2017). https://doi.org/10.1016/J.PCAD.2016.09.003
17. U.S. Department of Veterans Affairs: War Related Illness and Injury Study Center
18. Hermens, H., op den Akker, H., Tabak, M., Wijsman, J., Vollenbroek, M.: Personalized Coaching Systems to support healthy behavior in people with chronic conditions (2014). https://doi.org/10.1016/j.jelekin.2014.10.003
19. Elnitsky, C.A., Andresen, E.M., Clark, M.E., McGarity, S., Hall, C.G., Kerns, R.D.: Access to the US Department of Veterans Affairs health system: self-reported barriers to care among returnees of Operations Enduring Freedom and Iraqi Freedom (2013)
20. RURAL VETERANS - Office of Rural Health. https://www.ruralhealth.va.gov/aboutus/ruralvets.asp. Accessed 20 Jan 2024

21. Zulman, D.M., et al.: Making connections: Nationwide implementation of video telehealth tablets to address access barriers in veterans. JAMIA Open **2**, 323–329 (2019). https://doi.org/10.1093/jamiaopen/ooz024

22. Joo, J.Y., Liu, M.F.: A Scoping Review of Telehealth-Assisted Case Management for Chronic Illnesses (2022). https://doi.org/10.1177/01939459211008917

23. Ngo, V., Hammer, H., Bodenheimer, T.: Health coaching in the teamlet model: a case study. J. Gen. Intern. Med. **25**, 1375–1378 (2010). https://doi.org/10.1007/s11606-010-1508-5

24. VA Video Connect

25. Department of Veterans Affairs VHA, U.: Personal Health Inventory (2010)

26. Cornis-Pop, M., Reddy, K.P.: Integrative medicine and health coaching in polytrauma. Rehabilitation (2019). https://doi.org/10.1016/j.pmr.2018.08.007

27. Kligler, B., Khung, M., Schult, T., Whitehead, A.: What we have learned about the implementation of whole health in the veterans administration. J. Integr. Complement. Med. **29**, 774–780 (2023). https://doi.org/10.1089/jicm.2022.0753

28. Sforzo, G.A., Kaye, M.P., Faber, A., Moore, M.: Dosing of Health and Wellness Coaching for Obesity and Type 2 Diabetes: Research Synthesis to Derive Recommendations (2023). https://doi.org/10.1177/15598276211073078

What Works Well? A Safety-II Approach to Cybersecurity

Tommy van Steen[(✉)] [iD], Cristina Del-Real[iD], and Bibi van den Berg[iD]

Leiden University, Turfmarkt 99, 2511 DP The Hague, The Netherlands
t.van.steen@fgga.leidenuniv.nl

Abstract. The field of cybersecurity is used to focusing on what goes wrong. Threats, incidents, and impact are factors that are widely investigated, and the solutions presented often lie in correcting errors and mistakes. However, in many organisations, cybersecurity incidents do not happen, or at least not as often as the focus on incidents would predict. We argue that a focus on what works well, instead of focusing only on the incidents and what went wrong, can provide unique insights into how to improve cybersecurity in organisations. This focus, known as Safety-II in the safety science literature, aims to investigate what end-users, teams and organisations do well and what factors lead to incidents being prevented, or dealt with more swiftly. In this paper, we argue for a Safety-II approach to cybersecurity, and outline various topics of interest along an incident timeline. Furthermore, we discuss a research agenda: Which avenues should be explored further to improve cybersecurity in organisations using a Safety-II approach?

Keywords: Safety-II · Cyber Incidents · Behavioural Cybersecurity · Organisational Cybersecurity · PPDRG-Model

1 The Way of Working in the Cybersecurity Domain

Policy makers, politicians and the media regularly warn about the risk of cybersecurity incidents. The sense of urgency is sometimes expressed by claiming that a cyber or a digital Pearl Harbor [1] or some other form of 'cyber doom' [2] may happen any day now. Interestingly, in everyday life the number of large(r) scale incidents, and especially truly debilitating incidents, is actually very low. In the past 15 years there have indeed been big and impactful incidents such as Stuxnet or NotPetya, but the number of events does not appear to match the level of urgency and the rhetoric of fear surrounding this domain. As a matter of fact, when we take a step back and look at the highly digitalised and interconnected world we live in, it is actually very surprising that there are so few incidents. In the vast majority of cases, citizens, consumers and employees go through their days using an endless array of networked, digital systems that seem to operate with few disturbances from digital attacks or outages. In this paper, we choose to look at cybersecurity incidents at the level of organisations, to get a better understanding of why we witness so few large-scale and debilitating cybersecurity incidents today. Our starting point is that cybersecurity depends on the conjunction of a wide variety of different

D. D. Schmorrow and C. M. Fidopiastis (Eds.): HCII 2024, LNAI 14695, pp. 250–262, 2024.
https://doi.org/10.1007/978-3-031-61572-6_17

elements within organisations, including the digital networked technologies deployed there, the people that work with and use them, the governance landscape in which the organisation finds itself, and the organisational environment and culture within it. To understand better why the number of disruptive cybersecurity incidents is lower than expected, we need to first understand which lens is normally applied to cybersecurity, often without us realising that we do so.

2   From 'What Goes Wrong' to 'What Goes Right': Lessons from Safety Science

Over the past century, safety science has made significant contributions to increasing a broad range of societal domains, including transportation, public health, automation in industry, construction, infrastructure management and disaster management, to name but a few. Risk management has become the dominant paradigm for dealing with risk in public and private organisations [3]. At the same time, it has also received criticism from different directions. For the purpose of this paper, the most important line of criticism we will focus on is the fact that risk management, and safety science in general, tends to focus exclusively on the prevention of incidents by establishing all the many things that might potentially go wrong. Note that in this perspective, the aim is to find oftentimes rare and highly irregular occurrences, digressions from the ordinary that lead to (severe) incidents, and reduce the odds of their materialization. Under normal circumstances, after all, incidents usually do not materialize. Hollnagel provides an example of how this works [4]. Let's say we look at a sample of 10,000 events within a system. In 9,999 cases no incident will arise and operations will continue smoothly but in one out of every 10,000 events something goes wrong and some incident will materialize. By studying the causes of what goes wrong, scholars point out, the focus thus is on finding the one time in which an incident arises, rather than the 9,999 times when it does not [4]. Moreover, when the goal of safety science is to find the root causes of incidents and then remedy these so that future incidents of the same kind will be prevented, then by implication the percentage of the set of 10,000 events that leads to an incident will become ever lower – ultimately nearing zero. Erik Hollnagel calls this approach within safety science 'Safety-I thinking' and explains that this kind of thinking is driven by a 'causality credo': there is a clear and direct causal relationship between a vulnerability and a potential incident, and incidents may be prevented (or at least their likelihood and impact may be reduced) by addressing the vulnerability. This credo is also known as 'find and fix' [4].

Three elements of Safety-I thinking stand out. First, systems can be taken apart and reduced to a set of steps or elements that each play a consecutive role in the working of the whole. Incidents entail that one of the elements of the system has broken down, or that one of the steps has led to a faulty outcome. Second, as a result of this linear approach, systems either function, or they do not. Functioning is a binary thing: a system is either operational or it fails. Third, in the Safety-I perspective, human beings are at best considered to be one of many components in the sequential process, simply another 'cog in the machine'. At worst, they are considered to be the main cause of incidents, because human beings make mistakes [5]. Human beings, in this perspective, are considered to be the 'weakest link' in the system [6, 7].

Research has revealed that this perspective does not do justice to how systems within organisations function. Systems, in fact, are far more complex in their workings, and the level of interconnectedness within systems is such that the 'causality credo' falls short: many different factors may contribute to the rise of incidents at the same time, as well as to their prevention [8, 9]. A linear interpretation of incident causation, therefore, does not do sufficient justice to the reality of highly complex and interconnected systems. Moreover, systems do not simply function or stop functioning, they do not work or fail in a binary sense. Instead, systems may sometimes fail partially or insignificantly, or they may drift into failure over time [10] or they may degrade gracefully [4]. Both operation and failure are far more complex than a simple 'on' or 'off'. Finally, empirical studies show that human beings, in fact, oftentimes play a crucial role in preventing or stopping emerging incidents: because they are responsive, aware and creative, they may see when dangerous situations arise and step in to stop a chain of events from unfolding. By contrast, machines and devices lack this kind of flexibility: they simply keep going once a process is under way. Rather than seeing human beings as the weakest link in relation to incidents, therefore, one can also argue that human beings may act as the strongest link in the chain when critical situations arise [5].

These arguments show that the Safety-I approach falls short. Rather than focusing on what goes wrong, a more productive way of thinking about safety would be to focus on what goes right. As Hollnagel et al. argue: "the surprise is not that things occasionally go wrong but that they go right so often" [4]. Hollnagel calls this 'Safety-II thinking'. This perspective starts from the assumption that systems are highly complex and inter-connected, and that different elements in a system – including human beings – influence the workings of the whole in multiple ways and directions. Parts of a system may compensate for one another, or take over, or play a role in preventing incidents and thus creating a near miss. Moreover, there is much to be learned from the normal workings of a system: if only one in 10,000 instances of a process a failure arises, then the 9,999 cases when the expected outcome emerges give far more data to study on why and how safety is maintained.

While this paper uses a safety science approach, it is not the only field where learning from 'what goes well' is applied to improve understanding and designing effective solutions. For instance, scholars have similarly delved into understanding why, in many instances, individuals, communities, cities, and countries do *not* experience offline crime. The assumption that a motivated criminal is always present raises the question: why are they not invariably successful? Research across these fields has explored various facets of this question.

In a manner akin to the Safety-I principles, criminology often addresses the crime event itself, its execution, and the strategies for its reduction. However, similar to Safety-II advocates, other researchers have posited that some spaces exhibit specific design features that render them more defensible compared to others [11]. From this point of view, individuals, and their interrelations, are perceived as integral protective elements of the system, rather than as potential risks. Furthermore, certain attributes of the social system, such as the collective efficacy within neighbourhoods, have been identified as enhancing the protection and resilience of these areas [12]. Objects can also be designed to improve their resilience to crime. One example of this is the International Mobile Equipment Identity, a 17- or 15-digit code to uniquely identify individual mobile phones. In our discussion around Safety-II principles for cybersecurity, it is therefore important to not only adopt safety science methods to study this approach, but also learn from other disciplines in how to study success in organisational cybersecurity.

3 Putting Incidents Centre Stage: A Model for Cybersecurity in Organisations

When looking at the dominant set of activities with respect to cybersecurity in organisations today, it is striking to see that the majority of effort, whether it is focused on finding and remedying vulnerabilities or changing human behaviour, aims at preventing incidents from arising. Encrypting messages to ensure they cannot be accessed by unintended audiences, scanning networks for intruders and partitioning them so that intruders can only get into the outer shell of the organisation, patching software so that vulnerabilities can no longer be exploited, managing access so that information cannot be stolen – all of these activities are intended to lower, or ideally even fully eliminate, the likelihood of incidents. Safety-I thinking, expressed in risk management and the use of barriers for prevention, is at the heart of cybersecurity practices in organisations today. When viewed on a timeline, currently, one could argue, cybersecurity activities are predominantly focused on what in crisis management has been termed 'left of bang' [13] (See Fig. 1).

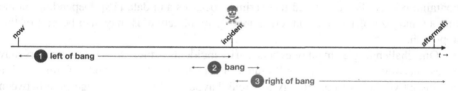

Fig. 1. Timeline of a cybersecurity incident, with subdivisions into left of bang (before the incident), bang (the incident) and right of bang (the aftermath).

However, in recent years there has been a growing awareness that due to the complexity and dynamic nature of cyberspace it is unwise to focus on prevention only as the dominant cybersecurity strategy.

Instead, the Prevent-Prepare-Detect-Respond-Governance (PPDRG) model states that in order to raise cybersecurity in organisations, the latter ought to focus on four different phases along a timeline, of which prevention is only the first [14]. While preventative strategies are certainly important, time and effort should also be invested in the detection of incidents, in preparing for incidents, in incident response and in the governance of all four. The PPDRG model posits these four activities on a timeline (See Fig. 2).

At the far left of the timeline, we find the notion of prevention, as discussed above. The following two phases are sometimes collectively called 'resilience'. This term refers

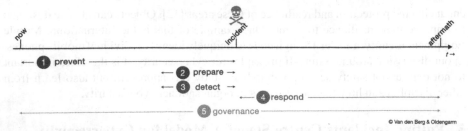

Fig. 2. Timeline of a cybersecurity incident with the various activities mapped on the 'left of bang' and 'right of bang' stages of the timeline.

to organisations' abilities to bounce back from incidents [15]. This entails for instance that organisations need to invest in redundancy in systems so that when one system fails another system can take over [16], or in the development of incident scenarios and large-scale crisis exercises to uncover weaknesses that may hamper quick recovery [17]. When looking more closely at the notion of resilience, it actually falls apart in two different elements. On the one hand, resilience refers to being prepared for incidents. This means for instance that organisations are aware of potential incident scenarios that may arise, and have equipment, manuals, procedures and roles and responsibilities in place that may be activated to deal with the incident as efficiently and quickly as possible. When plotted on a timeline, preparedness involves activities 'just left of bang'. On the other hand, resilience is about being able to recover quickly from incidents, so it involves what happens immediately after an incident materializes, i.e., 'right of bang'. Here, the focus is on incident response, which includes activities such as analysing the incident, containing it, eradicating it and recovering processes and data [18]. Depending on the impact and size of the incident, crisis management activities may also be part of this approach.

One challenging element of cybersecurity incidents is their detection. Intruders may access networks and systems and remain undetected for long periods of time, with a significant window of opportunity to wreak havoc. In 2023 the average time between intrusion and detection was 204 days [19]. This is partially due to the systems used for incident detection. These may provide security analysts with an overwhelming amount of information, often including a high number of false negatives. As a consequence, the skills required for detecting intrusions and emerging incidents are complex, and even for experienced security analysts detecting incidents is difficult [20]. Another reason why detection times are long is that organisations invest too little in this aspect of incident management. For many, the focus is on preventing incidents from happening, with fewer investments made into preparedness, detection and response capabilities. At the same time, incident detection, located immediately 'left of bang,' is where human beings may make crucial differences between (large-scale) incidents and near misses. 'Right of bang' lessons from incidents may lead to improvements in the prevention of future incidents, in preparedness for similar situations, in the detection of anomalies, and improvements on a general level with regard to processes, procedures, and behaviour.

Note that governance aspects are relevant for all stages on this timeline: for prevention, detection, preparedness, recovery and learning. Only with sufficient guidance, with adequate policies and procedures, with funds and available means can organisations implement interventions to increase their cybersecurity maturity. Proper governance facilitates and underpins all phases with regard to cybersecurity incidents.

4 Using the PPDRG Model to Get an Understanding of What Goes Right

The PPRDG model provides a clear-cut overview of the various phases related to incidents and is therefore a helpful starting point for organisation in increasing their ability to prevent and respond to incidents. It is also a useful tool in increasing our understanding of why incidents do not materialize, i.e., why things go right in organisations. This is so, because the insights from Safety-II thinking are not only applicable to the prevention of incidents, but also to detection, preparedness, recovery and governance. After all, human being may step in to detect incidents quickly or curb an emerging incident to prevent it from escalating, policies and procedures may increase resilience by providing guidance on secure and safe processes, and redundancy in (the elements of) systems may ensure that normal operations are solidified. The PPRDG model, therefore, provides a framework that can be used as investigative guidance for all phases that need to be addressed for cybersecurity maturity in organisations. We will explain how this works by discussing examples of research on cybersecurity from as Safety-II perspective in relation to prevention (Sect. 5), detection (Sect. 6), and preparedness and response (Sect. 7). We will end this article with a research agenda for future research into what goes right in cybersecurity using a Safety-II lens (Sect. 8).

5 Prevention from a Safety-II Perspective

5.1 Phishing

Traditionally, phishing is approached from a Safety-I perspective. Organisations are worried about people who click on links in emails and other forms of communication that can harm their organisation by sharing private information, installing malware and/or being a way in for criminals who want to perform a ransomware attack. Attempts to reduce the impact of phishing often rely on awareness campaigns and other means to reduce the 'click rate', the percentage of people who click on a link in a phishing test message [21–23]. In a typical test, 30–50% of employees click on the link in the test email and the organisation is then eager to take steps to reduce the click rate. A successful solution, for example through the use of behavioural change campaigns or training, might result in a click-rate of 20% or less. While the improvement is impressive from a behavioural science point of view, an attacker would on average only need to send out five emails to have one employee clicking on their malicious URL and divulge sensitive information. What changes when we instead focus on a Safety-II perspective in this case? As Safety-II focuses on why incidents do not happen, we would look at the employees who do not click on the URL, or, even more interestingly, the employees that report the phishing email to the relevant in-house expert. In a study on repeated clickers [24], Canham identified not only users who clicked on the link in a phishing test on every single occasion, but also a group of what he considers 'protective stewards', people who did not click on any phishing link and often reported these emails to the relevant security experts. Understanding why these people did not click on links from a behavioural science perspective, but perhaps also by looking at organisational and environmental factors can help shape solutions to improve reporting rates and speed, instead of focusing on reducing clicking behaviour.

5.2 Screen Locking and Clean Desk Policy

In addition to phishing, there are of course also other factors that end-users have control over that increase the security of their organisations. For instance, to combat insider threat or the impact of a successful site visit by a social engineer, adhering to a clean desk policy so that no confidential documents are lying around, and locking your screen when leaving your desk so that your system cannot be accessed and abused, are vital aspects of daily habits in the workplace. While attempts can be made to understand the causes of people not following these procedures, more interesting insights can be gained by focusing on the people who always lock their screen and follow the clean desk policy. These people might have taught themselves tricks to ensure that they will lock their screen, or perhaps have imprinted these behaviours into automatic 'muscle memory' responses when performing activities. However, it is also possible that they want to lead by example, are (overly) worried about potential risks, or see a personal danger instead of only a risk to the organisation. The latter could take the form of employees being afraid that colleagues might send messages to the board in their name, or can access their salary information when not locking their screen when leaving their desk. By understanding what drives the people who are exemplar employees in this matter, we can develop better cybersecurity solutions.

6   Detection from a Safety-II Perspective

Under the Safety-II paradigm, detection mechanisms are designed not only to identify threats as they hit the organisation, but also to understand the conditions under which its systems operate well. By proactively understanding and monitoring when systems are performing optimally, it should be possible to enable the early identification of deviations from these norms. On a technical level, scholars have examined the efficacy of machine learning and deep learning algorithms in detecting intrusions [25, 26]. The Safety II perspective would contribute to these developments by exploring tools that monitor systems based on evidence of a 'normal' situation, thereby allowing organisations to quickly respond to deviations that may indicate a security incident.

Beyond the technical aspects that have predominantly been the focus of incident detection literature, the Safety-II perspective underscores the crucial role of human actors in the detection process. A Safety-II approach involves examining organisations with shorter detection times to understand what sets them apart. Linking back to the phishing example in the previous section, the capability to detect phishing emails could be further supported by a culture of proactive reporting of actual clicking behaviour among employees. If employees are trained to identify threats and the organisation has effective, well-known mechanisms for incident reporting, the likelihood of accurately detecting incidents is significantly increased, and the lengthy average detection time of over 200 days can be reduced substantially. In this scenario, humans are seen not as a risk factor but as a safeguard for the organisation.

7 Preparedness and Response from a Safety-II Perspective

Finally, the PPDRG model advocates for a balanced approach to the preparation and response to cyber incidents, aligning it with the emphasis on prevention and detection. Current literature on the readiness and management of cyber incidents, including crises, is notably limited and predominantly concentrates on the technical facets of incident management such as the application of data analytics during an incident [27, 28]. Existing business continuity and disaster recovery frameworks echo the critique articulated in this discussion. They prioritize risk management during a cyber incident over delineating proven strategies that enhance response efficacy [29, 30]. Limited research in cyber incident management seeks to decipher the repercussions of data breaches on consumer behaviour or market dynamics [31], and to identify optimal strategies for stakeholder communication [32]. Yet, the exploration into organisational traits and employee behaviours that effectively reduce response times and limit organisational damage during a cyber incident remains largely uncharted. It would be advisable to explore, for example, whether it is possible to identify high reliability organisations in the context of incident response based on these characteristics [33]. These organisations, known for their high level of security and safety practices, are not only be better prepared and respond more effectively, but also show evidence of improvement with respect to the pre-incident situation due to effective learning and improved preparation for incidents. We propose to study what works during the preparation and response to cyber incidents, that is, what technical, human, and organisational factors are present when an organisation effectively responds to a cyber incident.

8 A Research Agenda for What Goes Right in Cybersecurity

Approaching cybersecurity from a Safety-II perspective allows us to not only view issues in a new light, but also helps in better understanding what mechanisms are underlying the various secure and risky behaviours and situations. Moreover, it provides insights that can be used to improve cybersecurity solutions across the board. In this section, we outline a research agenda that will help us describe, understand, and improve cybersecurity in organisations. We propose to investigate cybersecurity using a Safety-II perspective on three distinct levels: the end-user level, team level and organisation level. The offered research avenues are a first step towards more research into Safety-II solutions for cybersecurity and we hope that they can be a starting point for the community to further develop these, and other research ideas, from this point of view.

8.1 End-Users

Several steps can be taken to expand our understanding of end-users' cybersecurity behaviour in organisational settings. The earlier mentioned example of phishing is one area where a move towards Safety-II would play a large role in designing new solutions for behavioural cybersecurity topics. The protective stewards, or 'security champions' as others have named them [34, 35] are not only interesting from a behavioural point of view, but also in terms of cognitive processes, attitudes and values that these people hold. Understanding why they behave securely, and differentiating between aspects that are trainable (e.g., habits), and those that are not (e.g., personality) helps in finetuning solutions for both these aspects.

For instance, incorporating these scientific insights in cybersecurity training for end-users would greatly improve training effectivity, as currently little or no scientific under-pinnings are present in this field [36]. In terms of aspects that cannot be trained, these can still be of importance when working towards a more secure organisation. Perhaps these skills and abilities can be detected through the use of psychometrical methods. This could improve the security of an organisation in two ways.

First, using these methods can provide input in hiring decisions, as well as decisions as to where to place an individual and which tasks and job role to allocate to them. If a future employee is seen as a security champion, they can be placed in parts of the organisation where security is of the utmost importance, such as in departments that work with the highest level of classified data, or that are working on financial aspects of the organisation. But they can also be put in the position of an exemplar employee that can be a role model for people who are performing less securely. Mechanisms such as social contagion [37] could then lead to higher levels of security within the organisation, not only at the prevention level, but also at for example the detection or response levels.

Second, insights into what makes an employee successful in doing their work securely can help in deciding which behavioural cybersecurity solutions are more likely to be needed to avoid or report (detect) incidents, such as nudging and affordances [38] and a wider focus on access management for instance. On a governance level, they can also lead to an overhaul of existing security policies. Perhaps some policies are too stringent, and employees are likely to be too restricted by them, while they would still perform their tasks in a secure fashion when not hindered by these policies. Knowing what defines a successful end-user when it comes to cybersecurity is vital in developing solutions to make this success sustainable over time, especially when individuals, or whole teams, leave the organisation.

8.2 Teams

Sometimes focusing on individuals will not result in a successful improvement in cyber-security level within an organisation. However, by adopting a Safety-II perspective, we could also investigate why certain teams (or, on a higher level, whole departments) seem to adopt a higher level of cybersecurity than other parts of the organisation. For instance, perhaps the finance team is more focused on potential scams and fraud due to the nature or the work, or merely because of a focus on detail that might come with the job that acts as a support factor to improve cybersecurity at the same time. Investigating what makes secure teams successful allows us to improve other teams either by instilling the same values, skills and focus as the successful teams, or perhaps a successful team needs to be disbanded and the successful members spread over the other teams to share their insights and ways of working through social contagion principles mentioned earlier.

There are several aspects of teams that can result in high cybersecurity levels compared to other teams. For instance, it is possible that less successful teams suffer from higher levels of social loafing [39, 40], where team members expect that their lack of input or responsible behaviour will be covered by the team as a whole, and that a single person making a mistake is not disastrous. The successful teams might stand out, merely because they have the habit of double-checking decisions made by oth-ers, or feel comfortable asking a colleague for help while the lower performing teams might lack a team spirit or distrust others' perspectives. Furthermore, the successful teams might consist of a better mix of qualities within individual employees. These factors could include personality [41], demographic backgrounds, or past experiences within the same or other organisations. Teams that have a tight-knit community feel-ing might be more successful as asking fellow team members for help might come more naturally, or is encouraged through social processes. Understanding why these teams are successful not only helps in improving training and policies made by organ-isations, but can also be relevant when making hiring decisions by focusing on who would add an important security skill or mindset to an existing team, as explained in the section on the end-user level.

8.3 Organisations

While end-users individually or in teams can help to improve cybersecurity by preventing, detecting, preparing for and responding to incidents, on an organisational level the governance aspect of the PPDRG-model is key. High reliability organisations [42, 43] can be a starting point to improve understanding of what it is that makes organisations successful in dealing with security threats. By identifying these organisations, and studying the potentially unique aspects that make these organisations highly reliable, we can improve the standards being set and the ways of working of other organisations as well. To achieve this, three distinct aspects of successful organisations need to be addressed.

First, the structure of these organisations needs to be investigated. Perhaps the organisational structure allows for more (hierarchical) power for the security department over other departments, or the flow of information within the organisation is improved by a specific set of base rules regarding the organisational structure. Second, there might be specific cultural aspects that successful organisations have incorporated to achieve their level of security. This could be related to a 'just' culture [44], where people are not unduly punished for making mistakes, but where people are encouraged to speak up when they believe they might have made a mistake. But it could also be that employees are more confident in speaking up against their superiors, or feel the support of managers when bringing up doubts about new policies. Third and last, how organisations design, implement, and adhere to policies is of interest. While policies can be designed and implemented top-down, perhaps successful organisations are more likely to only adopt policies when there is wide support for these policies in the organisation. The implementation might also benefit from input from employees to decide how the policy is best implemented and, more importantly, what to do when the demands of the job clash with the policies at hand. To avoid shadow security practices [45], where people work around existing solutions to get the job done, a wider conversation about when to strictly adhere to a policy and when to find alternative solutions might be useful. Using

Safety-II principles to understand what successful organisations do differently is key in understanding which of these elements play a role in improving cybersecurity across the incident timeline.

9   Conclusion

In this paper we argued for a Safety-II approach to cybersecurity to tackle existing cybersecurity issues in organisations. While the need to understand what goes wrong is not diminished, the Safety-I toolbox should be expanded upon with tools using Safety-II principles. More research into understanding why the number of successful attacks is not so high as expected from a Safety-I perspective, and describing the underlying mechanisms of these protective factors will provide the cybersecurity community with valuable insights and, hopefully, tools to better protect the organisations of the future by focusing on the positive: What is going well and what can we learn from that? This question cannot simply be answered from a prevention focus only. Adopting a broad view including the preparation for, detecting of, responding to, and learning from incidents is key if we want to improve organisational cybersecurity across the board. To achieve this, we believe that we should not merely focus on policies, or only on end-user behaviour. Instead, we believe that it is likely to be the interplay between individuals, the teams they operate in, and the wider organisational structure, culture and way of working that is key in learning why some organisations do so well with regards to cybersecurity. Learning from organisational successes instead of failures is not only an exciting new way of approaching cybersecurity, but is also urgently needed to have a strong and effective response to future cyber threats.

References

1. Goldman, E.O., Warner, M.: Why a Digital Pearl Harbor Makes Sense. .. and Is Possible. Understanding Cyber Conflict: Fourteen Analogies (2017)
2. Lawson, S.T., Yeo, S.K., Yu, H., Greene, E.: The cyber-doom effect: the impact of fear appeals in the US cyber security debate. In: International Conference on Cyber Conflict, CYCON (2016). https://doi.org/10.1109/CYCON.2016.7529427
3. Dionne, G.: Risk management: history, definition, and critique. Risk Manag. Insur. Rev. (2013). https://doi.org/10.1111/rmir.12016
4. Hollnagel, E.: From Safety-I to Safety-II: A White Paper (2013)
5. Reason, J.: The Human Contribution: Unsafe Acts, Accidents and Heroic Recoveries. Routledge, London (2017). https://doi.org/10.1201/9781315239125
6. Kleinberg, H., Reinicke, B., Cummings, J.: Cyber security best practices: what to do? In 2014 Proceedings of the Conference for Information Systems Applied Research. Univeristy of North Carolina, Baltimore (2014)
7. Dunn Cavelty, M.: Breaking the cyber-security dilemma: aligning security needs and removing vulnerabilities. Sci. Eng. Ethics 20, 701–715 (2014). https://doi.org/10.1007/s11948-014-9551-y
8. Dahlberg, R.: Resilience and complexity. J. Curr. Cult. Res. 7, 541–557 (2015)
9. Woods, D.D.: Essential characteristics of resilience. In: Hollnagel, E., Woods, D.D., Leveson, N. (ed.) Resilience Engineering: Concepts and Precepts, pp. 21–34. Taylor and Francis Group (2006)

10. Dekker, S.: Drift into Failure. Taylor and Francis Group (2016). https://doi.org/10.1201/978
1315257396
11. Cozens, P.: Crime prevention through environmental design. In: Environmental Criminology
and Crime Analysis, pp. 175–199 (2013). https://doi.org/10.4324/9780203118214-19
12. Sampson, R.J., Raudenbush, S.W., Earls, F.: Neighborhoods and violent crime: a multilevel
study of collective efficacy. Science **277**, 918–924 (1997)
13. Baskerville, R., Spagnoletti, P., Kim, J.: Incident-centered information security: managing a
strategic balance between prevention and response. Inf. Manag. **51**, 138–151 (2014)
14. van den Berg, B., Oldengarm, P.: Een tijdlijn voor het denken over digitale incidenten. In:
Handboek Digitale Veiligheid. Wolters Kluwer (2024)
15. Linkov, I., Eisenberg, D.A., Plourde, K., Seager, T.P., Allen, J., Kott, A.: Resilience metrics
for cyber systems. Environ. Syst. Decis. **33**, 471–476 (2013)
16. Harms-Ringdahl, L.: Analysis of safety functions and barriers in accidents. Saf. Sci. **47**,
353–363 (2009)
17. Demchak, C.C.: Resilience and cyberspace: recognizing the challenges of a global socio-cyber
infrastructure (GSCI). J. Comp. Policy Anal. Res. Pract. **14**, 254–269 (2012)
18. Schlette, D., Caselli, M., Pernul, G.: A comparative study on cyber threat intelligence: the
security incident response perspective. IEEE Commun. Surv. Tutor. **23**, 2525–2556 (2021)
19. Petrosyan, A.: Global mean time to identify and contain data breaches 2017–2023.
https://www.statista.com/statistics/1417455/worldwide-data-breaches-identify-and-con
tain/. Accessed 26 Feb 2024
20. Ben-Asher, N., Gonzalez, C.: Effects of cyber security knowledge on attack detection.
Comput. Hum. Behav. **48**, 51–61 (2015)
21. Manoharan, S., Katuk, N., Hassan, S., Ahmad, R.: To click or not to click the link: the factors
influencing internet banking users' intention in responding to phishing emails. Inf. Comput.
Secur. **30**, 37–62 (2022)
22. Sutter, T., Bozkir, A.S., Gehring, B., Berlich, P.: Avoiding the hook: influential factors of
phishing awareness training on click-rates and a data-driven approach to predict email difficulty perception. IEEE ACCESS. **10**, 100540–100565 (2022). https://doi.org/10.1109/ACC
ESS.2022.3207272
23. Quinkert, F., Degeling, M., Holz, T.: Spotlight on phishing: a longitudinal study on phishing
awareness trainings. Presented at the Detection of Intrusions and Malware, and Vulnerability
Assessment: 18th International Conference, DIMVA 2021, Virtual Event, 14–16 July 2021,
Proceedings 18 (2021)
24. Canham, M.: Repeat clicking: a lack of awareness is not the problem. In: Degen, H., Ntoa,
S., Moallem, A. (eds.) HCII 2023. LNCS, vol. 14059, pp. 325–342. Springer, Cham (2023).
https://doi.org/10.1007/978-3-031-48057-7_20
25. Apruzzese, G., Colajanni, M., Ferretti, L., Guido, A., Marchetti, M.: On the effectiveness
of machine and deep learning for cyber security. Presented at the 2018 10th International
Conference on Cyber Conflict (CyCon) (2018)
26. Geetha, R., Thilagam, T.: A review on the effectiveness of machine learning and deep learning
algorithms for cyber security. Arch. Comput. Methods Eng. **28**, 2861–2879 (2021)
27. Naseer, A., Naseer, H., Ahmad, A., Maynard, S.B., Siddiqui, A.M.: Real-time analytics,
incident response process agility and enterprise cybersecurity performance: a contingent
resource-based analysis. Int. J. Inf. Manage. **59**, 102334 (2021)
28. Naseer, A., Naseer, H., Ahmad, A., Maynard, S.B., Siddiqui, A.M.: Moving towards agile
cybersecurity incident response: a case study exploring the enabling role of big data analytics-
embedded dynamic capabilities. Comput. Secur. **135**, 103525 (2023)
29. Zare, H., Wang, P., Zare, M.J., Azadi, M., Olsen, P.: Business continuity plan and risk assessment analysis in case of a cyber attack disaster in healthcare organizations. Presented at the

17th International Conference on Information Technology–New Generations (ITNG 2020) (2020)

30. Järveläinen, J.: IT incidents and business impacts: validating a framework for continuity management in information systems. Int. J. Inf. Manage. **33**, 583–590 (2013)
31. Algarni, A.M., Malaiya, Y.K.: A consolidated approach for estimation of data security breach costs. Presented at the 2016 2nd International Conference on Information Management (ICIM) (2016)
32. Kuipers, S., Schonheit, M.: Data breaches and effective crisis communication: a comparative analysis of corporate reputational crises. Corp. Reput. Rev. **25**, 176–197 (2022)
33. Weick, K.E., Sutcliffe, K.M.: Managing the Unexpected. Jossey-Bass, San Francisco (2001)
34. Beris, O., Beautement, A., Sasse, M.A.: Employee rule breakers, excuse makers and security champions: mapping the risk perceptions and emotions that drive security behaviors. Presented at the Proceedings of the 2015 New Security Paradigms Workshop (2015)
35. Gabriel, T., Furnell, S.: Selecting security champions. Comput. Fraud Secur. **2011**, 8–12 (2011)
36. Prümmer, J., van Steen, T., van den Berg, B.: A systematic review of current cybersecurity training methods. Comput. Secur. 103585 (2023)
37. Christakis, N.A., Fowler, J.H.: Social contagion theory: examining dynamic social networks and human behavior. Stat. Med. **32**, 556–577 (2013)
38. van Steen, T.: When choice is (not) an option: nudging and techno-regulation approaches to behavioural cybersecurity. In: Schmorrow, D.D., Fidopiastis, C.M. (eds.) HCII 2022. LNCS, vol. 13310, pp. 120–130. Springer, Cham (2022). https://doi.org/10.1007/978-3-031-05457-0_10
39. Harkins, S.G.: Social loafing and social facilitation. J. Exp. Soc. Psychol. **23**, 1–18 (1987)
40. Simms, A., Nichols, T.: Social loafing: a review of the literature. J. Manag. Policy Pract. **15**, 58 (2014)
41. Sackett, P.R., Walmsley, P.T.: Which personality attributes are most important in the workplace? Perspect. Psychol. Sci. **9**, 538–551 (2014)
42. Sutcliffe, K.M.: High reliability organizations (HROs). Best Pract. Res. Clin. Anaesthesiol. **25**, 133–144 (2011)
43. Roberts, K.H., Bea, R.: Must accidents happen? Lessons from high-reliability organizations. Acad. Manag. Perspect. **15**, 70–78 (2001)
44. Dekker, S.W.: Just culture: who gets to draw the line? Cogn. Technol. Work **11**, 177–185 (2009)
45. Kirlappos, I., Parkin, S., Sasse, M.A.: "Shadow security" as a tool for the learning organization. ACM SIGCAS Comput. Soc. **45**, 29–37 (2015)

Author Index

D. D. Schmorrow and C. M. Fidopiastis (Eds.): HCII 2024, LNAI 14695, pp. 263–265, 2024.
https://doi.org/10.1007/978-3-031-61572-6

Printed in the United States
by Baker & Taylor Publisher Services